Yiddish Cinema

THE SUNY SERIES
HORIZONS OF CINEMA
MURRAY POMERANCE | EDITOR

RECENT TITLES

Daniel Varndell, *Torturous Etiquettes*

Jason Jacobs, *Reluctant Sleuths, True Detectives*

Lucy J. Miller, *Distancing Representations in Transgender Film*

Tomoyuki Sasaki, *Cinema of Discontent*

Mary Ann McDonald Carolan, *Orienting Italy*

Matthew Rukgaber, *Nietzsche in Hollywood*

David Venditto, *Whiteness at the End of the World*

Fareed Ben-Youssef, *No Jurisdiction*

Tony Tracy, *White Cottage, White House*

Tom Conley, *Action, Action, Action*

Lindsay Coleman and Roberto Schaefer, editors, *The Cinematographer's Voice*

Nolwenn Mingant, *Hollywood Films in North Africa and the Middle East*

†Charles Warren, edited by William Rothman and Joshua Schulze, *Writ on Water*

Jason Sperb, *The Hard Sell of Paradise*

William Rothman, *The Holiday in His Eye*

Brendan Hennessey, *Luchino Visconti and the Alchemy of Adaptation*

Alexander Sergeant, *Encountering the Impossible*

Erica Stein, *Seeing Symphonically*

George Toles, *Curtains of Light*

Neil Badmington, *Perpetual Movement*

A complete listing of books in this series can be found online at www.sunypress.edu

Yiddish Cinema

The Drama of Troubled Communication

Jonah Corne and Monika Vrečar

Cover image: Still from *The Dybbuk* (1937), directed by Michał Waszyński

Published by State University of New York Press, Albany

© 2023 State University of New York

All rights reserved

Printed in the United States of America

No part of this book may be used or reproduced in any manner whatsoever without written permission. No part of this book may be stored in a retrieval system or transmitted in any form or by any means including electronic, electrostatic, magnetic tape, mechanical, photocopying, recording, or otherwise without the prior permission in writing of the publisher.

For information, contact State University of New York Press, Albany, NY
www.sunypress.edu

Library of Congress Cataloging-in-Publication Data

Names: Corne, Jonah, 1977– author. | Vrečar, Monika, 1984– author.
Title: Yiddish cinema : the drama of troubled communication / Jonah Corne and Monika Vrečar.
Description: Albany, NY : State University of New York Press, [2023] | Series: SUNY series, horizons of cinema | Includes bibliographical references and index.
Identifiers: LCCN 2022053653 | ISBN 9781438494210 (hardcover : alk. paper) | ISBN 9781438494197 (ebook) | ISBN 9781438494203 (pbk. : alk. paper)
Subjects: LCSH: Motion pictures, Yiddish—History. | Communication in motion pictures. | Mass media in motion pictures.
Classification: LCC PN1995.9.Y54 C67 2023 | DDC 791.43089/924—dc23/eng/20230411
LC record available at https://lccn.loc.gov/2022053653

10 9 8 7 6 5 4 3 2 1

Contents

List of Illustrations	vii
Introduction: "The structure of communication is the infrastructure of human reality"	1
1 Powers of Music: *A Little Letter to Mother* (1938)	9
2 Discourse and Dialogue: *The Living Orphan* (1939)	37
3 The Mass Media Family: *Kol Nidre* (1939)	69
4 The Battle of the Books: *Tevye* (1939)	93
5 Motherhood, Migration, and the Asylum: *Where Is My Child?* (1937)	125
6 "Silence which is communication": *Motel the Operator* (1939)	161
7 Groundlessness I (The Nation against the Jew): *The Wandering Jew* (1933)	191
8 Groundlessness II (Among the DPs): *Long Is the Road* (1948)	217
9 Mediating the Mystical: *The Dybbuk* (1937)	255

Coda	297
Acknowledgments	301
Notes	303
Bibliography	323
Index	335

Illustrations

1.1 The father stands behind his wife and child in a moment of paternal crisis, the three forming an ironic image of hierarchy. *A Little Letter to Mother* (1938). 19

1.2 The songwriter father finds a new livelihood selling socks from a street cart in the New World; the word "RADIOS" gestures at America as a space of technological modernity and mass media. *A Little Letter to Mother* (1938). 22

1.3 A superimposed shot of two notices in the Yiddish press that conveys the idea of a missed connection between a mother seeking her son and her son, now a famous singer, headlining a HIAS benefit concert. *A Little Letter to Mother* (1938). 29

1.4 As Arele—now the celebrated "Irving Bird"—performs at the HIAS concert, Dobrish mesmerically approaches the stage in recognition of her lost son. *A Little Letter to Mother* (1938). 31

2.1 Muni's deflated expression after his performance at the radio station. *The Living Orphan* (1939). 40

2.2 Amphitheatrical discourse. Vilém Flusser. 47

2.3 Theatrical discourse. Vilém Flusser. 47

2.4	Staying late for theater rehearsals, Freda pleads with her husband over the phone, while staring at a photograph of her child; the doubled image of her created by the reflection in the mirror symbolizes her split allegiance between the home and her career. *The Living Orphan* (1939).	51
2.5	In a mise-en-scène that evokes Flusser's model of "theatrical discourse," Benny sells newspapers in a musical street performance. *The Living Orphan* (1939).	57
2.6	Freda's position at the center of the final, familial image, expressing that she is the one in charge. *The Living Orphan* (1939).	67
3.1	Ignoring her father, Jenny switches on the radio. *Kol Nidre* (1939).	75
3.2	Despite her husband's sardonic opposition, Chassie affirms her desire to perform on the radio. *Kol Nidre* (1939).	79
3.3	Moishe suffers a bodily breakdown while uttering an excommunication of his daughter. *Kol Nidre* (1939).	82
3.4	As Sarah sings a regretful song about having children, the camera's rigorous inclusion of her mute husband in the frame creates the effect of a "phantom duet." *Kol Nidre* (1939).	86
4.1	A Gorky book placed in between Chava and Fedye: a potent mediator of desire. *Tevye* (1939).	96
4.2	The daughter of a Jewish farmer kisses a shy *yeshiva bokher* whom she's trying to seduce with her secretly acquired literacy; the placement of the writing tablet in between them mirrors the placement of the Gorky book in between the lovers in *Tevye*. *Green Fields* (1937).	97
4.3	Tevye critically examines the newest Gorky book that Fedye has gifted to Chava. *Tevye* (1939).	101

4.4	Unnoticed by her family, the excommunicated Chava observes her mother's death through the window. *Tevye* (1939).	111
4.5	Tevye rescues a book of psalms from underneath the official documents ordering his expulsion. *Tevye* (1939).	115
5.1	As Esther waits for a postman on the steps of the doctor's old home, Elick the "letter-carrier" arrives with favorable news. *Where Is My Child?* (1937).	138
5.2	Esther sings a lullaby to a photographic portrait of her lost son in the home of his adoptive parents. *Where Is My Child?* (1937).	141
5.3	Esther makes a swaddled baby—another surrogate object for her lost child—out of the bedding in her asylum cell. *Where Is My Child?* (1937).	149
5.4	Unnoticed in the background, Alice conveys an expression of devastation and anguish as she gives up her adopted son to his "real" mother. *Where Is My Child?* (1937).	159
5.5	As Victor embraces his "real" mother and fiancée, the trio of bodies eclipses his excluded, adoptive mother (situated invisibly behind them) from the image. *Where Is My Child?* (1937).	160
6.1	The workers in the garment factory perform a defiant work song. *Motel the Operator* (1939).	166
6.2	A strike-breaking gangster hits Motel over the head and knocks him unconscious. *Motel the Operator* (1939).	172
6.3	Reluctantly ushered out of the room by his adoptive mother, Jackie gazes empathically at the vagabond stranger, who he does not know is his birth father. *Motel the Operator* (1939).	179
6.4	Returning Jackie's gaze, Motel tearfully chokes back words and withholds revealing his true identity to his son. *Motel the Operator* (1939).	179

6.5	Motel and Mr. Rosenwald, Jackie's adoptive father, enter into an understanding about Motel's choice to remain silent and continue withholding his identity from Jackie. *Motel the Operator* (1939).	186
7.1	Arthur has a disturbing flashback to the book burnings, shown in a double exposure that creates the impression that he himself is being engulfed by the flames. *The Wandering Jew* (1933).	207
7.2	Arthur's portrait, *The Eternal Wanderer*, modeled on his dead father, comes to life and wanders off the canvas. *The Wandering Jew* (1933).	210
7.3	In a stop-motion animation sequence that recasts the book burnings, a book by the early nineteenth-century German Jewish author Heinrich Heine is dropped into the flames. *The Wandering Jew* (1933).	214
7.4	Out of the flames of the burning books, Arthur and the spirit of his father rise up unscathed. *The Wandering Jew* (1933).	215
8.1 & 8.2	In a loaded transition between scenes, the Yellins' challah bread cover with a Star of David dissolves into the hand of a Nazi officer drawing a Star of David on a map of the Warsaw Ghetto. *Long Is the Road* (1948).	227
8.3 & 8.4	On a train transporting Jewish prisoners, a Nazi officer surveils the inside of one of the boxcars through a slit in the wall. As this panoptic gaze comes across David, the latter manages to stare back and resist the objectification imposed upon him: a quiet communicative revolution. *Long Is the Road* (1948).	230
8.5	As Hannah searches for her son after the war, she drowns in an overwhelming bureaucracy, appearing double exposed over images of the vast archives at the various "tracing services." *Long Is the Road* (1948).	237

8.6	In the immediate aftermath of the war, Dora falls asleep on David's shoulder on the ruined streets of Warsaw: an image of the two homeless DPs finding shelter in one another. *Long Is the Road* (1948).	242
9.1	The hoi polloi trying to get a glimpse of the mystical practices of the zaddik and his followers. *The Dybbuk* (1937).	261
9.2	A medium between heaven and earth, the zaddik sits amid his followers and appears to draw invisible energy from a pile of closed books. *The Dybbuk* (1937).	262
9.3	During a speech about the Kabbalistic heights, the zaddik's followers strangely strain to hear him. *The Dybbuk* (1937).	263
9.4	A mystical wind causes Leah's wedding veil to billow, while the groom looks on in fear. *The Dybbuk* (1937).	281

Introduction

"The structure of communication is the infrastructure of human reality"

MARTIN BUBER, IN HIS enormous compendium of retellings of Hasidic legends, *Tales of the Hasidim*, recounts a characteristically spare, enigmatic tale entitled "Those Who Are to Hear, Hear." The story reads in its entirety as follows: "Once a great throng of people collected about the rabbi of Apt to hear his teachings. 'That won't help you,' he cried to them. 'Those who are to hear, will hear even at a distance; those who are not to hear, will not hear no matter how near they come.'"[1] Notably, the tale is stringently silent on what the teachings of the illustrious rabbi of Apt, which so many wish so zealously to hear, actually contain: a strategic withholding that directs us toward questions about the communicative act itself. In this way, the tale mirrors Franz Kafka's "An Imperial Message," a far more famous tale in which, similarly, nothing at all is revealed about the contents of an all-important message dispatched from a source on high, and accordingly the focus falls on the operations themselves of communicative transmission. In Kafka's short parable, a messenger, tasked by a dying emperor with delivering "a message to you, the humble subject, the insignificant shadow cowering in the remotest distance before the imperial sun,"[2] strives to reach his destination and yet faces mysterious difficulties, the space he is attempting to cross appearing to grow ever more vast the more he proceeds.[3] In a comparison of the two texts, it is difficult to say which is more pessimistic, or alternatively optimistic, about the possibilities of communication. In Buber, reception is assured, or so it is claimed, for "those who are to hear," for those who perhaps, to borrow a key Buberian concept that we'll discuss in the pages that follow, are "turned"—generously and attentively attuned, as it were—to the rabbi, regardless of—or more accurately, critically primordial to—considerations of proximity, of farness or nearness relative to the position of the speaker. Yet what about "those who are not to hear"? Are they not, according to the sagacious rabbi, as fated to be foiled in relation to the reception of the message as "the humble subject" in Kafka? Certainly, one expects bleakness from Kafka. And yet, at the end of "An Imperial Message," as the intended receiver sits by the window in the twilight and continues waiting for the message to arrive, she or he at least possesses the capacity to "dream"[4] the message to her- or himself. As it turns out, both tales make hermeneutic certainty just as elusive as the critical messages whose contents they never disclose, thus throwing us back, once more, on the naked operationality of communication, and more specifically on the notion that, in the human predicament being described, it is the (im)possibilities of communication that constitute the decisive factor.

Just as "Those Who Are to Hear, Hear" and "An Imperial Message" resonate with one another, so they both resonate with—and could be said to offer intimations of—the remarkable media philosophy of Vilém Flusser (1920-1991). A Prague Jew who escaped Nazi-occupied Czechoslovakia, lived in Brazil for the next thirty years, returned to Europe in the early 1970s, and gained a measure of international renown in the 1980s for his writings on electronic media (today sometimes regarded as "prophetic" texts in the field of digital culture), Flusser announces what had become, and remained, his core methodological tenet in a lecture series, "The Surprising Phenomenon of Human Communication," given in Aix-en-Provence in 1975-1976. Reflecting on the earlier installments of the series in the final lecture, he remarks: "I believe that a hypothesis is 'good' or 'bad' according to the extent that it allows to be worked with. A hypothesis is a tool, not a revelation. And what I attempted to do during the course of these lectures was to show you how our situation presents itself if we assume, hypothetically, that the structure of communication is the infrastructure of human reality."[5]

Such a hypothesis represents an evolution from an earlier phase in Flusser's intellectual trajectory in which he is preoccupied with the philosophy of language, and more specifically with the Wittgenstein-inspired view that language constructs human reality.[6] In other words, the lecture series signals Flusser's shift into a full-fledged media philosopher who brings a distinctly phenomenological approach (implicit in the emphasis on "the infrastructure of *human* reality") to an analysis of the extensive gamut of social and technological communicative structures within which we find ourselves embedded. In reaching this point, however, Flusser hardly displays an "agnostic" or "value-free" position. For him, the most favorable communicative arrangement is one that facilitates "dialogue": a view that bears the unmistakable imprint of Buber, one of his central influences whom, in the Prague of his late teens, he once indelibly heard speak.[7] Indeed, Buber's concept of the "I-Thou" relation, of an intersubjective, noninstrumentalizing, immanent yet divinely suffused relation between people,[8] colors Flusser's thinking all over the place. We find it in his writing on Jewishness (i.e., "To be a Jew is not just to be a Jew for oneself, but also for the others."[9]), on the figure of "the migrant" (whose potential for challenging the hardened norms of society he encourages openness toward), on the basic forms of communication structures (which he broadly sorts into the "dialogic" and the "discursive"), and far beyond.

This book seeks to offer a new, hopefully revivifying, exploration of Yiddish cinema, taking Flusser as its main theoretical guide, alongside several of the thinkers that directly inspired his "communicology." Among this latter group, we thus draw considerably on Buber, whose profound importance for Flusser we just mentioned; on Edmund Husserl, from whom he developed his phenomenological orientation; and on Hannah Arendt, whose claim, "Communication is not an 'expression' of thoughts or feelings, which then could only be secondary to them; truth itself is communicative and disappears outside of communication,"[10] strongly echoes his guiding "hypothesis." If our project might be conceived as the staging of a novel encounter between Yiddish cinema and Flusser, these two regrettably too-little-known entities, however, we wish to pursue such a "dialogue" with a sense of equal footing. For our aim is not simply to apply Flusserian concepts to Yiddish cinema, but rather to reveal Yiddish cinema as a kind of media theory in itself—a media theory that, like Flusser's, bears a distinctive Jewish character, and at the same time, unlike his, emerges strikingly "from below," from up out of the lowbrow realm of popular culture. (We should also point out that apart from Flusser and some of his key influences we also engage with several other thinkers whose concerns intersect with those of the films, including Gershom Scholem, Theodor Adorno, Emmanuel Levinas, Hans Kohn, Joseph Roth, Erving Goffman, Shoshana Felman, Judith Butler, Jacqueline Rose, and Zygmunt Bauman.)

In more specific terms, our central argument is that Yiddish cinema also propounds the idea that "the structure of communication is the infrastructure of human reality," and that it does so through an insistent focus on *troubled* communication. Consequently, we contend, the films offer exemplary testimony to what is often said about the revelatory powers of dysfunction: namely, that it is in their faltering and breaking down that we become most cognizant of the systems that sustain us, that we vitally rely on for our existence. Again and again, with archetypal frequency, in a manner reflective of the turbulent period of Jewish history in which they arise, Yiddish films revolve around characters who become treacherously cut off, disconnected, "excommunicated" (to use the term in a broad sense), and as a result are thrown into full-blown existential crisis, whose only means of resolution or mitigation appears to derive from a type of reentry into the world of communication. However, to describe these characters as grappling with "troubled communication," we realize, might court skepticism, if not resistance, within some corners of media theory. Along these lines, in *Speaking into the Air: A History of the Idea of Communication*, an influential, wide-ranging study that critiques the notion of so-called "perfect" communication, John Durham Peters argues that all communication is, at heart, troubled communication. For Peters, "perfect" communication, which he treats as synonymous with "the dream of communication as the mutual communion of souls,"[11] embodies a glaring contradiction, an impossibility, since communion obviates both the need and the potential for communication itself (in fact, for reasons that will become clear in our final chapter dealing with mystical modes of communication, what Peters describes as "communion" might better be described as "union"). Such a point dovetails with the interrelated media theory axioms that no communication is unmediated, and that no medium is transparent, a mere neutral container for information. Although we concur with Peters's sense of the inherently troubled nature of communication, what we would like to stress is that not all communicative troubles are the same. Once we leave the realm of abstract first principles and enter into specific contexts, certain forms of communication begin to look more or less troubled than, and differently troubled from, others. Accordingly, in Yiddish cinema, one finds a highly unique, highly emphatic iteration of troubled communication that stems from the particular social-historical predicaments that the films set out to capture—predicaments that, as mentioned, belong to one of the most turbulent periods in all of Jewish history (certainly European Jewish history). Mass immigration, the erosion of religious and familial traditions and the concomitant disorientations of modernity, labor struggle, the rise of political antisemitism that would lead to the Holocaust: all of these preoccupations, and more, inflect and ramify what Peters calls "the gaps of which communication is made," lending a distinctive cast to his conviction that "communication is a trouble we are stuck with."[12]

Harboring much hopeful, even utopian energy, Yiddish films feature a wide range of strategies and devices for dealing with the predicament of troubled communication. These include special, "metasemantic" modes of communication like music and silence; an ethics of "responsibility to the Other"; a certain approach to time that facilitates both memory and (possible) redemption; a sense of the portability of "home," a la Heinrich Heine's famous formulation regarding the Bible as a textual homeland; and an entertaining of the democratizing promise of mass media (which coexists with a series of misgivings about mass media), to name only a few. Nevertheless, the predicament recurrently proves stubborn, frequently failing to resolve entirely or with sturdiness at the conclusion ("negotiation" will be the watchword of our discussions of endings), and throughout manifesting in terms of what we call, in the only conceptual neologism that we've allowed ourselves, "hypercommunication." What we mean by this term is a mode of heightened activity infused with communicative yearning that acts not as a counterforce to troubled communication, in the sense of an enhanced or improved connectivity, but rather as a feverish symptom of unresolved blockage. This exaggerated form of communicative striving may lead to a measure of meaningful compensation, to a beating back against the instigating dilemma of excommunication, in the short or long term, but such a dialectical upshot is in no way guaranteed. Relatedly, the term "hypercommunication" also attracts us for the way it taps into the quality of excessiveness that is often attributed to Yiddish cinema. As J. Hoberman remarks, comparing Yiddish American melodramas to their Hollywood counterparts: "There is a stark, aggressively unmodulated quality to their [the former's] tear-jerking that suggests an entirely different tradition than that of the more genteel Hollywood weepies."[13] Along similar lines, Nahma Sandrow writes of the Yiddish theater, Yiddish cinema's most important aesthetic forerunner and frequent supplier of acting talent: "The popular style in Yiddish acting was unsubtle, broad, and electric. Yiddish actors to this day explain proudly that if there is one quality that sets them apart from their non-Yiddish fellows, it is the intensity and abundance of their temperament, which they also call energy, or presence."[14]

Given such observations, it is hardly surprising that the easily most prevalent genre in Yiddish cinema is melodrama, famously characterized as a "mode of excess"[15] by Peter Brooks in his landmark, championing 1976 study of the genre. Brooks serves as an important critical voice in what follows, especially regarding the recurrence of pathological states of "muteness" in melodrama. And yet, while we owe him a debt, we wish to point out up front that our consideration of specifically Yiddish melodrama compels us to adopt an important modification of his characterization of melodrama as a quintessentially Romantic and by extension "expressionistic genre."[16] As we argue, excess in Yiddish cinema functions not only in terms of a "pervasive concern with expression,"[17] but also, and even more importantly, given the recurrence of predicaments of disconnection, in terms of a pervasive concern with relation. Indeed, it would feel perilously incomplete to characterize a cinema all about reconnecting with others, reestablishing ties, and resuming a place within an accommodating communicative order, strictly under the banner of a movement—namely, Romanticism—that privileges the self and holds self-expression as a means in itself and the highest ideal.

A diasporic phenomenon produced in multiple countries—mainly Poland, the United States, Russia (with significant output after the 1917 Revolution), and Austria—Yiddish cinema began early in the second decade of the twentieth century, still early in the silent era, continued in various bursts across the divide into talking pictures, and reached a spectacular peak in the mid-to-late 1930s, before being abruptly cut off by World War II. After the war, it never fully recovered, never fully came back from its precipitous fall from what today is recognized as its "golden age," and for all the familiar reasons encompassed by the story of the decline of the Yiddish language more generally: the near-total destruction of the centers of Eastern European Jewish life in the Holocaust, the ascendancy of Hebrew as the official language of the fledgling Israeli state, and various forms of assimilation among Jews living around the world. In order to describe Yiddish's effective afterlife—a life by no means necessarily moribund, and yet at the same time clearly distinct from the life that was led earlier—Jeffrey Shandler has proposed the term "postvernacular."[18] From the beginning of Yiddish cinema until the onset of what we can thus describe as the postvernacular phase of the language—a phase extending into the present—around forty Yiddish features survive, the majority of which have been restored and circulate in periodic repertory or film-festival screenings and in home-video format.[19]

It is on this treasured archive of survivals that our book is based, while drawing most heavily on those titles from the "golden age" phase. Our justification for this makeup stems from an intention to produce extended, in-depth close readings of the films (obviously challenging to do with lost films), and from the fact that the "golden era" phase, inevitably, possesses a high quotient of representativeness. Accordingly, among the nine films that each receive a chapter-length treatment—and that all, in some way, specially captivated us during the course of watching and rewatching our way through the corpus of (existing) Yiddish cinema—one will find *The Dybbuk (Der Dibek)* and *Tevye*, arguably the two most famous Yiddish films, both prestigious adaptations of Yiddish theatrical/literary classics; a substantial share of highly obscure and in our opinion undervalued films on the spectrum of what is known as *shund*, a term of denigration and sometimes twisty affection that literally means "trash," and that covers a style of ultra-low-budget melodrama on steroids; a lonely voiced film that prophetically warns against Nazism at a startlingly early date; and a postwar film about Jewish DPs, made under extraordinary circumstances in the American-occupied zone of Germany (it is these last two films that respectively represent the earliest and latest of the films that we focus on, and that thus provide a loaded periodization, from 1933 to 1948, or from Hitler's rise to power to the founding of the state of Israel). In addition, as a way of mitigating the inevitable exclusionary costs of our focus, we have made considerable attempts to weave in allusions to, and short digressions on, several more

Yiddish films that fall both outside and inside the fertile mid-to-late 1930s period.

    A final word about method. Although we rely indispensably on the existing literature on Yiddish cinema, we depart from this body of research in a crucial way. All three monographs on Yiddish cinema—Eric A. Goldman's *Visions, Images, and Dreams: Yiddish Film, Past and Present* (1983, updated 2011), Judith N. Goldberg's *Laughter through Tears: The Yiddish Cinema* (1983), and J. Hoberman's *Bridge of Light: Yiddish Film Between Two Worlds* (1991, updated 2010)—move through the films, roughly speaking, "diachronically"; that is, following the chronology of the films, the books all show how Yiddish cinema developed over time; they are all, in short, histories of Yiddish cinema, which seek in their ways to encompass the entire phenomenon under investigation. Meanwhile, a number of articles published in journals and anthologies—notably among the latter, *When Joseph Met Molly: A Reader on Yiddish Film* (1999), edited by Sylvia Paskin—offer concentrated analyses of specific films or topics, and in this way necessarily dispense with any kind of encompassing optic. This book proceeds differently from, while at the same time sharing something with, both approaches. Namely, through an interlocking collection of concentrated analyses that are sensitive to historical context, we aim to provide a perspective on Yiddish cinema that is extensive, that treats Yiddish cinema as a kind of "total unit," and yet that takes conceptual matters rather than historical development as its through line. In this way, our approach can be likened to a "synchronic," or structural, approach, with the caveat that we retain a vantage on the whole of the material rather than on only a slice of it as it appears at a single point in time. Thus, while our chapters do not follow a consistent chronology, they refer constantly backward and forward to one another, revealing Yiddish cinema as a strikingly cohesive, Jewishly charged, dramatically embodied system of ideas about media and (ex)communication.

1

Powers of Music

A Little Letter to Mother (1938)

A Little Letter to Mother (*A Brivele der Mamen*) is the last, and most melancholy, of the four Yiddish films made in Poland by Joseph Green, a Yiddish theater actor, born in Lodz, who transplanted to America in the mid-1920s, spent time in Hollywood, and during the period of his turn to directing in the mid-1930s shuttled back and forth between his adopted and native countries.[1] Codirected with Leon Trystan—all of the films Green made in Poland were codirected—the film tells an epic story of familial disintegration that takes place between the years just before and just after World War I, and that stretches geographically from the shtetl to America. Like all of Green's Yiddish Polish films, which teem with musician characters and scenes of musical performance, the film exhibits a deep preoccupation with music, boldly announced by the film's title, a direct borrowing from a popular Yiddish ballad called "A Brivele der Mamen." Written in 1907 by the Minsk-born, American composer Solomon Smulevitz, the song tells the story (elements of which the film also borrows) of a Jewish mother in the Old Country who ends up dying tragically alone, after many years of waiting in vain for her son, who has moved away to America, to respond to her scores of pining letters.[2] Early on, as the son is preparing to embark on his emigratory voyage, the mother issues an injunction to "send a letter every week," a demand to stay in touch that each one of her subsequent "hundred letters" sent over the years effectively reiterates, and that the son strenuously fails to heed. Hence the final verses find the neglectful child in his lavish New York home receiving one last letter, one bearing news of his mother's death—or rather, receiving that missive and one more, for the narrator addresses the son in order to convey his mother's "last wish," which of course is but another version of the original injunction: "Say a little kaddish for your mother, / don't delay . . . / Your mother will hear the kaddish / from her grave. / You'll heal her pain, her bitter heart. / You'll delight her soul."

The heartbreak of the song derives, notably, not so much from the separation per se between the family members, but rather from the son's failure to oblige his mother's repeated appeals for communication. According to the logic of the song, that is to say, epistolary media might well serve as a means to keep a diasporically fragmented family intact, in some form. And indeed the concluding verse recapitulates such a hopeful belief, such a faithful investment in the ameliorative capacity of long-distance communication. For if the son were willing at last to obey his mother's desire for reconnection and say kaddish for her, then the prayer, the narrator assures him, would cross ontological boundaries and reach her in "her grave," connecting the two estranged family members and making up for all the son's excruciating nonresponsiveness when his mother was still alive. Given that we never find out whether the son does ultimately reform and say the prayer, that we are left on a note of uncertainty and prolonged troubled communication, however, it ultimately falls to Smulevitz's ballad itself to mourn and commemorate the mother. The tearjerker of a song itself, that is, becomes positioned to function as a form of kaddish and vehicle of remembrance for the mother—and, by extension, for all the Eastern European Jewish mothers who, amid the massive waves of immigration still unfolding at the time the song was written, have met with a similar fate.

As we'll see, this figuration of music as a potent bearer of memory is one that Green's film faithfully echoes and richly elaborates, thus partaking of a larger, pervasive trend in Yiddish cinema, where, again and again, we find music working as a medium specially endowed with vigorous powers of (re)connection, as a privileged channel that, when all other channels have failed, manages to supersede material obstacles, make impossible journeys across long distances, transcend ontological boundaries, among other incredible feats, and at last deliver the all-important message.

The Gesture of Listening to Music

What, however, accounts for music's extraordinary communicative prowess? In an exploration of "the gesture of listening to music," Flusser begins to answer this question by drawing a crucial distinction between the reception of music and the reception of semantically reliant forms of communication like speech: "Music is heard differently from speaking voices (*logoi*). With speaking voices, one hears as one deciphers, one 'reads.' . . . There is actually a deciphering in hearing music as well, for music is codified sound, and so a musical message is just as logical as that of the *logoi*. But it is no 'semantic reading,' no deciphering of codified meaning. Despite centuries of discussion, there is still no agreement about what is being deciphered when we hear music."[3] In listening to music, no "semantic reading" is necessary because it is the listener's *body* that is extensively "set . . . in vibration"[4] by sound waves and that receives the message. On account of this intensely physical type of reception, Flusser characterizes the gesture of listening to music as a deep "adaptation"[5] on the part of the receiver to the message received, or as he puts it: "In listening to music, the body becomes music, and the music becomes a body."[6] Further, this effect of being physically, transformatively "moved" by music comes with special implications on an emotional plane. As Flusser explains, reaching back to the original sense of the Greek word *pathein*, which literally means "to feel": "The reception of music in the belly (and chest, sexual organs, head—all body parts disposed to oscillation, in short) is *pathos*, and its effect is empathy with the message. The acoustic message alone literally has this pathetic character. In all other messages the effect is only metaphorical."[7] In listening to music, which requires an intensive effort of attention and arrest, wherein the listener "is not actually concentrating on himself but—within his body—on the incoming sound waves,"[8] the listener thus might be said to engage in an exemplary, radical form of receptivity to the Other. Indeed, as Flusser points out, because music circumvents the difficulties of semantic codification and overcomes the physical border between the listener's body and the surrounding world—vibrationally changing the body's skin "from boundary to link"⁹—such communication results in the world appearing "not as a contradiction between subject and object but as 'pure relationship.' . . . [The listener] experiences man and world relationally, that is, relative to one another, becoming one, 'pure intentionality,' as Husserl put it."¹⁰ Accordingly, as Flusser concludes, the gesture of listening to music is "the gesture of ecstasy," and music "the very greatest, most sacred mystery," paradoxically on account of the fact that listening to music embodies a "perfectly profane, perfectly technical, and perfectly public (unconcealed) gesture." Music, that is, "does not need to conceal itself, for in its magnificent, supercomplex simplicity, in mathematical simplicity, it is obscure."¹¹

Viewed in such a light, it is no wonder that Yiddish cinema prizes music so highly, repeatedly representing the medium as possessed of special, often mystical, connective abilities, and correlatively treating other media that tend toward instrumental efficiency, distinct code, and distanciation—that is, that lack music's unique capacity for metasemantic, highly intimate "touch"—with a wary, critical attitude. As we'll see, *A Little Letter to Mother* offers a case in point, though, notably, only by effectively, gradually coming around to the point and portraying, for much of the first part of the film, a juxtaposition between the aesthetic world of music and the practical world of everyday survival in which the former comes across as deeply fraught. Indeed, whereas the ballad on which the film is based focuses on the communicative predicament of a mother, the plot of Green's film devotes considerable attention to a father, and specifically to his communicative troubles within both the family and the shtetl, which arise from his unremunerative career as a songwriter, as a freelance composer of Jewish tunes or melodies known as *nigunim* (pl. of *nign*).

Beginning in Luboml in 1912, the film opens with what appears to be an outright, full-throated celebration of music. At dusk, in an atmosphere of languid dreaminess, the father, Dovid Berdichevski (Alexander Stein), a mild-mannered figure recalling a kind of flaneur (top hat, long overcoat, ornamental cane), strolls leisurely down a lively main street of the shtetl, while basking in a chorus of heavenly voices that streams in from offscreen and, in line with Michel Chion's famous account of "acousmatic" sound, or sound whose source remains invisible, throbs with a sense of mystery and magical potency.¹² By chance, Dovid runs into his youngest child, the adolescent boy Arele (Irving Bruner), who passes off to his friend the goat that he's *shlep-*

ping, dashes over to his father, and exclaims excitedly, "The shepherd's song is beautiful today." Concurring, Dovid gently shushes and stills Arele so that the two can better absorb and appreciate the music, so replete, as the father points out, with "soul," in a moment that offers a perfect analogue to Flusser's notion that "the listener [of music] can only listen well when he concentrates, that is, somehow turns his muscles and nerves off."[13] Next enters a friend of Dovid's, the beleaguered albeit steadfastly jovial tailor Shimen (Max Bozyk), who complains to Dovid: "You're lucky. Your Dobrish likes a song . . . My Malke doesn't understand such things . . . I must pretend to deliver pants in order to hear a little music. As if a tailor had no soul. One can live without a chicken in the pot, but not without a song. Life would be bitter." And next comes another friend, an unnamed cantor at the local synagogue (Simche Fostel), whose hasty, dismissive attitude toward the music—"It's a gentile melody," he objects—is swiftly overturned. Taking umbrage at the remark, Dovid retorts, "Anything can be sung our way," and proceeds, on the spot, to adapt the melody to a Hebrew verse, "Praise be the Lord, His mercy endureth forever," and this confection—which exemplifies the hybrid nature of cultural production in the diaspora, as well as the metasemantic operations of music (as per Dovid's retort, it is as if the words don't so much matter, are secondary to the intensely affecting/touching "pathos" of the music)—causes the cantor to reconsider. Indeed, the cantor reacts to the remediation of the melody with a fervent desire to "hear it again" and proceeds enthusiastically, along with Shimen, to learn the tune, guided by the obliging songwriter.

Continuing to evolve from its embryonic state, Dovid's composition later plays a crucial role in the plot, serving as an agent of climactic recognition and exhibiting the connective powers of music in a most spectacular fashion. The opening scene chimes with this eventuality and yet at the same time is laced with subtle (and eventually not so subtle) ambiguities regarding music, which aren't as easily dispelled as the cantor's initial resistance to the shepherd's song. Shortly after Arele passes off the goat and joins his father, for instance, he is swiftly re-preoccupied by practical matters, repeatedly reminding his father that his mother is expecting them, and thus that they must stop all the listening and talk of music and hurry home. By and large, Dovid ignores such pleas. Although Arele's first urging manages to move them along (however with no sense of alacrity in

Dovid), amid the second urging, the father is suddenly rivetted by a turn in the offscreen music and, with one hand restrainingly on the child's shoulders and the other raising his cane in the air, once more plunges into a state of rapt, suspended listening. In this way, Arele emerges as the more responsible, the more parental, of the two Berdichevskis, and indeed the force of his practical demands significantly escalates through the sudden appearance of Malke (Chana Lewin), Shimen's musically disinclined wife, while Dovid teaches the new *nign* to his friends. Aproned and irate, Malke scolds Shimen for tarrying in the delivery of the (fictitious) pants and drags him back to work, thus propelling the meeting between the men to a close. In short, while the men inhabit a world of music that fills them with romantic exhilaration, the scene more and more hints at the same space as one of problematic, unproductive, male escapism: a portrayal that, as we'll see, emerges out of broadscale shifts in the structure of traditional Jewish society and the traditional Jewish family.

Authority and the "Passive" Father

Unable to find a substantive audience for his music out in the wider world, beyond his immediate circle of friends and (select) family, Dovid's songwriting fails to bring in any money, and as a result, the role of provider in the Berdichevski family is assumed by Dovid's wife Dobrish (Lucy Gehrman), a capaciously resourceful woman, whose stout, earthy build contrasts distinctly with Dovid's slenderness and timidity, and who, all on her own, runs the family's dry goods store. Such a familial makeup, in which it is the mother who interacts with the world and economically sustains the family (in addition to managing the domestic sphere), while the father pursues effectively nonproductive ends, suggestively evokes the traditional Jewish family structure—a structure that, as Daniel Boyarin details in *Unheroic Conduct: The Rise of Heterosexuality and the Invention of the Jewish Man*, an influential study of gender in Jewish culture, crucially differs from the traditional Western European Christian bourgeois family structure. In Jewish culture, Boyarin points out, "the greatest value was placed specifically on the economically 'useless' practice of Torah study," a practice officially restricted to men, and thus it became not just necessary, but highly accepted for Jewish women, "through their labor and business acumen,"[14] to enable their husbands to partake in such highly valued, impractical scholarly activity.

In other words, taking a nonpathological attitude toward "passive" men and "active" women, who were (or often enough were) viewed by the surrounding culture respectively as "sissies" and "phallic monsters,"[15] Jewish culture effected a striking inversion of traditional Western gender roles. As Boyarin remarks, the Jewish structuring of gender according to which a woman works in order to support her husband's religious learning "issues in a reversal of the topoi of public and private that encode male and female within European culture. Although, to be sure, those topoi are themselves seriously open to question, they are nevertheless active as commonplaces and norms, and much of upper-class Jewish culture reverses them exactly, offering the private spaces of study and prayer as most appropriate to the male and the public spaces of getting and spending to the female."[16]

The Berdichevskis aren't upper class—they are, at best, struggling to hang on to middle-class status—but, as Boyarin stresses, the elite class provided an "ideal model"[17] for Jewish society writ large, and so it makes sense that we can recognize inflections of such a model in the Berdichevski family dynamics, in spite of the family's precarious economic standing. In fact, while Dobrish in her role as provider strongly recalls what Boyarin calls the "Glikl type"—after Glikl of Hameln, a deft Jewish businesswoman in early modern Europe, famous today for her pioneering Yiddish memoirs[18]—Dovid can be seen as a variation, in the form of an artist, on what Boyarin calls the *yeshiva bokher* type, which refers to the figure of the retiring, pensive, gentle yeshiva student, who plays a key role in Boyarin's deep genealogy, stretching all the way back to the Babylonian Talmud, of the feminized Jewish male. (Notably, a *yeshiva bokher* as such takes center stage in Edgar G. Ulmer and Jacob Ben-Ami's 1937 *Green Fields* [*Grine Felder*], though a rather atypical one—one not entirely satisfied with his life in the yeshiva study hall who ventures out into the luminous countryside in search of "true Jews."[19])

At the same time, as much as we can appreciate a resemblance between the Berdichevskis and the ideal/prototypical traditional Jewish family, it is important to bear in mind that Dovid's "passivity" is not quite the same as that of the traditional Jewish father. In the case of the latter, "passivity" is associated with the highly privileged, gender-restricted study of Torah, which grants the father a deep sense of authority within the family. To adapt Flusser's approach to understanding "the family unit"—which he treats as a variable type of communication structure "that aims at transmitting some essential cultural information from one generation to another"[20]—the unique knowledge to which the traditional Jewish father had access, and which he then mobilized and transmitted within the multigenerational domestic sphere, operated in the service of a hierarchy of family relations in which he occupied the top-most position. In other words, the traditional Jewish family structure, although importantly different from the traditional European family structure (in which the father derived authority from his exclusive working relationship with the world), still remained predominantly patriarchal in nature. What we find in the case of Dovid is a father whose endeavors do not transmit religiously based authority, while neither do they manage to make money and turn him into a provider. Dovid fails, that is, to occupy the patriarchal position of either the traditional Jewish father or the traditional European/bourgeois father. And the fact that he is a struggling "author"—a word, it is useful to recall, that bears a strong etymological tie to "authority,"[21] and that plays a central part in Flusser's characterization of the patriarchal father as "an authoritative memory, in the sense of being imperative, and in the sense of being an author of information"[22]—makes this twofold failure all the more significant.

A Little Letter to Mother dwells heavily on Dovid's problematic lack of paternal authority, portraying it across a series of scenes in which we are afforded an intimate glimpse into the dynamics of the Berdichevski family, which includes two other children besides Arele: an older son and daughter, both in their late teens or early twenties. We enter the home for the first time shortly after the opening scene, witnessing Dobrish arguing hotly with the daughter Miriam (Gertrude Bulman) and admonishing the pretty, headstrong girl against continuing an affair with her older, urbane dancing teacher: a relationship that threatens to sabotage Miriam's parentally approved—and likely prearranged—engagement with Shimen's son Yudke, who is away studying engineering in Odessa. In the midst of this squabbling, Dovid and Arele make their return, heralded by the offscreen sounds of Dovid's blithe, bouncy singing. At this point, the film pans from the table, where Dobrish and Miriam are seated, over to the doorway, forging a suggestive juxtaposition (which would have been lost, or at the very least diminished, by a cut from the table to the doorway) between the activities of the two familial pairs, and more specifically between the vexed, disciplinary seriousness of the maternal voice and the playful levity of the paternal voice. "Let's be very quiet, Father, or we'll both be spanked by Mother," Dovid trills to Arele, wagging a minatory finger at him. Dovid is kidding around, being parodic, of course, and yet the joke's implication that he has been reduced to a kind of disempowered infant within the family contains a strong dose of truth and continues to be borne out throughout the scene. First, quickly cutting off her quarrel with Miriam and throwing up a cheery, all-is-well façade as soon as Dovid and Arele enter the room, Dobrish protectively, "maternally" conceals from her husband all the disturbing *tsores* with which she has been trying to cope. Instead of alerting Dovid to what's going on with their daughter and soliciting his potential assistance, she says with tender indulgence: "Everything he sings, and why shouldn't he?" Next, in another gesture of seeming frivolity that betrays the tensions within the family and the reality of its topsy-turvy power dynamics, she points out to Dovid that his "tie is crooked" and proceeds, like a *mame* to her *yingele*, to set the tie straight—doing so with a marked forcefulness that compels Dovid to protest, with a pained series of *oy-oy-oy*s, "You'll choke me." Such a gesture reveals not so much the traits of a stereotypical overbearing (suffocating) Jewish mother as Dobrish's feelings of unconscious aggression toward her husband for his shortcomings, a resentment that coexists, uneasily and ambivalently, with her desire to protect Dovid and sustain the use of his "ever-singing" voice: a desire, of course, that only further undermines Dovid's authority and ensures the prolongation of his problems, for it is not as if singing allows him to assert his paternal role, his struggling career as a songwriter forming the crux of his paternal crisis in the first place.

The scene's tensions escalate considerably with the entrance of the eldest Berdichevski child, Meir (Izak Grudberg), a tall, brooding, aimless university student. Shirking any greetings or niceties as he sits down at the table, Meir briskly announces that he has yet one more time changed his course of study ("I've decided to drop pharmacy. I'll become a doctor"), which incites a rebarbative exchange with his sister. "He becomes and becomes, but meanwhile he's nothing," Miriam quips, to which he quips back, "And you only dance and dance," alluding to her affair with the dancing teacher, which, we now begin to realize, is far from a well-kept secret, at least for anyone paying attention. In many ways, the children appear to take after their father and his struggles and complications. Meir's fecklessness regarding his future occupation mirrors Dovid's challenges making a living. Like her father, Miriam exhibits a perilous attraction to the charms of art, giving herself over to beauty at the expense of practical matters; indeed, in preferring the dancing teacher to Yudke, she dashes a presumably secure future as the wife of a hard-working engineer. As Miriam excuses herself from the table in the middle of the meal, remarking in an attempted-blasé tone that she is "going out for a while," her brother casually undermines her suspicious circumlocution by exposing her true plans: "She's meeting that dancing teacher, of course!" The stating of the open secret triggers Miriam to storm out of the room, which in turn triggers her mother (notably not her father, who by this point has been cropped out of the frame by the panning of the camera) to spring out of her seat and shout through the doorway: "You're not going! YOU'RE NOT GOING!" Yet the command proves futile, failing to stop Miriam or draw her back inside the house. Hence, in the face of Dovid's failures, Dobrish may be thrust into the role of the head of the household, a role that she assumes heroically, but her occupying the power vacuum does not equate to filling it. Returning to the table to find Dovid sloping his head and vacantly making circles on the table with a spoon, Dobrish articulates her frustration at such a state of affairs, in an aggrieved mix of assertion and interrogation: "You're the father, and you sit there and say nothing." Indeed, what Dovid is able to say only justifies the circumstantial necessity of his silence. "A father who doesn't support his family *has* to look on and say nothing," he declares resignedly, before letting out a protracted, deflationary exhalation that brings the scene to a fade-out end.

Later, Dovid's troubles are brought much more decisively and cuttingly out into the open by Meir, who displays nothing of his mother's prevailing urge to protect her husband. In another domestic scene, Meir enters the room and, significantly neglecting to address his father, impatiently announces, "Mother, I'm going to Odessa," and proceeds to savage his father's vocation, denigrating the evolving, new song (which Shimen and the cantor have come over to practice) as a *"nign shmign."* Meir's latest plan, as he explains, is to become a dentist—a plan to which his mother reacts with anxious skepticism: "Always something else. What will become of you?" Here Dovid's friends, rightly sensing a row about to break out, bid their goodbyes in order to give the family privacy. "We're not rich, times are bad, mother works hard," Dovid chimes in hesitantly, attempting to get a foothold in the conversation, to which his son fires back: "Mother, mother! Of course she works! Why don't *you* do something? . . . If we had a father like everyone else, things would be different!" This harsh, out-in-the-open attack on Dovid prompts Dobrish, as usual the disciplinarian in the family, to step in and give Meir a vigorous, loftily primed slap in the face, crying out: "So your father is not good enough?! You're not worth the dust on his shoes." Dobrish then collapses in tears, and Arele rushes over and throws his arms around her in consolation, his alacrity underscoring his father's chronic passivity and failure to respond to the urgencies of the moment. Indeed, while Arele makes the dash over to his mother in the foreground, Dovid remains stock-still, immobile, in the background. The arrangement of these three bodies in the frame—stunned, Meir exits the room—makes for one of the most evocative mise-en-scènes in the movie. Together, mother, son, and father form a triangular shape, with Dobrish and Arele constituting the two lower points, and Dovid, at a distance behind them, forming the pinnacle (see figure 1.1). The shape evokes the notion of hierarchy, and yet with an ironic perversity, for, as we've seen again and again, Dovid functions in no way as the head of the family. Accordingly, the scene ends with the camera dollying in and framing Dovid's blankly mortified face in increasingly tighter close-up, showing him as isolated, cut off, a mere point stranded outside any structure of relations at all.

Figure 1.1. The father stands behind his wife and child in a moment of paternal crisis, the three forming an ironic image of hierarchy. Joseph Green and Leon Trystan, *A Little Letter to Mother* (1938).

Given all this, as well as a humiliating scene in which Dovid, like a wraith, incapable of intervening in the drama of his own life, spies on Dobrish through the window of the dry goods store and overhears some women gossiping about how Dobrish supports him and bears her "punishment from heaven" while refusing to "let anyone say a word against him" (once more the film thus conjures an image of the mother as supreme operator, controlling the switchboard of communications not only within the family but also between the family and the outside world), the struggling songwriter decides to abandon his situation rather than try to resolve or adapt to it. That is to say, Dovid secretly absconds for America, confiding only in Shimen, from whom he solicits financial help, and whom he tells that he is taking the step "for my children's sake." In fact, the film leaves it open whether Dovid's decision to emigrate embodies a genuine act of self-sacrifice, intended to benefit the rest of his family down the line, or a convenient means of escape, a ploy allowing him to flee the wretched, ego-ravaging situation in which he has been entrapped for so long—or, of course, and perhaps most likely, whether the decision serves as both of these things, in a tangle of conscious and unconscious motivations. Nevertheless, what isn't in dispute is the communicatively disempowered manner in which Dovid takes the step. Only once he arrives to America does he explain his actions, sending home a letter, whichIzed reads aloud to Arele ("When I've become a success here, I'll send for all of you. We'll all be happy here"), and which causes her to break down in anguished tears rather than gather reassurance. In other words, Dovid strategically avoids a face-to-face encounter with Dobrish and instead takes recourse to a mode of communication at a distance—namely, letter writing—that precludes the possibility of immediate response, and thus of his voice being, as it invariably is, overpowered by his wife's.

Transformative Absence

With the passage of time, Dovid's physical absence produces effects that, unlike those that result from his virtual or metaphorical "absence" as a father while he is still present in Luboml, work in a positive direction, sparking energies of familial togetherness and elevating his reputation in the shtetl. Such a phenomenon gradually becomes apparent during Passover, presumably the first big Jewish holiday to fall in the wake of his departure. As the remaining family members sit down for the seder dinner, the mood is bleak. Draped with the *kittel*, the white robe customarily worn by the leader of the service,[23] Dovid's seat at the head of the table sits throbbingly vacant, as the camera repeatedly emphasizes in a series of frontal framings. Meanwhile, during the *mah nishtanah*, the recitation known in English as "The Four Questions" that the youngest at the table is tasked with performing, Arele goes off script and poses an importunate, distressed, highly personal "*fifth* question"[24] to the paternal void: "Why did you leave us?" Here, via a brief travel montage consisting of stock footage of the New York skyline double exposed with the billowing ocean, the film transports us to America, where we find Dovid sitting on a park bench next to a fellow Jewish immigrant, who effectively recapitulates Arele's question: "Why *did* you?" Dovid offers a regretful explanation: "You like to think that on the other side of the ocean is happiness, a paradise. So you fly away from home, like a bird, and often you perish, like a bird that's lost its way. Oh, if I could only be home now with my wife and children . . ." However, the most important part of his response is what comes next: a yearning, sorrow-drenched rendition of the usually riotously upbeat, seder-concluding song "Chad Gadya [One Little Goat]." As Dovid sings, the film takes us back, via the travel montage from before yet played in reverse, to the table in Luboml, where the seder has come, with fateful synchronicity, to the end, and Dobrish is just waking up from having nodded off during the long service. In her dreams, it appears, Dobrish had been mysteriously able to hear Dovid's distant singing, for she fondly reminisces, "When father sang that ["Chad Gadya"] the whole town would listen outside." As if to relive the memory (likely tinged with some exaggeration: nothing that we've seen previously suggests Dovid receiving such bountiful appreciation for his music), she then leads the table—including Shimen, who turns up for a surprise visit—in an emotional performance of Dovid's version of the song. The result is a transformation of the mood into one of hopeful persistence (notably, even Meir, previously so disparaging of Dovid's music, belts out the tune with total surrender), in which the viewer gathers the impression of the family achieving a kind of provisional reunion in spite of the ocean that separates them. (In this way, the moment also looks ahead to the climax of the film, where the mystically inflected powers of music to reconnect people receive their fullest elaboration.)

As for Dovid's reputation in the shtetl, rumors circulate wildly, via the primitive broadcast system of gossip (the shtetl "radio," as it were), that he has become a "success" in a typical, rags-to-riches, American-dream-style manner. In a busy market scene, news that Dobrish has received a letter from Dovid along with some "*gelt* [money]" swiftly passes from one person to another, and in the process becomes radically embellished. Upon the distorted news reaching him, a man comments with jesting, would-be knowingness, "A man who couldn't skin a cat here, in America he's a Rothschild," to which another adds, "Over there Rothschilds are as thick as flies." The reality, of course, turns out to be something quite different, as the insight into the functioning of the shtetl gossip mill, so given to fantasies of America as a Land of Plenty, prepares us. Indeed, the next time we see Dovid, he is in the midst of selling socks from a street cart, parked in front of a storefront awning suggestively emblazoned with the word "RADIOS" (see figure 1.2), a highly deliberate bit of set design (the New York street is clearly a soundstage replica) that functions as a shorthand way of linking America with technological

Figure 1.2. The songwriter father finds a new livelihood selling socks from a street cart in the New World; the word "RADIOS" gestures at America as a space of technological modernity and mass media. Joseph Green and Leon Trystan, *A Little Letter to Mother* (1938).

modernity (specifically with modes of mass media), while nodding to the film's key theme of communication at a distance (discussed further in the next section).

Obviously, the nitty-gritty job represents a significant departure from songwriting, and yet it grants Dovid some much needed independence and serves to close the distance between him and his youngest son. As he explains proudly to his acquaintance from the park who eventually turns up on the scene, the work has enabled him to make a living and earn enough to send a steamship ticket back home for Arele. That is to say, it appears to make little difference that in reality he has to resort to the lowly occupation of hawking *shmates*, droning the same stock commercial phrases over and over to indifferent strangers in a foreign language he barely understands ("Two for a qvarter, two for a qvarter . . ."), in order to have become the "success" that he had promised in his letter. Accordingly, it is with this image of Dovid plying himself at the labor that has enabled him to become an "active," if hardly hypermasculine, "provider" of a father (a transformation that will prove to have a decisive influence over the family's future) that the film shows him, poignantly, for the last time.

Epistolarity and *Mame-loshn*

In his pathbreaking work on what he calls "accented cinema," Hamid Naficy explores the ways that movies by exilic and diasporic directors display a recurrent, shared preoccupation with epistolarity, writing: "Exile and epistolarity are constitutively linked because both are driven by distance, separation, absence, and loss and by the desire to bridge the multiple gaps."[25] Given its derivation, titular and beyond, from Smulevitz's "letter-song," and its status as a product of, and reflection upon, diasporic conditions, *A Little Letter to Mother* unsurprisingly, amply bears out such an observation. Indeed, following the moving moment of musical togetherness at the seder table, all of the Berdichevski children, one by one, end up taking leave of their mother and using epistolary means in the wake of the severance. Miriam is the first child to leave, eloping with the dancing teacher and leaving behind a letter, which Dobrish finds as she awakens from maternally intuitive, darkly oracular dreams (Dobrish's oneiric faculty, as we saw in the seder scene and as we'll see again, functions in its own right as a potent communication device, as a medium for the reception of critical messages), and responds aghast to the empty imprint on the bed next to her. As Dobrish begins reading the missive, the film cuts to a stock image of a hurtling train, implied to be carrying Miriam away, and then cuts back to Dobrish, devastated, at the end of taking in the words. Literally fragmenting the process of epistolary reception, the film suggestively if rather unsubtly undermines the lingering connection that the letter, despite giving an account of Miriam's exodus, sustains. Indeed, whereas Naficy points out that epistolary media often "work in opposition to transportation means, also frequently inscribed in accented films, that usually function to keep people apart,"[26] the moment inverts this equation and shows transportation means working in opposition to epistolarity and thus highlights disconnection rather than reconnection. (Eventually, Miriam returns repentant after the affair falls apart, marries Yudke as originally planned, and moves away with her new husband to Odessa, after which we never see her again.) Such a pattern also underlies Arele's leave-taking for America, which occurs after the arrival of the steamship ticket from his father. In a wrenching scene at a train station, as the young boy leans out the window of the incipiently moving vehicle, his mournfully clad, hankie-bearing mother cries out: "Remember, dear heart, when you arrive across the ocean, the first thing you do is send a letter to your mother!" Right in the midst of her entreaty, however, the film cuts to a close-up of the train's massive, implacably churning wheels, while the soundtrack fills with the shrill whistle of departure. In other words, the film once more disrupts the connective energies of epistolarity, embodied here in the urgent demand to write rather than in a letter itself. (Luckily for Dobrish, such a disruption proves not to be definitive, as Arele turns out to shirk the template of the neglectful son in the Smulevitz ballad and to fulfill the demand to write to her. Indeed, the letters that he sends supply her not only with information about him but with kissable, clutch-able objects that allow her to indulge in an enhanced, tactile sense of reestablished connection, wherein, as Naficy observes, "letters stand in for those who are absent and inaccessible."[27])

All of the letters that Dobrish receives—these letters to *mame*—bear a potent double meaning, take on a fascinating added layer of significance, from the specificity of the language in which they are expressed. As Hoberman remarks, writing about an even earlier Yiddish film called *A Brivele der Mamen*, a silent film with live sound accompaniment that toured around the Pale starting in 1911: "The appeal of Yiddish and the thematics of a Yiddish cinema are inscribed in the very phrase '*a brivele der mamen*' and the ballad of the abandoned Old Country mother. That Yiddish is known to itself as *mame-loshn* (mother tongue) only doubles the urgency of her cry."[28] It is as if when a Yiddish mother demands that you send a *brivele der mamen*, she is demanding not only that you stay in touch with your *mame*, but that you stay in touch with the very medium that makes it possible for you and her to stay in touch, and that presumably you become at risk of losing when you go away to places where Yiddish isn't spoken. Such a sense of multiple, reflexive signification ripples especially through the third instance of Dobrish's epistolary engagement with a child who takes leave of her. The last of the remaining children, Meir departs when he is drafted into the army at the outbreak of World War I. Throughout the war, at least as far as we see, Dobrish never hears from him, though she has terrible nightmares about his death, portrayed in a phantasmagoric montage sequence of bombs exploding and Meir getting shot by an offscreen enemy. Once more showing the mother's oneiric faculty as endowed with remarkably intuitive, communicative/receptive powers, the nightmares turn out to be true, as Dobrish finds out at the end of the war, by which time she is living with Shimen and Malke in Warsaw, where the three flee after Luboml is attacked and goes up in flames. As the streets break out in celebrations, a disfigured, one-armed soldier who fought with Meir at the front shows up at the humble apartment and informs Dobrish: "His last words were 'Mother.' He died like a hero." With this verbally conveyed "letter" from Meir, we find an even richer, even more multilayered, reflexive enfolding of meanings than in the letters from Miriam and Arele. For not only is the message addressed to the mother and in the *mame-loshn*, but it also consists entirely of the word *mame*.

Such ruminations can be pushed even further, however. In line with Yiddish cinema's predilection for melodrama, to which belongs the subgenre of the "woman's film" (which we discuss further in chapter 5), mothers—or else a character, most often a daughter, who takes on a surrogate maternal role in the event of a mother's absence or death—feature in Yiddish movies with staggering frequency. *A Little Letter to Mother* provides one example, to which could be added: *Bar*

Mitzvah (*Bar Mitsve*, 1935), *Love and Sacrifice* (*Libe un Laydnshaft*, 1936), *Where Is My Child* (*Vu Iz Mayn Kind?*, 1937), *Two Sisters* (*Tsvey Shvester*, 1938), *Mamele* (1938), *Mothers of Today* (*Hayntige Mames*, 1939), *Mirele Efros* (1939), and *The Living Orphan* (*Der Lebediker Yosem*, 1939). In the face of such prominence of the maternal, we might thus think of Yiddish cinema as aspiring to the condition of *mame-loshn* itself: a *mame-cinema*, or, tapping into and teasing out a punning possibility internal to the name of its actual medium, a *cine-ma(me)*.

Musical Reconnection

With Meir dead, Miriam (presumably) still relocated in Odessa, Dobrish displaced in Warsaw, and no news about Arele and Dovid in America (the war having severely impaired communication lines), the final section of the film moves toward a critical measure of familial reconnection, realizing such a beating back against the forces of atomization by coming back to the marvelously relational, intimacy-establishing "powers of music." At the same time, and in many ways as a logical corollary of this, the narrative enters into an extended engagement with modes of institutional bureaucracy and mass media, which, by contrast, as alluded to earlier, the film subjects to critique and exposes as wanting in regard to the fierce need for intersubjective (re)kindling.

Representing the chaotic post-WWI moment in which thousands of Jews, among many others, were displaced, the film shows Dobrish taking recourse to HIAS (Hebrew Immigrant Aid Society), the real-life Jewish support agency, in order to try to track down information on the whereabouts of her husband and son in America. While in no way contesting the value of the institution, the film expresses notable worry over the manner of its operation, recoiling at the prospect of granting assistance to people in a way delimited by the standards of bare mechanical efficiency. (Later in the book, in chapter 8, which discusses a film that deals with Jewish displacement in the context of the aftermath of the Second World War, we return to similar territory regarding postwar bureaucratic structures of assistance and tracing.) Accordingly, as early in her efforts Dobrish waits interminably in the crowded HIAS office, where a passing clerk, to whom she appeals, rudely brushes her off, the film cross-cuts to a backroom space, where a senior figure, Mr. Stein (Misha Gehrman), himself a one-time HIAS-assisted immigrant to America who has now returned to Europe to supervise the postwar operation, gives an impassioned lecture, infused with his own experience of being on the other side of the partitioned, bureaucratic counter, to a group of younger employees. "Instead of brotherly assistance I see nothing but formality," he laments, and urges, "Away with all this stiff formality, these private offices, these windows. You shut out people and their troubles. Open your hearts to their human needs." As it turns out, it is Stein himself who, putting his own humanitarian philosophy—which openly flouts the maintenance of official, impersonal, "professional" boundaries—into practice, takes a special interest in Dobrish's case and counteracts her initially chilly, inhospitable experience with the institution. That is, while only able to find out information about Dovid, who has sadly died in the interim, Stein helps Dobrish arrange a steamship ticket to America so that she can continue to search for her son and not be left behind by Shimen and Malke, whose family in America have sent tickets for them. And such assistance from the uncommonly empathetic *mentsh* (played, fittingly, by Dobrish's husband in real life), which, critically, instantiates a mode of interpersonal interaction that stands opposed to, or at any rate, above and beyond, brute administrative power, proves pivotal in moving Dobrish's communicative troubles toward a point of resolution.

However, once Dobrish arrives in America, that point still stands a ways off, entailing an entanglement with yet another large-scale institution of mediation. This time, it is a newspaper: a form of communication technology that intersects with the reference to "RADIOS" on the storefront awning behind Dovid's street cart and further cultivates the image of America as a space of modern mass media, in contradistinction to the more communicatively low-tech shtetl. Accompanied by the cantor, who has also made his way to the country (and whose appearance, now sans beard, has undergone significant Americanization), Dobrish visits the headquarters of an unspecified Yiddish paper to publish a notice about her search for her lost son. Before revealing her sitting outside the office of the editor of the paper, where, with shades of her experience at the HIAS office in Warsaw, she has been futilely waiting for a long time, the film takes us into the editor's room where Arele (Edmund Zayenda), now a celebrated singer known as "Irving Bird," is having his photo taken for an ad for a HIAS benefit concert that he is slated to headline. Forging for the spectator an identification between the grown-up, dapperly tuxedoed performer and the young boy from Luboml, Arele's wife adjusts his bowtie in preparation for the camera, causing him to remark chucklingly, "Just like my mother. She would always fix my father's tie." Tellingly, the gesture appears void of any of the tension and underlying aggression manifested in its previous incarnation, suggesting that Arele and his wife don't suffer from the same problems as Arele's parents, and thus that a certain generational meliorism has transpired within the new environment. The moment also serves to display further Arele's difference from the neglectful son in the Smulevitz ballad, showing that he has eagerly hoped to remain in touch with his family and does maintain a strong connection to his roots despite his prosperous life in America. Replying to Stein, who is there negotiating the placement of the ad and inquires whether he has any relatives in Europe, Arele says: "No, unfortunately. There's no word from my family. Our home was destroyed." Indeed, even though he believes none of his family members are still alive, Arele plans to embark on a journey to Europe with his wife right after the concert in order to visit his old home, or whatever is left of it—a plan that, with devastating irony, threatens to reverse Dobrish's efforts and once more put an ocean between them.

As Arele leaves the office and we discover Dobrish waiting outside, the two estranged family members cross paths and yet fail to recognize one another: a common, fatefully infused occurrence in Yiddish cinema that serves to delay the climax and gather anticipation around it. However, what is most germane to our argument is how this missed connection is critically recapitulated, rather than in any way rectified, in the brief, evocative montage—a quintessential sequence of "hypercommunication," embodying a turbulent response to and continued immersion in troubled communication—that comes next and that shows the publication of Arele and Dobrish's respective notices. The sequence begins with a stock footage flurry of machine activity: a newspaper printing press rapidly churning out scores of copies. Next, we jump ahead in time to Dobrish, seated next to the cantor in an undisclosed domestic setting, eagerly scanning one of the copies and pointing something out to her companion on one of the pages inside. Here, the film cuts to a precisely frontal close-up of the page—the screen filling all over with Yiddish text—that reveals what Dobrish is pointing to, though, critically, without conveying a sense that this is her (or any character's) point of view. What we see there, in bold, outsized font, is the article about Dobrish, headlined "Mother Seeks Lost Son." The film gives us a few seconds to read the text, or at least get the gist of it, and then, in a fusion of panning and dissolving, brings us over to another page of the paper that contains the ad for the HIAS concert, capped by the headshot of "Irving Bird" that we saw being taken the other day (see figure 1.3). In an act wrought by postproduction special effects, the two articles thus brush up against one another, but only phantasmatically, without any tangible result. Or to put it differently, the brute fact of the two texts being published in the same issue, of a mediatized proximity between mother and son, fails to constitute an uncovering of the relation between Dobrish and Arele. And indeed, Dobrish's taking recourse to the newspaper—this highly distanciated, distinctly coded mass medium—doesn't end up playing any role in her reunion with her son.

Figure 1.3. A superimposed shot of two notices in the Yiddish press that conveys the idea of a missed connection between a mother seeking her son and her son, now a famous singer, headlining a HIAS benefit concert. Joseph Green and Leon Trystan, *A Little Letter to Mother* (1938).

Rather, of course, it is the climactic musical event that does the trick. Along with her small circle of friends from Luboml (Shimen, Malke, and the cantor), Dobrish attends the HIAS concert, where Arele, in the last performance of the night, backed by a substantial orchestra, sings a song that he has written especially for the occasion entitled "Memories of My Old Home." The song, somewhat of a pastiche that conjures the lost world of his childhood with fierce nostalgia and strong currents of romanticization (in reality, as we saw, Arele's family life as a boy involved quite dark and disturbing elements), begins with a set of verses that zero in on his father and the crucial place of music: "I remember when I was a child, I walked in the fields with my father. How beautiful were the melodies of the shepherd's flute! Oh, my heart yearns to see my old home! The song of the shepherd's flute filled my heart with joy! I remember the holiday songs, as Jews prayed with deep devotion." In the middle section, the song switches tonal registers and shifts from one of slow, heavy lamentation to one of sprightly jubilation, as Arele launches into music directly from his childhood: namely, the distinctive melody that Dovid begins to compose in the opening scene of the film. Right away, the old *nign* causes Dobrish and her friends to perk up and look around at one another in stunned confusion, initiating a process of recognition regarding Arele's identity that, especially for Dobrish, gradually intensifies as the song draws toward a conclusion. Following the "Dovid" interlude, the song returns to a series of melancholy verses, and for its grand finale offers a variation on the eponymous Smulevitz ballad:

> Remember, children—forget it never, never.
> She sits there waiting, waiting—your old mother.
> She sits there waiting, and she weeps and weeps.
> And as she weeps her head droops,
> And in her eyes the tears brim over.
> Waiting, waiting—your old mother,
> Waiting for your letter.
> You promised you'd write her. You promised. Remember?
> "Write, my child, that you are well. To mother write a
>   letter."

As Arele sings the climax of the song, which doubles as the climax of the film, several cutaway shots of Dobrish with tears streaming down her face identify her, and reinforce her identification, with the mother of the lyrics. As well, in the very last moments of the performance, yet just shy of its actual conclusion, Dobrish anomalously gets up out of her seat and approaches the stage, walking down the center aisle of the auditorium in an utterly transfixed state, as if mesmerically drawn, and ultimately reaching the front row, where, in a mix of uncontainable elation and longing, she lists forward on the tips of her toes with outstretched arms (see figure 1.4).

It is the film's most ecstatic musical moment, in which the entranced mother's deeply physical, transgressive, audience-protocol-shattering movement toward the source of the music strongly evokes Flusser's sense of the extreme empathic connectivity involved in the gesture of listening to music. Indeed, it is as if we get a rare visualization of his notion that in listening to music, "the body becomes music, and the music becomes a body." (One slight clarification vis-à-vis bodily *arrest*, which Flusser argues is a necessary

Figure 1.4. As Arele—now the celebrated "Irving Bird"—performs at the HIAS concert, Dobrish mesmerically approaches the stage in recognition of her lost son. Joseph Green and Leon Trystan, *A Little Letter to Mother* (1938).

component of music listening: while Dobrish's wildly absorptive listening involves her getting up and walking toward the stage, this is a type of movement that, driven by hypnotic forces, might best be described as a kind of *movement within suspension*, or in other words that is eminently reconcilable with Flusser's point.) Accordingly, it is in this aurally transcendent moment that Dobrish finally receives the message from Arele for which she has been waiting so long, and which has failed to be delivered by so many other means: the tracing services, the newspaper, and the casual, conversational encounter outside the newspaper office.

At the same time, the performance asks us to reassess, or to continue reassessing, the communicative troubles of the father, the anguished voicelessness that Dovid grapples with all throughout the first half of the film. That is to say, whereas early on Dovid's unremunerative, scantly recognized career as a songwriter stifles his ability to wield paternal authority and creates all sorts of fractious conflicts within the family, in the concert scene his *nign* serves as a commanding agent of familial reintegration, while receiving a resplendent "broadcast" out in the wider Jewish world for which he had always hoped for his music. Indeed, the performance's attestation to the fact that Dovid's song has been indelibly passed down to Arele causes Dovid to shine anew in terms synonymous with Flusser's notion of the "family unit" as a communication structure "that aims at transmitting some essential cultural information from one generation to another," and of the patriarchal father as a figure who actualizes such a process in terms of "an author of information." Of course, the performance recuperates the father not only as an "authoritative memory," as a bearer and transmitter of "original" information, but also as an object of memory; and, accordingly, Flusser is relevant here not only in regard to his communicative conceptualization of the family that draws on a cybernetic sense of "memory" (cf. "I shall use the word 'memory' to describe the systems (persons) that are connected in the process of human communication. And I shall define 'memory' as any system that stores information. Thus, for the duration of this lecture, humans shall be information stores, just like libraries, museum, and computers, as well as society, which shall be a net that connects such memories through cables to be called 'channels' "[29]), but also in relation to his understanding of memory in Judaism. As he remarks in one of his many references to the critical role ascribed to memory in Jewish tradition (a theme that we treat in greater detail in chapter 9): "I think the fundamental Jewish idea is that my immortality depends on the other person. That it is the other person who is responsible for my immortality, and I am responsible for his. This may be why Jews say of a dead person: 'Let his memory be a blessing.' Which may mean: I am responsible for him."[30] It is precisely this kind of human-scale, interpersonal, Jewishly coded act of "immortalization"—shot through with a sense of gratitude for his father's taking of responsibility for him, for the struggles without which there would be no illustrious "Irving Bird"—that Arele's performance accomplishes for Dovid.

In fact, such a rich braiding of music, memory, and Judaism also strongly figures in a scene not long before that offers an important rehearsal of the interrelation. Whereas usually the low-budget Yiddish cinema is compelled to portray the quasi-mythic/epic act of transatlantic emigratory passage through brief shards of stock footage (just as we saw earlier in the travel montage played and then replayed in reverse during the Passover seder scene that goes back and forth between Luboml and New York), the film represents Dobrish's journey to America through an extended, elaborate, staged sequence that invests the trip with a deep, rare quality of phenomenological vividness. The journey falling over the high holidays, the sequence includes a scene in which one of the spaces on the ship is transformed into a kind of mobile, makeshift synagogue and a huge crowd of Jewish passengers—women and men, young and old, a group far exceeding the minimum requirements of a *minyan*—partakes of Yom Kippur services, communally *davening* under the leadership of a talented cantor who happens to be on board, pounding their hearts, and rocking back and forth (seemingly in synch with the waves outside, to which the film periodically cuts away). Following this religious musical set piece, the film cuts to a guardrail on the deck, where Dobrish and Stein arrive, assume a perch, and pensively peer out into the watery distance, visibly moved by what they have just experienced. Here Stein reflects, offering a crystallizing commentary on the event: "Today's prayers impressed me very much. A ship in the middle of the ocean, and Jews praying like our forefathers long ago in their old synagogues." As Stein suggests, through the refraction of his own memory, the prayers, in calling back to the distant forefathers, seemed to vibrate with a particularly potent mnemonic charge. That is to say, he draws attention to the same interplay of forces at work in the equally transcendent musical scene on the horizon—where it is the specific "father" of the Berdichevski family, rather than the proverbial "forefathers," who is impressively recalled—and sets the relationship in a vital, much broader, Jewish cultural and historical frame.

An Almost Happy Ending

It is necessary to say one last word on the ending of the film—the actual ending of the film, which isn't comprised by the climactic concert scene—and especially so since such further analysis opens on to the broader question of endings in Yiddish cinema, to which we return again and again. As we'll see, the "happiness" of Yiddish film endings almost always presents in a qualified manner, inflected by elements of instability, uncertainty, and/or incompleteness. Such a phenomenon speaks to the acuteness of the problems whose reality the films attempt to capture, as well as, consciously or unconsciously, to a cultural consciousness long accustomed to ordeals and misfortunes, and thus for which smooth, all-out resolution would have a ring of hollowness and inauthenticity. In this way, the pervasive crisis of troubled communication, though tending to be assuaged in the end (and often gloriously), also tends to persist in some form. Thus in *A Little Letter to Mother*, for one thing, the entire family is not in the end reunited (as one might expect, for instance, if this were a Hollywood film), owing to the deaths of Meir and Dovid, and Miriam presumably having a life in Odessa. As a result, the film provides only a partial reunion, consisting of just Dobrish and Arele, while adding a kind of virtual reunion involving the father via Arele's memorializing musical performance. Notably, however, the fragmentary nature of the reunion and the need to take recourse to memory are not the only challenges roiling the ending. As mentioned, the film does not end with the concert scene. Rather, as Arele is mobbed by the crowd at the end of the performance and whisked out of the auditorium, Dobrish desperately follows him out on to the streets, where the long-suffering mother is made, astonishingly, to suffer ever more. Namely, she is hit by a car, knocked down unconscious, at which point Arele leaps out of his limo, rushes over to her, and recognizes her as his mother. Next, we cut to a hospital, where Dobrish wakes up amid a flashback of images of Arele as a boy, knowingly collates these with the solicitous face leaning over her bedside, and, finally, completes the act of mutual recognition. All of which is to say: the film overstays its welcome, entering into a strange, jarring narrative prolongation, which indeed Green himself regretfully acknowledged. Asked in an interview in the late 1970s if he would have changed the ending of the film, he responded: "Yes. Yes, I would. To begin with, I would not let her [Dobrish] have an accident. That was an anti-climax. But the concert is all right, the melody, because . . . It should have ended there."[31] In other words, the concert in which Dovid remediates his father's *nign* more than adequately seals the reconnection between mother and son, producing in effect a proleptic impression of a reunion between them, and so the subsequent two scenes take on a sense of redundancy. Nevertheless, the fact of the "slip" is revealing, and worth attending to (as are all the involutions and peculiarities of Yiddish film endings), hurling us back into quandaries of troubled communication, now at the level of narrative form, and toward their reopening and working through in the body of Yiddish films at large.

2

Discourse and Dialogue

The Living Orphan (1939)

SET ENTIRELY IN AMERICA, where it was made, Joseph Seiden's *The Living Orphan* (*Der Lebediker Yosem*), also known as *My Sonny* (*Mayn Zundele*),[1] greatly expands upon *A Little Letter to Mother*'s evocation of the "modern" "New World," picturing America as a realm dominated by technology (especially technologies of mass media), capitalism, secularity, and a Western-bourgeois conception of the family. In other words, regarding this last issue, we find a world in which the traditional Jewish family structure (discussed in chapter 1), based upon the dynamic of a "passive" father and an "active" mother, has all but disappeared and been replaced, has undergone a kind of assimilative process, as Boyarin would put it, of un-queering, and it is this newer, "straighter" version of the family with which the central problematic of the film is acutely bound up. For, telling another story of familial disintegration, this time involving a stage couple and their young child, the film locates a major source of the crisis in the mother's career ambition, which subverts her expected role in the family as an "angel in the house" (viz., a mother whose activity is confined strictly to the domestic sphere, unlike the fusional, private- and public-acting "Glikl type"), and disruptively vies with the father's expected role as the sole breadwinner. Meanwhile, continuing the pervasive Yiddish-cinematic "critique" of mass media that we saw in *A Little Letter to Mother*, the familial (and patriarchal) breakdown also intriguingly emerges in relation to professional *success* in the music and entertainment industry, which both mother and father enjoy. That is to say, the highly touted careers of the couple emerge as laced with a dark, problematic underside, as—to borrow the key conceptual opposition from Flusser that animates this chapter—hazardously overinvested in "discourse" and not enough in "dialogue."

Discourse and Dialogue

In stark contrast to the opening scene in *A Little Letter to Mother*, where the shepherd's song creates a blissful pastoral atmosphere and somewhat nostalgically defines the public space of the pre-WWI shtetl in terms of pretechnological communication, Seiden's film tellingly begins with a radio broadcast, drawing attention to the fact that the story is placed in an entirely different public realm, one defined by highly technologized (mass) mediation. The first shot of the film takes us to the headquarters in New York of what was at the time the biggest Yiddish radio station in America, WEVD,[2] shown in a documentary shot of the façade of the building, emblazoned with the station's acronym in vertical neon lights. This establishing shot is followed by a brief cutaway to an anonymous female listener tuning in at home, or what we are meant to read as the radio program's prototypical audience member: a listener who is remote, dispersed from other listeners, and situated within private space (in contrast, recall Shimen's complaint in *A Little Letter to Mother* that he has to make excuses to his wife and come *out* of his workshop in order to hear a little music). What ensues is an exclusive, behind-the-scenes glimpse of what for those tuning into the program within the world of the film remains a strictly auditory experience. Amid a curtained, stagelike area inside the station, a bespectacled announcer sits at a desk and introduces "the great star, Mr. Muni Berger" (Gustav Berger), a dark-suited, solemn-looking man in his late twenties or early thirties, who proceeds to sing, with intense emotion, a piano-accompanied version of "his hit song, '*My Sonny*,'" a sorrowful ballad that takes the form of an address to the singer's child:

My child, little son,
May I protect you from any pain,
May you live long,
May you always be healthy.
When the sky is overcast,
With a dark cloud,
You open your eyes,
And my heart grows light.
You're the apple of my eye,
A blessing on your head.
My little son, my kaddish'l,
May your pain be mine!

While showcasing the performance in its entirety, the film takes full expressive advantage of the privileged, additional channel afforded by its own audiovisual medium. A medium shot of Muni, which abstracts him from the space of the stage and illustrates his deep absorption in the song, dissolves into a close-up of an infant in a crib sucking restlessly on a rattle, of what we are meant to assume is the object of the singer's engrossed imagining. Despite all the passion that Muni infuses into the song, however, the end of the performance is met by an awkward silence, owing to the absence of a live audience, and this lingering nonreponse causes a disconcerted frown to appear on Muni's face, prompts an ominous change that, of course, remains beyond the apprehension of his radio listeners (see figure 2.1). Meanwhile, following a brief sign-off, the announcer walks over to Muni and reports that a kind of response to his performance has in fact been made, via the supplementary channel that the station provides to its audience, and yet the news does nothing to reverse Muni's deflation:

ANNOUNCER: During your song we got over 100 calls. You sing with such love, such soul.

MUNI: When I sing, I see my son before my eyes.

ANNOUNCER: Yes, but you yourself are so sad.

MUNI: It's nothing, as long as the audience is happy.

Figure 2.1. Muni's deflated expression after his performance at the radio station. Joseph Seiden, *The Living Orphan* (1939).

Revolving around the radio broadcast of Muni's performance of "My Sonny," the opening sequence of the film right away establishes a conception of the father in communicative terms. Within these terms, however, the father's transmitted voice comes across as an intriguingly ambiguous entity. Clearly, "the great star, Mr. Muni Berger," possesses formidable communicative powers. As an "author" of information occupying the authoritative position within the structure of mass communications and speaking unidirectionally to the many, he commands great admiration from his audience—hence the "over 100 calls" that the station receives during his performance. At the same time, such a wild lighting up of the station's switchboard serves less to introduce a meaningful element of intersubjective connectivity into the situation than to quantify and buttress up Muni's authorial and authoritative success. Indeed, the fact that the channel by which Muni communicates so powerfully offers no substantive opportunity for the receivers to directly respond to him appears to give rise to a troubling emotional disconnect between the (sad) performer and his (happy) listeners, a rift that makes us rethink the performance as an ostensibly unqualified communicative triumph.

The film's representation of radio—whose communicative structure, in a move typical of Yiddish cinema, is repeatedly foregrounded—exemplifies Flusser's important classification of mass media as "discursive," and more specifically as "amphitheatrical." As Flusser points out, discursive media operate in a one-way fashion, aiming to distribute and preserve information; meanwhile, "amphitheatrical" discursive media exhibit a specific type of discourse structure in which a centralized broadcaster "emits information towards a circular horizon of mutually non-communicating receivers."[3] In such a scenario, "there is no existential rapport between emitter and receivers, nor between the receivers,"[4] and consequently "amphitheatrical discourse excludes dialogue, excludes revolution, and excludes 'progress'"[5]—a lack of opportunities for dynamic, immediate interchange between any of the participants in the communicative process that constitutes a source of concern for Flusser. As he writes, contrasting discursive media with dialogic media (i.e., two-way media that aim to produce new information), and pointing out the difference between the two types in terms of their (in)ability to cultivate "responsible" human relations (as we'll discuss later, Flusser's pervasive concern with "responsibility," or "response-ability," finds a place within a larger tradition of Jewish ethics):

> Responsibility is not an immediate answer, but the capacity for an immediate answer, and the accent should be on the word "immediate." Of course: we may be capable of answering even the messages of discourse through one medium or another. One may send letters to newspaper editors or use the phone to call TV stations. But in dialogue it is the medium itself that permits our answer. Responsibility is this immediateness of our capacity to answer. This is why discourse fosters an irresponsible attitude in the receivers, while dialogue provokes a responsible attitude even during reception (responsibility is of course a political attitude; it is the capacity and readiness for publication).[6]

It is important to point out that Flusser, avoiding setting up a crude binarism, affirms that discourse and dialogue cannot so easily be distinguished from one another, that they are in fact comprised of inescapable aspects of one another, the perception of which depends heavily on what he calls the "'distance' of the observer."[7] As he writes: "[A] book on a scientific subject may be considered, if observed in isolation, to be a discursive communication. If observed in the context of other publications, it may be considered part of a dialogue: the scientific 'debate.' And if observed from an even greater distance, it may be considered part of that scientific discourse which flows ever since the Renaissance and characterizes our civilization."[8] At the same time, Flusser reminds us, "at certain places and certain moments one structure prevails over another,"[9] and thus the opposition ultimately does possess a productive, practical descriptive value. Accordingly, in the case of mass media, it is obvious that a discursive structure predominates, and so Flusser taxonomizes mass media (i.e., print, radio, television) under the banner of the discursive. At any rate, his underlying point—that the structural organization of a communication process along either discursive or dialogic lines strongly informs an audience's attitude toward the information that they receive, and toward the author of such information—resonates strongly with the opening radio sequence of *The Living Orphan*. A big part of Muni's troubled connection with his audience appears bound up with the medium through which he communicates with them, and through which they cannot communicate back. Just as in the examples of amphitheatrical mass media that give a false appearance of two-sided interaction by allowing the audience to "respond" through an additional channel not inherent to "the medium itself" (i.e., newspapers that permit us to send letters, TV stations that allow us to call in), Muni's fans vigorously phone into the radio station and yet remain insuperably disconnected from his true feelings. As distances between communicators increase through technology, it seems, an "existential rapport between emitter and receivers" becomes more and more difficult to establish, with the result that "the participants do not recognize themselves nor their partners as 'humans'"[10] within their communicative contexts. Celebrity authors turn into idols, and audience members, listeners, turn into numbers.

Regarding the musical content of Muni's performance, this notion of the dehumanizing effects of amphitheatrical discourse provides another way of saying that the audience loses its ability to empathize with the "pathos" of the message, which Flusser holds to be an essential feature of musical communication. As one will recall from the previous chapter, Flusser understands music as a communicative mode that resonates with receivers on a physical, visceral level and thus possesses the ability to "touch" an audience in a special, empathic way that transcends semantics, so long as listeners adopt the requisite stance of arrested openness toward the sounds. In *The Living Orphan*, the radio broadcasting of Muni's performance appears to effect a radical transformation in "the gesture of listening to music" that traditionally transpires in a live, face-to-face situation. Technically speaking, various relays distort the song, disembodying the original message and inescapably introducing media-specific noise into the equation (information is added and lost). Or, as Adorno puts it in his writing for the Princeton Radio Research Project, carried out in exile in the 1930s through the early 1940s, and especially concerned with the broadcasting of live music, which at the time constituted the overwhelming majority of radio music: "Good reception is by no means identical with reproduction suitable to the original work."[11] Indeed, Adorno sketches out a whole series of disjunctions in the radio situation worth pointing to in the context of Seiden's film and Flusser's notion of amphitheatrical media. Taking up radio's endless returning to certain "standard" or classic works, Adorno elaborates acidly on how this repetition is liable to banalize such works and reduce them to mere household background noise: "When they [standard works] are played again and again, they can no longer uphold the dignity of the occasion. . . . They show . . . a tendency to mingle in his [the listener's] everyday life because they can appear at practically every moment, and because he can accompany brushing his teeth with the Allegretto of the Seventh."[12] Along similar lines, Adorno points out that "the intensity of musical 'statement,' which is so important for the impressiveness of the symphonic movement, is lost as soon as it is lowered to the acoustic conditions of a private room,"[13] and thus that such loss leads to an attenuation of attention that—shades of Flusser—music requires for its proper reception. As Adorno explains, contending that time tends to come undone in the live music situation (where, say, an hour can seem, almost magically, to pass by in a moment): "As soon as this intensity is lacking [on account of being transmitted over the radio], the symphony drops out of its suspension; it, so to speak, falls back into time. The concentration vanishes; the listener may concentrate upon certain details or parts, but it is most unlikely that he will be able to realize the relation between the part and the whole as well as he could with the intensity of presentation of every moment. Thus the symphonic work, in a way, will be atomized when presented by radio."[14] In other words, the radiophonic flow of music into private spaces does not convert such spaces into concert halls, and this nonidentity results in a raft of impoverishing, unnerving consequences.

Interestingly, Adorno fleshes out his dark analysis of radio technology, in its existing deployment by the monopolistic American broadcasting industry, by considering the ways in which listeners attempt to push back against the communicative situation in which they find themselves, against what he terms "ubiquity-standardization." Such resistances include techniques such as selectively toggling between different stations, fiddling with the dials in order to improve reception, sending fan mail, and simply switching the radio off. In the case of fan mail, which is worth delving into for the way it stands in analogous relation to the phone calls to the radio station in *The Living Orphan*, Adorno is particularly struck by the deeply forthcoming tenor of the letters, by the tendency of the writers to disgorge a torrent of personal details in the act of providing ostensibly "objective" feedback on matters like programming and scheduling. Attempting to unravel the puzzle, Adorno writes:

> The problem, then, is: why does an individual who pretends to be making objective suggestions, write about himself to an institution with which he has no personal connection when he knows that he cannot expect any real personal interest (even though the station's stereotyped answers carefully uphold that illusion). Apparently these letter-writers feel somewhat lost and neglected in the face of "ubiquity-standardization." Thus, even while they are criticizing the phenomenon, they compensate for this lost feeling by attempting to re-establish personal participation in the phenomenon and by trying to attract the attention of the institution from which it originated.[15]

In other words, to translate into Flusser's terms, fan mail exposes a desperate thirst for dialogue in the dialogic desert of amphitheatrical media. And yet, anticipating and gelling with Flusser's comments on the limits of response-ability in the practice of sending letters to newspaper editors and making phone calls to TV stations, Adorno offers a wary, deflating view of the modes of resistance that he considers, since, as he argues, each one remains ultimately, futilely bound within the framework that it attempts to resist. Indeed, even turning the radio off, which gives a strong impression of triumphant, willful escape, in fact offers no such thing, according to Adorno: "It creates the illusion of might and power, but it really means only that the rebel is withdrawing from contact with the very public events that he believes he is altering."[16] Once more, then, for Adorno, as for Flusser, mass media are inclined to create a potent dissonance between author and audience rather than establish a meaningful bond between them. (To look ahead for a moment, such a point regarding radiophonic disconnection might appear to contradict what we say in chapter 7, where we discuss how the acoustic properties of radio make it a perfect propaganda machine. Yet the two arguments are in fact complementary. Radio propaganda does not attempt to create an "existential rapport" between the author and the audience but rather works to create an "irresponsible" arousal of excitement that fosters a sense of what McLuhan would describe as "tribal" unity among atomized masses.)

Comparing Arele's overwhelming, empathic connection with his audience in the face-to-face performance scene at the end of *A Little Letter to Mother* with Muni's sullen isolation and loneliness at the end of the opening radio performance scene in *The Living Orphan*, one can't help but notice a staggering transformation. That is to say, in the more contemporary world of Seiden's film, where it has undergone a process of mass-mediatization, music seems no longer to act as an unqualified source of transcendent connection; the ritualistic, (Jewish)-community-building function of song seems now taken over by a narrow entertainment function (pertinently, as Flusser writes regarding the amphitheatrical discursive structure, "it should not be forgotten that its prototype is the circus, like the Roman Colosseum"[17]). Accordingly, almost all of the songs performed by the Berger family members throughout the film serve to vent tensions that they are experiencing in the private realm rather than to ameliorate such troubles. As we will see, both Muni and his wife Freda compensate for their shortcomings in the private sphere by acting out versions of their assigned family roles in the public sphere, which at the same time opens up questions concerning the authenticity of their acts. Again and again, interwoven with criticism of the frivolous and individualistic entertainment industry in America, the film points up a discrepancy between the couple's irresponsibility in the home and their expressions of loving responsibility to their family in musical performances that feed their professional success. Freda's hit show is called *Mother Love*, and yet the problem is precisely that her love of theater seems to be compromising her maternal duties. Muni pours out his heart to his child in the musical performance on the radio, and yet he seems not to be able to protect his son or successfully play a father. (This duality also ends up manifesting in their son, who, when he grows into adolescence, plays the part of a poor orphan in order to sell more newspapers, while in reality he not only has a father but is even in charge of their household.)

If the film provides a critique of the discursive medium of radio precisely through a discursive medium (namely, cinema), however, we also need to bear in mind an important difference between the specific type of discourse structure embodied by radio and the specific type of discourse structure embodied by (traditional, publicly screened) cinema, especially since the distinction plays a critical role in the narrative of *The Living Orphan*. In contrast to "amphitheatrical" media like radio and TV, other types of discursive media *do* offer the possibility of immediate audience response, as the critical scene to be discussed later demonstrates. In what Flusser calls "theatrical" discourse (i.e., a screening at a movie theater, a theatrical performance, a lecture, a concert), "emitter and receiver face each other during the discourse"[18] (see figures 2.2 and 2.3). For Flusser, such "facing" means that the author and the audience members, or just the audience members themselves, share the same space, and so a dialogic "revolution," where an audience member breaks with convention and speaks back to the author and/or in place of an author to the other audience members, becomes eminently possible. Notably, as Flusser points out, theatrical discourse also provides the model for the communicative structure of the bourgeois family;[19] that is to say, although the bourgeois family embodies a highly hierarchical arrangement in which the father assumes the authoritative position and is expected not to be questioned or contested, the nature of theatrical discourse does not fully protect his voice from being answered and defied. Such a fact is highly apropos to Muni's other key role in the film as a (would-be)

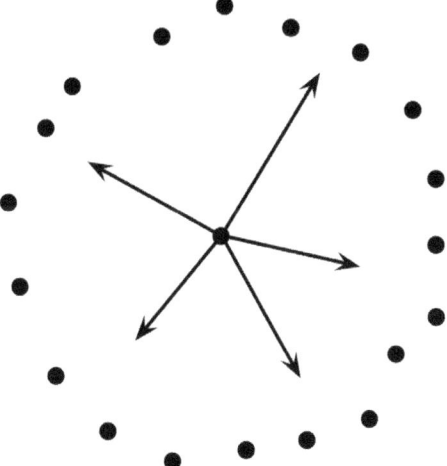

Figure 2.2. Amphitheatrical discourse. Vilém Flusser.

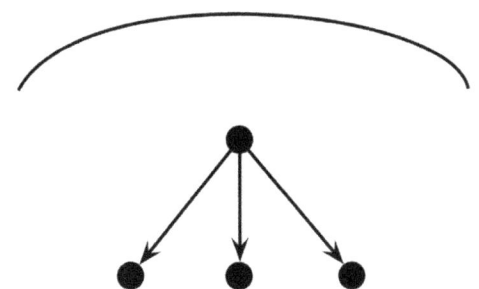

Figure 2.3. Theatrical discourse. Vilém Flusser.

bourgeois patriarch. For, as we'll see in the next section, the famous radio father is again and again forced to contend with a subversive responsiveness coming from within the family unit that deeply rattles his claim to authority in the private sphere.

Discontents of the Stage Couple

Music in Yiddish cinema, as we discussed in the previous chapter, regularly functions to combat troubled communication and, often with supernatural capability, forge connections between separated loved ones. Contemplated in relation to this trend, Muni's passionate performance of "My Sonny" raises a key question, namely: Why in the first place does he feel the need to reach out to his son with such profound, practically telepathic intensity? What sense of separation might he be compensating for, and what is the nature of the rift? No ocean stands in between him and his son, as is the case with Dobrish and Arele throughout a significant stretch of *A Little Letter to Mother*. Nevertheless, it is as if such a gulf exists, even though he and his son live on the same continent, in the same city, under the same roof. In modern American life, it seems, an atomizing distance reconstitutes itself *within* the home.

In both subtle and glaring forms, signs of domestic discontent accordingly permeate the first part of the film. After his performance, Muni does not rush back to see his son, the object of his monumental longing, but instead opts to go out with the announcer to an "exotic" Romanian restaurant (Muni's choice), hinting at an anxious avoidance of home, of the familial and familiar realm, and a knowledge, conscious or unconscious, that his domestic problems will require much more than mere physical reunion to resolve, or are perhaps on some level intractable. Further, the first time we are taken into the Berger house, the scene is marked by the conspicuous absence of both parents. Instead of Muni and Freda, we find Muni's mother (Ida Borkin), who is babysitting their infant child and singing him a lullaby, as well as Muni's sister Malke (Jennie Cashier), who is listening to the radio, which her mother implores her to turn off lest the noise—swing music—wake the baby. In this way, the film once more suggests that there is something problematic about the radio, which Muni's mother fails to consider as a channel that might transmit Muni's heartfelt address to his son. Meanwhile, Muni's sister proceeds to articulate a critical double standard regarding gender that becomes a major motif in the film: "I thought my brother's dear wife was here. Her only concern is becoming an actress. Muni is also an actor, and famous, yet he is so dear and good to me. I wish all men were so good." Although both parents are absent from home due to their careers, Malke only feels compelled to chastise Freda for it, revealing her own longing for a traditional, patriarchal-bourgeois familial arrangement, while, interestingly, her suitor, Leibke (Jacob Zanger), is a chronically unemployed quasi-intellectual and socialist dreamer, who, in a throwback to the traditional Jewish family, appears to have no problem letting a woman be the breadwinner, as we later see once he is married to Malke and they have three children to feed.

Picking up the thread introduced by his sister, Muni elaborately extends Malke's (unequal) critique of his wife. In a later scene, we see Muni at home for the first time, seated uneasily on the arm of a couch next to a framed picture of his baby son (positioned insistently at the center of the frame) and confiding to Chaim Green (Harry Field), an earnest, struggling immigrant singer whom he met at the Romanian restaurant and promised to help out career-wise: "I'm a lucky man, but . . . When a poor man comes home, his wife is there, they can talk, eat together. But as for me: theater, just theater. This is my son. And where is his mother? Theater, theater." Clearly, Muni's domestic situation contrasts starkly with his position as an in-demand radio star and respected performer in the public realm—a situation for which he interestingly blames an institution of public performance itself, or as he repeatedly puts it (the word acting like a stammer, a source of vocal trouble), the "theater." Muni insinuates that the theater, or at any rate his wife's involvement in the theater, somehow fundamentally contests the integrity of his family: a notion left lingering and reverberating as the film cuts to a behind-the-scenes glimpse into the "theater" in question. Here for the first time we see Muni's glamorous wife Freda (Fania Rubina), or as she is known in public, "Freda Walters," a stage moniker that significantly effaces all traces of her marriage and reveals a conspicuous split between her public and private worlds. Sitting in her dressing room in front of a large vanity that reveals her attractive, made-up face to us while her back is to the camera, Freda gazes at a framed picture of her baby— the same one that Muni picks up to show to Green in the previous scene—and smilingly kisses it. The fact that both parents address a picture of the child rather than the child himself provides yet another indication of the forces of disconnection roiling the family. However, while the mirror-induced splitting of Freda sitting alone and holding a mere mediation of her child suggests that she is leading a dizzying and fragmented life, her buoyant smile suggests that it is a life that she ardently chooses to live, in spite of whatever anguish it causes her.

The cruelly binary dilemma that Freda is faced with—either devote herself to her career *or* to her domestic life—is of course familiar from many instances of the "woman's film" of the same era—an era in which Western society as a whole was seeing more women enjoying (or expressing the desire to enjoy) freedom to cultivate lives beyond the home. Regarding this fraught transition, *The Living Orphan* asks us to think about why Freda's success as an actress so disturbs her husband's authority within the family, and by the same token, why Muni fails to assume a "successful" paternal role as long as his wife resists dedicating herself entirely to the domestic realm. One answer lies in the fact that in the bourgeois family, the father's authority depends on his possession of an exclusive, working relationship with the world, on his singular affiliation with the public sphere—consequently coded masculine—that invests him with the status of the family's main transmitter of critical information, to continue to use the terms of Flusser's treatment of the family unit discussed in the previous chapter. To clarify, it is not that females don't socialize with one another and exchange information, but rather that their exchanges aren't considered "politically" consequential. (Silvia Federici traces this devaluation of female friendship and voice through the suggestive shift in the meaning of the word "gossip." The word initially meant "god-parent." With the strengthening of patriarchy and the suppression of the female voice in European society that Federici traces back to the late Middle Ages, the word took on a pejorative meaning, signifying vacuous, often malicious, "women's talk."[20]) What "political" means in this context strongly encompasses a sense of the "dialogic," if we recall that, for both Flusser and his key influence Arendt, dialogue lies at the foundation of political life. Accordingly, through participation in the public realm, the father is able not only to confirm the validity of established values but also "dialogically" to synthesize new information, which he can then "discursively" pass on within the private realm. The reason why such a social arrangement perpetuates the father's authority within the private realm is thus because the other family members have no other access to such knowledge, no option for acquiring it other than to simply trust the father's judgment, which in turn determines the activity and future of the household. Bearing all this in mind, one can see how when a married woman flouts the once self-evident imperative to dedicate herself exclusively to the private realm—that is, when she begins to acquire and synthesize new information in the public realm, information that she could then use to engage with her husband in dialogue—the violation causes a drastic disruption in the communicative structure on which the patriarchal, bourgeois family is based.

As the scene with Muni entertaining the struggling singer over at his house continues, such a dynamic comes into focus ever more sharply and intriguingly metastasizes with the introduction of another modern communication technology that plays a recurrent role in the film. Muni invites Green to stay for dinner—a meal that ought to be a celebratory one, since Malke and Leibke have just announced that they are going to be married. Yet, as everyone sits down at the dinner table (always a highly symbolically charged locus in Yiddish film, a kind of microcosmic stand-in for the domestic sphere overall, as we saw earlier in the seder scene in *A Little Letter to Mother*), the one conspicuously missing from the table phones to say that she needs to work late, and that her absence will be indefinitely prolonged. Hence the film cross-cuts back and forth between Freda in her dressing room, her gaze trained on the photograph of the child (see figure 2.4), and Muni at home in a state of increasing distress:

Figure 2.4. Staying late for theater rehearsals, Freda pleads with her husband over the phone, while staring at a photograph of her child; the doubled image of her created by the reflection in the mirror symbolizes her split allegiance between the home and her career. Joseph Seiden, *The Living Orphan* (1939).

FREDA: Muni, please understand, we have a lot to do for the premiere.

MUNI: But we have guests today. Malke is engaged to Leibke.

FREDA: Dear, believe me, I'm longing for you and Benny. But try to see . . . You're an actor too . . . You know how the theater is.

Unlike the other way around, Freda attempts to engage with Muni, trying to mitigate his apprehensions ("I'm longing for you and Benny") and strike a negotiation with him based on mutual empathy ("You're an actor too"). In this way, she subversively assumes a "political" stance within the structure of familial communication. Refusing to treat listening as a form of obedience in the sense that a wife must "listen" to her husband, she asserts her right to dialogue. Or to put it another way, while Muni attempts to transmit his paternal authority across the line, Freda refuses to receive it and instead attempts communication with him as an equal. Revealingly, Muni expresses his frustration with this move by his wife by prematurely cutting off the conversation, slamming the phone down, and then once again repeating the cursed word "theater." In pointed contrast to the earlier scene where he communicates powerfully to anonymous scores of admiring listeners over the discursive medium of the radio, his voice suffers a radical diminishment over the dialogic medium of the telephone. This is because, as we've been stressing, dialogic media allow for the quite literally live possibility of contestation (not coincidentally, Flusser cites as examples of dialogic communication both "the telephone network" and "fighting"[21]). The moment also helps illuminate Muni's lingering resentment toward the theater, which as a discursive form of communication (like the radio) serves as a rivaling means of amplification of his wife's voice within the public sphere, whose implications critically carry over into the private sphere. (In the next chapter, which discusses a film in which a supporting female character, an effervescent aspiring singer, dreams of being on the radio, and by so doing deeply threatens her husband's authority, we'll expand further on this democratizing potentiality of media in relation to gender and the family.)

Freda refuses to be cowed by her husband's pressures. Presented with the opportunity to go to Chicago for six weeks to star in the production of *Mother Love*, she takes it, despite Muni's demands that she remain at home and attend to their (mildly) sick child. Nevertheless, characteristically, the decision is far from an easy one for her, and she struggles deeply with what she understands essentially as a conflict of responsibilities. After an intimate maternal moment in which she sings a lullaby to Benny about the importance of not forgetting one another—a song that seemingly aims to create a sonic imprint in the child that will allow him to recall their bond and derive comfort in the future—Muni enters the room and, inflating the severity of Benny's illness (which a doctor diagnoses as merely a cold), gives Freda an ultimatum that if she goes on tour she'll never see her child again. Interestingly and ironically, such a demand prompts Freda to start playing mother to *Muni*, whom she accuses of "talking like a spoiled child" and reminds that "a cast of sixty could lose their living." In other words, pointing out that she possesses attachments and responsibilities beyond her own family to a second, "theater family" that Muni can't or won't acknowledge, Freda casts his ultimatum as a manifestation of infantile narcissism (a diagnosis that foreshadows his more explicit regression later on); and indeed, she isn't able to get anywhere or engage in any meaningful dialogue with him. As her plump, typical show-biz, bottom-line-oriented manager Mr. Salkin (Herman Rosen) shows up at the house to pick her up, she appeals with undiminished warmth once more to Muni to understand and yet in response receives only a derisive chuckle about the name of the play.

Once Freda is gone, Muni enters into a second telephonic encounter in which he undergoes radical blockage in trying to assert his fatherly authority. After sending Freda two telegrams and not hearing back, all the while having the doctor pay another house call to check up on Benny (whose condition worsens, though not severely, not spelling anything like the immediate mortal danger that Muni makes it out to be: as the doctor reassures him, "Don't worry, your son will recover. You should move to California with him. The air here is dangerous. His lungs need dry air. California would be perfect"), Muni attempts to reach Freda via an alternate communicative channel and puts in a long-distance phone call to the Palace Theatre in Chicago. The call, however, is answered by Salkin, who, we swiftly deduce, has also been responsible for similar acts of interception in the case of the telegrams. In reply to Muni's mountingly urgent protestation about the telegrams, about how his and Freda's child is "deathly ill," and about how he must speak with his wife, Salkin (seated at his desk in the production office in front of a poster for *Mother Love* in which a glitzy Freda regally waves a white-gloved hand) diverts the conversation into a jocular account of the smash success of the play and claims that to connect Muni with his wife would be "impossible," as if he were simply carrying out the orders of an unchallengeable institution (i.e., the theater) that exists above the telephone and the telegram, and that overwrites the dialogic capacities of such media. Indeed, partaking of the unidirectional, hierarchical arrangement of discursive structures like radio and theater, Salkin's behavior suggestively recalls the treatment of the telephone in the opening scene of the film at the radio station. Just like the phone operators at WEVD, he acts as a relay that militates against direct communication between author and audience. In both cases, the dialogic medium of the telephone becomes subordinated to a larger discursive structure to which it forms an appendage. Acting as the guardian of Freda's authoritative voice in the theater, Salkin treats Muni as just another annoying fan and hangs up on him abruptly, in a move that represents another disquieting power of technologically enhanced, long-distance communication. As Flusser points out: "The technical structure of the telephone networks permits a gesture no other dialogic medium permits: it is possible to silence the other by hanging up the receiver."[22] Echoing the earlier scene where Muni brutally slams down the receiver on Freda to protect his own voice, Salkin here, protecting Freda's voice, gives Muni a dose of his own medicine.

Thus stymied, Muni descends into a reeling state of hypercommunication and accordingly makes a desperate bid to recover his troubled communicative authority, doing so via a reactionary imposition of excommunication on Freda. That is to say, he resorts to the drastic measure of attempting to eradicate the subversive element from the structure of familial-communicative relations entirely (the films discussed in the next two chapters present similar scenarios, though the object of excommunication in these films is a transgressive daughter rather than a transgressive wife). Banging his fists down on a low bookshelf, Muni pronounces that he'll be taking Benny to California the next day, to which Malke retorts, coming to Freda's defense in spite of her generally coolly contemptuous attitude toward her sister-in-law, "She's his mother," to which Muni fires back, sternly correcting his sister: "Benny has no mother. He's an orphan [*yosem*]. I, his father, will nurse him back to health . . . My son means more to me than all the theaters!" Revealing intriguing tensions and instabilities in both the utterance and the utterer of excommunication (a pattern that we also find in relation to the face-saving, power-reconsolidating attempts of the excommunicating men in the films in the next two chapters), Muni's declared excision of Freda from the family raises a number of important questions. First, why does he all of a sudden consider Benny to be "an orphan," a term that implies the elimination of *both* of Benny's parents? Second, if we do grant that Benny is an orphan, then how does this square with Muni's assertion of *himself* as Benny's parent ("I, his father . . .")? And third, how does Muni's strident declaration of fatherhood square with the maternal associations of his promise to "nurse" Benny back to health? It is as if Muni simultaneously figures himself as a null father, an absolute father whose claim to fatherhood requires no more than a mere statement of self-evident fact ("I, his father"), and a father who adopts the role of nurturing, maternal father. In short, Muni's excommunication of Freda reveals him as radically confused about which of these versions of the paternal role to play; and, as we'll see, it is a confusion that only becomes more and more aggravated as the cutting of Freda out of his and Benny's lives plays out.

When Freda eventually returns to New York—as she does in a hurried panic once the run of *Mother Love* concludes and Salkin finally turns over Muni's stale-dated telegrams—her attempts to track down Muni and Benny, who have long since decamped for California, fruitlessly result in the total dissolution of her private world and provide a further opportunity for the film to critique the modern world. After a stranger greets her at her old house and informs her that the previous tenants left a month ago with no forwarding address ("He [Muni] withheld word," she gasps to herself in the lingering aftermath of the encounter), Freda goes to the police. Yet, as is almost a rule in Yiddish cinema, an impersonal, bureaucratic, official body proves to be of virtually no help in reuniting family members despite its apparent power and exclusive access to information. Sitting at an imposing, judge-like desk, a directory-like tome next to him and a map on the wall behind him, an officer at the station informs her (his speech beginning in English and quickly switching to Yiddish, in the manner characteristic of state officials in Yiddish American movies): "Sorry Madam. We can't help you. They've vanished without a trace . . . America is a big, free country. Everyone may come and go as he pleases . . . Maybe you should try a private detective agency." Notably, the officer figures individual liberty, arguably the quintessential American value, as an agent of antagonism, or at best indifference, to the family, while his suggestion about the private—that is, commercial, for profit—detective agency perfectly captures a (capitalist) system that lacks any sense of social welfare and responsibility.

As Freda takes the officer's advice and indefinitely awaits the detective's findings, she throws herself back into work, which instead of serving as a means for taking flight from, or working through, her problems, becomes a vehicle for the endless traumatic repetition of her real-life separation from her child. Indeed, after ten years pass, a period in which she takes *Mother Love* around the world and becomes an international star (a rise portrayed in a montage of flashing marquees and grand halls), she returns to New York for yet another run of the show and laments to Salkin backstage: "I can't go on. Every evening I have to play that scene onstage, when I see the baby lying dead in the cradle. It rips me to pieces. I realize how I would feel if it were my own child, my Bennele. I can't do this play anymore. I just can't." Guarding against the penetration of new information, the discursive structure of the theater works against the play progressing or swerving off in different directions, and thus the actress becomes trapped in a stereotyped representation of tragic motherhood seemingly unable to be mitigated or changed from within. In this way, repeated night after night, Freda's role in *Mother Love* becomes a metaphor for her ongoing inability to establish dialogue with her husband and her son, and move on from their troubled past.

Newspaper Boy, Messenger Boy

Over the course of the same ten-year period, unable to restore his authority within the truncated family unit, Muni loses his standing as an actor and a singer and deteriorates into a lowly drunk, into a kind of deadbeat dad whose adolescent son is forced to work in order to support them and maintain their penurious existence, back in New York, in an archetypally grim tenement on the Lower East Side. Regarding this work, the rugged, streetwise, precociously grown-up Benny (Jerry Rosenberg), critically and suggestively, like his parents, earns his money in a media-related capacity—or rather, in multiple such capacities. Reintroducing him after the passage of ten years, the film shows him at work as a newspaper seller, peddling his goods on the street to a large, spontaneously assembled crowd and gaining a competitive advantage over the other urchin sellers (whom we later see jealously bullying him) by performing a mawkish musical number. In a mise-en-scène that provides an uncanny instantiation of Flusser's model of theatrical discourse, whose prototype he designates as the classical Greek theater (viz., a structure in which the author/emitter is positioned in front of a convex wall and surrounded by receivers on three sides[23]), Benny stands in front of a drugstore façade and wails to the crowd that forms a semicircle around him (see figure 2.5), playing

Figure 2.5. In a mise-en-scène that evokes Flusser's model of "theatrical discourse," Benny sells newspapers in a musical street performance. Joseph Seiden, *The Living Orphan* (1939).

(up) the part of a pathetic orphan: "Good people, buy a paper! Help me out! Everyone has a mother, who cares for her child. But I never had a mother, I was born of a stone! Good people, buy a paper! Don't let me go to the devil!"

In spite of the total absence of professional media infrastructure, Benny manages to transform the street into a virtual theatrical space, and, like his parents, deploy performance in the public sphere in a (somewhat awry) attempt to work over the tensions and conflicts of the private sphere. Yet, Benny's "success" in the public sphere perhaps most resembles his mother's success earlier on, since it works to bring about a usurpation of the father, a rivaling takeover of the traditional bourgeois paternal role of provider. That is to say, especially in light of the fact that Muni is no longer the celebrated singer that he once was, Benny's attention-grabbing routine comes across less as an inheritance than an arrogation of his father's voice. And, indeed, much in the film works to figure him explicitly as the "man of the house." For instance, as he returns home from work, Benny finds Leibke in the apartment, where the latter, now operating as a quasi-choral figure, and, too, trying to make money in a media-related capacity (rare is the character in the film, it seems, who isn't involved with a media institution), is engaged in writing a chronicle about the Berger family that he plans to sell to a newspaper. Sharing some lines from his work in progress, Leibke reads aloud to Benny: "Your father, a former actor, disappointed with life, gave himself up to drink . . ." However, as it dawns on him that if the article is published it will humiliate his father, Benny tears the pages away, rips them up, and threateningly affirms: "Nobody laughs at my daddy!" Of course, the irony is that in stepping into such an aggressively protective role it is Benny who emerges as the father in the family, as a father to his father who is consequently thrust into the role of a child to his child—all of which is reinforced by the landlady Mrs. Steinberg, who, entering the room to hassle him for the long overdue rent, sardonically yet not inaccurately addresses Benny as "Mr. big breadwinner."

As for his second (official) media-related line of work, Benny is employed as a telegram messenger, exemplifying Yiddish cinema's rich, recurrent fascination with messenger characters, whose occupations reflexively announce the films' preoccupation with communication, and more specifically with troubled communication, which creates the need for such special mediatory figures in the first place. (Already we've encountered one messenger—the returning soldier who conveys Meir's last words to his mother in *A Little Letter to Mother*—and we will encounter many more, in various guises, in the chapters ahead.) In a fantastic, fateful coincidence characteristic of *shund*, Benny is tasked with delivering a telegram message to his estranged mother—and, of course, it is not just any message, but one from the detective agency relating to the ongoing search for him. Accordingly, while the message is effectively empty, containing no news of his whereabouts, it has the effect of making Benny *himself* present to Freda, thus creating a delicious opportunity for the two to reconnect. In this way, even as mother and son fail to recognize one another on a conscious level, a sudden, mysterious intimacy, an unwitting mutual magnetism, arises between the two that embodies what Peter Brooks refers to as melodrama's "celebrated topos of the *voix du sang*—the secret impulse by which parents and children and siblings are drawn to one another despite mistaken and lost identities."[24] Specifically, as Freda shares with the messenger boy, "My Benny would be about your age," and is overtaken by a surge of unfulfilled maternal longing, she embraces Benny, causing his "hard" demeanor to melt away and him to confess: "This is the first time I ever felt so good." Nevertheless, the moment doesn't result in any further disclosures. Pressed by Freda to reveal his name, the smartly uniformed Benny instead throws up a chirpy professional façade and explains: "A messenger boy doesn't talk. He sees, he listens, but he keeps his mouth shut." Elaborating the problem and persistence of troubled communication, while stressing the critical importance of one's specific positioning within a given communicative arrangement (an emphasis that echoes Flusser's central "hypothesis" regarding the structure of communication as the infrastructure of human reality), Benny's status as a messenger boy thus presents an interesting shift of communicative perspective. That is to say, deviating from the film's previous repeated attention to authors and authorship (Muni singing on the radio, Freda acting on the stage, Benny performing on the street, Leibke writing a newspaper article), Benny here emerges as occupying a laboring space between senders and receivers that, as he says (speaking only insofar as it accounts for his imposed speechlessness), necessarily deprives him of *the right* to speak.

Communicative Revolutions

The first significant break with the tenacious spell of troubled communication that hangs over the Berger family occurs in a performance scene in which Freda's well-guarded voice faces a dialogic challenge from her audience, thus demonstrating what Flusser describes as the characteristic form of communicative "revolution" that remains a possibility within the theatrical discourse structure. As Flusser writes, again drawing on his crucial sense of responsibility as response-ability:

> Although it is relatively well shielded against outer noise, it [the theatrical discourse structure] is unprotected against noise from the inside. The receivers can turn around during the discourse, and, since they face the emitter, they can also turn around the channels and "answer" the emitter. The theatrical structure places the receivers in a "responsible" situation, that is, in a structure from where they can answer, and thus introduce noise into the original information. Which of course means that the original information is changed into a new one, because the discourse is changed into a dialogue.[25]

Playing a charity event at the "Bialystoker Home for the Aged," where the crowd consists of elderly immigrants reminiscing mistily about their lives in the old country, Freda, bedecked in crown and fur stole, performs what Salkin describes in his impresario's introduction as "her hit song, 'Give Me Back My Child,' " a number in which she once more autobiographically vents her private pain in public and remorsefully addresses the perils of following a "false ideal." At the conclusion of the song, however, something unusual happens. Amid the enthusiastic applause, Muni's aged, now completely blind mother—who, unbeknownst to Freda, has come to live in the home, and has been sitting in the front row the whole time—stands up and, equipped with special insight into Freda's former private life, into the circumstances of the actress's real-life loss of her child, mounts a potent challenge to the performance, shouting out: "A lie! She speaks a lie! She does not have a mother's heart, only a heart of stone." Enacting the potential for response-ability latent within theatrical discourse, Muni's mother "turn[s] around the channels and 'answer[s]' the emitter," "introduce[s] noise into the original information," and as a result "the original information is changed into a new one, because the discourse is changed into a dialogue." Indeed, the "revolutionary" act completely diverts the presiding direction of the performance, swiftly prompting others in the audience to join the mutiny and respond with accusations of *"shande* [shame, disgrace]," which deeply rattle Freda (who just moments ago was ensconced in a seemingly invincible celebrity glow) and cause the reactionary Salkin to call for the instigator of the disturbance to be thrown out of the auditorium. Nevertheless, the challenge ultimately proves fruitful for the original "author," who in turn keeps the unexpected, eccentric exchange going. Frantically, Freda descends from the stage, approaches her mother-in-law, and poignantly rearticulates the eponymous line from the song, now in the context of "life" rather than "art," and begs for information of Benny's whereabouts (that is to say, for information that evidently, in the wake of the fact-finding failures of both the police and the detective agency, only a personal relation can provide). And Muni's mother—though sorely, stubbornly requiring the prodding of the nurse sitting next to her, who reminds the old woman of her stalwartly stated belief in forgiveness—obliges, passing Freda a piece of paper with Muni and Benny's address, and refusing (unlike Muni in his absconding with Benny to California, and Salkin in his machinations to keep the show running in Chicago) to "withhold word." In short, the grave situation originating in a dialogic breakdown between two famous "authors," Freda and Muni, undergoes a dialogic breakthrough.

Yet as much as the revolutionarily challenged performance results in progress, much more is still necessary to bring the film to a resolution, or at least to a point of resolution. Finally in possession of their whereabouts, Freda rushes over to Muni and Benny's tenement in her limousine, recognizes Benny as the anonymous messenger boy from earlier on, reveals herself as his mother, showers him with gifts, and pleads with him to come live with her in her "beautiful home": an offer of lavish providing that would effectively allow the prematurely grown-up child to resume being something of a regular child again. Despite being strongly enticed, however, Benny rejects the offer, instead opting, self-sacrificially, to keep playing a father to his needy father. Indeed, as Freda reluctantly leaves the apartment in tears, Benny bids her the iciest of farewells, toggling bilingually out of Yiddish and declaring in English: "Good-bye, lady." Refusing in the same stroke to call Freda *"mame"* and to continue addressing her in the *mame-loshn*, Benny thus conveys his rejection of his mother with striking, added, communicative force, in a manner that showcases another inventive mobilization of the deep-rooted association between the maternal and the Yiddish language (discussed in chapter 1).

To recap, Freda's discovery of the information about Muni and Benny leads to the disclosure of true identities, but not (yet) to the piecing back together of the family unit. Or in other words, the film decouples recognition and reunion: a narrative gambit that is in fact relatively rare in *shund*. Accordingly, part of what else is required for the family to get back together is a "revolutionary" change in Muni, particularly regarding his fraught paternal relation to Benny—and this transpires in an involved series of plot turns. In a precipitous communicative fall from his previous radio star heights, Muni returns to the Romanian restaurant as a cabaret-style act that has him, dressed in a clown costume reminiscent of the degraded professor played by Emil Jannings in Josef von Sternberg's *The Blue Angel* (1930), singing a raucous, misogyny-fueled song of protest against the evils of *"froyen* [women]." After the performance, the club owner fires Muni for his reckless, obvious drunkenness, and yet backstage Muni reencounters Chaim Green, now a big star, who wishes to repay Muni for his earlier kindness and thus goes on to arrange an audition for Muni at a radio station. The night before this opportunity to restore his former broadcasting glory, however, Muni goes out on an all-night drinking bender—an act of self-sabotage that causes Benny, especially concerned over his father's heart condition that requires medical attention that they can't afford (here as elsewhere, *shund* displays a strong inclination toward metaphorizing illness, or what Brooks describes as the use of "extreme physical conditions to represent extreme moral and emotional conditions"[26]), to steal money from Mrs. Steinberg, who catches him in the act and threatens to call the police and have him sent to a reformatory. This daunting prospect of Benny becoming a ward of the state and an orphan *for real* instantly sobers Muni up and causes a striking shift in his deadbeat dad demeanor. Not wanting Benny to "grow up a tramp, a liar, a thief, a loafer," Muni adopts the posture of an authoritative father, and, in the middle of the night, drags Benny over to Freda's posh house, where he believes the child will be protected against the fate of orphanhood-cum-criminality.

It is a genuine turning-point for Muni, but also one that, like most upheavals of the bottoming-out variety, is highly tentative and fragile. Indeed, in the very moment of the shift, outraged in his sweat-soaked undershirt, Muni overcompensates wildly for the lack of authority that has been plaguing him the entire film, resorting to violence and not only twisting Benny's arm in order to get the boy to surrender the stolen money but responding to Benny's tearful reaching out for forgiveness with a wallop in the face. Such aggressive acts conceal a latent, persisting insecurity, or as Arendt puts it in a famous formulation: "Where force is used, authority itself has failed"[27] (that is to say, authority finds its true basis in obedience, such that when smoothly functioning it has no need of violence: blows, threats, ultimatums, etc.). As well, the film insists upon something irremediably façade-like about Muni's imposing, authoritative behavior. After Benny disappears into Freda's house, for instance, the scene concludes with a close-up of Muni in which the stern face that he has assumed since the theft suddenly falls away, as if a mask, and is overtaken by his familiar, blank-eyed, bobbly-headed face of drunken stupor. Taking all of this into account, one is hardly surprised to find that Muni undergoes a radical escalation in his condition of troubled communication in the wake of protectively ceding Benny to Freda. The next day we see him back at the tenement, laid up in bed and ministered to by his distraught sister, who reveals to Green (who has come over to check on his friend) that the night before he attempted suicide and has since been in a dire state. "See for yourself. He lies in bed, won't talk . . . ," she explains, to which Green concernedly replies, "I don't want him to give up the opportunity to appear on the radio." Interestingly, the exchange creates the impression that Muni's whole being is somehow suspended between two radical vocal polarities—a fatal muteness and a revitalizing acoustic mass mediation—as if communication were not simply a matter of life and death but the very force upon which life and death depend. (In fact, Muni can still speak, and yet he only does so in order to dwell morbidly on his disconnection from Benny, and to enter into evidently mystical, long-distance communication with the child. "We were like two hearts beating together, but I cut them apart and they bleed . . . At night, I lie here crying, and my heart calls out for Benny. And I hear him crying, calling, 'Papa,'" Muni whimpers, at which point the film cross-cuts to Benny in bed at

Freda's and substantiates the numinous, telepathic exchange, showing the boy issuing the crying call to his father, to "Papa," in the midst of uneasy dreams.)

Beating back against Muni's renewed fall into suicidality and (conditional) muteness, both Green and Benny make critical mediatory efforts that supply the remaining ingredients of the family's reunification. Green goes back and forth between the two households, reassuring Muni that he will bring Benny back and Freda that he will explain to her husband the truth (which he has since found out from Salkin) behind her unresponsiveness to the belatedly delivered telegrams in Chicago. Meanwhile, stealing away in the middle of the night to return to the tenement, Benny leaves a note for Freda in which he expresses his longing to live neither without his father nor his mother and begs her to "come back to Papa and let us all be together": a wish that comes to pass. In a scene unfolding in a single shot, Freda urgently arrives at the tenement, Benny begs his father to let him have a father and a mother, Green reminds his friend that he is an "understanding" man, and Muni mercifully extends a hand to Freda, who presses it to her face in joyous relief, at which point the scene concludes with all the assembled characters forming a chain stretching from one side of the frame to the other: an evocative tableau of reconnection. In this way, Green fulfills his responsibility to the person who earlier showed such immense responsibility toward him, demonstrating Yiddish cinema's unique penchant for interpersonal, nonindividualist modes of overcoming (a subject to which we will return in later chapters); and Benny, at last, fulfills his communicative promise as a messenger that earlier his official position as a "messenger boy" so resonantly, constitutively denied.

The Mother in Charge

As usual in Yiddish cinema, however, unruly elements lurk in the happy ending, and these emerge, strikingly, in a brief denouement that on the surface of things would seem to work to fortify resolution and the restoration of the destabilized and broken family unit.

After the fading out of the bedside reconciliation scene, the film fades into a scene in which a trio of anonymous young women (representing an exponential increase from the one female listener pictured at the beginning of the film) sit in front of a round-arched, cathedral-style radio, whose speaker emits the voice of an English-speaking announcer: "And now, after an absence of ten years, the celebrated artist Muni Berger will again sing for you his famous song, 'My Son.'" The film then cuts to Muni at the radio station, or other performance venue, where he reprises the opening song of the film, yet on a much grander, much more ornately curtained stage, accompanied by a full orchestra rather than a lone pianist and donning a tuxedo rather than an ordinary suit and tie. All of this thus conveys not only that Muni has recovered his health and celebrity—filling in the gaps in the narrative ellipsis, we deduce that he must have nailed the audition facilitated by Green—but that his fame is now even greater than it was before he originally lost it. Indeed, despite that in reality much of the announcing on WEVD was done bilingually,[28] the fact that the announcer is speaking English, in contrast to the Yiddish-speaking announcer at the beginning of the film, hints at the possibility that Muni is appearing on a more mainstream, English-language station, as if in his comeback he has become so successful that he has come to be known and featured beyond the ethnically "narrowcast" networks of Yiddishland. Accordingly, in such an intimation lies another fascinating Yiddish-cinematic eccentricity. For whereas in reality the success of Jews in the media industry usually entailed an assimilation-driven shying away from explicitly Jewish content (as Neal Gabler tells in his account of the Jewish moguls who "invented Hollywood"[29]), the English-language announcer evokes the idea of a Jewish performer achieving widespread fame in America while at the same time still performing in Yiddish and taking up explicitly Yiddish themes. In other words, phantasmatically distorting the historical reality, the move allows for an envisioning of mainstream mass culture as effectively an extension of Yiddishland—a portrayal, one might add, that also obtains in relation to Freda (who achieves national and international stardom through her role in *Mother Love*), as well as, on a more implicit level, to the renowned "Irving Bird" in *A Little Letter to Mother*.

Yet to return to the treatment of the comeback performance itself, the film at one point cross-cuts to another domestic space of reception, where we find Benny and his grandmother listening to the broadcast in a state of beaming rapture. Indeed, although nothing indicates a *shund*-appropriate, miraculous restoration of Muni's mother's sight, the withholding of an optical recovery appears to matter little in the moment of ecstatic auditory immersion. However, another lack does significantly ruffle the image. Namely, we are compelled to wonder, where is Freda? Her conspicuous absence from the blissful image of domestic audition suggests that Muni's revivified voice doesn't have quite such a powerful effect on *her*, that its capabilities do not so simply translate to, and hold sway within, the private sphere, and that the image that ostensibly embodies the home to which Muni will return after his performance in fact remains troubled for him. In short, there remains something incomplete about the triumphal return of the "Voice of the Father."

Further hints of the instability of Muni's reasserted voice follow the performance. Back at home—which is to say, the posh home bought by Freda with her riches—the reunited family leisurely relax together, characteristically in relation to some form of media. Freda sits on a recliner reading; Benny browses a bookshelf and takes down a volume for himself; and Muni, in the most loaded component of the tableau, plunks out the melody to "My Sonny" on a piano. Slow, spare, faint: Muni's restatement of the melody creates a profound sonic contrast with the massive fullness of the orchestral treatment of it in the preceding scene. Consciously or unconsciously, Muni seems to be trying to assert his big radio voice at home but can only manage an attenuated, tremulous, nonverbal reverberation of it, playing the song almost as one might imagine it being played by a child just learning how to play the piano. Moreover, giving an impression of overcompensation, Muni crowingly remarks to Freda: "And dear, they almost tore my clothes, until I signed all their autograph books," to which Freda replies, meeting his brag: "Yes dear, I know what fans are like! Why once, in Paris, I was just leaving the stage, when—" Here a maid enters the room and interrupts the exchange to deliver a "cablegram" to Freda, who reads the message aloud: "From Salkin, in London: 'May I book the Berger Family, husband and wife, for a joint world tour? Reply immediately.'" Although Muni responds to the message enthusiastically ("Great. Our chance to tour the world together! Let's cable him right away"), Freda puts an executive kibosh on the offer, finally bringing the film to an end by taking her husband and son by the hands, pulling them down toward her on her chair, and declaring: "Yes, I'll cable him. We're not going. Theater cost us bitter years of unhappiness. My new career will be as a happy mother, to both my dear boys!" No doubt, Freda's stark volte-face choice of motherhood over career strikes a deeply conservative note. At the same time, however, the film slyly manages to implant the decision in a context in which Freda, once more, emerges as the one in the family calling the shots, the one making the key decisions: a point emphasized both by her getting the last word and by her positioning at the nucleic center of the familial image (see figure 2.6).

Further, and perhaps most tellingly, her self-description as a "happy mother, to both my dear boys [*tayer boyes*]" once more infantilizes Muni (albeit affectionately), and thus all the sudden rehashes, and suggests the persistence, of his troubled paternal status. In the end, the willful exclusive embrace of motherhood does not have the restoration of patriarchy as its necessary corollary, does not necessarily land everyone in their proper roles within the structure of the bourgeois family unit. Finally, the film proffers a convolutedly matriarchal picture of the discursive structure of the family, in which, so we might

Figure 2.6. Freda's position at the center of the final, familial image, expressing that she is the one in charge. Joseph Seiden, *The Living Orphan* (1939).

read her final line, Freda engages in a paternally destabilizing, cryptic adoption of the father, as if the idea of the *yosem* secretly applies, after all, most powerfully to Muni.

3

The Mass Media Family

Kol Nidre (1939)

JOSEPH SEIDEN, APTLY DESCRIBED by Hoberman as a "Hollywood mogul writ small,"[1] churned out within the single year of 1939 an impressive three films: *The Living Orphan*, *Kol Nidre*, and *Motel the Operator* (*Motl der Operator*). Taken together, the three can be regarded as a loose, unofficial trilogy, particularly in the way that they all feature a troubled father against the backdrop of contemporary America. At the same time, the connection between *The Living Orphan* and *Kol Nidre* goes even further, for both films not only take up the theme of the destabilized patriarch in America but interweave it with a strong focus on technological media: a focus perhaps not surprising in the work of a director extensively experienced in the technical side of film. Prior to starting his own production company, Judea Pictures, in the late 1920s, Seiden worked variously as a projectionist, cameraman, and film-sound equipment dealer.[2] However, whereas the father in *The Living Orphan* is a younger man, and a musical performer on the radio whose phenomenal vocal amplification in the public sphere fails to connect him meaningfully to his audience and who remains critically ineffectual in the private sphere, the father in *Kol Nidre* is an older, middle-aged man, who belongs definitively to a first generation of immigrants and is propelled into a full-on *clash* with the radio, which, as a quite literal force of home invasion, threatens to divest him of, and usurp, his paternal authority. Moreover, the latter film also intriguingly complicates its "critical" representation of radio (the reigning broadcast technology of the 1930s: a status that reflects the recurrence of radio in the films discussed in this book) by drawing attention to the medium's progressive, emancipatory potential, particularly in relation to gender. That is to say, for certain women in the film—namely, a rebellious daughter, one of the main characters, and a rebellious wife, one of the supporting characters—the mass medium of radio offers up a bracing democratic promise. Yet, as we'll see, the film ultimately makes a desperate effort to iron out such ambivalence, meeting the liberatory energies of radio with an arsenal of fervent suppressions and neutralizations.

The Mass Media Family

In order to grasp the familial power struggle at the heart of *Kol Nidre*, it is useful to turn once more to Flusser's essay "Family Unit," which provides an evocative account of how, in the era of broadcast mass media, the bourgeois family, the prevailing family structure in the West, underwent a key transformation. As we've discussed, in the bourgeois family, information of the highest importance was typically conveyed—or "broadcast"—by the father, who functioned as the exclusive negotiator between the family and the outside world (in the traditional Jewish family, one will recall, we find a similar, patriarchal information flow, yet one in which the father derives his critical, exclusive information not from the public sphere but from the sources of religious authority, that is, from Torah study). However, with the advent of broadcast mass media (radio and, later, television), which heightened the capacities of earlier mass media, information encroached upon the private sphere and flowed into the home that was new for all members of the family. Accordingly, the father no longer occupied a place at the head of the table, as it were, but rather came to be seated on a level on par with the rest of the family members, joining the rest of the family in what Flusser, delineating the shape of the newly emergent "mass media family,"[3] describes as a semicircle gathered around the apparatus.

Within this new family communication structure, the apparatus replaces the father as the authoritative transmitter of knowledge without merely reoccupying his former position. Within the patriarchal, bourgeois family structure, which as we recall assumes a "theatrical" discourse structure, dialogue between author and audience is discouraged yet not impossible; communicative "revolution" on the part of the audience, though frowned upon, can never be ruled out. In the mass media family, on the contrary, any direct interaction between the author and receivers of information is structurally disabled, while any dialogue between receivers is "restricted to a minimum because it interrupts a practically continuous TV transmission."[4] In short, the authoritative messages of broadcast mass media work very differently from the authoritative messages of the patriarch. As Flusser writes:

> The TV is an authoritative transmitter, in the sense of being imperative, and in the sense of allowing no answer. But it is an authority quite unlike the one the "father" memory possessed in previous family structures. It does not provide original information, but stereotyped information. There is no hierarchy within the members of the family: father, mother, and children are on the same level of passive receivers of imperative behavior patterns. Therefore, if we were to call the previous family structures "patriarchal" ones (because they were based on a "father" authority), we may call the mass media family structure a "fratriarchal" one (because it is based on TV authority which is disruptive of hierarchical orders). The TV is not a father, but a big brother. The result is that every member of the family disposes of the same information and has the same competence to transform it into action.[5]

Accordingly, with the father no longer acting as the authoritative transmitter of information, the fulcrum around which the family's activity revolves critically shifts beyond the bounds of the family unit. Whatever action the family members might take in relation to the information that they receive, whether in the private or public sphere, "this action functions on behalf of a memory which lies outside the horizon of the family members."[6]

According to Raymond Williams in his influential 1974 book *Television*, which treads similar ground as Flusser's essay, the notion that broadcast media serve as extrafamilial influences on the construction and operations of the family is hardly without historical precedent. Writes Williams:

> Many people who are aware of the manipulative powers of radio and television, or of its apparently inexhaustible appeal to children, react in ways that implicitly suppress all the other history of communication. Thus it is often indignantly said that television is a "third parent," as if children had not in all developed societies had third parents in the shape of priests, teachers, and workmasters, to say nothing of the actual parents and relations who, in many periods and cultures, intervened to control or instruct.[7]

Williams, however, enacts a too glib conflation between broadcast media and earlier "third parent" candidates. For can one really say that "priests, teachers, and workmasters" possess, like radio and television, an "apparently inexhaustible appeal to children"? Certainly there are instances of children enthusiastic about their religious and educational authority figures (about their workmasters, one can be less sure . . .); and yet within the broadcasting era, what we often—if not most commonly—find is children being enticed with the pleasureful *reward* of mass media engagement for fulfilling the presumably less-than-desirable institutional obligations of church, school, and so on. Further, Williams ignores important differences in the structure of communication, which Flusser precisely highlights. Unlike priests, teachers, and workmasters, radio and television allow for no possibility of dialogue between author and receiver, for no possibility of "revolution" within the communicative arrangement. In this way, to follow Flusser, broadcast media really do present something novel. They are not simply subsumable into a readymade parental category; rather than adding another, authoritative yet potentially contestable, third parent (specifically, a second father) into a relatively stable patriarchal mix, they level the playing field between parents and children entirely. Hence Flusser's important point about the shift from a family based on hierarchy (that is, patriarchy) to one based on "fratriarchy": a notion of brotherhood that complicatedly encodes both an intrafamilial, democratic potential (i.e., the downgrading of the father, and the correlative upgrading of all the other family members, in a relation of *fraternité*), and an extrafamilial, antidemocratic, even authoritarian, potential (i.e., TV as a "big brother," evoking Orwell).

Of course, Flusser's account of the emergence of the "mass media family" is highly abstract and overneat. As he himself readily admits, the new model does not become dominant all of a sudden and all at once: some aspects of the bourgeois family stubbornly resist usurpation, while other aspects falsely appear to persist as a result of lingering "ideological masks"[8] that embody a deep—sentimental, nostalgic—attachment to the old model and prevent recognition of the new one. Moreover, characteristically invested in human freedom, Flusser ends the essay by pointing out that while "the tendency toward a mass media family structure is determined by, among other things, the technological development of communication apparatus, . . . it is still possible to divert such a tendency toward a different sort of family structure, if there is a sufficiently strong will to do so." That is to say, he affirms the possibility of human "free will" stepping in, perhaps at the infrastructural level, to thwart or disrupt "the victory of totalitarian mass culture."[9] To such caveats to any purported smooth transition to the mass media family, one might also add a none-too-surprising resistance coming intrafamilially from the father, whose authority is threatened fundamentally by the newfangled apparatus, and who thus stands to lose the most as a result of the transformation. Indeed, as we'll see, the father in *Kol Nidre* exhibits precisely this sort of opposition—in addition to the sort of ideological blinkeredness described by Flusser—such that the film can be regarded as providing a fascinating portrait of a fraught, *transitional stage* in the cultural movement toward the mass media family.

Disruptions and Promises of Radio

Intergenerational conflict is a classic theme of Yiddish cinema, and, of course, of many episodes in the history of cinema. Yet what is so distinctive about the treatment of the theme in *Kol Nidre* is the way in which the film imbricates strife between parents and children with media, and in fact puts media right at the center of the dissension. Focusing on the Dorfmans, a Jewish American family, the film tells the story of a daughter, a svelte, recent college graduate named Jenny

(Lili Liliana), who is seduced by a hedonistic, modern American lifestyle—notably channeled by the radio—that radically conflicts with the worldview of her father Moishe (Joseph Schoengold), a traditional, bearded, kippah-wearing man who appears, owing to his baggy dark suit, somewhat dwarfish. Accordingly, Jenny is triangulated between an upstanding, recently minted rabbi whom her father wants her to marry, Joseph Goldstein (Leon Liebgold), and a frivolous, fun-loving, hyper-Americanized libertine whom she prefers, Jack (Menasha Oppenheim). Indeed, in the first of the film's many musical numbers, as Jack entertains the crowd at a graduation party with a jazzy song that toggles not between the usual poles of Yiddish and English but rather, with libertine energy, between Yiddish and French ("No one girl's enough for me, I'm determined to be free! *Cherchez la femme? Jamais, madame!*"), Jenny twirls a hand to the rhythm and appears in a state approaching rapture, tellingly unalarmed by—or hypnotically blind to—the object of her affection's swaggering, effective affirmation that he will never settle for her alone.

Setting up the portrayal of the father's crisis of authority, the film reveals a far different atmosphere in the Dorfman house. The first scene set there begins with Moishe sitting at a desk reading solemnly aloud from a Hebrew book, while his wife Sarah (Bertha Hart) tidies up the room like a typical housewife, putting Moishe's tallis away and fixing the sofa cushions. This then gives way to a conversation about their daughter in which Moishe relates the rabbi's desire to marry Jenny and wishfully muses, before taking his wife by the arms and dancing with her: "We should be able to celebrate a wedding like in the old country [*heym*]. If only my dream would come true. We would be the luckiest people in the world." The next time we enter the home, however, immediately following another musical scene in which Jenny and Jack sing a romantic duet while on a tryst in a secluded wood, Moishe's dreams are revealed as drastically myopic. Pacing around the room in nervous agitation and impatiently awaiting her return, he vents his well-warranted suspicion that Jenny is "running around with that loafer Jack again," while his wife largely attempts to stay out of the brewing fracas and continues with her dutiful housework. Once Jenny does appear, her entrance is instantly striking, for she walks straight past her distressed father without greeting him, as if he weren't even there, and makes a beeline over to the radio, which, despite Moishe's forbidding finger-wagging (unnoticed by her), she switches on (see figure 3.1). Here, in a new shot that cuts Moishe out the image, such that he is required to step back inside the frame and make a concerted effort to establish his presence, a quarrelsome exchange ensues:

> MOISHE: Stop playing the radio. I want to speak to you.
>
> JENNY: Benny Goodman and his orchestra are on. I want to listen to his program.
>
> MOISHE: Benny Goodman, big deal—a *klezmer*! Listen to your parents. Stop running around with that loafer. Rabbi Goldstein is a real match for you.

Perhaps owing to constraints in the low-budget film's sound mix, and/or to copyright issues, the Benny Goodman broadcast fails to enter into the aural composition of the scene, and yet the (ghostly) sound

Figure 3.1. Ignoring her father, Jenny switches on the radio. Joseph Seiden, *Kol Nidre* (1939).

of the famous Jewish swing bandleader (who importantly, in contrast to Moishe, embodies a modern, highly assimilated Jew) plays a critical role, functioning as that to which Jenny listens in lieu of "listening" to her parents. Or, as McLuhan puts it, in a passage regarding the sensory demands of radio that is especially, uncannily germane to the absence of radiophonic sound in the radio-centric scene: "Given only the *sound* of a play [on the radio], we have to fill in *all* of the senses, not just the sight of action. So much do-it-yourself, or completion and 'closure' of action, develops a kind of independent isolation in the young that makes them remote and inaccessible. The mystic screen of sound with which they are invested by their radios provides the privacy for their homework, and immunity from parental behest."[10]

Indeed, under the influence of radio, Jenny remains defiantly distant and sealed off from her parents, vowing that "the sooner we assimilate, the better we will be," and ultimately declaring, "I'm tired of listening [to you]. You cannot understand this modern world," before making an exasperated, fed-up exit from the room. In this way, Jenny's choice of listening-object, of the radio rather than her parents, and more particularly her father, indexes a critical reshaping of the Dorfman family structure—a reshaping, that is, toward a "mass media family" structure—and this shift causes Moishe to react in a most suggestive manner. "You'll do as I say. Remember!" he commands his daughter, in a sudden upsurge of apoplectic rage. Yet, conspicuously, the demand is fired off several beats after Jenny has already left the room, only once she is presumably far removed from the site of face-to-face communication. Hence, in an aggressive, defensive maneuver, Moishe appears to be trying to communicate at a distance *like the radio*, to leech and repurpose the powers of the modern mass medium precisely in the name of the father and the old familial regime. As McLuhan writes, resonating with the family-centric world of Yiddish cinema: "For those whose entire social existence is an extension of family life, radio will continue to be a violent experience."[11]

In *Entertaining America: Jews, Movies, and Broadcasting*, coauthors J. Hoberman and Jeffrey Shandler include a reprint of a fascinating, revealing 1924 article from the *Jewish Daily Forward* entitled "Radio-Phonograph: That's the Bone of Contention in Jewish Families These Days."[12] A reflection on how the two different acoustic media are impacting the Jewish family, and more specifically on how they are differently regarded by different generations, by those born in the old country and those born in America, the piece dovetails with a McLuhanite-Flusserian sense of the disruptive force of the introduction of broadcasting: "As with most inventions and machineries, the radio has brought unhappiness to many a poor home. Indeed, it is a new source of jealousy, futile longing, broken hearts and pocketbooks. . . . In many a poor family, the problem now arises as to what to buy, a phonograph or a radio. The price is about the same; the benefits are not." It then goes on to observe "an interesting division": namely, between the older generation, those "born on the other side . . . [who] talk English more or less fluently, but . . . converse in a still better Yiddish or Russian or German . . . [and] enjoy a Yiddish or Russian show, . . . have a taste for the best in literature, . . . [and] an ear for music," and the new generation, those "boys and girls who were born and brought up in in this country . . . [who] have no taste nor desire for the subtle, the fine, the nuances . . . [;] children of a young and vigorous soil . . . [whose] faculties are young and pulsating."[13] Accordingly, whereas the former prefer the phonograph, which enables them to "listen to their heart's content to Jewish tunes and pieces by Jewish comedians" (this is at a time before Yiddish broadcasting), the latter prefer the radio, which allows them to explore beyond the Jewish/traditional sphere of their immigrant parents/elder siblings and "get in touch with any broadcasting station and open floodgates of noise and merriment and dance themselves into physical exhaustion."[14] The article chimes resonantly with *Kol Nidre*, whose rebellious daughter, drawn to mainstream radio, and her illicit paramour (whose opening number also includes a glorification of sports and physical activity) are well accounted for by the piece's characterization of rambunctious, sensation-seeking, American-born, young people. Indeed, although appearing fifteen years later, the film represents precisely the same sort of familial-mediatic conflict described by the piece still very much at work.[15]

Radio also plays a crucial, unruly role in the relationship of Moishe and Sarah's friends Chassie and Shmelke Shmelkevitz (Yetta Zwerling and David Lederman), a bickering, middle-aged married couple who offer some comic relief from the tragic seriousness of the central plotline, while reflectively and refractively invoking several of the same concerns that occupy the main narrative thread. Immediately following Jack's risqué number at the graduation party, the film cuts to a scene in the couple's bedroom, where the effervescent Chassie sits at the vanity doing high-pitched vocal exercises, practicing excitedly for an audition for a singing contest on the radio. Yet her husband is wildly unsupportive, to say the least. "Stop your screeching. You're piercing my eardrums," he intervenes, while going on to attack the radio directly, remarking with acidic irony, "You have talent. To eat . . . to gossip. Just imagine, darling, we'll soon have Television, and I'll look at your sweet face on the Radio. It'll make me dizzy," and, "If I meet Marconi, I'll murder him for inventing Radio. Why did he do that to me? He poisoned my wife and ruined my life!" Like Jenny in the later scene revolving around the radio, however, Chassie refuses to stand down against the threatened male's objections to the apparatus, which here emerges as possessing a liberating potential for women in terms not only of reception (i.e., that which is demonstrated in the radio scene with Jenny) but also of emitting, of being able to accede to the other end of the broadcasting chain of transmission and disseminate one's own messages. As Walter Benjamin writes, seeing a progressive potential for the masses embedded in the radio medium, yet lamenting society's inability, so far, to mobilize such a promise:

> The crucial failing of this institution has been to perpetuate the fundamental separation between practitioners and the public, a separation that is at odds with its technological basis. A child can see that it is in the spirit of radio to put as many people as possible in front of a microphone on every possible occasion; the public has to be turned into the witnesses of interviews and conversations in which now this person and now that one has the opportunity to make himself heard.[16]

Or, as Benjamin puts it in his famous essay on art and mechanical reproducibility, making a similar claim in relation to cinema: "*Any person today can lay claim to being filmed*,"[17] such that "the distinction between author and public is about to lose its axiomatic character."[18] Deeply invested in "the opportunity to make [herself] heard" described by Benjamin—and effectively bringing a missing gender dimension to his Marxist-inflected analysis, which is largely preoccupied with the subject of the working-class masses—Chassie rebuts her husband's initial attempt at shutting her down, pridefully affirming, "I'm going to sing on the air" (see figure 3.2), and continues to assert her com-

Figure 3.2. Despite her husband's sardonic opposition, Chassie affirms her desire to perform on the radio. Joseph Seiden, *Kol Nidre* (1939).

municative rights, in spite of the fact that, as her husband repeatedly, savagely points out, she may not have a very good voice. "Like the Americans say, 'Never mind the voice, you just have to put it over,'" she volleys resiliently in the face of his put-downs, exhibiting a pragmatic insouciance in relation to traditional aesthetic standards that gels with Benjamin's sense of the revolutionary, shattering promise of mass media.

Chassie's pièce de resistance of antipatriarchal rebellion, however, comes in the aftermath of her husband's exit, in a stridently feminist, solo musical number, a fiery complaint on behalf of all women, performed bluntly to the camera as she finishes getting fancily dressed up for the audition. "*Oy, di mener* [Oy, the menfolk]," runs the choral refrain, while the verses intriguingly synthesize the feminist sentiment with currents of Yiddish sweatshop socialism and labor activism (of the sort that we'll see more of in chapter 6). Calling for a *Lysistrata*-style sex strike in a vision that extends her desire to subvert her husband's authority within the family into a desire to subvert the patriarchal organization of society as a whole, Chassie sings:

> Every man thinks he's a big shot—
> he's in charge no matter what.
> He's the master, we're his servants,
> that is every woman's lot . . .
> Just like poison I despise them,
> they think that pants mean they're on top.
> Come on ladies, let's surprise them,
> let us strike and close up shop!
> Let us organize and picket,
> no more women's pain on earth!
> Let the husbands all get pregnant,
> let them suffer giving birth!

The film neglects to show, or even mention again, Chassie's radio audition, to say nothing of her actually appearing on the air. Hence the "*Oy, di mener*" number serves, cunningly, to give her an opportunity to put her much-maligned, musical-communicative aspirations on display and into practice nonetheless—for us, the mass audience of cinema spectators, to whom she directly addresses the song. In other words, the film itself comes to stand in for radio, to serve as a kind of quasi-radio, in an act of reflexive intermediation, and this allows Chassie, in a manner, for the moment, to get her wish and make herself heard.

The Scandal of the Speaking Body and the Text of Muteness

As we've mentioned, melodrama indulges habitually in a metaphorics of illness, deploying pathological states of the body to represent its characters' "extreme moral and emotional conditions."[19] Very much in line with this tendency, Moishe's crisis of paternal authority comes to assume a most spectacular physical form, manifesting in a bodily paroxysm—likely a stroke or heart attack but never specifically named, never pinpointed in concrete medical language, thus enriching its metaphoric effectivity—that results in him being paralyzed, confined to a wheelchair, and unable to speak, afflicted by a disorder of muteness far more extreme than we saw in the case of Muni after his suicide attempt in *The Living Orphan*. In another heated confrontation scene in the home, like the one earlier centering on the radio, Moishe discovers a secret that Jenny has been harboring for some time and has been compelled to disclose, particularly in response to his increasing pressure to marry Goldstein: that is, she and Jack have eloped, and she has become pregnant. As if possessed with a darting, literally wounding power, the disclosure causes Moishe to grip his chest, stagger backward, and lower himself in a recliner—at which point he laments to Sarah, suggestively refusing to face Jenny and respond to her directly: "Well, Mother, glad tidings, you've married your daughter. Our life's dream, and she's destroyed it. She killed us but didn't finish the job." And he continues, managing to stand up yet needing to stabilize himself using his desk, and still refusing to look at Jenny even while now obliged to address her: "Go. I never want to see you again. You have no parents. You are dead to us." As in the earlier scene with the radio, Jenny makes an exit mid-scene and storms out of the room, though, importantly, she does so not in obedience to her father's banishment but in outrage over his unbudgingly hostile, unempathetic response to her revelations, while paying no heed to her mother's distraught entreaty *not* to go. Meanwhile, in the wake of her exit, Moishe continues to dwell on Jenny's insubordination, brooding further on the sabotaging of his nuptial dreams ("Musicians play. Louder, stronger. Mother will dance the wedding dance. I will sit Shiva. She is dead to us, dead"), and attempting to cement the banishment with an added, religious dimension of formality. Raising a shaking fist with one hand and clutching his chest with the other, he thus declaims with quintessential Yiddish-actorly energy: "Blessed is God, the righteous judge . . ." In the mist of this articulation, however, Moishe is suddenly interrupted, thrown into a fit of seizures—his face contorting grotesquely, his fist unraveling into a chaos of twitching fingers—that results in him collapsing unresponsively onto the couch, as Sarah cries out for a doctor (see figure 3.3).

The scene's disastrous, broken-off expulsion embodies another vital fixture of Yiddish cinema also brought up in chapter 2—that is, the archetypal moment of excommunication, of transmission of a paradoxical *"message that proclaims: 'there will be no more messages'"*[20]— that it is now an apt time to say some more about. As J. L. Austin,

Figure 3.3. Moishe suffers a bodily breakdown while uttering an excommunication of his daughter. Joseph Seiden, *Kol Nidre* (1939).

the founder of speech act theory, points out, an excommunication is a type of speech act that is not only "performative," that not only "does something" (i.e., in opposition to a mere description or postulation of fact) but that more particularly fits under the rubric of "exercitives": speech acts whose "consequences may be that others are 'compelled' or 'allowed' or 'not allowed' to do certain acts,"[21] and that accordingly "confer powers, rights, names, &c., or change or eliminate them."[22] As one might anticipate from such a definition, exercitives are commonly used by "arbitrators and judges,"[23] and thus involve a particularly pronounced display of authority upon which, as Pierre Bourdieu has argued in a famous sociological critique of Austin and analysis of performatives in terms of "authorized language" and "rites of institution,"[24] all performatives rely for their success. Indeed, this emphatic authority exhibitionism strongly typifies excommunication scenes in Yiddish cinema, which frequently function as critical testing grounds for the powers of a contested authority figure. In *Kol Nidre*, which is exemplary in this respect, the besieged father flunks the test in a host of ways. First, the daughter displays her own kind of authority, embodied in her disclosure to have, as it were, "excommunicated" her parents from her crucial life choices and gone ahead and married whom she pleases; second, Sarah's plea to Jenny that the latter not leave subverts, or completely ignores, what her husband has just a moment ago commanded in thunder, revealing that she doesn't really take her husband's dictates all that seriously, doesn't really take them as binding; and third, of course, Moishe totally physically breaks down in the act of ratifying the expulsion. Regarding this last and most spectacular index of performative failure, the film offers a striking instance of what Shoshana Felman, another influential commentator on Austin's work, has called "the scandal of the speaking body."[25] As Judith Butler explains, usefully explicating and unpacking the implications of Felman's concept (in the next chapter, we turn to Butler's own reflections on the instability of performative speech acts):

> For Felman, the body that speaks is a scandal precisely because its speech is not fully governed by intention. No act of speech can fully control or determine the rhetorical effects of the body which speaks. It is scandalous as well because the bodily action of speech is not predictable in any mechanical way. That the speech act is a bodily act does not mean that the body is fully present in its speech. The relationship between speech and the body is that of a chiasmus. Speech is bodily, but the body exceeds the speech it occasions; and speech remains irreducible to the bodily means of its enunciation.[26]

As Moishe utters the forbidding performative intended to excommunicate his daughter, his body produces excessive, unpredictable "rhetorical effects" that radically destabilize what he is trying to say/do and cause his imposition of social death ("You are dead to us") to wildly backfire and nearly kill him on a quite literal level. Indeed, it is this unleashing of unruly corporeality that comes to be distilled in Moishe's dire state of wheelchair-bound paralysis and muteness, which the film reveals, in a shock close-up of his frozenly contorted, grimacing face, when it picks up a year later.

Like excommunicatory speech acts, conditions of muteness constitute another staple of Yiddish cinema (in fact, unsurprisingly, as in *Kol Nidre*, the two are usually linked in some way), and now is a good time to say more about this recurrent feature too. Developing his observation about the notable reliance on extreme physical states in melodrama, Brooks points out that within the genre's "gallery of mutilations and deprivations . . . the mutes have a special place."[27] This special emphasis on *speech* pathology within the range of possible physical disorders is something abundantly shared by the pervasively melodramatic Yiddish cinema. In Yiddish cinema, however, those afflicted by some form of muteness or speech disorder (and we will encounter many more besides Moishe and Muni, on both the giving and the receiving end of excommunication, in the pages that follow) tend to function in a manner somewhat different from that which Brooks describes, or rather, with an important additional dimension. Parsing what he calls "the text of muteness," Brooks writes:

> Melodrama appears as a medium in which repression has been pierced to allow thorough articulation, to make available the expression of pure moral and psychological integers. Yet here we encounter the apparent paradox that melodrama so often, particularly in climactic moments and extreme situations, has recourse to non-verbal means of expressing its meanings. Words, however unrepressed and pure, however transparent as vehicles for the expression of basic relations and verities, appear to be not wholly adequate to the representation of meanings, and the melodramatic message must be formulated through other registers of the sign.[28]

In other words, what appears to be a paradox is in fact no such thing, since, in line with his overarching thesis about melodrama's deep, driving expressionistic nature, the "non-verbal means" to which the genre takes recourse still serve in an expressive capacity, signifying in an *alternative* manner to language rather than giving way to nonsignification. Indeed, for Brooks, such nonverbal means (his primary examples are gesture and tableau, which often work in tandem) are capable of far *outstripping* language in terms of expressive, semantic output. Grasping gesture in melodrama in the context of eighteenth-century debates about the origins of language—a speculative, burning topic taken up by Diderot and Rousseau, among other prominent thinkers of the time—he writes: "The use of mute gesture in melodrama reintroduces a figuration of the primal language onto the stage, where it carries immediate, primal spiritual meanings which the language code, in its demonetization, has obscured, alienated, lost."[29] On a certain level, Moishe's muteness conforms well to this perspective, conveying to the audience his profound, ineffable anguish over the break with his daughter that he himself has instigated. Yet the Brooksian maneuver by which muteness is translated back into—newly enriched—communication, signification, decipherability, and so on, misses what is most important and characteristically Yiddish-cinematic about Moishe's condition: that is to say, its brute, literal status *as* muteness, which critically instantiates his ongoing troubled communication (viz., his continuing lack of an authoritative paternal voice).

The film underlines this sense of blockage qua blockage in one of the most extraordinarily grim musical numbers in all Yiddish cinema, one that innovatively interweaves muteness into the very fabric of the song being performed. Near the end of the sequence reintroducing Moishe in his impaired state, with just the two of them in the living room, Sarah appeals to her husband amid hopeless bawling: "*Oy Moishe*, is it worth having children?" The inevitable nonresponse then prompts her to attempt to answer the question herself, which she does in the form of a somber, hankie-clutching ballad that serves as another instance of raw, outspoken female complaint (recall Chassie's "*Oy, di mener*"):

> Is it really worth having children? No, not worthwhile at all.
> Children? We ought to strangle them when they're quite small.
> Children are fine when they're young at home,
> As soon as they're older, they'll leave you all alone.
> Is it worth having children, giving them all we own?
> Instead of children, I should have borne a stone.

Strikingly, in each of the four shots that comprise the number, the film includes Moishe in the frame (see figure 3.4), creating the insistent impression of what we might consider a phantom duet: a song for two in which one of the voices remains uncannily, conspicuously absent. Or in other words, with every inclusion of the father in the musical image, the film drives home Moishe's communicative obstruction in

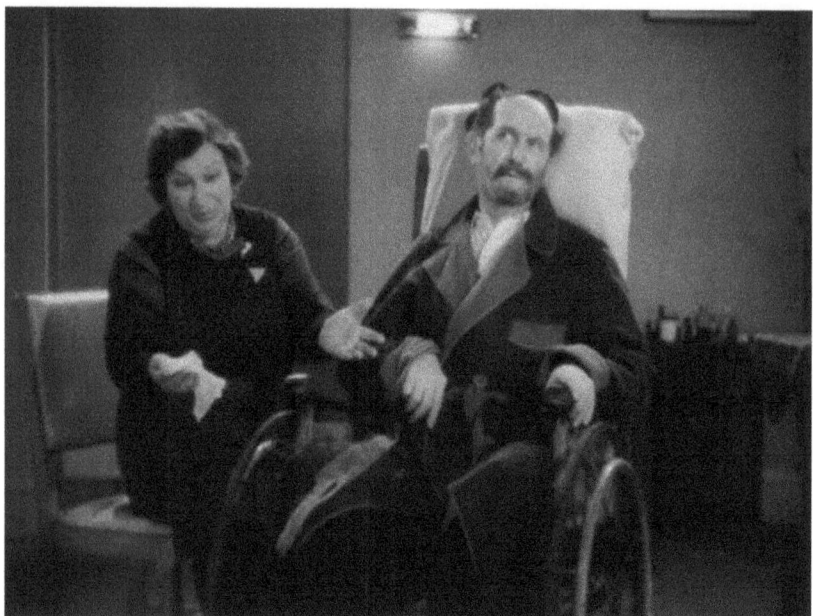

Figure 3.4. As Sarah sings a regretful song about having children, the camera's rigorous inclusion of her mute husband in the frame creates the effect of a "phantom duet." Joseph Seiden, *Kol Nidre* (1939).

itself, the very fact of his inability to sing, or indeed to produce any kind of smoothly deliberate verbal sound. Accordingly, once the song concludes, Moishe does become audible, and yet hardly articulate, vainly striving to say Jenny's name in a disturbing, protracted, moaning stammer, which provides a fittingly macabre coda to the number.

That Yiddish cinema plays out—with emphatic force—the fixation on muteness found in melodrama makes perfect sense given its larger preoccupation with troubled communication. Further, we can read into the phenomenon, into the movies' endless return to ailments of speech, resonant traces bearing on the history of the Yiddish language itself. As Dan Miron tells in his pivotal study of the rise of modern Yiddish fiction, Yiddish writers in the nineteenth century formatively grappled with a view that the language that they were mobilizing was problematic, inferior: a view that can be traced to the *maskilim*, the torchbearers of the *Haskala* (Jewish Enlightenment), whose preferred Jewish tongue was the allegedly "pure" Hebrew.

Writes Miron: "This opposition [to Yiddish] carried the full authority of the venerated Moses Mendelssohn (1729–1786), the fountainhead of the *Haskala* and its undisputed hero at least until the 1870s, . . . and was propagated by the members of the Mendelssohnian circle, who vilified Yiddish as a linguistic hodge-podge, a jargon that barred Jews from contact with their neighbors and doomed them to isolation from civilization."[30] For Mendelssohn, as he wrote in the introduction to his German translation of the Pentateuch, Yiddish was "a language of stammerers, corrupt and deformed, repulsive to those who are able to speak in a correct and elegant manner."[31] Along similar lines, heightening the case with an iteration of an oft-repeated claim regarding an imputed scarcity of vocabulary, the Hebrew poet Avrom-Ber Gotlober wrote, in the 1860s, that Yiddish lacked "enough words for expressing one correct idea, especially in the field of the sciences, where it is completely impotent, so that a person who speaks no other language can be regarded as no better than a mute."[32] Meanwhile, as Sander Gilman has recounted, such internal negative attitudes toward Yiddish were paralleled by a potent strain of external negative attitudes arising from elements in the dominant gentile culture invested in an antisemitic othering of Jewish languages.[33] Seen in the context of this history of manifold denigrations, a history in which Yiddish repeatedly comes up against the accusation of embodying in itself a kind of speech pathology, the stammering, muttering, howling mutes of Yiddish cinema present a metamediatic redounding upon the language of which they have been deprived. Their aphasic traumas dredge up, to aggravating effect, Yiddish's own traumas.

Returning to Tradition

Despite all the drastic destabilizations that Moishe suffers, the film ends by making a hypermoralistic, cautionary attempt to reinstate a sense of paternal authority, and thus to roll back whatever effects may have been produced by the advance of the mass media family. This reversal kicks into high gear in a scene that portrays a performance of the eponymous prayer, a piece of music sung at the inception of Yom Kippur, and famous for its elegiac beauty (indeed the Kol Nidre service normally comprises the most anticipated event in the whole liturgical calendar). Outside the synagogue where the prayer is being sung—by the real-life cantor Louis (Liebele) Waldman, a recurrent presence in Yiddish cinema who gives a characteristically virtuoso performance, accompanied by a large all-male choir, while Goldstein, ostensibly the presiding rabbi, stands behind him on the podium next to the ark[34]—Jenny fatefully appears garbed in all-black with her baby in her arms, on her way to commit suicide (at this point, in a dramatic deterioration of her situation, she and the baby have been abandoned, left penniless and about to be evicted, by Jack, who after the marriage neither stopped philandering nor materialized into the great business success that he had promised). As the film cross-cuts from the interior of the packed synagogue to Jenny just outside the temple gate, we see the outcast mother overhearing the transcendent music in a state of rapt attention, and declaring in a plea for mercy appropriate to the penitential occasion of Yom Kippur (aka "The Day of Atonement"): "Kol Nidre! What a holy melody! Lord God, forgive me for my sins, for the sin I am about to commit." Critically bearing on the film's treatment of the mass media family, the moment provides a striking counter to the earlier moment in which Jenny insists on listening to the radio rather than to her father's voice. Now, she is in thrall to sounds that embody her father's attachment to tradition, and that, moreover, for her, appear disembodied—acousmatic—like those on the radio. And such a current only grows stronger as the film hurtles toward the requisite "happy ending." In a providential intercession typical of *shund*, a cop, happening to walk by, stops Jenny from going through with the desperate act of killing herself and the baby; at the Social Service, to which she is referred from the police station, a caring female employee who knows Goldstein tells the rabbi about her and lets him "handle the case"; Goldstein shortly proposes marriage, anchored in the assurance that he will be a father to the child; Jenny joyfully accepts (while her previous marriage is conveniently dissolved by Jack fatally drunk-driving off a cliff, a spectacular accident shown in a rapid insert nakedly repurposed from another film); and, at last, poised to serve as what his doctor describes as "the right medicine" for Moishe, Jenny returns home with Goldstein and the baby, and, in the closing shot of the film, gains her father's forgiveness.

Such an ending presents a restoration of patriarchal authority far more pronounced than in the films discussed in chapters 1 and 2. However, a number of key factors still cast doubt on our sense of Moishe's rehabilitation as a father. First, there is the especially hurried way in which the father's momentous exoneration of his prodigal daughter is arranged (all of approximately six minutes transpires from the time that Jenny fails to commit suicide until the end of the film). Second, although the doctor promises that the reunion with his daughter will provide the antidote to his illness, we never actually witness Moishe's recovery and the restitution of his voice. Following his sluggish few words of forgiveness to Jenny, which he is able to utter only with immense laboriousness, the film offers no denouement or epilogue showing him with his symptoms lifted. Third and most importantly, the film effects a critical displacement. Far beyond taking on a paternal role within his new family and acting as a father to Jenny's child, Rabbi Goldstein serves, via his profession, as a father figure to the broader "family" of the Jewish community. Not only is this type of "fatherhood" invested with far greater communicative potentiality than ordinary fatherhood, but it is a position at which, the film goes to great lengths to show us, Goldstein excels. In between the radio scene where Jenny spars with her father over wanting to listen to Benny Goodman and the excommunication scene where Moishe suffers his collapse, the Dorfman family go to the synagogue for a benefit concert for German Jewish refugees: an event similar to the one at the end of *A Little Letter to Mother*. As the first act of the evening, Goldstein delivers a lecture on the importance of Jewish history keyed to the threats and exigencies of the present moment (recall, it is 1939). He opens: "Dear Friends, I speak today for the first time as a rabbi. Our youth are neglecting the proud past of their people. Our duty is to teach them the beauty of that history. This people have stood steadfast through the ages. Today more than ever we must face our enemies. Jewish youth and tolerant Christians will build a better world." He then proceeds to illustrate his argument through a series of exemplary stories from the Old Testament, which the film illustrates for us through a montage of recycled footage from biblical silent films.[35] Despite this being his first time publicly speaking as a rabbi, the novice performs expertly, as demonstrated in a cutaway to the rapt audience during his opening remarks. In stark contrast to Moishe's voice, Goldstein's voice transmits authority—the authority of the biblical teachings, and of the highest authority of all, that of the supreme father, God—with almost effortless effectiveness. Indeed, it is his voice, which delivers the commanding narration to the repurposed footage and which we hear uninterruptedly for the duration of his lengthy lecture, that proves the real star of the scene.

With Jenny's decision to marry Rabbi Goldstein, the film thus manages to reestablish all dimensions of patriarchy around her without relying on her actual father. Authority migrates from the father to the son-in-law/husband, exemplifying a model of displacement that (unlike the displacement of the father's authority by the mother's in *The Living Orphan*) preserves the essential dynamics of the power structure of the patriarchal family. Unable to resolve her wretched situation on her own or in some other way, Jenny ends up relying on and embracing Goldstein, despite her previous dreams of a repletely modern lifestyle. Meanwhile, Jenny's abandonment of the subversive "promise" offered by the radio is interestingly inflected by what happens to Chassie, who not only doesn't realize her dreams of radio stardom (as mentioned, the film never again refers to her audition after allowing her the chance to impress us with her singing) but is soundly rebuffed when pursuing another "broadcasting" opportunity. After the benefit concert, acting uncharacteristically on his wife's behalf, Shmelke visits Goldstein in his office and asks if Chassie might be able to join the synagogue's choir, to which Goldstein responds with polite misgivings and an ultimate refusal, making the excuse "I have no women in my choir." In this way, despite the fact that when Chassie enters the office Shmelke awkwardly lies and assures her under his breath that the rabbi has agreed, there ultimately proves no space for her within the traditional performance structure. Her voice remains stranded, its broadcasting possibilities cut off on all sides. Whereas she sees herself as the rabbi's communicative equal—"Your speech held the audience, just like when I sing," she remarks to him on her way out the door—Goldstein remains incapable of imagining such parity, saying to himself with a bemused smile once the couple exits: "A strange woman." In sum, in the case of Jenny, the reformation of the rebellious daughter—her ultimate willing marriage to the rabbi—gives in to a kind of reactionary fantasy. Jenny's renunciation of the disruptive, liberating force of mass media is shown to be a happy, positive development, as is the concordant arrest and reversal of the restructuring of the family into the mass media family. At the same time, in the case of Chassie, female rebelliousness is again tamped down (the radio audition going nowhere/being erased, the attempt to penetrate the all-male choir proving fruitless); and yet, unlike Jenny, Chassie never ultimately concedes to the forces of neutralization. One can well imagine her, stretching beyond the bounds of the ambivalently messaging film, continuing her quest to get on the air, to get into the choir, and so on, and finally, *justly* make her eccentric voice (so disturbing to her husband, so baffling to the rabbi) heard.

4

The Battle of the Books

Tevye (1939)

LIKE THE MORE WELL-KNOWN 1964 American musical *Fiddler on the Roof*, the 1939 Yiddish American film *Tevye* is an adaptation of Sholem Aleichem's *Tevye the Dairyman*, an immensely popular cycle of Yiddish stories set in the late nineteenth/early twentieth century (that is, at the same time as the stories were written: 1895–1916) in the Pale of Settlement, the sprawling ghetto in western Imperial Russia to which Jews were legally confined from the late eighteenth century until the Bolshevik Revolution. Written and directed by—and also starring—Maurice Schwartz, the founder of the prestigious Yiddish Art Theatre in New York, the film elides and condenses much of the original story cycle, focusing on the most contentious of Tevye's daughters' romantic leave-takings: that of Chava, who is wooed by, and runs off with and marries, a local gentile. The film, accordingly, reflects *Kol Nidre* in portraying a daughterly rebellion against patriarchal authority, and yet its treatment of fatherhood is notably differently from that in the Seiden film. Schwartz's Tevye never comes across as preposterous or grotesque in the way that Moishe (fulminating to the point of physical meltdown) often does, and indeed, of all the troubled fathers who feature so prominently in all the films discussed up to this point, the eponymous patriarch emerges in the end as the most "intact" (we might think of Dovid, Muni, Moishe, and Tevye as forming a kind of quartet). Behind this leading position is almost certainly the film's sustained attempt to engage its own historical moment and channel the dire situation unfolding in Europe (by the time of the film's release, in late 1939, the Nazis had already invaded Poland)—a move whereby the tribulations of Jews in Tsarist Russia are made to resonate, obliquely though unmistakably, with those of Jews in the present. In other words, the film appears compelled to offer a bracing, reassuring message to its Jewish audience amid dark times; radical imperilment, in the film's treatment, precisely *necessitates* a radical show of fortitude in the famous paternal protagonist, a character who was originally conceived as significantly more resigned and passive—if by no means under a negative valence—in the face of rising troubles. At the same time, and in a manner that instructively distinguishes the film from the English-language *Fiddler* (made into a movie, fascinating in its own right, in 1971 by Norman Jewison), a concern with forms of media and mediation takes center stage and can largely be understood in terms of, and in relation to, what we wish to call "the battle of the books"—our focus in this chapter.

The Battle of the Books

In its original literary incarnation, *Tevye the Dairyman* takes the form of a series of vibrant monologues delivered by the titular character to the authorial persona of Sholem Aleichem (a pseudonym for the real-life author Sholem Rabinovitch), thereby producing an embedded, covert yet all-enveloping tension in the work between tradition (embodied by the rural dairyman speaker) and modernity (embodied by the writer-intellectual auditor). The film foregoes this narrative structure, doing without any framing and adopting the equivalent of an "omniscient" third-person narration. However, the tradition/modernity tension is not scuttled by extension but rather reinscribed in, or displaced entirely onto, the relationship between Tevye, on the one hand, and Chava and her suitor, on the other, wherein the latter derive an outsized share of their knowledge and motivations from a contemporary source—namely, Russian literature—that lies largely outside of Tevye's purview and to which, in his minimal familiarity, he is resistant. In this way, Russian books function analogously to the radio in *Kol Nidre*, prompting a similar destabilization of paternal authority, while speaking to an earlier historical moment in which the predominant form of mass media was embodied by print.

Books permeate the opening sequence of the film. Glisteningly blonde, strappingly high-booted, riding on horseback through the countryside, Chava's suitor Fedye Galagan[1] (Leon Liebgold) enters the film as if *out* of a book, as if a knight from a chivalric romance. Further, once he finds the ebullient, dark-haired Chava (Miriam Riselle) feeding ducks on a small wooden dock by a pond, he takes her by surprise, kisses her vigorously (despite her concerns about keeping their relationship a secret), and, supplanting her earthy, rural pastime with a more sophisticated, urbane one, presents her with a book by the Russian author Maxim Gorky. In *The Jewish Century*, an influential history that deals with the younger generation of Russian Jews in the early twentieth century and their profound, often parentally frowned-upon attraction to the wider world of Russian letters and culture, Yuri Slezkine writes: "In the 1910s, Gorky was Russia's most celebrated writer, most revered prophetic voice, and most articulate and passionate Judeophile."[2] In both the stories and the film, this Judeophilia is clearly reflected in Chava's paramour, as his passion for Chava suggests, and indeed both the stories and film go to significant lengths to reinforce the Gorky/lover association. In Sholem Aleichem, Chava's suitor is himself a writer, whom she describes enthusiastically to her father as a "second Gorky,"[3] while she carries around a portrait of the famous author in her pocket. In the film, taking a lingering look at the frontispiece of the gifted book, Chava observes, thrillingly, that Fedye looks just like Gorky (even though, unlike his precedent in the stories, he isn't explicitly a writer) and goes on to note, also with delight, that his poetical, high-flown speech radiates a literary aura:

> FEDYE: You're so beautiful, my little girl, like the dreamy skies of our Ukraine.
>
> CHAVA: You speak so beautifully, Fedye, just like in the novels.

In both the stories and the film, that is to say, Chava's attraction to her suitor is framed as stemming from something much larger than him. What entices the young, intelligent, curious, independent-minded Jewish girl is an entire field of communication different from and rivaling the one she is used to. Accordingly, within the sphere of her relationship, and working in a two-way fashion, Russian books serve as potent mediators of desire: a point reinforced and tangibly illustrated in the film when, during their exchange, Fedye puts his hand on the book that Chava holds, and *only then* onto her florally bloused upper arm, as if the text were a necessary station in the progress of his caress; and again when, in the final moment of the scene, Fedye moves in to embrace Chava more fully, and the book winds up positioned directly in between them, at the dually heart-throbbing center of the frame (see figure 4.1).

Notably, we find a similar treatment of literary-mediated desire—or in this case, literacy-mediated desire—in Ulmer and Ben-Ami's *Green Fields*, where the wandering, typically shy *yeshiva bokher* is taken in by a family in the countryside and is pursued by their contrastingly forward, illiterate daughter, who attempts the seduction by means of a clandestine absorption of the reading and writing lessons that the scholar has been giving to her younger brother. At one point, seeking to impress the scholar and flaunt her new skill, the daughter makes

Figure 4.1. A Gorky book placed in between Chava and Fedye: a potent mediator of desire. Maurice Schwartz, *Tevye* (1939).

him close his eyes while she writes his name in chalk on a wooden board. However, in the midst of the demonstration, she takes the opportunity of his sight-deprived, redoubled passiveness to plant a kiss on his cheek. Strikingly, as this happens, the two jointly hold the chalk board in between them and thus form a triangular romantic-mediatic circuit that strongly mirrors the one that we find in the scene just described in *Tevye* (see figure 4.2).

As for Chava's father, it is not at all that he is opposed to books per se, but rather that he is opposed to the particular type, the particular *content*, of books that exert a special fascination on his daughter. Indeed, Tevye attempts to cultivate a relationship with Chava through books just as much as Fedye. First, he talks to her—and, admittedly, to everyone—in a manner whose most distinctive feature is a rampant

Figure 4.2. The daughter of a Jewish farmer kisses a shy *yeshiva bokher* whom she's trying to seduce with her secretly acquired literacy; the placement of the writing tablet in between them mirrors the placement of the Gorky book in between the lovers in *Tevye*. Edgar G. Ulmer and Jacob Ben-Ami, *Green Fields* (1937).

reliance on citationality. His speech interweaves countless quotations, or most often, to comical effect, misquotations, from the Bible and other religious texts. Second—and, importantly, constituting a detail that does not appear in the stories, that belongs uniquely to the film—Tevye explicitly supplies Chava with a book of his own liking (as we'll discuss further in a moment). It is in this way that what we are calling a "battle of the books," part and parcel of a larger rivalry of communicative modes and infrastructures, takes shape between Tevye and Fedye, and in which the former faces a serious disadvantage. For Chava is far more drawn to Fedye's remediatory Russian-novelistic voice than to Tevye's remediatory Judaic voice, perhaps detecting, as Dan Miron points out, "how much of a defense mechanism his [Tevye's] clever pseudo-scholarly discourse is," how it is often employed as a means of evasion and cover-up "as soon as a serious issue is to be discussed or a difficult decision made."[4]

Just as is the case with Fedye, Tevye's gifting of a book to Chava occurs in his first scene with her, cultivating a kind of counterpoint. Arriving home in his wagon from a day at work selling milk in Boyberik, Tevye first greets his older married daughter Tseytl (Paula Lubelski) and her two young children Shloimele (Vicki Marcus) and Perele (Betty Marcus), who have showed up for a surprise visit. He then turns to Chava and presents her with a "*bikhele* [little book]" that he pulls out of his breast pocket. Although Chava responds to the gesture with gracious excitement ("A book! Thank you, father"), her mother instantly frowns upon the gift ("What does she need books for?"), compelling Tevye to defend himself with one of his signature quotations: "Golde, I thought you agreed not to meddle in my affairs? As the Rabbis say, 'What is mine is thine, and what is thine is mine.'" And yet, what Tevye doesn't know, and doesn't bother to find out, is that his wife's frustration at her daughter's love of books is heavily informed by her disapproval of Fedye's textual courting of Chava, as she earlier anxiously explains to Tseytl in a brief tête-à-tête ("Do you know that young goy, Fedye Galagan.... He gives her books to read. They stand at the gate for hours and talk, and talk, and talk"). Evidently, Golde senses it is dangerous for Tevye to help cultivate a readerly passion that also provides building blocks for Chava's relationship with Fedye—an intuition that, as the next scene demonstrates, proves deeply justified.

As the family eats a meal in the yard, Chava and her father sit at opposite ends of the table, in a subtly conflictual spatial arrangement.

Further, Chava's head is buried in a book, yet apparently not the book that she just received, with a show of enthusiasm, from Tevye.

TEVYE: So, Chava, what do your books preach?

CHAVA: Papa, I thought you agreed not to meddle in my affairs? As the Rabbis say, "What is mine is thine is thine . . . is thine."

TEVYE: Said like a real ignoramus! But, you're right. One shouldn't meddle in the affairs of others. What would happen if we'd meddle in your mother's borscht?

GOLDE: Stop being silly! The borscht is ready and he's singing.

Strikingly, in the short span of time elapsing between Tevye's arrival and the meal, Chava has already effectively forgotten the book that Tevye has given her, is already immersed in another book, presumably the Gorky that Fedye has given her, or something by another luminary from the pantheon of Russian literature. As for what book has passed from father to daughter, one can confidently assume that it is something Jewish in content, such as the popular vernacular prayer books for women known as *tkhines*.[5] However, the film never makes this clear, in a lacuna that expresses the lack of weight that the book bears for Chava and that stands in flagrant contrast to the great fuss that she makes over the authorship of the book from Fedye. Such undermining of Tevye's gift is also reinforced by the conversation at the table, which underlines the gap—once more reminiscent of *Kol Nidre*—that exists between the respective sources of the father's and the daughter's knowledge (i.e., Tevye is utterly clueless about what Chava's "books preach"), and reveals Chava momentarily usurping her father's voice, comically impersonating him with the same quotation that he uses against her mother, despite a few struggles with the Hebrew. Such a hijacking of Tevye's famous, citational verbal style allows the daughter to play the father and thrusts the father into the position of his wife: an emasculating slide that recurs throughout the film, and against which Tevye anxiously attempts to defend himself.

The "battle of the books" that emerges through Chava's text-saturated interactions with her lover and her father only escalates as time goes on, and with increasing consequences. Later on, Fedye pays a furtive nighttime visit to Chava. Tapping on a window to get her attention, he draws her outside onto the porch and presents her with yet another book by Gorky. Before he can lead her away on a stroll, however, Chava notices her father leaving the stable, and Fedye flees with a hastily snatched kiss. Then, as Chava tries to sneak back into the house, she is hailed by her father, who has clearly seen Fedye run off and starts a sort of interrogation, utterly devoid of the joking tone of their previous exchange at the table, that continues the focus on books:

>TEVYE: What was he [Fedye] doing here?
>
>CHAVA: Nothing. We talked. He brought me a book.
>
>TEVYE: A book? So it's books, is it?

Tevye clearly senses trouble brewing, having been introduced to the idea of "losing" his daughter to a non-Jew at the end of the meal scene, when the Priest (Julius Adler) shows up and, no doubt knowing about the affair between Chava and Fedye, ominously warns Tevye that Jewish women who marry into the Christian faith fall into "our domain." Accordingly, as the two move from the porch to a bench in front of the house, Tevye continues pressing Chava about Fedye and the books that he gives her, while continuing to display deep avoidance and/or ignorance regarding his daughter's situation (see figure 4.3).

>TEVYE: Let's see what kind of books he brings you. Books are important. Books tell you what's going on all over the world. But why doesn't he bring the books into the house instead of jumping over the porch? Is it one of those books banned by the Tsar?
>
>CHAVA: No, it's a novel by Gorky.
>
>TEVYE: Gorky? Who is this Gorky?
>
>CHAVA: A writer. A Russian writer. Second only to Tolstoy.

Figure 4.3. Tevye critically examines the newest Gorky book that Fedye has gifted to Chava. Maurice Schwartz, *Tevye* (1939).

TEVYE: Who?

CHAVA: Tolstoy. Count Tolstoy. The one whose portrait hangs in my room.

TEVYE: Oh, Tolstoy. The one who says that if they slap you in the face, you should say, "Thank you. Many happy returns," and turn the other cheek? Oh, yes, Tolstoy! And what does he preach, this, what's his name, Gorky?

CHAVA: Gorky is a great man, father. This is his portrait [flips to the book's frontispiece].

TEVYE: That's him? He looks familiar. I'd swear I'd seen him somewhere.

If the resemblance between Fedye and Gorky were fully to enter into the father's consciousness, he might deduce that his daughter's admiration for the famous writer speaks volumes about her affection for the author's rural lookalike. However, Tevye again shows his limitations. Not only is he unable to make the connection between the writer and the suitor, but he also possesses insufficient knowledge of the world that his daughter is attracted to, and thus he is unable to dissuade her from that world. What he is mainly concerned about is whether the book is political contraband—a not insignificant concern, given that being caught with revolutionary material would be especially perilous for Jews, who occupy a precarious position in the Russian Empire. However, it is also a concern that ironically overlooks the possibility that it might be precisely *Jewish* literature and/or literature *by Jews*, and not the other way around, that would constitute illegal writing. For Jewish ethical teachings, including the many that Tevye himself spouts, contain a strong strain of universalist humanitarianism (embodied by concepts such as *tikkun olam* and responsibility to the Other, which we'll be exploring in later chapters) that readily lends itself to potentially subversive causes aimed at liberation and justice. As well, regarding the real-life historical context of the narrative, in the early twentieth century, Jews in Russia, and in Eastern Europe more broadly, participated in socialist and communist causes in disproportionate numbers relative to the rest of the population, and/or had a reputation for doing so, as historians like Slezkine, and Alain Brossat and Sylvie Klingberg in *Revolutionary Yiddishland*,[6] detail. Handily, Slezkine quotes a passage from Gorky that captures, in highly romantic tones, the first of these points, while perhaps providing intimations of the second:

> This idealism [of the Jews], which expresses itself in their tireless striving to remake the world according to the new principles of equality and justice, is the main, and possibly the only, reason for the hostility towards Jews. They disturb the peace of the satiated and self-satisfied and shed a ray of light on the dark sides of life. With their energy and enthusiasm, they have given people the gift of fire and the tireless pursuit of truth. They have been rousing nations, not letting them get rest, and finally—and this is the main thing!—this idealism has given birth to the scourge of the powerful; the religion of the masses, socialism.[7]

In the stories, the Jewish revolutionary Perchik, whom Tevye's other daughter Hodl follows after he is arrested and cast into Siberian imprisonment, embodies this kind of sentiment and would thus presumably cue Tevye into the possibility of a Jew penning a book, even a very Jewish book, scourging the powerful and opposing the Tsar. However, the film skirts over Hodl's fate—a casualty of adaptive, narrative compression—and so Tevye's overlooking of the possibility doesn't come off as implausible. In any case, Chava assures her father that the book isn't in fact forbidden and goes on to lionize Gorky and Tolstoy in such a way that enhances the parallel that we've been trying to draw between the interplay of media and family in *Tevye* and the interplay of media and family in *Kol Nidre*, where Jenny idolizes the modern, assimilated Benny Goodman, whom her father dismisses as a mere *klezmer*. Once more, an extrafamilial, mass media source transmitting a type of content coded as non-Jewish disrupts the father's authority, rendering problematic the maintenance of his own powers of influence. Just as Moishe faces off against the radio, which broadcasts the secular forces of American modernism as embodied by Goodman's jazz, Tevye faces off against a particular mobilization of print, which "broadcasts" what are in his eyes the radical and/or Christian forces of Russian literature as embodied by Gorky and Tolstoy's novels. In each case, the daughter reveals a deep inclination toward listening to the voice of the patriarch's mediatic rival, who represents an extension of the communicative realm of her "inappropriate" suitor.

For Chava, the fact that her father shows a poor understanding of *her* textual influences confirms the erroneousness of his worldview, and accordingly, while pushing back against his dismissive ignorance of Gorky and ridicule of Tolstoy's Christian pacifism, she also goes on to refute his harsh characterization of the Galagan men (whom he refers to as boars, drunkards, wife-beaters, potato-peelers, and pig-breeders) and to question his warning about antisemitism:

> CHAVA: But you always say there's one God for all mankind.
>
> TEVYE: Of course, you're right. All men are equal before God. "All Israel has a share in the world to come." Jews and Gentiles alike. The Torah teaches us to love all people, but also to remember forever Amalek, who harmed us.
>
> CHAVA: What do you mean, father?

TEVYE: I mean if there should ever be a pogrom, all our fine friends wouldn't hesitate to join in, and throw some stones in our windows.

CHAVA: I don't believe that father.

For the audience of the film, Tevye's evocation of an antisemitic eruption characterized by the smashing of windows would irresistibly conjure up an image of *Kristallnacht*, which occurred not long before the film's release, on November 9th and 10th of 1938. That is to say, such an allusion lends Tevye's warning an aura of prophetic justification, while casting Chava's resistance to believing in the possibility of such an event as hopelessly naive. At the same time, Tevye also partakes of myopic wishful thinking, continuing to ignore or repress the extent of his daughter's involvement with her non-Jewish suitor. At the end of the scene, he asks Chava, "Would you ever do such a thing that would drive your parents to the grave?"—to which she replies, "*Neyn, tate* [No, father]," but only after a long, tense pause, and with a quavering voice and somber face that telegraph enduring distress. Although finally able (albeit in a thinly disguised, roundabout way) to ask his daughter the critical question about whether she would run away with Fedye and marry him, Tevye completely misses the obvious signals embedded in her nominally negative response, going into the house with impatient excitement to share the good news with Golde, while Chava breaks down into tears outside. In short, whereas Chava's vision of the future is blinkered with respect to antisemitism, Tevye's vision of the future is blinkered with respect to assimilation, failing to take into account those aspects of the "host" culture that do not exclude or antagonize, but precisely appeal to, his children.

The Battle of the "Fathers"

Following Chava's running away from home, Tevye and Golde try to reclaim their daughter from the Priest's house on the day of her wedding, and yet what happens is another intricate, communicative face-off in which the "voice" of the Jewish father languishes. At the beginning of the scene, a brief montage shows glimpses of the boisterous village festivities taking place in celebration of the nuptials:

traditional Ukrainian folk music and dancing, wrestling, beer-drinking. All of this functions more than merely to paint the larger contours of the scene, generating a wall of noise that gives the impression of Tevye and Golde being sonically drowned out—muted—as they approach the grand house in their dark, mournful clothes. Indeed, even when the sound switches from the diegetic hullabaloo to melancholy underscoring in tune with the distraught parents, the sense of vocal amputation is made to linger and intensify. As the two wait at the door for someone to answer, Golde warns her husband, "Be careful what you say, Tevye. It'll all be lost if you start citing one of your quotations. Speak softly, Tevye, don't yell," knowing that her husband is now operating in a highly unaccommodating communicative context, one in which his exuberant voice, stitched with Jewish quotations, is powerless, and his authority, reliant on Jewish tradition, holds no sway. After a few moments, the imposing, long-bearded Priest appears, not at the door but rather through a window beside the door, and tells Tevye and Golde that he'll join them on the porch for tea. Tellingly, the Priest does not invite the couple inside the house, intimating the dangerous conditionality of whatever hospitality he is prepared to accord to them in apparent reciprocity for the generous hospitality that Tevye had accorded him earlier. "Make yourself at home," the Priest remarks to Tevye, showing him to a table as a servant brings out a samovar. However, Tevye refuses to sit and drink, and, despite his wife's warning, irresistibly reverts to his old verbal habits and asks the Priest: "Do you remember the story in the Bible about the rich man who stole the poor man's lamb?" This moral allusion to the Old Testament fails to elicit the slightest bit of sympathy from the Priest, causing Tevye to grow increasingly agitated and, with trembling hands, frenziedly make one of Yiddish cinema's most recurrent demands: "Give me back my child!" Here, as Golde had well foreseen, the accumulation of communicative effronteries provokes a disastrous response from the Priest. In an expressive long shot that shows a repeating multiplicity of carved-out Orthodox crucifixes adorning the porch railing (a reminder that Tevye and his wife are in unfamiliar territory where they are an outnumbered minority), the Priest stands up, walks tauntingly toward the couple, and thunderingly invokes the institutional power that he represents in order to silence Tevye: "How dare you speak to me this way! Do you know before whom you stand? You stand before a servant of the Tsar! Before the protector of the holy church!"

Such an irreconcilable clash between Tevye and the Priest, and their respective communicative modalities, makes for a striking juxtaposition with an earlier scene between the lovers. "Differences were invented by evil people. We are above all faiths. You are my faith," Fedye rhapsodizes to Chava in the fields, invoking another, more secularist current of universalism in order to try to allay her worries about their union. As the fraught interaction between Tevye and the Priest demonstrates, however, such ideas turn out to be wildly idealistic insofar as the couple is compelled to make their relationship official through matrimony. Indeed, contrary to Fedye's beaming assurance that he and Chava can exist "above all faiths," it becomes more and more clear that their wedding has been arranged in a radically asymmetrical manner. For instance, erasing Chava's Jewish origins, the whole affair has been arranged with the involvement of only one set of parents, Fedye's nakedly antisemitic father Mikita (David Makarenko) and unnamed mother (Helen Grossman)—who encounter Tevye and Golde leaving the Priest's house and refuse to recognize the couple not simply as in-laws but as human beings, branding them as "pest[s]," with unsettling, exterminatory undertones.

In fact, the only person inhabiting the Christian "domain" capable of receiving Tevye's voice is Chava, who awaits the ceremony with Fedye in an upper room of the Priest's house. As Tevye frantically demands the return of his child and calls out for her, the film crosscuts to Chava—decked out in an ornate traditional Ukrainian wedding dress and crown—throbbingly pierced by his cries and plunged into full-blown regret over her broken promise to her father. "I hear my father's voice," she affirms wailingly, before abortively attempting to flee the room and being restrained by Fedye. With tragic irony, Chava desires to "listen" to her father at precisely the moment that he most desperately grapples with the castration of his voice, and that she can no longer translate her receptivity into effective outward action. The machinery assimilating her into her fiancé's culture is already too strongly in motion, reinforced by imbalances of power in the social structure: Christians dominate Jews, and men women. Of course, Fedye's dominance over Chava is far from completely stable. To reinvoke Arendt's argument about violence as an index of the shakiness of authority, one must ask why Fedye needs to restrain, to resort to force against, his fiancée (something that he does again toward the end of the scene, as bridesmaids fill the room and distant church bells beckon, and Chava again makes a failed attempt to run for it). In any case, from the point of view of Tevye, who remains ignorant of all the activity in the room upstairs, Chava's *apparent* nonresponsiveness to his calls can easily be interpreted as a further rejection of him and his faith, and a willful submission to Fedye and the Priest and their "domain."

Excommunication and the Family Organism

In the stories, consistent with his style of resilient resignation, of coping with supposedly inevitable misfortunes through a religiously informed, philosophic acceptance, Tevye does nothing more to try to counteract Chava's marriage following his fruitless encounter with the Priest. In the film, however, he does not so easily settle into defeat. Devoting the afternoon of the wedding to "running like a madman from one official to another" (as Golde recounts to Tseytl), he departs from his literary predecessor in terms of an enhanced—or superadded—drive to action. Such a quality accords with what we have been describing as Tevye's notably more "potent" representation in the film, and extends into the highly elaborated scene of excommunication that occurs later on the day of the wedding. Indeed, performing that recurrent speech act in Yiddish cinema by which an end to communication is paradoxically communicated and challenged authority figures are so often put to the test (recall the stern, severing pronouncements of the defied, troubled fathers in chapters 2 and 3), Tevye significantly shores up his flouted paternal powers, although in a far from straightforward manner.

The expulsion of Chava from the family unit takes place, suitably, at home. Golde returns there first, by herself, walking through the door in a wide master shot that conveys Chava's gaping absence from the space, that makes the interior appear, despite its lowly, modest dimensions, positively cavernous: an impression of voidness that recurs throughout the scene. Tseytl arrives next, commiserating with her tearful mother and listening to the account of her father's dogged yet vain efforts to impede the marriage. And finally comes Tevye, stumbling and clutching his heart in a daze as he approaches the gate outside—his body telegraphing his emotions in classically melodramatic, symptomatic fashion. Once he enters the house, he walks laboriously to his chair and bitterly acknowledges his previous blindness and the bleakness of the present situation, and yet he refuses to "hold a grudge against the Lord." Instead, he dutifully attends to his religious obligations, performing the *Havdalah* ceremony that marks the Sabbath's end, in a series of close-ups that he shares with the symbolically freighted (vital, persevering), flickering flame of the specially braided *Havdalah* candle, held up by Tseytl just offscreen. (As the ceremony alerts us, the wedding has taken place on Shabbat, adding insult to injury.) With his responsibilities to God taken care of, Tevye then turns to his own private affairs and performs the excommunication in an extended, semi-ambulatory monologue, while Golde and Tseytl quietly weep:

> Chava is no more. She is dead. "The Lord hath given and the Lord hath taken away." "Blessed be the true judge." You can cry now. But not me! Nonsense! Tevye doesn't cry. Tevye isn't a woman. The law requires that we mourn her death . . . for just one hour. For just one hour. We'll sit and cry and then forget about her. As if she were dead. Even more than that. One at least recites kaddish after the dead. One observes the anniversary of their death. But Chava "shall neither be remembered nor mentioned." Such children should never be mentioned: "neither remembered nor mentioned." Do you hear? I want no mention of the name Chava. She's dead. She never existed.

Notably stressed and repeated in the film, the religious injunction that the offending party "shall neither be remembered nor mentioned" is culled from Sholem Aleichem,[8] aptly aligning with an overarching Yiddish fixation on communication, and indicating that Chava is not simply barred from the family but from all the family's future *mediations*. The first of these negative, mediatic commandments—the moratorium on remembrance—derives its wounding power from Judaism's distinctive valorization of memory (recall our discussion of what Flusser calls the "fundamental Jewish" idea—that is, the idea that "we shall survive in the memory of others"—in chapter 1). The second—the prohibition on mentioning—generates its bite from the particular nature and predilections of the speaker of the monologue, who, famously, loves nothing more than to mention, to employ the medium of speech.

For a Jew not to be remembered, and for Tevye, the arch-verbalist, to refuse to speak of you: both are daunting prospects, supercharging the excommunicative act, which indeed appears strikingly radical in both the stories and the film when set beside the handling of the Chava affair in *Fiddler*. In the film adaptation of the musical, Tevye not only utters a relatively abbreviated excommunication ("She's dead to us. We'll forget her"), and proceeds straightaway to launch into a nostalgic number that directly violates the injunction against memory ("What a sweet little bird you were, Chaveleh . . ."), but, in one of the most (in)famous departures from, and Americanizing transmutations of,[9] the source material, he in the end *accepts* the intermarriage, if in a cannily grudging way. That is, amid the mass expulsion of Jews, although he still refuses to speak directly to Chava, who approaches him and explains that she and her husband can't bear to stay in an intolerant place and so are moving to Kraków, Tevye utters a quiet blessing of the couple (subsequently shout-relayed by Tseytl) as they walk away into the distance.

To return to the Yiddish film, however, the excommunicatory moment sets Tevye off on a twisted trajectory toward the recovery of his paternal authority. Reflecting a psychological complex amply displayed in the stories, Tevye's boasting insistence that he possesses an unimpeachable "masculine" ability to keep his emotions in check ("Tevye doesn't cry. Tevye isn't a woman") betrays an obvious, overcompensating defensiveness and vulnerability, which Schwartz's performance brilliantly accentuates. Whereas at the start of the monologue Tevye is calm, self-possessed, consonant with his idealized self-image, he becomes increasingly discombobulated, his hands shaking wildly, as if in isolated fast-motion. In other words, in his strenuous psychic act of splitting or disassociation necessary for him to tamp down his enduring, inextinguishable feelings of love for his daughter and utter the excommunication against her, Tevye's speech act begins to go haywire, ushering in a threat of imminent bodily collapse, as in the analogous scene of excommunication in *Kol Nidre*.

An equation between the two fathers only goes so far, however. Unlike Moishe, Tevye is able to rally from his frenzy before he finishes his speech. He is not finally struck down by a paralyzing stroke that erodes his very personhood. The measured voice with which he begins the monologue returns at the end, and he punctuates his closing words by bringing his trembling hands under control and making a deliberate wiping gesture that expresses that he is through with Chava, that he has washed his hands of her. To be sure, such a recovery is far from absolute. Clearly showing that he remains unmoored by the events of the day, Tevye continues to walk with a treacherous wobble as he goes over to the corner of the room to fetch a stool. And as he proceeds to sit down on the tiny seat in order to take off his shoes, he is quite literally brought low. Also, his faith appears deeply shaken. Posing a question that lingers unresolved in the final moments of the scene, he implores: "God, where are you?" Nevertheless, the film everywhere makes efforts to modulate such instabilities. As Tevye sits on the stool, Golde and Tseytl join him, though they sit even lower, on the bare floor, creating an evocative mise-en-scène that conveys the persistence of his role as the head of the family: the stool, meager as it is, plays against the idea of an all-out paternal dethronement. Moreover, the camera tracks in and frames him in the midst of his spiritual crisis in low-angle close-up, denying us the chance to look down on him and investing him with an aura of indissoluble dignity.

With Tevye's paternal authority thus reconsolidated, the only considerable familial decline that continues to take place is that of the family unit as a whole. Indeed, the film, like many Yiddish films, presents an intriguing vision of the family as a kind of radically interdependent organism, wherein disturbances to individual parts fatefully affect the entire structure (recall Muni's remark in *The Living Orphan* that he and his estranged son "[were like] two hearts beating together, but I cut them apart, and they bleed"). Over time, Golde falls gravely ill, which Chava interprets as a direct result of her taboo marriage: "My mother was always a healthy woman. I am the cause of her death," she catastrophizes to Fedye in response to receiving the news of the sickness. The film then recapitulates this line of thinking in a heartbreaking scene where Chava pays a secret visit to her old home. While the rest of the family members are gathered around Golde's deathbed, Chava appears at the window in the pouring rain, and, unnoticed, observes the grim situation from behind the glass. In a striking tableau, all of the family members are "there," forming a circular chain within the frame, and yet since Chava is partitioned off from everyone else, it appears as if her mother is dying precisely on account of such a disruption to the overall familial system (see figure 4.4)—an impression intensified by Chava calling out *"mame"* at the moment of her mother's death without Golde (or any of the

Figure 4.4. Unnoticed by her family, the excommunicated Chava observes her mother's death through the window. Maurice Schwartz, *Tevye* (1939).

other family members) being able to hear her. Indeed, the film reinforces the muteness of Chava's cry—which consists of a single word metonymically aligned with the language to which it belongs (like the *"mame"* missive in *A Little Letter to Mother*)—by situating the camera and the corresponding audio perspective on the inside, so that the sound of the cry fails to reach us too.

Sovereign Performatives and Insurrectionary Speech

In the wake of Chava's marriage, the greatest threat to Tevye's authority lies beyond the family realm, in the antisemitic decree that he is to be expelled from the village. In this way, the father who subjects his daughter to an excommunication becomes himself subject to an excommunication—by the state. However, while this latter speech act, to which the film devotes enormous energy, belongs to the class of "exercitives" discussed earlier in the context of scenes of familial expulsion, it also comprises what Judith Butler calls a "sovereign performative": a type of performative that functions on behalf of an institution of state power, and accordingly whose utterer necessarily embodies a mediating *proxy* for such power.[10] That is to say, this is unlike the case of a "patriarch" who banishes another family member, where it is the speaker himself who embodies the authority upon which the speech act relies for its effectiveness.

The communication of the expulsion order intersects vigorously and suggestively with the film's elaboration of the "battle of the books" theme. Just prior to the arrival of the village council, the first layer of state proxies who appear at his house to inform him of the decree, Tevye sits down with Tseytl's near-Bar-Mitzvah-aged son and insistingly teaches the boy how to recite the psalms from a small volume, how to declaim them in the proper, intricate, plaintive manner, while the boy's younger sister sits on the other side of her grandfather and looks and listens on (by this point, Tseytl's sickly husband has died, making Tevye into the sole provider for his eldest daughter and her children, into an effective father for the nuclear unit that no longer has a father). As usual, much ado is made over the communicative act, over this quintessentially "patriarchal" transmission of traditional— Hebrew-based, male-restricted—knowledge from one generation to another. Covertly absorbing the lesson intended for her brother, just as the enamored daughter does as a means of pursuing the retiring scholar in *Green Fields*, the precocious granddaughter chimes in unbidden with a pitch-perfect verse, which amazes Tevye before his allegiance to tradition swiftly takes over: "God bless you! Did you hear that? But the psalms aren't for women. The psalms are for men. *He* should study them." Albeit relating to a different textual dynamic, one that lies entirely within the remit of Jewish culture rather than entailing an opposition between Jewish and non-Jewish spheres, the brief moment evokes and is of a piece with Tevye's earlier attempts to police Chava's reading life, insinuating that in the future he will likely face yet *more* female dissidence and trouble in the project of raising a girl. Nevertheless, the question of the granddaughter's exclusion from the scene of Jewish learning is left dangling, supplanted by the broader state decree of exclusion aimed at Jews as a whole.

Resonantly disrupting and cutting off Tevye's educative, communicative act, the council imparts its excommunicative message with a notable disavowal of individual responsibility. "We came to tell you,

Tevye, that you must leave the village. The council says so," the head of the council declares matter-of-factly, standing at the front of the group with a large medallion around his neck, and making sure to speak on behalf of—to attribute agency strictly to—the bureaucratic organization. Further, when Tevye protests by referring, with contrasting concreteness and personalness, to his history of neighborly relations ("You're driving me out of the village? But in the fifty years I've lived here I've never robbed or harmed anyone"), the head goes on to appeal, now in quasi-apologetic tones, to ever higher registers of officialdom and authority: "The Tsar has decreed that Jews be driven out of all the villages." Nevertheless, Tevye keeps protesting, inquiring: "And if people cut their noses off in all the villages, you'll do that too?" In this way, Tevye enacts that characteristically Jewish, "questioning" modality that, as Benjamin Harshav points out in his illuminating study *The Meaning of Yiddish*, came to infuse Yiddish speech writ large. Writes Harshav, in a passage that bears particular relevance to the moment in the film:

> Whether the source [of a Jewish penchant for asking questions] lies in religious learning, in the precarious Jewish existence—the question marks it raises, or the need for evasive behavior—in the relativism of a marginal group, in the skepticism of a people exposed to bitter experiences throughout the ages, a set of attitudes has crystallized and become typically "Jewish," incorporated into typical Yiddish speech. It seems that these attitudes, transferred to secular situations and to other languages, became the basis for what could be seen either negatively as the Jewish "inquisitive" or "argumentative" behavior, or positively as a questioning, "scientific" attitude, challenging any authority.[11]

From his sarcastic line of questioning, however, Tevye shifts into a more somber and introspective register as the head of the council continues with the dubious, self-distancing apologetics and assures him: "If it were up to me, you could stay here, even die here." The reference to death touches something in Tevye, who is moved to pull back and contemplate his situation: "When it comes to dying, you'd all do it much better. You all have ranks and medals. You will all have luxurious funerals. I'm just a poor Jew. They'd take me to the city to look for a Jewish cemetery. No, I still have to live. I have to provide for my orphaned grandchildren." The remarks provide a telling window into Tevye's motivation, revealing not only that his imperative to persevere hinges on his responsibility to the remaining members of his family, but that, as he understands it, his very existence in the village has up to this point constituted a potent act of resistance. As he points out, even if he were allowed to stay, he would be expelled anyway in time—at the time of his death; and so, merely to live in the place that he lives is to forestall the day of that eventual removal, to refuse to cede control over the locality of his body, or more specifically, given the restrictions on Jewish mobility within the Empire, over *all* control over the locality of his body.[12]

Instead of the rather ambivalent members of the village council who know him, the actual ordering of Tevye's expulsion is carried out by an entirely unsympathetic Tsarist officer (Boaz Young), bedecked in full imperial regalia, who shortly turns up at the house, attended by the clerk Zuzuya (Al Harris), a bumbling, almost Gogolian figure who walks with a stiff, mechanical limp. Gripping the handle of his long, holstered saber at his side, the officer curtly sums up the meaning of the order:

> OFFICER: Tevye, you must leave within twenty-four hours. Understood?
>
> TEVYE: What's so hard to understand? It's such a hard thing? You are granting me twenty-four hours to catch my breath, to sell my belongings, to pack up, and remove our sinful feet from this sacred village.
>
> OFFICER: Stop blabbering! Zuzuya, read the edict and let him sign it.

Although Tevye is able to maintain a semblance of conversation with the members of the village council, who stand behind the officer, the more direct representative of the state simply dismisses all of his words as nonsensical; and indeed this gesture of communicative dominance receives visual reinforcement as Zuzuya slaps a massive folder of official, bureaucratic documents directly down on top of the comparatively diminutive book of psalms, which remains open on the table, and which Tevye consequently rescues by moving out of the way (see figure 4.5). It is here that a series of explicit disruptions to the official proceedings arises.

As Zuzuya goes to pull out the relevant document from the folder, he is suddenly overcome by an uncontainable urge to sneeze, which a moment later he ends up discharging all over his superior. Next, searching for his glasses, which he needs in order to read the edict, he extensively pats himself down and rummages his pockets, before, of course, finding the glasses resting squarely on his forehead. It is only then that he finally begins to deliver the decree, which is in Russian: "By order of his imperial highness . . ." At this point, however, taking advantage of the mood of disturbance, Tevye interrupts the recitation with a scornful critique of its style, of its unnecessary complexity ("Never mind the rest. I understand perfectly. The council decrees that I leave. Why take so long? You can say it in three words: Tevye, please leave"), which incites the officer to respond with a repressive, authoritative bark that once more reduces the Jew's communication

Figure 4.5. Tevye rescues a book of psalms from underneath the official documents ordering his expulsion. Maurice Schwartz, *Tevye* (1939).

to nonsense: "Stop blabbering. Sign it!" Further, despite proceeding to agree to adhere to the command, Tevye manages to invest his "compliance" with a stark insurgency, standing up and wagging the quill at the officer like a loaded weapon and imparting a charged warning: "Be careful. I'm signing." Yet, as we shift from speech to writing, this is far from the end of the communicative disruptions. While Tevye writes his name, Zuzuya surveils him over his shoulder and, both irked and irksome, screeches, "Stop scribbling! Dip the pen into the ink," before promptly undermining his very own demand, which transfers the denigration of Jewish communication onto the plane of textuality (i.e., scribbling as the textual equivalent of babbling). In a condescending demonstration of how to use the quill, he in the process accidentally sprays ink into his superior's eyes, thus triggering the village kids, who have gathered around to watch, to burst into laughter, and the momentarily blinded officer to roar, "Idiot!" Ultimately, Tevye completes the formal procedure, although his mode of communication continues to disconcert Zuzuya, who inspects the document—signed, it is likely, in Hebrew rather than Cyrillic script—and comments with a disapproving shake of his head: "They always scribble."

In this way, the scene returns us with a vengeance to Felman's concept of "the scandal of the speaking body." As we saw in chapter 3, a striking exemplification of the concept appears in the scene in *Kol Nidre* where Moishe suffers a stroke in the act of expelling Jenny from the family, and indeed, the same dynamic appears earlier on in *Tevye*, when Tevye shakes violently (and yet eventually brings his body under control) in the act of excommunicating Chava. Similarly, the sneezing, spraying, nasally whining, hobbled Zuzuya struggles drastically with his body in the case of delivering the expulsion order to Tevye. Meanwhile, throwing the clerk's bodily disorder into relief, Tevye appears to become more and more corporeally composed as the scene goes on (i.e., standing up and brandishing the quill in the preamble to signing), even as he outwardly submits to the excommunication. In all of these cases, the body strikingly destabilizes the speech act, demonstrating how, to return to Butler's commentary on Felman, "speech, precisely because it is a bodily act, is not always 'knowing' about what it says."[13]

In the case of Tevye's expulsion, however, the destabilization of the performative occurs, too, at the level of language. Drawing on

Derrida, another key interlocutor of Austin, Butler points out that the performative is intrinsically citational or "iterable" in structure. What this means is that performative speech acts aren't cued to specific examples but always appear in conventionalized, generalized, decontextualized form. Think, for example, of the policeman's fixed declaration upon putting someone under arrest: "You have the right to remain silent . . ." Butler points out that it is precisely this independence from context that constitutes "the force of the performative, beyond all question of truth or meaning."[14] In regard to Tevye's expulsion, such an insight helps us understand how deeply the decree relies on its linguistic formality. Although directed specifically against Tevye, the decree intentionally disregards the specificity of his case (recall how the head of the council justifies the decision by referring to the broader, nationwide expulsion measure against Jews). Such detachment befits sovereign performatives in particular, with their reliance on evermore removed proxies and agents for their execution/utterance—a feature that invests them with a deliberate means of protection, guarding them from any possible objections (e.g., in Tevye's case, his status as a respectful member of his community, his good neighborly relations, his responsibility to provide for his family, and so on). Grasping well the operations of the sovereign performative, Tevye doesn't try to counter the decree with objections of this type but rather by attacking its very linguistic mechanism. Making fun of the document's long-winded, obfuscatory style, he proposes that the legalistic language, which he lacks the patience to listen to in its entirety, be cut down to "three words," to its basic core of injustice. That is to say, he bitingly rearticulates the edict in his own words, and in such a way that he grounds the injurious, necessarily overformal and abstract language within the specific context at hand ("Tevye, please leave"). It is thus that Tevye engages in what Butler calls "insurrectionary speech," her term for the phenomenon that arises when "the word that wounds becomes an instrument of resistance in the redeployment that destroys that prior territory of its operations,"[15] when a person subject to an oppressive sovereign performative manages to use such language against itself, to hijack it for subversive ends. Accordingly, while the expulsion order compels Tevye to leave the village, his acidly black-comic, concretizing redeployment of the excommunication does produce important, nourishing, and bracing effects for himself and the film's audience—indeed, one imagines, especially for the film's contemporary audience in 1939. As Butler writes, "Insurrectionary speech becomes the necessary response to injurious language, a risk taken in response to being put at risk, a repetition in language that forces change."[16]

Meanwhile, the fact that the entire antisemitic sovereign performative, aside from Zuzuya's brief, disrupted recitation of the decree, is carried out in Yiddish, a language that both the Tsarist officer and the clerk, along with all the non-Jews in the film, speak with magical fluency, wildly enhances such effects on a metalevel. Pointing out this strange, poignant phenomenon, Hoberman writes of how "each Yiddish movie offered the imaginary fulfillment of a new *Yidishland*," conjuring phantasmatic "realms where Jewish peasants tilled the soil and even police or party officials might address the spectator in *mame-loshn*."[17] (Here we should add that when Zuzuya attempts to recite the decree, his grasp of Russian comes across as flagrantly shaky and stilted, as if the Yiddish that he speaks normally were his native tongue.) In this way, by its very representational operations, the film couches the injurious speech that the state directs against Tevye within a linguistic fabric that simultaneously invests such words with a swerving, subversive dimension. Overwhelmingly unfolding in Yiddish, the excommunication of Tevye is forced to rely on the very communication system that binds Jewish communities together and fosters their sense of internal interconnection and belonging.

Textual Homeland and the Consolations of Exile

Tevye's expulsion is offset by yet one more factor—one that lies beyond the scene of the utterance of the sovereign performative. That is, the news of the expulsion shocks Chava and spurs the immiserated wife, finally, to take leave of the realm from which there was supposedly no return, and to return to her father. In this way, being expelled plays a surprising, critical role in rectifying the crisis that so unsettles Tevye's paternal authority in the first place, ultimately leading to an imbuing of his paternal status with a previously unrivaled sense of strength and stability.

Over time, Chava's life in the Galagan household drastically redoubles what can be considered a condition of spectrality. Not only does she emerge as a ghost in the scene where she mutely and invisibly cries out to her mother at the moment of Golde's death, but she also becomes a ghost in her new domain. At the Galagans, Chava finds not the thrilling world that she imagined from her reading of Russian novels but rather a hypertraditional Slavic household, ruled by her in-laws, where she is thrust into domestic servitude. The film underscores her invisibility in this respect when, in a scene following Tevye's expulsion, one of the members of the village council, fresh from the fire sale where Tevye is selling the family's possessions, visits the Galagan house and, incredibly, while Chava is right there in the room, brags about stealing her dead mother's Sabbath dress—an object that, as it turns out, contributes to snapping Chava out of her submissive invisibility and prompting her to take action. For once the coast is clear, she secretly steals the dress back and flees to her old home that is about to be no more, treating the garment like a sacred totem, a crucial means for staying connected with the past and with the dead (all the more important in the precarious moment of uprooting). Analogously, just prior to this, as she remains inside during the fire sale and packs the few belongings that the family plans to take with them, Tseytl comes upon her mother's candleholders, which she proceeds to wrap solicitously and carry off like a swaddled child, in a swirl of commemorative maternal energy.

Such relations with objects reflect the key role that sacred, richly mediating, distinctly transportable objects have played in the longstanding exilic history of the Jews—a dynamic that the film taps into even further. As George Steiner writes in "Our Homeland, the Text," a key essay that explores the profound relationship between Judaism, exile, and the written word:

> In post-exilic Judaism, but perhaps earlier, active reading, answerability to the text on both the meditative-interpretive and the behavioural levels, is the central motion of personal and national homecoming. The Torah is met at the place of summons and in the time of calling (which is night and day). The dwelling assigned, ascribed to Israel is the House of the Book. Heine's phrase is exactly right: *das aufgeschriebene Vaterland*. The "land of his fathers," the *patrimoine*, is the script. In its doomed immanence, in its attempt to immobilize the text in a substantive, architectural space, the Davidic and Solomonic Temple may have been an erratum, a misreading of the transcendent mobility of the text.[18]

The film offers a striking distillation of this notion of textual homeland right after Chava's escape with the Sabbath dress. Unaware that his daughter is on her way back, Tevye packs up his library—his collection of religious texts that, like Golde's candleholders, has been deemed indispensable and will go along with the family on the road. Flipping through the books on the upper shelves, he muses to Tseytl, who has asked him why he has proposed, preliminarily, that they go to "*Erets Yisroel* [the Holy Land; lit., the Land of Israel]": "Where else can I go? To America? What would I do there? They don't know my language, and I don't know theirs. So we can either go to Argentina, Palestine, or the Holy Land."[19] Resonating with his response to the village council, Tevye exhibits here a strong interest in bodily locality, in the geography of where he and his family, as refugees, might go. It is interesting, however, that amid all the talk of territory, what concerns Tevye the most is the language spoken in the possible destinations. America is dismissed out of hand because "they don't know my language, and I don't know theirs"—a remark that encodes a strong dose of self-reflexive irony given that the actor playing Tevye is standing in Long Island, where the film was shot. Such stress on communicative potentiality naturally gels with Heine's classic formulation of the Jewish homeland inhering in script, and indeed, despite Tevye's eager expression of interest in visiting various biblical sites in the Holy Land (the destination he clearly appears to favor), the bulk of the scene is preoccupied with Tevye's loving inventory of his book collection. Taking the volumes down one by one and dusting them off, he enumerates: "The Five Books of Moses. A prayer book [*siderl*]. The penitential prayers [*slikha*]. Lamentations [*kinah*]. What is this little one? Grace after meals [*bentsher*]. We'll take it along. These are the riches [from the *goles*, the exile] we're taking to the Holy Land." Blessedly mobile, Tevye's books take center stage in the moment of unhousing and accordingly assume the status and function of home—an impression reinforced by the fact that we never ultimately find out where Tevye and his remaining family wind up following the expulsion. The film, like the stories, concludes in the open-ended, ongoing act of leave-taking.

Via the securing of the rich diasporic archive, Tevye meaningfully prepares his family for the departure. Accordingly, in contrast to Muni and Moishe, the fathers from chapters 2 and 3, who are both still radically ailing in the moment of reunion with their children, Tevye remains crucially operative as the head of his home when his prodigal daughter returns. Bearing her mother's precious Sabbath dress, Chava finally encounters her father just after Fedye catches up with her outside the house and she apologetically explains to him that she "must be among my own" and that "it will never work . . . we are worlds apart." At first, her reappearance deeply flusters Tevye, who persists in his anger and remains impervious to her pleading reassurance that "the Priest's words did not touch my soul. My soul remained pure." However, he eventually becomes more receptive as Tseytl repeatedly begs him to show mercy (*rakhmones*), and as Chava continues with her words of penitence and explanation: "I didn't betray our faith, father. I always thought of you, and longed for you. I thought everything was better there than here among us. I was wrong. Your old faith is deeper and greater. I realize that now. Father! I want to come home. I can no longer live without you. My soul belongs to you. Wherever you go, I will go. Your life is my life, your plight is my plight." Intriguingly, in her account of her marriage to a Christian, Chava figures herself as a kind of Marrano. As Jacqueline Rose writes, "A Marrano is a Jew, forcibly converted to Catholicism in Spain or Portugal at the time of the Inquisition, who cultivates her or his Jewishness in secret. The Marranos cherish their identity as something to be hoarded that also sets them irrevocably adrift."[20] According to Chava, although she undertook it willingly, her marriage functioned like a conversion to which, inwardly, she refused to subscribe. Hence her claim that the Priest's words did not touch her soul, that her soul remained pure, that she did not betray her father's faith; or as she puts it earlier to Tseytl before entering the house: "My body was there but my soul was here with you." In this way, Chava indirectly dredges up traumatic Jewish history and employs the inquisitorial period as metaphoric scaffolding for her to convince her father that she never ultimately fell under the communicative sway of his religious rival. As well, she infuses her appeal for forgiveness with Tevye's own citational speaking style—a tactic that, not surprisingly, proves particularly effective in persuading the radically verbocentric father. As Tevye responds, manifestly moved and removing his glasses from his welling-up eyes: "Our life is her life, our plight is her plight. Those are the words of the book of Esther . . . I mean Ecclesiastes. Our people are her people. Our God is her God. That's how Tevye's daughters should speak. I only wish one thing—that the officer and Zuzuya could hear those words." Like she has heard her father do a million times, Chava quotes scripture, and thus remediates his very habit of remediation, crucially doing so in solemn tribute rather than affectionate parody (as earlier at the table in the yard before her marriage). Of course, Tevye introduces a disruptive ripple into the moment by initially blundering and misattributing the quotation—something that he often does, as Dan Miron points out, in order to "undermin[e], for the fun of it, the sacred sources to which he professes loyalty."[21] Nevertheless, while continuing to indulge his characteristic scriptural *détournement*, Tevye admits that it is precisely the reformation in the way his daughter "speak[s]"—her uttering of "those words," which he wishes his expellers could hear, as if to further turn up a nose at their absurd and unfair decrees—that wins him over. Chava speaking like he does cinches for Tevye that, finally, she has listened to him, that she has opted for *his* textual resources. Indeed, moments later, in a shot that increasingly tightens and ends in an intimate close-up of the two, Tevye accepts Chava's peace offering of the dress and embraces her in exoneration. Meanwhile, he joyfully and relievedly rasps on the borderline of becoming *verklempt*, imagining God as a communicative entity and calling on Him to carry on the vital verbal flow: "O, Lord. What do you say?"

The conclusion of the film strongly underscores that what matters, above all, in the face of trying and oppressive circumstances, is the togetherness and perseverance of the family unit. In the final moments, the reunited family sets off on their exile on a windy road, packed into Tevye's milk cart along with their few belongings. As the wagon jostles along, a small item of furniture falls out of the back, and yet no one notices except for the poor little goat, tied to the back of the wagon, who must negotiate a way around the unexpected hurdle. Evidently, the loss of such an object (which unlike the dress, the candleholders, and Tevye's books, relates to the physical space of the home), doesn't matter at all as long as the family is on its way together. And it is Tevye, installed in the driver's seat and piloting the cart with a modest whip, who leads his husbandless daughters and fatherless grandchildren into the future, who "communicates" (to use the term in its archaic sense of conveyance and transportation[22]) the family from the village into the future. Finally, after a series of convulsions, Tevye's paternal authority persists despite, and even because of, the fact that he suffers a great blow in the world. That is to say, the increasing hardships to which his family is subject makes his role as their guardian and caretaker that much more important. At the same time, the expelled father does prove to have some power in the world. Critically, Chava's ultimate return to him and revelation that she remained under his influence all along register an important victory for Tevye against his oppressors, even if the likes of Zuzuya and the officer remain, vexingly, unaware of the full magnitude of the triumph.

5

Motherhood, Migration, and the Asylum

Where Is My Child? (1937)

DIRECTED BY ABRAHAM LEFF and Henry Lynn, the Yiddish American *Where Is My Child?* (*Vu Iz Mayn Kind?*) presents a fascinating, *shund*-ified synthesis of two major strains or subgroups of the classical Hollywood "woman's film": the maternal melodrama, which focuses on the threat or actuality of separation between a mother and her child, and what might be termed the medical melodrama, in which a disturbed female finds herself enmeshed within the spaces and discourse of medicine, propelled into the care or custody of a doctor, who, practically as a rule, is male.[1] The film weaves into the mix, too, and vitally foregrounds, the theme of migration, for the trials of the long-suffering protagonist—an impoverished, widowed, young mother who is manipulated into putting her newborn baby up for adoption, and then, in the midst of her arduous journey to recover the child, is wrongfully committed to an insane asylum—extend directly from her condition of being a new immigrant to America. In this way, in focusing on a character who becomes stripped of *all* relations, or in other words who becomes an out-and-out social outcast, the film introduces us to a new kind of figure, one who importantly differs from the procession of cut-off, disconnected characters whom we have encountered so far in Yiddish cinema. In *A Little Letter to Mother*, the Berdichevski family grapples with a relentless process of atomization, and yet each individual family member retains ties of other kinds, while sometimes maintaining familial communication at a distance. In *The Living Orphan*, *Kol Nidre*, and *Tevye*, none of the transgressive women excommunicated from their families are left totally alone: Freda still has her theater family and fans; Jenny still has Jack; Chava still has Fedye. As for the troubled, excommunicating fathers and husbands in those films, what they lose, or risk losing, is their authority, not every social bond: though reduced to a feckless drunk, Muni still has Benny; though reduced to a paralytic mute, Moishe still has his wife and friends; though smarting from the loss of Chava, Tevye still has the rest of his family, which he manages to continue guiding. Concentrating on an outcast, on an especially abject outlier in relation to this group of characters, *Where Is My Child?* thus gives way to a forceful philosophical concern with "the Other," and more specifically with a Judaically coded "responsibility to the Other" (or as Flusser would say, teasing out the communicative dimension of the concept, "response-ability to the Other")—a relation that gets introduced through another character who eventually comes along, takes an interest in the protagonist, and restores her to the realm of relationality and dialogue. Such a dynamic between an ill-fated outcast and a model humanitarian in fact comprises another key paradigm of Yiddish cinema—as we'll see in the next chapter, it repeats in *Motel the Operator*—and provides the film with an overarching frame for its uniquely interwoven treatment of motherhood, migration, and the asylum, whose operations this chapter seeks to illuminate.

Migration and Motherhood

It is no wonder that the figure of the outcast haunts Yiddish cinema, a cinema obsessed with connectivity. In *Where Is My Child?*, this haunting is made all the more powerful by the fact that the protagonist, Esther Liebman (Celia Adler, luminary of the Yiddish American stage), inhabits a ramifying multitude of outcast positions: immigrant, single mother, asylum inmate. For now, let us delve into the first and second of these positions, which are active right from the beginning of the film (Esther's confinement in the mental institution doesn't occur until about two-thirds of the way in). On a phenomenological level, an immigrant is a person who chooses or has been compelled to cut herself loose from critical, identity-forming bonds—bonds that derive from what Flusser, in his writings on the figure of the migrant, which are heavily informed by his own experiences with migration (to be discussed at length in chapter 7), refers to as the immigrant's "heimat": a German word that "allows for connotations such as home, homeland, and region (of one's origins), often accompanied by notions of nostalgia, even myth."[2] Detaching from her heimat, the immigrant takes leave of a whole array of vital communication structures (language, culture, family, etc.) and must enter into new structures—a task that famously involves colossal effort. In addition, as Flusser stresses, the immigrant is also challenged by the consequences of the challenge that she poses *to* those in the new milieu, which of course all-too-commonly results in reactions of xenophobic ire and aversion:

> The secret codes [of heimat] are not, in general, conscious rules but rather are spun largely from unconscious habits. . . . To be able to settle in a new heimat, an immigrant must first learn the secret code consciously—and then forget it again. If the code becomes conscious, then its rules are exposed as something banal and not sacred. For the native who is settled, the immigrant is even more alien and strange than the migrant outside his door because he exposes as banal what the native considers sacred. He is worthy of hatred and he is detestable because he reveals the heimat's beauty as prettified kitsch.[3]

Importantly, the native's xenophobia stems not from fear of the immigrant's values but rather from a disturbing realization about his own entrenched values. Accordingly, in this risky scene of communicative encounter where the native becomes conscious of the artificiality of his naturalized codes, Flusser identifies three emergent possibilities, which (as becomes glaringly clear in the film) are inescapably influenced by imbalances in power between the two sides, wherein the immigrant often finds herself up against giant institutional mechanisms that function to keep her on the margins and aggravate the dissolution of her identity and world (irresistibly, one thinks today of the panoply of immigrant detention camps that exist around the world). Writes Flusser: "A polemical dialogue develops between the beautiful native and the detestable immigrant, which can end either in a pogrom, a change in the heimat, or the native's liberation from his own attachments."[4]

Regarding Esther's predicament as a mother, Jacqueline Rose's incisive, insightful book *Mothers: An Essay on Love and Cruelty* provides an eminently fitting guide, and especially so since it begins with a discussion of mothers who, like Esther, are both single mothers and immigrants. Rose cites a sensationalistic 2016 article from the British right-wing press in which the immigrant single mother is portrayed as a kind of parasite, as a figure who is somehow, paradoxically all at once, deeply calculating and deeply reckless. For Rose, the piece offers an exemplary illustration of her overarching argument that motherhood in the West functions as "the ultimate scapegoat for our personal and political failings, for everything that is wrong with the world, which it becomes the task—unrealizable, of course—of mothers to repair."[5] As Rose points out, the real problem is the (ongoing) global migration crisis, in all its horrific, geopolitical specificity, and yet the newspaper covers this up by offloading blame onto the immigrant single mother herself. Inevitably, Rose goes on to discuss other maternal figures who, on the contrary, are radically revered: classic "maternal imagos,"[6] for instance, like Niobe and the Virgin Mary, celebrated for their profound suffering over the death of a child. "But," Rose observes in regard to such bereaved mothers, "the mother must be noble and her agony redemptive. With the suffering of the whole world etched on her face, she carries and assuages the burden of human misery on behalf of everyone. What the pain of mothers must never expose is a viciously unjust world in a complete mess."[7] In other words, the idealization of Niobe and Mary ends up serving a similar function as the reactionary media's demonization of immigrant single mothers; again, in what amounts to a staggeringly consistent historical pattern, the mother is used "to deflect from our awareness of human responsibility for the world."[8]

As Rose makes clear, mothers throughout Western history have gotten a raw deal, but, as she also points out (and thereby turns the depressing point around), the sheer enormity of the effort that goes into the stereotype against mothers betrays the instability and hollowness of the stereotype. Indeed, the very rigorousness with which mothers are policed (the first part of Rose's book is titled "Social

Punishment") alerts us to their status as figures who threaten to expose the societal pitfalls for which they are (spuriously) held answerable. As Rose proposes: "Mothers, we might say, are the original subversives, never—as feminism has long insisted—what they seem, or are meant to be."[9] In this way, Rose's conception of the mother provides a striking analogue to Flusser's conception of the migrant, envisioning a similarly subversive figure who, threatening to reveal and desacralize society's cherished codes, encounters powerful repressive pressure.

Crisis of Disconnection

Where Is My Child? announces its concern with immigration straightaway. In the credit sequence, evoking the point of view of someone peering over the side of a moving ship, shots of churning, whitecapped water filling the screen produce a resonant metonymy for what, in the Eastern European Jewish American imaginary, is the near-mythic, central rite of "passage": the transatlantic voyage undertaken by millions in the period of the Great Migration—that is, from the early 1880s, or the time of the assassination of Tsar Alexander II, which brought down an intensification of restrictions on Jews in the Russian Empire, to the mid-1920s, when the institution of the Immigration Act drastically curtailed the number of immigrants allowed into the United States. Written in aptly bumpy English, as if by a new immigrant, a scrolling prologue follows the credits: "Esther Liebman, young, beautiful, and with her husband Joseph, after the usual hardships in Russia, leave for America with high hopes for a happy future. On the boat, Joseph Liebman takes suddenly ill and dies. He finds his grave in the ocean. In America, Esther gives birth to a child. She leaves the hospital penniless and destitute. She has no friends . . . no relatives to turn to."

The text emphasizes that Esther's main problem as a new immigrant is that she finds herself without relations (excepting, of course, her newborn child), while also providing important details concerning the fate of her husband, who is kept confined to the film's backstory, dying in an unceremonious state of statelessness, in between the country from which he flees, where he belongs to a minority facing numerous restrictions, and the country toward which he is heading, where he hopes for a better life. Indeed, the husband's failure to be physically "communicated" to America finds a suggestive correlate in his inability to be communicated with any sort of actorly directness or immediacy *by the film*. Or as we might otherwise put it, Joseph's failure to become a citizen in geopolitical terms is echoed by his failure to becomes a citizen, as it were, in the world of the dramatis personae.

Bringing us into the action in a state of feverish, almost climactic in medias res, the opening scene fleshes out the prologue's nightmarish evocation of the immigration experience. Dressed in a dark dress and hat evocative of mourning, the young widow stands on the shore of the East River in New York, cradling her white-swaddled baby and gazing upward at the Queensboro Bridge, which had been built only a short time before the moment in which the film is set (a superimposed title informs us that the year is 1911). Strikingly, the new and imposing bridge, a symbol of connectivity, of the modern industrial city's exemplary powers of circulation, works to point up Esther's radical disconnection. Bridging—the transposition of relations that would provide her with some stability in her new context—is precisely what she has been unable to achieve in her brief time in America. Accentuating such failure, the film positions her far below the structure—which consequently gives the impression of an impossible ideal—and aligns her instead with the lowly water. Indeed, images of the water eventually appear undulatingly on top of Esther in double exposure, conveying the flooding of her distraught mind by suicidal impulses, by the urge to engulf herself, along with the child, in the water, in the same element in which her husband lies entombed.

As Esther walks along the bank, the soundtrack richly contributes to the dark mood. A barge making its way down the river blows its horn and produces a long, low, droning roar that sounds almost as if it were coming from beneath the surface of the water. Clearly added in postproduction, the sound effect jarringly interrupts, and momentarily supplants, the film's tension-ratcheting, staccato underscoring, in an apparent breach of diegetic boundaries. Most likely, the technical reason for the breach is that the film, despite having a credited sound recordist, lacks a proper sound *mix*, recalling the transitional period of sound film (a period lasting from the mid-1920s to the early 1930s), when the editing of multiple tracks was not yet an established norm.[10] Such a "primitive" audio modality, whose old-fashionedness would have screamed out to a Hollywood audience of 1937 (the development of quite sophisticated sound film having occurred quite rapidly), is perfectly of a piece with the "poverty row" conditions of production of *shund*: faster and cheaper not to mix, even though the technology exists. However, the filmmakers choose a marvelously fitting moment to flaunt the technical-economic constraint under which they are operating. Creatively mobilizing the restriction, they evoke a sense of restriction *as such*, and in this way generate a potent, highly evocative metaphor for the crisis of disconnection into which Esther is thrown.

Performative Abuse

Esther's primary nemesis is one Dr. Reisner (Morris Strassberg), a characteristically mustachioed villain who intervenes at the last minute and "saves" her from taking the suicidal/infanticidal plunge and then proceeds to plot a scheme in which her child will be, without her consent, adopted away to a rich couple, Morris and Alice Gross (Morris Silberkasten and Anna Lillian), who have just lost a child of their own. As the dejected, well-dressed Mr. Gross remarks to Reisner outside the hospital where the doctor works, relating what he has been told by a (presumably psychiatric) "Professor": "Her [Alice's] only cure is to adopt a child. It would help her forget the child she lost." Notably, shortly led out of the hospital by a nurse, the ballasted, bereft Alice is not brought into the conspiracy between the men, is not told the truth about the dubious mechanics behind the adoption, which requires her husband ponying up a large sum of money. And though she later becomes afflicted by nervous suspicions about the story that she has been told, it seems questionable whether she would have gone along with the plot in full consciousness of its nature—the maternally idealizing film loath to portray a mother *directly* committing such a nefarious act against another mother (as we'll discuss further on, Alice ultimately—and unsurprisingly, with immense pain and ambivalence—sides with the aggrieved birth mother and relinquishes the "curative" child whom she lovingly raises). On the other hand, Alice's husband's unmistakably conscious collusion with the corrupt doctor reveals an important dimension of the film's treatment of villainy. Namely, Reisner is by no means an anomaly. Rather, he is a representative of a whole institutional system—governed at the highest levels by men—that is crooked, unjust, blindly interested in its own perpetuation, and structured against the powerless, the outcast, the

Other. In this way, the film encourages us to envision the manifold establishment figures who become involved with the plot as effective versions of one another.

As instructed by the deviously stage-managing Reisner, Esther takes her child to the Ohel Zedek Orphanage, a "private institution" (as a bilingual sign reads) where the superintendent is a similarly corrupt, venal friend of the doctor's. At first, Esther cautiously reconnoiters the space, approaching a tall metal gate off to the side of the main building, and proceeding to peek through the bars at the activity taking place on the grounds inside. Represented through a pair of wonkily match-cut, seemingly repurposed images, what she glimpses—a group of adolescents playing ball, a group of toddlers lounging on a blanket—is a far cry from the glittering images in Aleksander Ford's nearly contemporary Yiddish documentary *Children Must Laugh* (*Mir Kumen On*, 1935), which takes the viewer on a tour of the renowned Medem Sanitorium, the orphanage—located just outside of Warsaw and run by the Bund, the legendary socialist Jewish organization—that provided invigorating relief and valuable lessons in self-governance to Jewish children living in dismal urban conditions. Nor do the images give any indication of the sort of tender, ministering support and care exhibited by the orphanages in *We Live Again* (*Mir Lebn Do!*, 1946) and *Our Children* (*Unzere Kinder*, 1948), postwar Yiddish documentaries that focus on Jewish children tragically orphaned by the Holocaust. Nevertheless, the optics of the institution give Esther an impression that might fairly be described as decent; and this construction of a front of viable safety is important since, it must be kept in mind, she is being deceived about what leaving her child at the orphanage would entail. In her mind, the arrangement would only be temporary, allowing her to take back her child at a later date once she was able to provide for him on her own. Moreover, Esther is under the perfectly understandable belief that being consigned to the orphanage would in no way translate into a total stripping away of the child's familial origins. This is demonstrated later when she instructs the adoption officials to call the child "Joseph" "in order to let his father's name live on." Accordingly, such an allowance for retaining a basic measure of personal identity is why sociologist Erving Goffman expresses reservations about designating the orphanage as a type of "total institution," which, as we later discuss, imposes on the inmate a complete break with his or her civil identity.[11]

Once Esther overcomes her anxious tarrying and enters the office, she signs the contract, foisted upon her by the superintendent, with massive reluctance (of course, even a temporary, needful separation from the child is agonizing). Further, in an all-too-common predicament in the highly administered life of the immigrant, she does so without reading the documents, presumably on account of them being in English and therefore incomprehensible to her. What Esther thus believes she is agreeing to is, as mentioned, a merely conditional separation from her child, whereas what her signature on the papers actually entails, or rather effects, is a total abrogation of her maternal rights. In this way, the film presents us with yet another type of excommunicatory speech act, one that Austin would classify as an example of "performative abuse," a category that represents one of two ways in which a performative can "go wrong" or be "infelicitous." "Performative misfires," Austin explains, refer to speech acts that do not prove binding: for instance, to adapt one of his famous examples, strolling around a harbor, I proclaim that a ship, which in no way belongs to me and with which I have nothing to do, shall be renamed the *Queen Elizabeth*. "Performative abuses," by contrast, refer to speech acts that do prove binding despite some miscommunication, misunderstanding, or bad faith being involved in the utterance: for instance, I enter into a loan agreement with a bank that I have zero intentions of repaying.[12] In the same way, even though Esther fails to grasp the full implications of the signatory act—this act by which she effectively excommunicates *herself* from her child—the speech act proves binding, as it is backed by "legitimate" authorities. (To cite another notable example of performative abuse in Yiddish cinema, yet one that appears in a comic context: in Sidney M. Goldin's silent *East and West* (*Mizrekh un Mayrev*, 1923), Molly Picon plays a mischievous, secularized Jewish American who visits the Old Country with her father and orchestrates a mocking exchange of vows with a *yeshiva bokher*, a "faux" ritual that, to her and her father's dismay, results in her inadvertently getting married to the less-than-desirable mate for real.)

Strikingly, once Esther signs the papers, the orphanage personnel treat her in an utterly changed manner. Suddenly, they see her as an effective nobody, a (non)person not only without maternal rights but without any rights whatsoever, exhibiting a transformation that drives home that her communicative legitimacy existed for them only insofar as she was still legally attached to her child. After painfully surrendering the baby to the nurse, Esther collapses in tears against the door through which the child is taken, and within seconds, through the same door, a second nurse appears, who tauntingly backs her out of the office in clenched-mouth silence. Whereas earlier, as the superintendent plies Esther with lies and false reassurances in order to compel her into signing ("We take good care of the children here"), the film cuts to a close-up of the first nurse, who nervously turns away and averts her eyes, as if a sense of female solidarity were suddenly churning up and threatening to burst through, any such empathetic inklings are utterly absent from the severe, matronly, second nurse, who handles Esther at will like a mere expendable object, thus anticipating the mechanical orderlies—extensions of a full-fledged total institution—who later come for Esther and haul her away to the asylum.

Return of the Repressed

The radical intimidation that Esther faces at the orphanage, this extreme need to get the poor immigrant mother out of the way, reveals her paradoxical, subversive power. Indeed, again and again throughout the film we find Esther reappearing in the face of her oppressors in the manner of a classic, destabilizing return of the repressed. Her first return comes not long after she is ejected from the orphanage. Later that same day, she reappears at the institution in a changed mood, beaming and recovered, and announces that she simply can't live without her child and wants him back. Unsurprisingly, the request prompts the superintendent once more to attempt to dismiss and discard her, which he does by taking recourse to the massive legal-bureaucratic apparatus into which she has become ensnared. "You signed away all your rights to him [the child]," he remarks, conveniently explaining what he never explained before and appealing to the authority of the law, and by extension of the state, which grounds and enforces laws (one could draw a parallel with the moment when Tevye shows up at the house of the Priest on the day of Chava's wedding, demanding the return of his child, and the Priest shuts him down by reminding him that he—the Priest—speaks with the authority invested in him by the Tsar). Encountering resistance from Esther, the superintendent then goes on to reveal that her child is no longer on the premises, having already been "adopted by a rich family." The disclosure shocks Esther and impels her to demand the family's whereabouts—the first of many such acts that come to constitute a vast, long-term, maternal detective operation. However, the superintendent again trots out the law in order to thwart her, informing her that to provide any information to birth parents about their children's new lives is strictly "illegal" and thus making her brutally aware of the full extent of the contractual excommunication imposed upon her.

The rupture between Esther and her child, and the silencing that, as a defenseless immigrant, she undergoes at the hands of the orphanage, a relatively powerful institution backed by the legal apparatus of the state, necessitate radical efforts to overcome such compounded troubled communication. Or in other words, to come back to that recurrent complex in Yiddish cinema, Esther's situation of excommunication propels her into a state of hypercommunication, which she expresses in bravura fashion. Battening down and appearing to transfigure herself into a supra-legal, indomitable force of (mother) nature, she thunderously vows: "I'll go from door to door to find him! I'll break down iron doors. Nothing will stop me from finding my child. I'm going to find my child!" The spectacular protestation provides further intriguing resonance with Rose's discussion of the representation of immigrant single mothers in the reactionary media. As Rose points out, the caustically punning title of the article she cites, "Here for Maternity," "echoes the title of the 1953 Fred Zinnemann film *From Here to Eternity*, a phrase which has passed into common parlance in the English-speaking world to evoke a love that will follow its object to the ends of the earth, even if the price is death."[13] Hence, Rose continues, the title performs a play on "eternity" and "maternity" that furthers the piece's misogynist, xenophobic agenda by suggesting "that, without drastic action, we are stuck with this problem, with these mothers, for ever."[14] An active threat to rather than (stereotypically alleged) passive burden on the system, Esther, however, transforms the reactionary association between eternity and maternity into a trenchantly dissident relation.

Esther's hypercommunication, too, comes to infuse the film on a formal level. In a pattern that we'll see again in chapter 8 when we discuss *Long Is the Road* (*Lang Iz der Veg*), another film that involves parent-child separation, the film represents the all-consuming project of searching for a lost family member via a rapid, densely layered montage sequence. Immediately following her fist-brandishing, chest-pounding pledge to find her child, the sequence (which condenses the passage of the next six years) double and triple exposes mobile shots of Esther walking toward the camera—her head swiveling from side to side in probing sweeps of the area, her face increasingly careworn yet unflaggingly determined—with a flurry of documentary shots of the bustling city, whose masses remain utterly indifferent to her quest. Thus the exorbitant image track mirrors Esther's exorbitant exertions to overcome her troubled communication; or in other words, visual excess plays the same kind of expressive role that the mix-lacking, sonic disruption does in the opening scene by the East River. Further, there is a paratextual dimension to Esther's state of hypercommunication. Attempting to reproduce something of her electrifying delivery, the film's original English subtitles, hard-encoded on the print, resort to a flagrant, typographical stressing effect for the line, "<u>I'm going to find my child</u>!" Indeed, such accentuations appear frequently in the original English subtitles of Yiddish films, including (in addition to underlining) all-capitalization and variations in font size and font type: features that draw attention not only to the general challenges of subtitling (i.e., how to convert sensuous, tonally variegated speech into relatively homogeneous blocks of text) but to the particular challenges of translating Yiddish, a language whose expressive force and punch are legion among its users.[15] As Harshav writes:

> Yiddish speakers have always felt that theirs is quite unlike any other language and provides them with a highly charged means of expression. The difference was conspicuous when compared with the rational, well-ordered, and intellectual but detached or bureaucratic language used in post-Enlightenment western societies. Not growing out of high culture and a refined literary tradition but out of a homogenous folklore world, steeped as it was in irrational discourse, quintessential formulas of folk wisdom, and highly charged intimate family attitudes, the language was suddenly—in the lifetime of one or two generations—confronted with a pluralistic and specialized modern world and with elitist culture. Speakers, making that leap, either despised their "primitive" language or saved from it precisely the unusual,

irrational, folkloristic, or symbolic elements, carrying over their full semantic weight into the new, "European" context: the very strangeness of Yiddish expressions and gestures when used in another language served as an emotive, untranslatable "spice" for the initiated as well as a substitute for an authoritative "Bible of quotations" for the new texts.[16]

By the same token, one often hears today from non-Yiddish speakers that certain Yiddish words (particularly insults: i.e., *glomp*, *puts*) somehow don't *require* translation in order to be effectively understood, as if their meanings were viscerally immanent to their sounds. In any case, whether inflected by a sense of the impossible or the superfluous, the task of translation in Yiddish cinema emerges as an added site of communicative trouble, as the conspicuously hardworking, typographically involved rendering of Esther's dialogue testifies.

Letter Carrier and Whistleblower

Constituting another vital bond with other Yiddish movies, *Where Is My Child?* features a remarkable messenger figure (one will recall the one-armed solider in *A Little Letter to Mother* and the "messenger boy" in *The Living Orphan*). Following the hypercommunicative montage sequence, Esther, who has been searching all alone and in vain for her child for the last six years, finally gets some assistance from a secondary character named Elick (Ruben Wendorf), a chronic wisecracker who over the course of the film comes to be employed, as the other characters macaronically refer to him, as a "letter carrier." In this specific emissary capacity, Elick resonantly calls to mind the chapter on epistolary communication in *Does Writing Have a Future?*, where Flusser meditates on the infrastructure that has historically sustained the transmission of letters:

> I don't know whether anyone has written a postal philosophy. It would have to start from an analysis of waiting. Letters are things one waits for—or they arrive unexpectedly. Of course, waiting is a religious category: it means hoping. The post office is founded on the principle of hope. Postal

carriers, these functionaries who seem practically medieval, are angels (from *angeloi*, "messages"), and what they carry are evangels (good news, with respect to the hope that sustains the post office).[17]

For Esther, Elick embodies precisely such an angel, a representative of an institution that, exceptionally in the film, does not harm her and indeed proves beneficent. Picking back up with her, the film shows Esther sitting and leaning tautly forward on the steps of Reisner's old home, where she is waiting eagerly for a postman himself (that is, rather than for one of his letters), who she hopes can tell her the doctor's new address and advance her tireless, yet evidently stalled-out, search (see figure 5.1). Not surprisingly, Elick is fully capable of delivering on this request—addresses are the stock-in-trade of his job—and yet, knowing much more about the doctor and his social

Figure 5.1. As Esther waits for a postman on the steps of the doctor's old home, Elick the "letter-carrier" arrives with favorable news. Abraham Leff and Henry Lynn, *Where Is My Child?* (1937).

circle, he provides Esther with far more information about the doctor than she had hoped to obtain. Relating that she won't find Reisner at his new home, and writing out the more relevant address, he spills: "You can find him at Gross's house. It's their boy's first day at school. They adopted him when a baby through Dr. Reisner . . . from the Ohel Zedek Orphanage. He [Reisner] does favors—for money."

Interweaving with his status as an "angelic" messenger, Elick also embodies a kind of subversive, authority-puncturing "whistleblower," as his purveying of the extra information to Esther suggests. In fact, not only do we find this suggestion earlier on in the film, when Elick goes to see Reisner for a physical exam (necessary for applying for the letter-carrier job) and continually skewers the doctor ("They insist I find out how my heart is. Really, I never saw my heart. Though they say people live without hearts . . . I heard you haven't a heart. It's made of stone!"), but the film also evokes it in suggestively literal terms following Elick's encounter with Esther on the steps. As Malke (Blanche Bernstein), the Grosses' amiable maid whom Elick is wooing, ecstatically remarks to Reisner, "The sound of Elick's whistle always thrills me"—at which point, right on cue, Elick announces himself from offscreen with a high-pitched blast of the whistle. In this way, Malke, too, ardently "waits" for the letter carrier, while her excitement over his "whistleblowing" transposes the anticipation over the recent, and still-to-come, revelations into the realm of desire and the erotic. We might thus more generally think of Elick as forming an opposition with Reisner, contrasting the latter's meddling, divisive "bad mediation" with a form of "good mediation" that acts to bring Esther and her child closer together. Accordingly, Elick foreshadows the humanitarian figure who later takes an interest in Esther, and who, as we'll see, acts as a force of reformation in the context of an institution that, unlike the quaint, "practically medieval post office," functions, as per usual in the world of the film, as an instrument of oppression against Esther.

Lulling a Photograph

Let us now turn to a type of media only fleetingly addressed so far in these pages. In both painted and photographic form, still images feature prominently in Yiddish cinema, serving as reminders or vestiges of absent loved ones, and often, via special effects or a simple offscreen voice, "coming alive" as part of a dream and/or supernatural vision. Such a mystic phenomenon appears in a key scene in *Motel the Operator* and contributes pivotally to the plot in *The Wandering Jew* (*Der Vandernder Yid*), as we discuss in later chapters.[18] It plays a role, too, in the treatment of still images in *Where Is My Child?*, though in the form of an inventive negation.

The relevant moment comes once Esther arrives at the Grosses' house, which she does only after several complications. Equipped with the address from Elick and attempting to navigate the unfamiliar, upscale part of town, she at first fatefully encounters her son himself, now named Victor, outside his school playing football with a group of boys. However, while she is intuitively drawn to the boy, crying out, "My lost child," and embracing him, she doesn't appear to recognize the child as specifically her own lost child (recall the similar, *voix de sang* moment in *The Living Orphan* when Freda observes that the anonymous "messenger boy" is about the age that her son would be and embraces him). Thus the "real" child ironically serves as a surrogate for the lost object, for the child that Esther *hopes* to find. In any case, before she is able to explain herself to the baffled, somewhat creeped-out boy, the interaction is swiftly broken up by a passing cop, another male figure of oppressive institutional authority, who also, shortly afterward, discovers Esther "prowling around" the Grosses' house—which she manages to locate after asking several strangers for directions—and drags her inside to the living room. (Notably, the cop speaks entirely in English, fittingly failing to understand the communicatively troubled immigrant's protestations—which appear to him as mere babbling, nonsense—and creating a momentary gap in the imaginary Yiddishland that the film otherwise constructs.) It is here that Esther encounters, on a side table next to the sofa where she has been seated, a framed photographic portrait of Victor, who appears neatly coiffed, dressed in a white suit, and contentedly half-smiling. With urgent impatience, the mother grabs hold of the portrait and pronounces her excitement over the prospect, "I'll soon embrace him, hear him call me 'Mama,'" laying stress on the importance of the child's communication of his relation to her, of his addressing her via that most loaded word in the *mame-loshn*. Meanwhile, like the unrecognized child in the schoolyard encounter, the picture serves as another surrogate for the lost object, which the film indeed goes on to multiply. Deftly dismissing the cop and putting into motion a plan to entrap her, Reisner promises Esther that she will shortly be reunited with her child and dispatches her into an adjoining room. There, the mother's gaze falls on a mundane pile of Victor's toys—a football, a tennis racquet, a batting glove—that she proceeds to treat as quasi-religious relics, caressing the objects with wild, devoted belief in a kind of sympathetic magic, with a sense of wonderment over the fact that "his hands touched them."

Eventually, Esther turns her attention back to the photograph, further indulging its surrogate affordances. She cradles the object in her arms and rocks it to and fro, substituting in her mind the image with its referent, with the child himself—or more specifically, with the child not as he is now but as he was as an infant (Esther, clearly, is to a large degree traumatically entrapped in the long-ago moment of separation). Continuing this absorbed, fantasy-fueled activity, the mother then bursts into a song addressed to the child (see figure 5.2),

Figure 5.2. Esther sings a lullaby to a photographic portrait of her lost son in the home of his adoptive parents. Abraham Leff and Henry Lynn, *Where Is My Child?* (1937).

into a musical number generically entitled "The Lullaby Song," composed by Ludwig Satz, the well-known Yiddish comic actor and star of Goldin's early talkie *His Wife's Lover* (*Zayn Vaybs Lubovnik*, 1931). It is Adler's only musical number and in fact only one of two musical numbers in the entire film (the other being a romantic duet between Elick and Malke that makes ingenious use of the postal theme[19]), as if the film were loath to temper or modulate its gritty, dire plot with too many explicitly "unrealistic" departures. Accordingly, Adler's lone song is crucial, as is its status as a lullaby, a quintessential maternal musical genre (where the music acts as a kind of aural equivalent or accessory to "the Breast," aiming to provide slumber-inducing soothing) that corresponds with the film's own generic status as a maternal melodrama.

Yet what is most striking about the number is how the film repeatedly cuts away to close-ups of the photograph, which, because Adler's performance is addressed to the person "in" the photograph, stand in the position of reaction shots. That is to say, the editing primes us to expect the embedded image of the child to react to—to be, in the most literal sense, *moved by*—the passionate outpouring addressed to his real-life signified. Indeed, this expectation is all the more powerful in the context of Esther's belief that she is on the verge of being brought into the presence of the child himself, as well as in the broader context of Yiddish cinema, where, as mentioned, still images frequently *do* spring to life, especially in the face of an ardent musical appeal (cf. the musical number/dream sequence in *Bar Mitzvah* where the young boy, rising out of his sleeping body in ghostly double exposure, calls out to the full-length portrait of his "dead" mother on the wall—she in fact turns out not to be dead—and this triggers the mother, also via superimposition, to appear and take over the song, offering a spate of melodious maternal guidance). However, such a process of mystical enlivening is precisely what *doesn't* happen in the number in *Where Is My Child?* The film denies the expectation it so assiduously sets up, leaving the photograph to remain a photograph, and thus barring it from acquiring those qualities—mobility, presence, animation, life—conventionally attributed to cinema when set in opposition to photography.[20] At the same time, one can't discount the possibility of such a process happening *within an invisible register*, along the lines, for instance, of Ariella Azoulay's provocative, ethically charged political theory of photography, which calls for "watching" rather than "looking at" photographs, for a process of interpretation and reading on the part of what she calls "the civil spectator" that entails the reinscription of time and movement into the still image, and thus that cultivates a heightened sense of obligation and responsibility in the viewer.[21] One can well imagine, accordingly, a "cinematic" processing of the photograph of the child in Esther's powerfully churning imagination. Yet the film's thwarted flirtation with the motif of the enlivened still image; its refusal to allow Esther's lullaby any manifest effects of "response-ability"; the fact that the wide-eyed child in the photograph fails, as it were, to be lulled asleep by the song, his eyes *remaining* wide open: all of this invests the lullaby with a dark undercurrent that critically reminds us of the lingering disturbance of Esther's communicative abilities, which, as we'll see, undergoes a radical intensification in the immediate aftermath of the impassioned performance.

(Ex)Communication in the Asylum

In 1961, Erving Goffman published *Asylums* and Michel Foucault published *Madness and Civilization* (*Histoire de la Folie*), unleashing onto the world two radical critiques of the modern mental institution that became pivotal in the antipsychiatry movement, and that, as we wish to explore, resonate in a series of striking ways with the portrayal of the asylum in *Where Is My Child?* Indeed, like Goffman and Foucault, the film approaches the mental institution not so much as this or that particular mental institution but rather as a distinctly paradigmatic entity, as if wishing to go beyond the parameters of its narrative frame and say something of general sociological import about the operations of asylums. When Reisner phones up the asylum and arranges for the apprehension of Esther (whom he portrays as a dangerous lunatic, as a person under the delusion that "someone stole her child," and thus, with cruel irony, as a person who poses a risk of perpetrating exactly the crime perpetrated against her), the word "Asylum" momentarily flashes up on the screen in superimposition in order to clarify the action for the spectator. And, again, the word appears, now diegetically, on the gate of the evidently well-fortified grounds of the institution, to which we are brought after Esther is hauled away from the Grosses' house by a pair of menacing, expressionless, robotic, white-clad orderlies and a brief montage conveys the passage of the next twenty years. Hence, unlike the Ohel Zedek Orphanage, the asylum where Esther is committed lacks a proper name, is presented as merely the type or genus of institution to which it belongs.

In addition, "Asylum" sparks an important connotation by virtue of being an English word. That is to say, while everyone within the institution, staff and patients alike, "speaks" Yiddish, in accordance with Yiddish cinematic convention, the word, like the strictly English-speaking cop, exudes an aura of unfamiliarity—and this crucially transfers to our sense of the strictly Yiddish-speaking immigrant mother's predicament, making her incarceration in the space appear even more distressing and alienating. Meanwhile, in the oral register of the film, or at any rate at least when Reisner is referring to it during his phone call, the mental institution goes by the Yiddish term "*meshugoim-hoyz* [lit., madhouse]." In this way, and in a way typical of Yiddish (if we recall the previous quote from Harshav), a specially puissant "charge" appears superadded to the referent. For "asylum" and "madhouse" are by no means equivalent or easily interchangeable terms. The latter pulsates with harsh, "barbaric" overtones, while the former, especially when set beside the latter, gives off an almost genteel feel. (Of course, such an element of politesse in the English term by no means automatically translates into a positive, or even neutral, valence. For both Goffman and Foucault, the modern-day mental institution embodies a uniquely dismaying zone of domination, despite—and in many ways precisely on account of—its operational departures from the "madhouse" of earlier eras.)

In Goffman's *Asylums*, the central guiding term is "total institution," a phrase that he elucidates in the opening sentence of the study. Signaling his focus on mental hospitals, but also citing prisons as a choice example, he writes: "A total institution may be defined as a place of residence and work where a large number of like-situated individuals, cut off from the wider society for an appreciable period of time, together lead an enclosed, formally administered round of life."[22] Such a condition of being "cut off" bears particular relevance to Yiddish cinema, so rife with characters in the grip of states of excommunication—and indeed Goffman goes on to detail an enmeshed multiplicity of ways in which inmates of the total institution suffer disconnection. Paramount among these, and in homologous relation to their being severed from "wider society," is the subjection of inmates to being severed from *themselves,* or more accurately, from the assemblage of previous social roles that, within Goffman's highly relational, sociological model of identity, precisely constitute the self. "In our society, they [total institutions] are forcing houses for changing persons; each is a natural experiment on what can be done to the self,"[23] he writes, and goes on, addressing the critical admission phase: "In the accurate language of some of our oldest total institutions, he [the inmate] begins a series of abasements, degradations, humiliations, and profanations of self. His self is systematically, if often unintentionally, mortified. He begins some radical shifts in his *moral career,* a career composed of the progressive changes that occur in the beliefs that he has concerning himself and significant others."[24] Bearing in mind such forces of depersonalization (which Goffman refers to in terms of "role dispossession,"[25] "civil death,'"[26] and "personal defacement,"[27] among others), one can easily see why confining Esther within a total institution provides Reisner with a superlative means of dealing with his pressing dilemma. On one level, if Esther were left out in the world, one can easily imagine her going on to approach Gross's wife Alice, to whom she could potentially make a convincing appeal, and Victor himself, who is old enough to begin to grasp something of the scandalous truth of his origins. Removing Esther from "wider society" thus would presumably take care of such potentialities. On another level, how perfect from Reisner's point of view for Esther to become, in line with the total institution's central operational thrust, estranged from her prior identity and consequently to forget that she was ever a mother at all? On both levels, the total institution facilitates Reisner's project of getting Esther out of the way, of keeping her "outsider" voice, which threatens to subvert the order of his privileged world, rigorously silenced.

The film reveals the staggering excommunicatory dimensions of the asylum as it takes us on an atmospheric tour of the space in the lead-up to reintroducing Esther. In an interior shot dissolved into from the exterior shot of the gate, a middle-aged, male doctor greets his younger, rather dashing, male colleague (Mischa Stutchkof), remarking, "Dr. Gross," and thus swiftly identifying for us the latter character with Victor all grown up. (Of course, the coincidence that Esther's child winds up working at the very place where his biological mother is being held captive embodies just the kind of fantastical destiny mechanics that we have come to expect in the universe of *shund*.) Poised to begin their rounds, the two white-coated doctors stand in front of a door marked "123": a number that, like the generic name "Asylum," is striking on account of its blankness, giving the apt impression that the means of regimentation at the asylum has *itself* undergone a kind of depersonalization. In any case, what the two men shortly behold behind the door, which becomes thrust open in a jarring jump-cut (perhaps an artifact of damage to the original print), is a tableau of punishing isolation constituted by three manifestly disturbed patients of the all-female ward. Wearing drab, one-piece garments, the women stare off in three completely different directions (up aslant, across aslant, out aslant), demonstrating that, despite living in close, even claustrophobic, quarters, they inhabit distinct, hermetically sealed-off psychological worlds. At the same time, the shot generates an important effect from embedding an act of looking. That is, we see the doctors observing the redolently Charcotian scene of female madness.[28] And moreover, we see them doing so in a radically, even supremely, detached manner, for they are positioned, like the camera, on the outside of the room, standing at the doorway, which consequently frames the scene within the room and reinforces its status as an image.

Of particular relevance to such a moment, Marianne Doane writes that in the subset of the "woman's film" involving the familiar dynamic of a female patient in the custody of a male doctor, "the erotic gaze becomes the medical gaze"[29]—a formulation that contrasts the classic, fetishistic "male gaze" theorized by Laura Mulvey with a different species of (male) gaze theorized by Foucault. As Foucault points out, "the medical gaze," whose origins lie in the eighteenth century with the rise of the teaching hospital or "clinic," and which defines a new kind of perception in the field of medicine, takes vision—and more specifically, radically aloof vision—as its organizing principle in the relation between doctors and patients. Writes Foucault in *The Birth of the Clinic*, the book he published right after *Madness and Civilization*, "The observing gaze refrains from intervening: it is silent and gestureless."[30] In this way, "the medical gaze" in fact recapitulates in broad outline the trajectory that Foucault traces in *Madness and Civilization*, where he accounts for the increasingly repressive shifts and mutations in how Western society has treated "the insane" from the end of the Middle Ages until "the birth of the asylum" in the nineteenth century. As he writes, regarding an early fault line:

> In the Renaissance, madness was present everywhere and mingled with every experience by its images or dangers. During the classical period, madness was shown, but on the other side of the bars; if present, it was at a distance, under the eyes of a reason that no longer felt any relation to it and that would not compromise itself by too close a resemblance. Madness had become a thing to look at: no longer a monster inside oneself, but an animal with strange mechanisms, a bestiality from which man had long since been suppressed.[31]

And further, regarding another fault line, one typified by psychiatric reformists like Philippe Pinel in France and William Tuke in England:

> The proximity instituted by the asylum, an intimacy neither chains nor bars would ever violate again, does not allow reciprocity: only the nearness of observation that watches, that spies, that comes closer in order to see better, but moves ever farther away, since it accepts and acknowledges only the values of the Stranger. The science of mental disease, as it would develop in the asylum, would always be only of the order of observation and classification. It would not be a dialogue.[32]

Sounding unexpectedly in these passages a bit like Buber (whom we explore more at length in the next chapter), Foucault underscores a troubling foreclosure of intersubjective relations and consequent strict hierarchy of subject and object (that is, a posture of deep objectification on the part of a unilaterally acting subject), which captures incisively the dark, dominant mood of *Where Is My Child*'s conjuration of the asylum.[33]

This shutting down of "relation," "reciprocity," "dialogue," and so forth, extends into the scene's aural sphere, as the female patients provide the doctors with phenomena not only to behold but also to hear. One of the women in the "123" room, with long, let-down,

Ophelia-like hair, exclaims frantically and apropos of seemingly nothing, "No one else shall have my groom. He's mine," while one of the other women remains mute and immobile, as if ossified, and the third fumbles with the buttons on her gown, mouth dazedly agape. In the next room, "124," which the doctors eventually reach in their walk down the bare, antiseptic corridor, another unsettling combination of silence and outburst greets them. While one woman sits at the back of the room in a pose of frozen contortion, as if pinned to the wall by some invisible force, another woman stands at the doorway and spasmodically declares: "I'm Hitler's mother-in-law. Get out!" And in a third room—a full-fledged cell with bars, atavistically recalling the "madhouses" of yore—another inmate, desperately throwing her arms up against the barrier, pleads with what appears to be incontestable mental lucidity, "I want to do good. Let me out!" Yet a moment later, in a sudden, schizoid swing, she punctuates the entreaty with a blast of discordant noise, a howling "cockle-doodle-doo," which produces visible horror in Victor's superior and causes him to recoil, as shown in a quick cutaway shot. The doctors do not assign any sense to these verbal eruptions, in keeping with their carefully maintained position on the outside of the spaces of confinement, where the camera, as mentioned, is located, and consequently works to create a momentary "free indirect" identification with the medical onlookers. However, it is regarding this kind of failed response and reception that an insight of Goffman's concerning precisely the intelligibility—or more specifically, the elusively *displaced* intelligibility—of inmate communication finds acute pertinence: "The student of mental hospitals can discover that the craziness or 'sick behavior' claimed for the mental patient is by and large a product of the claimant's social distance from the situation that the patient is in, and is not primarily a product of mental illness."[34] In other words, the (mis)perception of inmates' words as vacuous or illogical often results from no more than a radical divorce between inmates and their usual context; it is, finally, the patients' condition of social isolation that determines their speech as "nonsense." Accordingly, we need only think of Esther's example to try to imagine what it would mean for the anguished cries of the other inmates to be restored to the original milieux from which they have been torn. We may even suspect that, just like in Esther's case, the reason for committing the women, indeed for subjecting them to such radical, multileveled excommunication (not only locking them up and cutting them off from the world but stripping away their very personalities), pertains to the unwelcome significance of their "erratic," "hysterical" speech in the outside world.

Illicit Relationality

Nevertheless, Esther manages to engage in a striking form of communicative resistance within this environment of seemingly boundless communicative deprivations and assaults. Just before the doctors arrive at her room, which she alone inhabits, the film provides a brief opportunity for us to observe her unobserved. In a shot notably taken for the first time from within one of the rooms, and in which the camera slowly tilts up to reveal her dramatically aged face (dark under-eye circles, unkempt gray hair), Esther sits on a bed and rolls up the covers into a simulacrum of a swaddled baby, which she proceeds to cradle and rock back and forth mollifyingly, there-there-ingly (see figure 5.3).

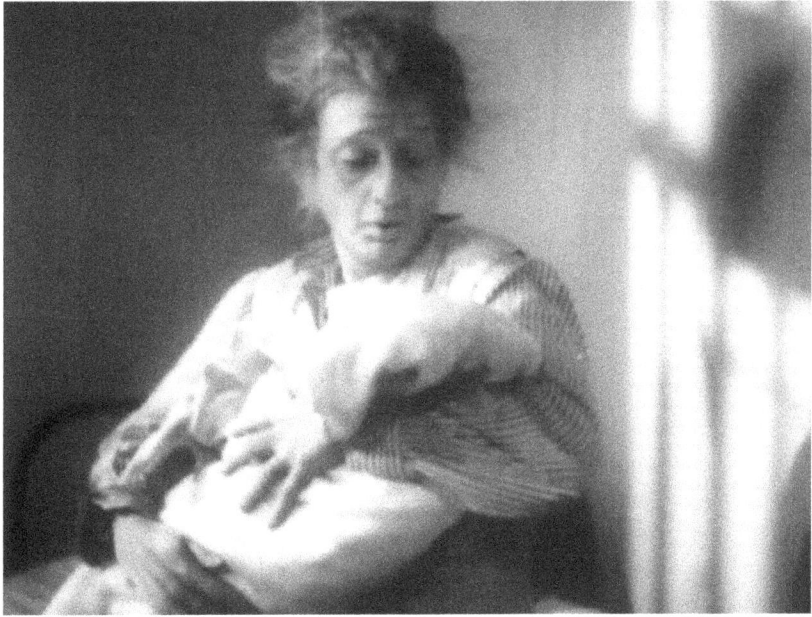

Figure 5.3. Esther makes a swaddled baby—another surrogate object for her lost child—out of the bedding in her asylum cell. Abraham Leff and Henry Lynn, *Where Is My Child?* (1937).

The moment recalls the earlier one during the lullaby number when Esther performs a similar gesture with the framed portrait of Victor and improvises a tactile, ersatz version of her lost child. Addressing the (substitute) child, she appeals over plaintive violin underscoring: "I'm not crazy, my child. You'll get your mother out of here. Surely, you'll rescue and protect me." While of course not wholly separable from a hallucinatory acting out, from her entrapment within—and compulsion to repeat—her traumatic history, this performance with the blankets also functions for Esther as an essential strategy of coping and survival. And indeed it is one that is all the more remarkable in the face of the stringent paucity of resources available to her, of the total institution's policy of inhibiting "object relations" in the most literal sense of the term. Upon entry, the inmate is stripped of all private property and provided with the bare minimum of replacements: clothing, bedding, and so on. "These substitute possessions," Goffman points out, "are clearly marked as really belonging to the institution and in some cases are recalled at regular intervals to be, as it were, disinfected of identifications."[35] In resistance to such practices, Esther incredibly, phantasmatically transforms the "standard issue"[36] blankets into her own (once) most intimate possession. In this way, such an object (like the portrait and the toys earlier, but in a much more striking manner given the fact that, unlike the portrait and the toys, it bears no prior relation to the child) takes on the status of a specially purposed media device: a device, that is, by which Esther is able to fantasize the lines of communication between her and her child as still operative, and thus to retain a form of connection to him, and to her own self—to the maternal identity that so powerfully, indeed with delirious totalizing force, defines her pre-institutional self.

The iconic, sustaining moment is short-lived, however, recalling and further elaborating the communicative trials of asylum life. In what would appear to be a familiar pattern, as soon as she realizes that she is being watched by the two doctors at the doorway (to which the film cuts away in the middle of her address to her child), Esther anxiously falls silent and attempts to conceal all traces of the performance by throwing the blankets back down onto the bed and hastily smoothing them out. In this way, the scene demonstrates what Goffman, laying out a common, particularly cruel, punitive dynamic, calls "looping." "Looping," explains Goffman, occurs when an inmate's techniques of self-preservation are effectively turned around against him or her by those deputized by the total institution: "An agency that creates a defensive response on the part of the inmate takes this very response as the target of its next attack. The individual finds that his protective response to an assault upon self is collapsed into the situation; he cannot defend himself in the usual way by establishing distance between the mortifying situation and himself."[37] Accordingly, the very act that defends Esther, indeed that explicitly involves her calling on her son to "rescue and protect" her, only exposes her to further persecution, reflecting and intersecting with the vicious double bind that she finds herself in owing to Reisner's lie about her being out to steal someone else's child.

Esther's (mis)fortunes, however, begin to shift with our further (re)introduction to Victor, who turns out to embody a glaring exception within the ranks of the asylum. As if in answer to his mother's surreptitiously voiced appeal for help, he breaks away from his colleague, as well as from his professionally prescribed role as a scientifically detached observer, and enters Esther's room. There, sitting close to her on a chair next to the bed, he unleashes a torrent of questions and exhortations—"Please tell me your name. Why can't you speak? Maybe I can help you. Don't be afraid! Please tell me your name. Why are you here? Who put you here?"—that calls back, in hyperbolic form, to what Foucault describes as the distinctive premodern approach to doctoring in the West, wherein the doctor attends to the patient herself rather than to the illness afflicting her. As Foucault writes, memorably distilling the new structure of the clinic by tracing a key shift in the doctor's manner of discourse: "This new structure is indicated—but not, of course, exhausted—by the minute but decisive change, whereby the question: 'What is the matter with you?,' with which the eighteenth-century dialogue between doctor and patient (a dialogue possessing its own grammar and style), was replaced by the other question: 'Where does it hurt?,' in which we recognize the operation of the clinic and the principle of its entire discourse."[38] Thus it is as if the asylum sequence enacts an inversion of this historical trajectory, beginning with a dynamic in which the doctors appear in no way to regard the subjectivity of the patients, in which their only concern appears to be with an objective, pathological "it," and eventually shifting toward a dynamic on the plane of intersubjectivity, in which Victor regards Esther concertedly as a "you" ("Why can't *you* speak? Maybe I can help *you* . . . Please tell me *your* name. Why are *you* here? Who put *you* here?"). Or, as we might otherwise put it in Buberian language, the sequence moves from a demonstration of the "I-It" relation to a demonstration of the "I-You" relation: a formulation in which we can observe a further resonance between the Jewish philosopher and Foucault, whose opposition between "Where does *it* hurt?" and "What is the matter with *you*?" strikingly echoes Buber's central conceptual opposition.

In a Goffmanian register, Victor's unusual attempt to make intimate contact with Esther appears to signal the initiation of an "involvement cycle,"[39] a process in which the staff member of the total institution falls prey, in the sociologist's wry formulation, to the ever-lurking "danger that an inmate will appear human."[40] To treat patients as humans, as "objects . . . of sympathetic concern,"[41] poses a threat on a foundational level to the total institution, which precisely depends, as discussed, on an evacuation of the inmate's personhood. Yet Victor's attempt to create a bond with Esther magnifies this threat exponentially, intensifies it far beyond the bounds of a standard-fare involvement cycle, given the unwitting familial relation that the two possess to one another. That is to say, as Goffman points out, the total institution and the institution of the family stand in mutually exclusive relation to one another. The "force" of the total institution in civil society, Goffman writes, "will in part depend on the suppression of a whole circle of actual or potential households. Conversely, the formation of households provides a structural guarantee that total institutions will not be without resistance. The incompatibility of these two forms of social organization should tell us something about the wider social functions of them both."[42] For certain, such incompatibility tells us much about why *Where Is My Child?*—which, like all Yiddish films, lionizes the family and treats the family as fundamental in the construction of identity, just as Goffman treats the total institution as fundamental in the deconstruction of identity—portrays the asylum as the very epitome of hell, as well as why the bringing about of the mother's liberation from the asylum should, in the main, fall to her son. At the same time, Esther's frightened slide back into silence and fretful reluctance to respond to Victor's caring interrogation—a state that persists all the way to the end of the sequence (which breaks off abruptly in the midst of the heated, one-sided interview) and effectively grants her a place in Yiddish cinema's vast assembly of characters grappling with predicaments of "muteness"— allows Victor to enact a Jewish ethics of responsibility, an instantiation of the ideals of *mentshlekhkayt* (humanity) and *tikkun olam* (repair of the world), that transcends a basis in "mere" filial obligation. For the time being, despite mutual stirrings of the *voix du sang*, the patient remains a mystery to the doctor, assuming the form of an Other rather than his very own mother.

Rescue and Reconfiguration

As the film moves toward a conclusion, Victor becomes more and more strident in resisting the dictates of his workplace, evoking Flusser's pervasive concern with the problem of "the functionary." For Flusser, as Cesar Baio explains, "the perfect functionary is an object that functions in conformity with the purposes of the apparatus."[43] Accordingly, the functionary "is not capable of making moral or ethical judgments about his/her actions, precisely because he/she does not question what the apparatus produces (ontological question), or what it should produce (deontological question). The functionary only asks him- or herself how the program of the apparatus can be realized in a more effective manner (technical question)."[44] Back at his parents' house after work, Victor acts in a way radically opposed to such a model of behavior, refusing to accept the asylum as a system governed by supposedly natural, fixed rules, challenging the legitimacy of the order that invests him with authority, making explicitly moral/ethical proclamations about the "apparatus" in which he is embedded, finding meaning where normally none is acknowledged, and so on. Sitting at the piano in the refined living room and addressing a rapt audience made up of his adoptive mother (Alice), the postman (Elick), and the maid (Malke), he righteously, indignantly pronounces about the asylum inmates: "What sane thoughts come from these people! I often ask myself why we keep them there. Who are the evil people who put them there?" Further, in a scene slightly later on, Victor reveals a plan that wildly ups the stakes of his transgression of the protocols of the total institution. In an intimate tête-à-tête scene in his old boyhood bedroom that conjures visual echoes of the earlier scene in Esther's room at the asylum, he sits on the bed next to his adoptive mother and requests the latter's permission to invite Esther over to the house, where preparations are underway for a party to celebrate his birthday. "She'll be paroled on my responsibility," remarks Victor of the mysterious patient, figuring that if he can temporarily remove her from the asylum, then the change of surroundings might alleviate her fear and allow her to speak openly about her pre-institutional identity. In this way, Victor takes advantage of a kind of distinctive "insider-outsider" position with respect to the asylum—he at once belongs to the institution and remains deeply critical of its workings—and thus can be seen to embody Flusser's realist-pragmatic vision of the modern subject's relation to apparatuses: namely, that while the modern subject cannot exist fully outside of apparatuses, "a gap between the human being and the perfect functionary . . . has not been entirely bridged," and so possibilities for resistance can be found in "trying to embed values and human awareness into apparatuses," in "invading th[e] internal structure [of apparatuses] in an ironical attempt to corrupt them from the inside and reprogram them, in a kind of utopian game of freedom."[45]

Amid such a subversive effort of humanistic reprogramming, Victor's choice to seek out the blessings of his adoptive mother rather than his adoptive father is immensely significant. The choice, or perhaps the gravitation, seems to stem from a dim, unconscious awareness on Victor's part of his adoptive father's complicity with the "original sin" of his being taken—effectively abducted—from his birth mother. At the same time, Victor's pursuit of maternal permission also comports with a key dimension of the film's treatment of gender. To come back to Doane on the medical subset of the "woman's film" of the 1940s, such films, in which the woman becomes an object of the detached yet penetrating, masculine-coded medical gaze, typically involve "the need . . . for the figure of the doctor as reader or interpreter, as the site of a knowledge which dominates and controls female subjectivity."[46] Thus Doane points to films like *Shock* (1946) and *Possessed* (1947), where we find traumatized, communicatively troubled (i.e., mute, amnesiac, etc.) female patients, who only (re)gain the ability to "speak" about their pasts via the doctors whose jurisdiction they fall under. Unpacking the structure of flashbacks and embedded female narration that consequently arises out of such a dynamic, Doane writes:

> Within the encompassing masculine medical discourse, the woman's language is granted a limited validity—it is, precisely, a point of view, and often a distorted and unbalanced one. The quasi-magical, and at the same time scientific,

ability of medicine to discover the truth is evidenced by the popularity of the notion of the truth serum in these films. In *Shock*, a female victim of amnesia is also [as in *Possessed*] given an injection so that the doctor can discover what she knows, what she has seen (here the speech-inducing agent is scopolamine, in *Possessed* it is "narcosynthesis").[47]

In *Where Is My Child?*, Victor might be said to "control" his traumatized, institutionalized mother's subjectivity and language in so far as he serves as an (unconscious) extension of her otherwise deprived voice. Indeed, this nonpharmacological mediation seems particularly to be operative as he delivers his nonconformist speech that speaks "the truth" about what the unfortunate patients at the asylum have likely, unjustly borne. However, the film also seems a considerable degree less reactionary in its gender politics than the portrait that Doane paints of the Hollywood films with which it corresponds. That is, the film goes out of its way to construct a significant base of female support behind Victor's rescue and relational restoration of Esther: a move that importantly resists investing the powers to resolve the crisis of the narrative strictly and solely in a man. Accordingly, Alice *grants* Victor permission to go through with his plan, momentarily managing her haunting anxiety that the woman of which he speaks might somehow *be* Victor's real mother. As she proclaims, decisively getting up from the bed and grasping Victor by the arms, as if the plan were not so much Victor's as her own: "My son, bring this woman here!" (Germanely, just before the scene in the bedroom, Alice's ambivalence toward Victor's birth mother is on full display as she lights a *yahrzeit* candle for the "holy soul": a gesture that seems intended at once to honor the woman *and* convince herself that the woman, as per the fallacious story fed to her by Reisner and her husband, *is* in fact dead and no longer a live threat to her own status as a mother.) And then there is Victor's fiancée and Reisner's daughter, the pretty, ultimately principled Julia (Ceril Arnon), who eventually reneges on agreeing to her father's instructions to convince Victor to "give up the asylum." Listening to her future husband launch into another of his fiery orations about conditions in the asylum, she declares to her father, "For every word, he deserves a kiss. I agree with him": a flagrant act of anti-paternal defiance that, unlike in films like *Kol Nidre* and *Tevye*, entails no ensuing appeal for mercy or forgiveness, that requires no rapprochement with the (amoral, ongoingly machinating) father.

In fact, by the time we arrive at the final, climactic scene at the Grosses' house, in which all the members of the main cast are gathered, we have learned that Reisner has undergone a drastic fall in status and erosion of authority. As Elick reveals in a slightly earlier scene in which he continues to acidly confront the doctor, Reisner has in the intervening years lost his medical license, forming a pointed contrast with Victor's astonishing, rapid professional ascent: a rise that Elick, too, informs us about, in another earlier scene, tapping on a newspaper and bringing up in conversation with Alice the glowing, *naches*-bringing articles that have been written about the young doctor. (In his capacity as a messenger, it is most apt that Elick "delivers" such newspaper stories to the viewer; like the messenger boy/newspaper seller Benny in *The Living Orphan*, as a representative of one media institution, he possesses the easeful ability to act on behalf of another.) Reisner's sullying descent is critical since his words no longer hold any weight at the critical juncture in which Esther, brought over to the house and beginning to surmount her fear of speaking out, recognizes him and Mr. Gross as the men who "ruined my life" and violently demands an answer to the eponymous question that she has spent a lifetime rehearsing: "WHERE IS MY CHILD?" (to borrow the emphatic, all-caps of the original subtitles). Indeed, even though at this point Reisner attempts to defuse the situation, as he has done so many times before, and declares Esther *meshugena*, now no one pays the slightest attention to the accusation. Meanwhile, as the exposure of his guilt strikes Mr. Gross dumb and he fails to respond to Victor's urgent demand for answers, the film leaves it up to Alice to disclose to her adopted son the secret of his origins, again accentuating her important role in restoring Esther's bond with Victor. In a continuation of her transformation into a decisive agent, she pronounces, gesturing at Esther with uplifted hands: "Now I understand all. Victor, this unfortunate woman is your mother! Your real mother!" Taking stock of what undergirds Esther's liberation, we thus find an array of critical factors rather than a single, simply localizable one. Victor growing up into a flourishing, humane doctor; Alice reckoning with the haunting possibility of Victor's birth mother still being alive; Julia gradually rejecting her father's dictates; Reisner losing his professional standing: all of these elements contribute vitally to the long-awaited vindication of the maltreated immigrant single mother. In other words, it is as if Esther's persistent struggle against injustice is of no effect until an alteration occurs in virtually the *entire communicative structure* from which she finds herself excluded. In this way, the film marks a sharp difference from the majority of Hollywood movies (not just instances of the "woman's film," but Hollywood films writ large), which, informed by an American ideology of individualism, tend to depict characters climbing out of marginal positions and up the social ladder through their own ingenious and industrious efforts. By contrast, it is practically a rule in Yiddish cinema that an outcast protagonist is (re)integrated into communal life thanks to another person becoming responsible for her or him, among other things. Deeply informed by Jewish ethics, Yiddish cinema again and again insists that a person's plight, good or bad, fortunate or misfortunate, is never something that only that person has brought about or can change.

The reunion between birth mother and son is emotionally seismic for both parties. In an intimate two-shot that extracts them from the larger space and cast of characters, that gives them a kind of momentary world of their own, the two drop down onto the couch in a sobbing, mutual embrace. "They took my young mother away from me—And now—But you are dear to me—So dear," Victor declares to Esther, going so far as to echo her sense of loss with a deep sense of loss of his own, suggesting that even though he was given a loving surrogate mother, he was nevertheless profoundly affected by the wrongful separation. And he goes on to declare his burning intentions to "go [away] from here" and to devote himself to Esther: "I'll guard and protect you from evil. I'll share my life with you." From a realist perspective, needless to say, such an extreme, instantaneous form of rebonding between two people who only seconds before believed one another to be strangers is aggressively implausible; it is a far cry, for example, from the notoriously difficulty-laden, real-life situations of lost, kidnapped, or fostered Jewish children who were reunited with their surviving biological parents after the Holocaust.[48] The operative question here is one that Emma Wilson poses in her illuminating study of the pervasive theme of the missing child in contemporary independent and art cinema, *Cinema's Missing Children*, namely, "the question of whether any missing child who returns could be entirely and easily recognized as familiar."[49] As we see in *Where Is My Child?*— and this is the case in *shund* films more broadly dealing with missing children—any such concern about the "seeming non-identity between a child and his later . . . self"[50] is instantly dispelled at the moment of reunion. Yet instead of regarding this feature as an index of the immaculate nature of the happy ending, one might, on the contrary, take its exorbitant implausibility as a sign of roiling overcompensation. That is to say, the very perfection of the reunion doubles as precisely its imperfection—its oddness or off-ness—speaking to an underlying, not fully worked out anxiety about separation and the ills of troubled communication, and the need to launch into hyperbolic wish fulfillment in order to paper such anxieties over.

However, the ending of the film in fact exhibits an even more flagrant element of persistent irresolution, hinging on Victor's relationship not to his birth mother but to his adoptive mother. More specifically, while Victor's zealous reunion with Esther and strident declaration that he will "go [away] from here" is unproblematic in relation to his adoptive father, who is now fully exposed and besmirched in his eyes, such actions inevitably raise questions about his future relationship with Alice, who up to his moment he always believed was his birth mother. "Mother—what shall I do? She [Esther] needs me now," Victor appeals to Alice, continuing to address her by the same old maternal epithet and to seek her advice and approval. In turn, in an act of self-sacrifice that radically escalates her agential conversion, and perhaps receives empathetic galvanization from her own experience of having lost a child, she responds: "Do what your heart dictates. I'll be happy in the thought that I brought up a lovely son for your real mother." Despite this keeping-it-together affirmation of being "happy" vis-à-vis the situation, however, happiness is the furthest emotion conveyed by her face a moment later; instead what we find is an expression of utter calamity, which indeed strikingly recalls Esther's expression of unmooring anguish as she reluctantly surrenders her child to the nurse in the earlier scene at the orphanage (see figure 5.4).

Rather than participating in the "happy ending," Alice thus flounders in unignorable, seemingly unappeasable devastation, as if in giving up Victor to his "real mother" she is effectively plunged back into a version of her original tragic predicament of child loss that adopting Victor was meant to ameliorate. Or in other words, the film seems to make the restoration of Esther to relationality contingent upon the violent excommunication of another, to reopen the whole crisis of vetoed maternal rights just at the moment of the apparent resolution

Figure 5.4. Unnoticed in the background, Alice conveys an expression of devastation and anguish as she gives up her adopted son to his "real" mother. Abraham Leff and Henry Lynn, *Where Is My Child?* (1937).

of such a crisis, and to do so in a deeply resonant, highly elaborated manner that resists being reducible strictly to a failure on the film's behalf to imagine a family structure sufficiently elastic to accommodate two mothers (a nontraditional arrangement that the ending of the film that we discuss next in fact gestures toward). Indeed, the film drives home Alice's sense and condition of exclusion via a startling reconfiguration of blocking and mise-en-scène in its lengthy final shot, which includes and runs beyond the adoptive mother's self-sacrificial pronouncement and revelation (to us) of her abysmal pain. Toward the end of the shot, Alice winds up positioned visibly in the background behind the trio of Victor, Esther, and Julia. Yet, as Victor enfolds his newly discovered birth mother and recently minted fiancée in a gratified, dual embrace, the ensuing huddle of bodies collectively walks toward the camera and consequently blocks Alice entirely out of the image with which we are finally left (see figure 5.5). Such a

Figure 5.5. As Victor embraces his "real" mother and fiancée, the trio of bodies eclipses his excluded, adoptive mother (situated invisibly behind them) from the image. Abraham Leff and Henry Lynn, *Where Is My Child?* (1937).

visual distillation of Alice's inability to be assimilated into the joyous, old/new family unit of husband, wife, and mother dovetails with what we might describe as Esther and Victor's fantastical *overassimilation* to one another, similarly conveying the film's ongoing grappling with its central dilemma of troubled communication—a dilemma that, as so often in Yiddish cinema, only finds resolution in a conditional or imperfect way. Hence, even as Esther recovers her child at long last and would now appear to have a much brighter future ahead of her in America, her predicament undergoes a kind of reanimating displacement: the unsettling figure of the outcast, agonized mother haunts the screen still further.

6

"Silence which is communication"

Motel the Operator (1939)

Like Sidney Goldin's earlier *Uncle Moses* (1932), Joseph Seiden's *Motel the Operator* (*Motl der Operator*), the third and final Seiden film discussed in this book, evokes the classic Yiddish preoccupation with labor and working-class politics, setting part of its action at a sweatshop. In contrast to Goldin's film, however, which focuses on a domineering owner, played by Maurice Schwartz, who ultimately softens and concedes to his employees' demands, Seiden's film focuses on a lowly laborer, whose dire working conditions not only fail to be improved but result in him being propelled into a far worse social position and communicative predicament. Indeed, from a routinely exploited industrial worker in capitalist America struggling to support his family, the eponymous protagonist descends into a hobo without a penny, home, or relation to anyone at all, including his former self, the memory of which fades into oblivion. As intimated at the beginning of the last chapter, the film thus reflects *Where Is My Child*'s concern with the figure of the outcast. And indeed, for those familiar with *Where Is My Child?*, the overarching plot structure sparks an unmistakable sense of déjà vu. For, once again, the protagonist is rescued and restored to relationality by a lost child who had been adopted away in infancy and is unaware that the marginal figure, the mysterious Other, is his biological parent. Nevertheless, despite such shamelessly glaring, practically plagiaristic borrowings, which are of course entirely kosher by *shund* standards, our main concern in this chapter is with a key difference between the two films in terms of how they respectively bring the shared narrative material to a point of "resolution." Namely, in Seiden's film, the rescued outcast parent does not use his newly recovered voice to reveal himself to his child and reestablish their original bond (which is what happens in the earlier film), but rather he subjects that voice to a strategic, ethically charged withholding. That is to say, it is a film that, from the evocation of the grueling, early twentieth-century Jewish immigrant labor experience in New York, veers into a rich, complex exploration of the productive potential of silence.

"Silence which is communication" and Turning

As composer and foundational sound theorist R. Murray Schafer instructively points out, Western culture's relation to silence is one that has typically tended to be dominated by fear. In a section entitled "Western Man and Negative Silence" in his 1977 book *The Soundscape*, Schafer writes: "Man likes to make sounds to remind himself that he is not alone. From this point of view total silence is the rejection of human personality. Man fears the absence of sound as he fears the absence of life. . . . In Western society, silence is a negative, a vacuum. Silence for Western man equals communication hang-up."[1] By and large, Yiddish cinema easily accords with such an antipathetic, even phobic, attitude toward silence. Recall the massive, nefarious collaboration of institutions mobilized to silence Esther in *Where Is My Child?*, or the silencing of the ambitious, sparkling Chassie from the airwaves and the synagogue choir in *Kol Nidre*, or any of the anguished fathers struggling with the loss, or tottering, of their traditionally authoritative voices in *A Little Letter to Mother*, *The Living Orphan*, *Kol Nidre*, and *Tevye*. Recall, too, the failure of anticipated messages to arrive and the distressful silence that lingers in the aftermath (for instance, in *The Living Orphan*, Freda returning to a home inhabited by strangers and discovering that Muni "withheld word"). Or—and one could go on—the several jubilant, long-awaited, late-narrative moments of familial reunion that reverse a trend of silence and involve passionate verbal outpourings (of identity, of pleas for mercy), and that often enmesh with a resounding musical performance.

In the face of this pattern, *Motel the Operator* constitutes a striking exception, for the film imagines a positive use for silence, reclaiming the phenomenon in a manner that accords with Martin Buber's under-glossed notion of silence as a potent species, and even foundation, of dialogue. As Buber writes in a section called "Silence which is communication" in the 1929 essay "Dialogue": "Just as the most eager speaking at one another does not make a conversation . . . , so for a conversation no sound is necessary, not even a gesture. Speech can renounce all the media of sense, and it is still speech."[2] The only thing required for dialogue, Buber goes on to explain, is what he calls "turning": "Even if speech and communication may be dispensed with, the life of dialogue seems, from what we may perceive, to have inextricably joined to it as its minimum constitution one thing, the mutuality of the inner action. Two men bound together in dialogue must obviously be turned to one another, they must therefore—no matter with what measure of activity or indeed of consciousness of activity—have turned to one another."[3] For Buber, "turning," this critical act that both embodies and institutes dialogue, and may transpire in complete silence, entails an attunement to another person on a kind of intuitive plane. As he remarks, regarding a person elusively turned/attuned to another: "Nothing that he believed he possessed as always available would help him, no knowledge, no technique, no system and no programme; for now he would have to do with what cannot be classified, with concretion itself. This speech has no alphabet, each of its sounds is a new creation and only to be grasped as such."[4] In this way, Buber's "turning" can be regarded as a metasemantic communicative process, similar to Flusser's "the gesture of listening to music," which one will recall also takes place on a level beyond the register of language and signs, and entails a deep, concerted effort of attention devoted to another. Notably, to further the link between the two thinkers, one suspects that Buber's "turning" provided a critical template for Flusser's key concept of "turning *around*," that is, of "revolution" in a given communicative organization, previously discussed in chapter 2 in relation to the pivotal scene in *The Living Orphan* where an audience member in a "theatrical" discursive structure "turns around," responds to the performer on stage, and thus realigns the situation in a dialogic direction. Indeed, Flusser's elaboration of communicative "revolution" in *Does Writing Have a Future?* greatly reinforces the connection. In a chapter on "Books," offering an evocative phenomenological reflection on the wall of the library as it is encountered by the reader, or more accurately the proto-reader, he writes:

> The spines of the books, lined up beside one another and over one another, form a secondary wall, positioned in front of the actual wall. Between the spines of the books and the actual wall is a zone of paper, where . . . numerous arms are trying to take hold of us. They can only do this if we ourselves stretch out an arm in their direction, pull a spine out from the wall, and turn the book around, to allow ourselves to be taken in by it.
>
> *Turning around* is a synonym for *revolution*. Two things happen with the pulling out and turning over of the book. First, the actual wall becomes visible behind the book that has been pulled out. Second, the arm of another, stretched out toward us, can be grasped. *Revolution* surely means to become aware of the walls that separate us, to be able to take hold of the other (be it a stranglehold, an intellectual grasp, or a mutual holding of interest).[5]

As we'll see, *Motel the Operator* enacts a powerful analogue to Buber's conception of the distinctively relational possibilities inherent in the absence of (conventional) speech, in the "mere" act of "turning," showing how a destructive repression of voice is able to give way to a constructively elected silence—a silence that enables its protagonist to (re)enter into "the life of dialogue" via an unexpected route and with unprecedentedly vigorous effects of responsibility.

Marx and the Talmud

Played by Chaim Tauber, who is also credited with writing the story of the film, the central character of *Motel the Operator* derives his identity, as his moniker suggests, from his status as a working-class laborer, as a sewing machine "operator," and the first part of the film traces his struggles to articulate and assert his rights in such terms. Bringing us into a factory on the Lower East Side, the opening scene introduces us to Motel, clad in a carcerally striped shirt, furiously pedaling away at a manual sewing machine, and, for a brief moment snatched from the relentless, monotonous work routine, wiping the *shvits* from his sopping brow. Meanwhile, over the soundtrack, a nondiegetic ballad assumes narrational duties and provides the basic details of his hard life:

> Motel the Operator, in the shop, sews all day long.
> Year in year out he tows the line.
> He spins the wheel, and sweats by the machine.
> Motel is a fine young man.
> Motel has a wife and child. He toils for them.
> But the harder he works, the richer the boss gets,
> And Motel remains a pauper.

As so often in Yiddish cinema, the main character finds himself in the grip of a merciless system characterized by gross imbalances in (communicative) power. Accordingly, it is notable that the "villains" of the films, rather than being anomalous, stand-alone, so-called "evil individuals," almost invariably bear the stamp of one social institution or another, which they thus stand in for as representatives: for example, the doctor Reisner in *Where Is My Child?*, the theater manager Salkin in *The Living Orphan*, and, as we'll see, "the boss," as he is typologically listed in the credits, in *Motel the Operator*. Within the particular oppressive context represented in *Motel*, however, the subjugated protagonist possesses a perhaps more than usual amount of potential for resistance and the maintenance of dignity, given that the system of oppression, namely, the factory production process, directly relies on his participation. Such a possibility comes into view once the ballad about Motel concludes and, the sonic dimension of the scene shifting into a diegetic register, the workers perform a defiant work song in a classic call-and-response mode. Initiated by Motel's friend, neighbor, and coworker, the plucky Yosl Frumkin (Jacob Zanger, a Seiden regular who also plays Muni's socialistically inclined brother-in-law in *The Living Orphan*), and accompanied by the rapid tap-tapping of the machines, which keep a kind of metronomic rhythm, the song goes as follows (see figure 6.1):

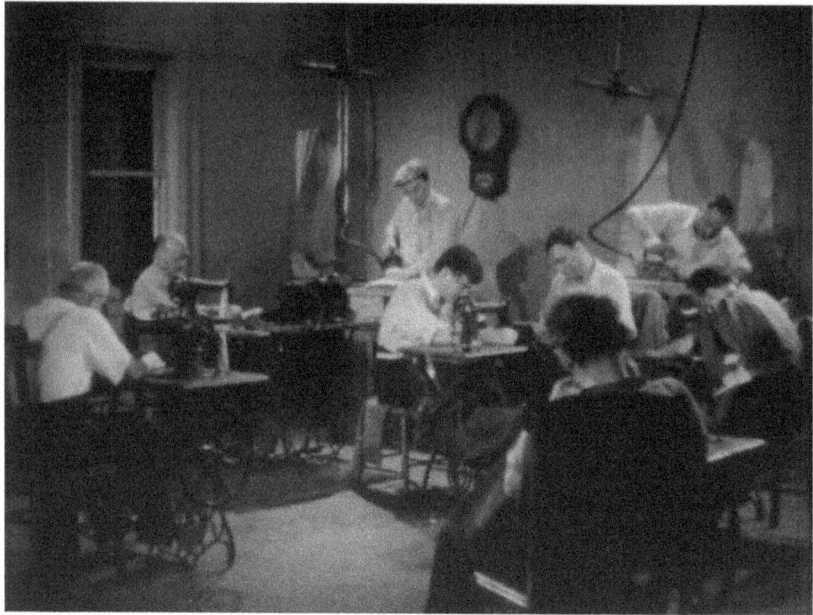

Figure 6.1. The workers in the garment factory perform a defiant work song. Joseph Seiden, *Motel the Operator* (1939).

[Chorus] Here's how a tailor sews, here's how a tailor toils.

[Yosl] When the days are cloudy for us poor tailors,
We don't sew clothes for ourselves,
We sew only for strangers.

[Chorus] Here's how a tailor sews, here's how a tailor toils.

In fact, the song is the same one used in Edgar G. Ulmer's *The Singing Blacksmith* (*Yankl der Shmid*, 1938)—a film similarly preoccupied with labor yet set back in the shtetl—in a scene in which the eponymous protagonist (Moishe Oysher, the well-known entertainer, cantor, and star of two other musically oriented Yiddish films) visits a small tailoring shop and sings along with the all-female workforce as the latter perform their needlework. (Notably, in a slightly earlier scene, the sewing women sing another work song, one in a melancholy key and choral mode, that tells of a poor female tailor whose lower-class status has forestalled her prospects for marriage, and thus for being liberated from the drudgery: "I sew and sew, / For someone else, not me. / I am already an old maiden, I have no dowry.") Lamenting the process of "how a tailor sews" (that is, not for "ourselves" but "only for strangers"), the work song featured in the two films vaunts a nakedly Marxist message regarding the alienation of the laborer.[6] Further, though the appearance of the song in Ulmer's film suggests non-nostalgically that tailors (or at any rate, female tailors) were prone to exploitation back in the Old Country, Seiden's transplantation of the song to a more industrial-style factory in America gives the song a different resonance, seeming to imply the disappearance of a time when tailoring, that quintessential Jewish profession, did have a better, more economically equitable and warmly artisanal and communitarian profile. Back then, it's possible to read between the lines of the song, a tailor would have been intimately connected with his manually produced products and with his customers, and would have derived a large share of his reputation within the community directly through his professional role (for instance, recall Dovid's friend Shimen in *A Little Letter to Mother*, who goes around personally delivering handmade garments to his customers). Now, it appears, all such bonds have been severed. No longer does tailoring provide the foundation for a meaningful identity, unless perhaps, as the film will soon explore, a form of collective action can radically transform the exploitative arena of production. In line with all this, in *The Singing Blacksmith*, there is another work song, "Strike the Hammer," a highly memorable solo tune sung by Yankl in his workshop in which he ecstatically compares himself to "a bird, free," and extols "the joy of work"; that is to say, the song's potently positive, almost utopian vision of labor almost unquestionably has to do with the fact that, unlike the tailoring men and women in the two films, Yankl is his own boss, owning and controlling the means of his production. Indeed, in this way, we might imagine the better-off, Old Country tailor seemingly evoked by the remediation of the work song in *Motel the Operator* as someone very much like Oysher's blacksmith.

    The narrative of *Motel the Operator* begins, as one can retroactively deduce from superimposed dates provided later on by the film, in that quaking year of world history, 1917, the year of the Bolshevik Revolution. Given the ethos of the year, in conjunction with the Marxist work song, it isn't surprising that when the factory boss (Izidor Frankel)—a harried, nebbishy figure—enters the scene, he instantly attempts to shut the song down:

> Boss: Hey! What's this singing? Get back to work. Stop staring at the ceiling. There are no birds up there, and no angels will be dropping pennies to you.
>
> Yosl: But for you, boss, they drop thousands!
>
> Boss: What? Did you say something?
>
> Yosl: Not I. But the Talmud [*gemore*] says the shofar will sound.

As in the work song, which he leads, Yosl again takes the initiative in challenging the boss's authority. He responds to his superior's sarcastic remark with a sarcastic remark of his own, drolly plays along when the boss denies his voice, and quotes the Talmud to subtly stinging effect. Indeed, Yosl's Talmudic evocation of a messianic blowing of the ram's horn evokes a thunderous blast of sound, as if to remind the boss that while he may have managed to silence the work song, and refuses to hear the workers even when they simply speak, his oppressive actions will ultimately be judged by a higher power that treats the voices of capitalists and workers as holding equal weight. (Like Elick in *Where Is My Child?*, Yosl recurrently utters such hard truths that others would rather keep suppressed, and thus, too, acts as a subversive, whistleblower figure.)

Moreover, Yosl's allusion to the Talmud works to ground the socialist energies of the scene in Jewish thought. As Abraham Cohen, in his interpretative study of Talmud, points out: "The relationship between employer and employee is strictly defined by the Talmud, and the responsibilities of each are very clearly specified. The matter is viewed as a contract between the two parties which must be scrupulously honored by both. For the master to withhold from the workman what is due to him, or vice versa, is denounced as fraud."[7] Indeed, the Talmud is full of demands for fairness and mutual responsibility in the relationship between workers and employers. Concerning the workday, for instance, it exhorts: "He who engages workmen and orders them to start early or continue late, in a place where they have custom not to start early or continue late, is not permitted to compel them (to exceed the usual hours of labor)."⁸ Resonating with this very demand, an unnamed worker, branded as the "ringleader" for threatening that everyone will "become socialists" and go on strike, rebuts the boss's command of "Enough talk!" with the counter-command of "Enough work!"—a reminder of the limits on the workday that the boss clearly has no intentions of respecting. Such ease with which Marxist and Talmudic ideas commingle makes ample sense, for, as Levinas, whose ethical philosophy of the Other (which we discuss more at length later in the chapter) is deeply grounded in the Talmud, points out: "In Marxism, there is not just conquest; there is recognition of the other," albeit of an atypical sort that "consists in saying: We can save the other if he himself demands his due."⁹

Broken Strike

When the workers at Motel's factory do demand their due, when they deliver on the ringleader's threat and go on strike—that resounding, radical act in response to a condition of troubled communication—everything up to that point in the film (the work song, Yosl's back talk, the ringleader's warning) has prepared us for a show of continued spirited defiance. For instance, we expect scenes akin to those evoked by that pivotal, legendary episode in Jewish American labor history, the shirtwaist makers' strike of 1909–1910, an action of some twenty thousand female employees, "most of them girls in their teens or early twenties, and about two thirds of them Jewish,"¹⁰ in which one young Jewish woman, Clara Lemlich, played a particularly catalyzing role. As Irving Howe tells of a meeting of the workers, union heads, and leaders of the Jewish socialist movement at Cooper Union on November 22, 1909, Lemlich eventually stormed the platform and "burst into a flow of passionate Yiddish which would remain engraved in thousands of memories: 'I am a working girl, one of those striking against intolerable conditions. I am tired of listening to speakers who talk in generalities. What we are here for is to decide whether or not to strike. I offer a resolution that a general strike be declared—now.'"¹¹ As for the strike itself, Howe quotes a contemporary newspaper account in the *Sun* that evokes a similar image of bold, boisterous resistance: "The girls, headed by teen-age Clara Lemlich, described by union organizers as a 'pint of trouble for the bosses,' began singing Italian and Russian working-class songs as they paced in twos before the factory door."[12] In *Motel the Operator*, however, as the film cuts from the opening scene inside the factory to a shot of the strikers outside on the street, we get a very different image of a strike. The previously created mood of upbeat feistiness undergoes a drastic deflation, heralding Motel's later descent into depersonalized outcasthood. In long shot, Motel and three other strikers, wearing Yiddish placards hung around their necks, pace back and forth on the grimy, trash-strewn pavement, in what resembles a funeral march. Nowhere to be seen is Yosl, who later abandons the strike to look for work elsewhere. The overall impression is one of staggering communicative enervation and impediment. Neither singing nor shouting, the workers flatly, intermittently state their appeals for support and "fair conditions." Indeed, the ambient urban background noise constitutes the loudest consistent sonic element of the scene (a result of questionably calculated, yet highly fitting, mic placement), containing the footsteps of an indifferent passerby, but none of those of the pacing strikers. In this way, the workers appear unable to make themselves heard, as if subject to an encroaching ghostliness, a metaphor to which the film later returns.

The film oscillates between the woeful scene outside the factory and a woeful scene at Motel's home, where his distraught wife Esther (Malvina Rappel) exhibits the dire ripple effect that the strike is having on the domestic sphere. Without any money coming in, Esther can't buy the food and medicine necessary to sustain her and Motel's infant son Jackie, who has fallen ill. Just after a doctor pays a house call to the tenement and gives his diagnosis, she goes over to a shelf above the stove, takes down a tattered box, and tilts it upside down over a pot—yet in vain, not even one crumb spilling out. As we discover, such scenes of distress are general among the workers' wives. For when the film returns to the strikers, a black-shawled woman, a kind of Lower East Side Cassandra, bursts on the scene and with trembling hands appeals to her husband: "Yone, please go back to work. The children are starving. You should all give in!" And she continues, in response to Motel's dug-in, idealistic commitment to the strike and chastisement that "a worker's wife shouldn't speak that way": "I speak. My troubles speak. I have four small children at home. They are speaking." Conjuring an image of proliferating speech, of the collateral distress of the wives and the children speaking volumes, the remark underscores the striking husbands and fathers' relative scarcity of voice, provides one more indication of the communicative fiasco of the workers' protest. Indeed, even when Motel appears in the domestic sphere, he is wrapped in an aura of alarming silence. "Motel, I didn't even hear you walk in!" Esther exclaims, after failing to notice him for several moments after he enters the room. To which he replies, recalling the drowned-out inaudibility of the strikers' footsteps on the picket line: "My shoes are worn out so I walk quietly." And he goes on, with a wretchedly drooped head, addressing Esther's disclosure that the drugstore refused to give them more credit, and driving home his sense of spectral absence and helplessness: "Believe me, I would sell myself into slavery for you and Jackie. But no one wants to buy me."

The situation reaches a fever pitch of catastrophe in another, and what will turn out to be the last, scene on the picket line. It is a scene to which the newspaper account of the shirtwaist makers' strike again offers an instructive anti-parallel. The article continues: "Of a sudden, around the corner came a dozen tough-looking customers, for whom the union label 'gorillas' seems well-chosen. 'Stand fast, girls,' called Clara, and then the thugs rushed the line, knocking Clara to her knees, striking at the pickets, opening the way for a group of frightened scabs to slip through the broken line."[13] In the scene in the film, one such "gorilla" lies in wait for Motel. As Motel stands in front of the factory door, a gangster hired by the factory boss comes out and hits him over the head with a bottle, knocking him unconscious and sending him tumbling to the pavement (see figure 6.2). Unlike Clara, whom the article represents as putting up intrepid, steadfast resistance to the incursion of strike-breaking violence, Motel is shown as an utterly vulnerable sitting duck. Even after the gangster appears and opens the door and winds up to deliver the blow, Motel remains completely motionless with a hand in his pocket, not suspecting a thing; and he never does get an idea of what hits him, going straight from such ignorance to unconsciousness.

Characteristically for Yiddish cinema, the film emphasizes the communicative, or more accurately excommunicative, dimension of Motel's victimization. As in the initial part of the opening scene, the soundtrack is taken over by a narratorial, nondiegetic song. "Motel stands in the picket line. A gangster with a bottle. He fell there," run the blunt lyrics in their entirety (jarringly, the scene is less than ten seconds long). We thus hear nothing of the action that the scene depicts: not the sound of the bottle thudding against Motel's skull,

Figure 6.2. A strike-breaking gangster hits Motel over the head and knocks him unconscious. Joseph Seiden, *Motel the Operator* (1939).

not the frantic shouting of the other strikers who rush over to him in the aftermath of the attack, nothing. It is as if the whole world of the narrative is suddenly, drastically silenced along with Motel, who ends up suffering a complete breakdown of his communicative faculties as a result of the traumatic blow to his head. Moreover, the placement of the Yiddish placard—hanging around his neck and communicating the message of the strike—at the very center of the frame reinforces the sense of violence being done to Motel as a specifically communicative agent: as Motel tumbles to the ground and out of the image, so his message vanishes along with him.

The Abandoned Mother and Phantasmatic Communication

Whisked away in an ambulance and taken to a hospital, yet another institutional setting, Motel next appears, thick bandages swaddled around his head, lying in a bed in a state of dire communicative impairment: semiconscious, staring out with blankly dark-circled eyes, only able to murmur to himself, to spew a temporally slip-sliding series of fragmented, traumatic (dis)articulations in the presence of his visiting wife and friends. With Motel thus incapacitated, the film turns to Esther, who as a result of the medical emergency is plunged into a parental crisis analogous to the one faced by her widowed namesake in *Where Is My Child?* Like Esther in the earlier film, Motel's suddenly abandoned wife cannot support her child and therefore confronts the prospect of putting the child in the care of others. Importantly, however, for the mother in *Motel the Operator*, such a prospect means putting the child up for adoption outright, in full consciousness of the process and what it entails. In other words, the second Esther is made to understand the full implications of the contract that she would be signing: that is, the total abrogation of her maternal rights. In this way, the film registers another divergence from *Where Is My Child?* and defines the mother's dilemma in terms of a sharply delineated sacrifice of her own rights for those of her child, instead of a deceptive intrusion by a third-party that breaches both her own and the child's rights (recall Victor's claim that, despite the loving family that raised him, he was nevertheless powerfully damaged by those who took his young mother away from him). "Have you the right to deny your child's happiness?" asks Mr. Benson (Joseph Schoengold)—a shady, mercenary agent from an adoption society, essentially the equivalent of the villainous Dr. Reisner in the earlier film—in response to Esther's initial expression of dismay at the prospect of "a struggling, suffering mother . . . giv[ing] up her child forever." Nevertheless, despite Benson's dishonorable intentions, even the "good" and merely morally "neutral" characters impart much the same message to Esther. "You must consider your child's happiness, [his] life," the doctor implores her in a similarly reproving manner. Meanwhile, the adoption process itself is put into motion by Yosl's well-meaning wife Chana Beile (Yetta Zwerling), who offers a nugget of folkloric wisdom passed down from her mother: "Better a rich man in a strange place than a poor man at home." (As we'll see, a version of the same agonizing, sacrificial dilemma that Esther finds herself in repeats vis-à-vis Motel later on.)

Ultimately, Esther goes through with giving up her child for adoption, and the result is a straightaway plunge into morbid mental derangement. Once Benson and a female assistant leave the apartment with little Jackie and the adoption papers (which the mother had signed lifelessly, in an alarming cessation of weeping, with the agent hovering over her and deviously manipulating her fingers), Esther is impelled into phantasmatic dialogue with her incommunicado husband, to whom she had paid one more visit at the hospital, begging him to talk and offer counsel and receiving only distracted babble in return ("The machines are knocking. They turn and turn. Faster and faster"). Amid the commencement of ominously brooding underscoring, a disembodied voice from offscreen calls out Esther's name and asks, "Where is our child?": a virtual name-check of the film's crucial predecessor. Meanwhile, in between the calling out of her name and the question, the film cuts to a close-up of a framed photo of Motel—an image in which he appears as if out of a horror movie: creepily somber and rigid, dressed up in a redolently Gothic, starched suit and tie, buttoned all the way up to the top—presumably located somewhere in the room and serving to drive home the identity of the voice. Thus the film activates the motif of the still image "coming alive" that, as we discussed in the previous chapter in relation to the lullaby that Esther sings to the photograph of her missing child, appears throughout Yiddish cinema. Here, however, although the image does effectively, aurally "come to life," the phenomenon works in a manner similar to the photograph inexorably resisting animation in the earlier film. That is to say, once more, the photographic interaction ultimately withholds relief and points up disconnection.

In fact, however, the scene's allusive calling back to *Where Is My Child?* goes even further. Intensifying the chain of intertextual references, Esther responds to Motel's question by reenacting the unforgettable moment in the earlier film where the mother creates a substitute child out of the bedding in the asylum. "Our Jackie is here, right here," Esther replies, as she goes over to the freshly empty cradle and picks up a pillow, which she proceeds to cradle, rock, kiss, and address: "Dear sweet child, your mother will never give you up." In contrast to the corresponding scene in the previous film, however, the phantasmatic act is outright disturbing: an indication of ever-further-encroaching insanity and suicidal self-destructiveness rather than preservation of sanity and self (much of the difference hinges on the fact that one mother persistently holds out hope of recovering her child, whereas the other believes such a recovery to be impossible). And indeed, as she goes through with the adoption, so Esther goes through with the suicide. Closing the window, locking the door, and switching on the elements on the stove, she does so by evocative means of the very gas that, as we learn earlier, is slated to be turned off because of an accumulation of missed payments. Perversely, it is as if the utility company holds off on cutting off the supply of gas just long enough to allow Esther to complete the fatal act. As with the portrait, the phantasmatic interaction with the pillow thus only further exacerbates Esther's isolating condition, failing to help her withstand or resist the forces working to keep her separated from her family.

Responsibility to the Other: Levinas and Buber

In the wake of Esther's pitiable suicide, the film turns its focus back to Motel, making two big leaps ahead in time that eventually bring him and his son back into a species of contact, which in turn initiates a flurry of complex ethical relations between the two—relations that, as we'll see, traffic resonantly in Levinasian and Buberian notions, and ultimately assume a form that align most closely with the latter. In the first temporal jump, spanning three years, Motel emerges from his practically catatonic state, only to encounter a series of disorienting revelations that swiftly propel him into yet another spiral of depersonalization. The doctor and nurse at the hospital, seemingly anxious about re-devastating their freshly recovered patient, conspiratorially refrain from informing him about the death of his wife and the adoption of his child. When he returns to his old address, however, what he discovers is not simply a house without Esther and Jackie but rather the total physical annihilation of the building where the family used to live—a pile of wreckage that sensationally seems more like the product of wartime aerial bombing than ordinary peacetime slum clearance (one will recall this trope of a return to find no home from *The Living Orphan*, and we will encounter it again in *Long Is the Road*). The ruins succinctly metaphorize the wholesale loss of Motel's world, induced by the strike-breaking episode on the picket line, and affirm its uncertain prolongation. Indeed, as Motel stumbles away from the ruins, the film launches into its second major leap ahead in time, expressed via a montage spanning from 1920 to 1940 that evocatively consists of close-ups of Motel's feet no longer pedaling laboriously, like they did at the factory, but rather wandering in an increasingly aimless and faltering manner, and concludes (with the camera tilting up from his feet to his face in a formal echo of his initial introduction) with an image of Motel transformed into a hobo living on the streets: nestled up against a stoop, garbed (flimsily) in a ragged coat and crumpled hat, his beard now speckled white, owing to aging and/or exposure to the wintry elements. The shift is incredible, for it appears that over the course of the two decades since coming out of the coma Motel did not, or could not, track down a single relative or coworker or friend who might have helped mitigate such an extreme descent into nonrelationality. It is almost as if all forms of media—telephone, postal service, city records—that might have assisted him in connecting with anyone from his former life beyond his immediate family were stringently denied to him. Worse, as becomes clear, Motel forgets his entire identity, possessing no recollection of ever being "Motel the Operator." All that remains of his selfhood is a whittled-down nub of pain, a traumatic core by which he can access his past only in an abstract, quasi-mythological way. Selling flowers on the street in order to survive, he sings a ballad to a street crowd:

> I will tell you a story,
> How the white flower was born.
> Once a father and a mother
> Lost their only son.
> The mother died,
> The father left all alone.
> He hasn't anything to live for anymore.

And yet, in a seesawing of fate extreme even by *shund* standards, Motel soon *re*-regains his selfhood, for a second time since the strike-breaking incident, not long afterward. To recap the baroque involutions by which this comes about: Benson, the adoption agent, who it turns out has for years been blackmailing Jackie's wealthy adoptive father, Benjamin Rosenwald (Maurice Kroner), and threatening to reveal Jackie's true origins, encounters Motel on the street, makes a superficial show of kindness toward him, and conscripts him into a new stage of the blackmail process necessitated by the adoptive father finally refusing to be extorted any longer. With no clue as to the identity of the tramp—who himself doesn't know who he is—Benson takes Motel out to a restaurant, plies him with food, and instructs him to come with him to the Rosenwalds and play a role: "Tell them that you are Motel Friedman. You were called Motel the Operator. And your wife's name was Esther Friedman. And your son's name is Jackie." Motel doesn't recognize his own name, further illustrating his dissolution of self over the years in which no one called him by his name or took any interest in him. Yet the names of his wife and son do not similarly elude him, managing to bring back an awareness of the past, which he quickly, strategically conceals from Benson. "Come with me, but remember who you are," the wily stage manager instructs, to which Motel excitedly responds, as if waking up from another lengthy coma, and not only recalling who he was but also affirming who he still is: "Of course I remember. I am a father. Motel Friedman, Motel the Operator. I am going to see my son, Jackie. My son."

Everything is thus prepared for the disclosure of the relations between the adopted child and the biological parent, and consequently for the reunion of the two long-estranged family members. However, it is at this point that the film embarks on its major divergence from the plot pattern of *Where Is My Child?* As we learn earlier, Jackie (Seymour Rechtzeit) has grown up into a thriving young man: a handsome law school grad, recently made a partner at his father's firm, and engaged to a girl from another well-off family, Ruth Frumkin (Gertrude Krause), coincidentally, the daughter of Motel's old friend Yosl, who in the years since the strike has built a successful pants manufacturing business. As Motel in a state of trembling anticipation enters the living room of the Rosenwalds' upper-middle-class house—where, in an evocation of cheerful familial contentment, Jackie and Mr. Rosenwald have been playing chess under the watch of Mrs. Rosenwald (Bertha Hart)—the sight of his son instantly overwhelms Motel, causing him to swoon and collapse to the floor. Amid the ensuing commotion, it is the conscientious Jackie who takes the lead solicitous role, calling for a glass of water, and proceeding to feed the distressed stranger sips. Such an interaction between the father and son radiates with mysterious connective energy, which continues to flow powerfully as Mr. Rosenwald (who for obvious reasons wants to resolve the situation in private) urges that Jackie leave the room. Accordingly, as he is being reluctantly led out of the room by his mother, Jackie rivetedly stares at the stranger, at which point the film cuts to an extreme close-up of Motel gazing intensely back at his child, his dark-pitted eyes welling up with tears, his fluttering, dumbly parting mouth seeming to choke back words (see figures 6.3 and 6.4). It is tempting to read the moment, particularly the poignant close-up of the wretched vagabond, in terms of Levinas's famous notion of "the Face," a strongly spiritual formation assumed by the Other that acts as the medium through which the demand for responsibility is made upon the I. According to Levinas, the Face involves the I in "a relation to the absolutely weak—to what is absolutely exposed, what is bare and destitute."[14] Or more specifically, and surprisingly and strangely, such a sense of radical vulnerability in the Other paradoxically calls up in the I a temptation to *murder* the Other *and* a resistance to that very temptation, an opposition embodied by the biblical commandment of "Thou Shalt Not Kill."[15] Within this scenario of complicated ambivalence, the I's responsibility to the Other takes on a form that Levinas conceives as "infinite," that is, as effectively unattainable (thus something ever to be striven after) and nonreciprocal (thus operative entirely independently of whatever the Other's own relation to the I may be). As Levinas explains, illustrating his "central idea" by contrasting his ethical philosophy with Buber's:

> And you see (and this seems important to me), the relationship with the other is not symmetrical, it is not at all as in Martin Buber. When I say *Thou* to an *I*, to a me, according to Buber I would always have that me before me as the one who says Thou to me. Consequently, there would be a reciprocal relationship. According to my analysis, on the other hand, in the relation to the Face, it is asymmetry that is affirmed: at the outset I hardly care what the other is with respect to me, that is his own business; for me, he is above all the one I am responsible for.[16]

Indeed, if we view matters from the outside, the asymmetry that Levinas describes appears ever more evident in the relationship between Jackie and Motel, as the son goes on to devote himself with ever more extreme selflessness to the father, whose already dire situation grows worse and worse.

However, equipped as we are with an insight into Motel's secret, we can appreciate that the relationship is in fact intensely dialogical. As he is being ministered to by Jackie, it begins fully to sink in for

Figure 6.3. Reluctantly ushered out of the room by his adoptive mother, Jackie gazes empathically at the vagabond stranger, who he does not know is his birth father. Joseph Seiden, *Motel the Operator* (1939).

Figure 6.4. Returning Jackie's gaze, Motel tearfully chokes back words and withholds revealing his true identity to his son. Joseph Seiden, *Motel the Operator* (1939).

Motel what a splendid *mentsh* his son has turned out to be in the prosperous, loving environment, and thus he decides, crucially, to break with his meta-dramatically redoubled role as Motel Friedman and to stay silent about who he really is, so as not to disturb the family peace. In other words, Motel freely gives up his paternal claim—piercingly, just at the moment of the opportunity of restoring it—in order to enact his fatherly responsibility on a deeper level. Accordingly, the close-up of his face (Face) as he and Jackie attune to one another and lock gazes conveys the difficult psychic and emotional maneuvering entailed by such an act of generously protective withholding, and by extension evokes not so much Levinas's vision of a radically asymmetrical responsibility to the Other but rather a paradigmatic instance of Buber's "turning," of "the mutuality of the inner action" that both institutes dialogue and reveals dialogue as already in process.

Makeshift Identity and Parental Rights

From this point on, the film devotes itself to an elaboration of such "turning," which it portrays as not only beginning in but also potently remaining bound up with silence, and which hinges on another sensational plot twist. Namely, Benson ends up being killed when, in a tussle with Motel that takes place after Mr. Rosenwald exits the living room in an exasperated, desperate surrender to an indefinite continuation of the blackmailing, the villain's revolver (a hardly out-of-place prop in the pulpish world of *shund*) accidentally goes off. In this way, Motel gets rid of the greatest immediate threat to his secret, and at the same time, unable to explain himself to the authorities without giving himself away, becomes a suspect in the death. Accordingly, he finds himself in yet another imposing institutional setting: this time jail, where he awaits trial. Nevertheless, Motel's newest predicament, one in which he faces the likely possibility of being convicted of murder, proves significantly less distressing than being an exploited factory worker or a comatose hospital patient. This is because now, in prison, as a way of enacting his responsibility to his child, he actively elects silence and withholds his voice, instead of enduring its externally instigated repression or loss. Meanwhile, since such a process appears on the outside to effect a dramatic escalation in his unfortunate condition, it in turn causes his child to take more and more responsibility for him. That is to say, Jackie volunteers to take Motel's case, functioning analogously to Victor in *Where Is My Child?* as a mediating voice for the voiceless outsider, as a uniquely humane professional in an arena (here law instead of medicine) that just so happens to coincide with that in which the enigmatic "nobody" requires aid. Indeed, Jackie launches into the case with zeal, notably dismissing his parents' concern over him becoming further embroiled in the scandal. "A lawyer's duty is to help the unfortunate, and defend the innocent," he righteously protests, as the next day the three pore over a copy of the Yiddish newspaper *Der Tog*, which, as if Motel's muteness has whipped up a hypercommunicative press frenzy over his mysterious motivations, contains coverage of the fatal incident.

Once we are taken inside the jail, represented minimalistically through a spare section of cells, the film shows Motel doing everything in his power to deflect Jackie's penetrating inquiries into his identity (i.e., "Open your heart to me as if I were your son") in order to sustain his sacrosanct course of silence. Indeed, he even goes so far as to defensively, at the last second, improvise an entirely *new* identity for himself when the interrogation risks becoming too overpowering: "Mot—oh, my name. Harry . . . Harry Greenspan." Despite its emergence within a story of fantastic proportions, such a fabrication, uttered under the pressures of legal duress, speaks to something all-too-true regarding the history of the early twentieth-century Jewish experience. As the essayist and novelist Joseph Roth writes in his endlessly incisive book on the state of Eastern European Jews in the interwar period, *The Wandering Jews*, first published in 1927: "To stick to one name that might not be his but would be a plausible and believable name anyway. The police have given the Eastern Jew the idea of concealing a true but tangled set of circumstances behind bogus but tidy ones."[17] No doubt like many immigrants, Jewish immigrants (the quote from Roth comes from a chapter on Jewish "ghettoes" in Vienna, Berlin, and Paris) often felt the need to resort to "simplified" identities in the face of impatient authorities, who perceived their factual, but bureaucratically unruly, information as convoluted, confusing, or incredible. Interestingly, however, Motel's invention of a new identity works at the same time to further his project of personal legitimation—a result that another of Roth's insights, this time on the relationship between Jews and names, can further illuminate. Explaining "the Jews' lack of attachment to their names," he writes: "For Jews their names have no value because they are not their names. Jews, Eastern Jews, have no names. They have compulsory aliases. Their true name is the one by which they are summoned to the Torah on the Sabbath and on the holy days: their Jewish first name, and the Jewish first name of their father. Their family names, however, from Goldenberg to Hescheles, are pseudonyms foisted upon them. Governments have commanded Jews to have names."[18] In a strange twist on this trend, the "pseudonym," the "compulsory alias," that Motel adopts in place of his Jewish first name, for the sake of satisfying Jackie's interrogations, works to enable him to pursue his course of silent responsibility and thus precisely to perpetuate what he believes to be his "true" identity. For Motel, the substitution of his all-important first name allows him to assume that name ever more deeply. (Relatedly, in an extension of this concern with names and identity beyond the main plotline, Yosl and Chane Beile also come to assume new names, yet as part of their dramatic economic ascent, which comes across as entailing a certain assimilationist smothering of religious and class origins. Yosl becomes "Joseph," and Chana "Annabella." At the same time, however, in line with Roth's point, neither appears terribly attached to the new, more English-friendly moniker. Indeed, in a musical number, a rollicking, klezmer-style duet, the two jokingly toggle back and forth between the old and new names in a spirit of giddy amusement.)

Aside from his fabricated identity, Motel "divulges" nothing more of any substantial nature to Jackie, only breaking out of his silence once he is left alone and engages in a phantasmatic conversation with Esther, his dead wife. Shortly after the lawyer departs, invoked by her husband as he grips the bars of his cell, Esther materializes in a superimposed, locket-like iris shot, appearing strikingly composed and dignified (white blouse, hair pulled back, gentle smile), in deep contrast to the last time that we saw her, in the earlier scene of phantasmatic "dialogue," in which, on the brink of suicidal madness, she is addressed by the haunting photograph of her husband. Coming to the heart of the matter—as we realize, the real purpose of the conversation is for Motel to debate his silent course of action regarding Jackie—Esther implores him, "Motel, he [Jackie] must know everything . . . You have a right to your son. You have a right to be happy." Esther's conscription of the language of rights and happiness in order to make her case recalls her own experience with Jackie earlier on, that is, her sacrifice of her maternal rights for the sake of the child's right to happiness. However, Esther urges Motel to take a different path from the one she took, and consider not only his paternal rights but also his *own* right to happiness: a recommendation made eminently defensible by the difference between the two sets of circumstances, by the fact that the present moment is a far cry from the long ago moment when the sick, malnourished child would have been put fatally at risk by staying in his destitute mother's custody. Nonetheless, Motel remains steadfast, implicitly insisting on the equivalence between their predicaments, imagining that if he were to disclose himself to Jackie he *would* in a sense be risking Jackie's life, which is the only life that the child (consciously) knows: "No, God forbid. He mustn't [know everything]. It would break his heart. He told me that he loves his parents very much, Mr. and Mrs. Rosenwald . . . Oh, Esther. It is too late for my happiness. I am so tired. My life will soon be over. I will soon be with you . . ." In this way, Motel emerges from the phantasmatic communication all the more emboldened in his decision not to disclose himself to Jackie, while the interaction, which once again evokes, via the portrait-style framing around Esther, the motif of the still image "coming alive," works, in spite of the anchoring of the exchange in a difference of opinion, in the way that such interactions most often do in Yiddish cinema—that is, to bring the separated that much closer together.

The Silent *Sheliekh* and the Two Fathers

Throbbing with complicated, unexpected communicative potential, Motel's silence takes center stage at his trial, an official, state proceeding that, of course, is conducted in Yiddish (save for a handful of intermittent bilingual toggles into English: "Your honor . . . ," "Gentleman of the jury . . . ," ". . . Thank you"), and involves a jury, a group of sternly contemplating men, blatantly repurposed from another, much grainier, film. Up on the stand in a state of nervous agitation, Motel is grilled by the aggressive, bespectacled DA, who puts a distinctively negative spin on the defendant's silence, harping upon it, demanding to know why Motel perpetuates it, and arguing for its fundamentally incriminating nature: "Your silence confirms your guilt." However, since Motel refuses to budge, it is left to Jackie, a conveniently dazzling, gifted orator (like Victor in *Where Is My Child?* and the young rabbi in *Kol Nidre*), to paint a persuasive counterpicture of his unforthcoming client. In his rousing closing statement, appealing to the jury's "sense of humanity. . . . [to] what is right, just, and humane," Jackie thus argues that Motel acted in self-defense against a man who was manipulating and terrorizing him, and in so doing not only deserves no blame but in fact performed a feat of divine justice: "No, gentlemen, that man [Motel] is no criminal. He is no murderer. He is a messenger of the Supreme Judge. He who judges us all. He carried out the sentence that Benson justly deserved. The verdict of the highest judge has been carried out. In the name of that high justice, I beg you—no, I demand that your verdict be 'Not guilty.'" In his characterization of Motel as a "messenger," Jackie uses the Hebrew-derived word *sheliekh* (from *shaliach*), whose synonyms include "envoy" and "emissary," and which is replete with traditional, religious connotations; moreover, the related word *shlikhes* can mean "mission" and "assignment,"[19] as well as "responsibility."[20] Employing this rhetorical tack (which intersects with the motif of the messenger in Yiddish cinema more broadly, and evocatively transforms the "American" trial into a full-blown, theologically invested Jewish trial), Jackie recasts Motel's silence, which the DA treats as a void that implies monstrous things, as itself a form of communication, and indeed, of the most vital sort: a form of communication bearing a message from God Himself. It is a move perfectly calibrated to the universe of Yiddish cinema—a universe, that is, in which communication is all important—and thus not surprisingly wins the day, persuading the jury and absolving the "mute," higher-order messenger of all the charges against him.

Rescued from his legal quagmire, Motel undergoes a kind of rebirth, emerges from the situation (in Mr. Rosenwald's words) a "new man," revived in body and spirit, and continuing to go under the name of "Harry Greenspan." However, what still lingers in uncertainty is the status of his (re)connection with Jackie going forward, and it is this question that the film's final scene takes up. We are brought, at last, to a wedding, namely, Jackie's, which previously the virtuously dutiful lawyer had delayed so that he could more fully commit himself to the trial. Naturally, Motel is invited, and when we first see him—handsomely put together, dressed in a respectable suit, his former scraggly beard trimmed into a well-managed moustache—at the event at the Rosenwalds' house he is approached by Mr. Rosenwald, who finds him amid the bustling celebrations "all alone." Swiftly invoking the critical question mentioned earlier, Motel veers the mutual exchange of pleasantries and congratulations into a rare request, which he formulates in his shy, sincere manner: "As Jackie, your son, embedded himself in my heart, [and] saved my life, I would like to give him my blessing before he goes to the wedding canopy." Generously, Mr. Rosenwald agrees, allowing another to carry out, or at least share in, this task that traditionally would be reserved for himself; and though we don't see Motel impart his blessing to Jackie, the film drives home his status as a kind of "second" father to the groom during the representation of the remainder of the ceremony. Captured in a long shot of the crowded scene around the chuppah, Motel is permitted to stand right next to the fathers of the couple, in the inner familial circle as it were. Further, in the same moment, Motel's course of responsible silence, through which he instantiates his fatherhood, is brought to the fore once more. In a series of close-ups that call back to the vital close-up of him during the tumultuous, initial reencounter with Jackie, he weepingly spills over with emotion while appearing to "say" something in a distinctly noiseless fashion—his mouth a-flutter, though without anything coming out. Indeed, Motel's special silence appears *more* silent here than ever before, thrown into relief by the soaring, full-throated, chorally backed prayer of the officiating rabbi/cantor (Liebele Waldman, whom we encountered before in *Kol Nidre*).

At this stage in the narrative, the only remaining threat to Motel's course of action would seem to come from his old friend and coworker at the factory, Yosl, the father of the bride, and the film confronts this potential source of spoliation head-on in its final moments, finessing and negotiating it in such a way that sheds further light on the future of Motel's relation to Jackie, as well as to the Rosenwald family as a whole. In fact, the threat posed by Yosl would seem to be particularly extreme, given that the character, as mentioned earlier (and consistent with his tendency to act as a wise-cracking deflator of postures of arrogance and power), displays an attitude of ironic detachment toward his newfangled status as a wealthy, cigar-chomping magnate. That is to say, as Yosl never forgets or develops an embattled relationship to his past—compare his remark, which invokes the traditional Jewish stress on memory and brings it to bear on the phenomenon of immigrant upward mobility: "As the Talmud says, remember the covenant. It is fine to remember the old tailoring troubles"—he would seem to be all the more likely to recognize Motel. And indeed, lo and behold, in the aftermath of the ceremony, he does, causing a commotion amid the crowd and crying out, while pointing a shaking, identifying finger alternately at Motel and himself: "This is Motel Friedman. My old friend, Motel the Operator." However, despite his good memory for Motel, Yosl is unable to go a step further and make the vital connection between his old friend and Jackie; in other words, perhaps forgetting that Motel's son was named Jackie, he fails to grasp the true significance of his revelation. At the same time, such an understanding *does* arrive for Mr. Rosenwald, who, having earlier learned the name of Jackie's real father from Benson, puts the pieces together.

Thus becoming the only person to know Motel's secret, Mr. Rosenwald hastily pulls Motel aside, shuffling him off into the other room, where, in an uninterrupted two-shot, the last shot of the film, over the celebratory music faintly streaming through the walls, the two have a private, tearfully emotional exchange, whose hashed-out agreement is sealed with a handshake that melts into an embrace (see figure 6.5).

Figure 6.5. Motel and Mr. Rosenwald, Jackie's adoptive father, enter into an understanding about Motel's choice to remain silent and continue withholding his identity from Jackie. Joseph Seiden, *Motel the Operator* (1939).

MR. ROSENWALD: You knew that Jackie is your son?

MOTEL: Yes, I knew.

MR. ROSENWALD: And you kept silent?

MOTEL: Yes, and I will remain silent until my death. I will not disturb your happiness. You are good people. Be happy.

MR. ROSENWALD: How will I be able to thank you?

MOTEL: I have my thanks, Jackie is happy. I ask only one thing, Mr. Rosenwald. Invite me to visit from time to time. So I can see him, even if from afar.

MR. ROSENWALD: You are a good and noble person. You will be with us always.

It is instructive to compare this closing moment with that of *Where Is My Child?* In the earlier film, as we spent considerable time analyzing, the reemergence of the birth parent results in a painful usurpation of the adoptive parent, a dire excommunication of the latter from the newly formed, intimate structure of relations, tragically despite her loving and being loved: a state of affairs driven home in the final shot in which the devastated adoptive mother is quite literally pushed out of the picture, visually eclipsed by the interlocked unit of birth mother, son, and fiancée. *Motel the Operator* winds up somewhere considerably different, if not quite offering a binarizing, polar opposite conclusion. Namely, on conditions facilitated by Motel's vital, enduring silence, and by, in turn, Mr. Rosenwald's affording of Motel a place in the family (a place still considerably undefined but perhaps more involved than Motel's request merely to see Jackie "from afar"), *both* the birth parent and the adoptive parent are permitted to remain in the picture: a state of affairs that the final image of the film, too, like the final image of *Where Is My Child?*, renders on a literal plane, via the static composition in which both of the characters retain a place in the frame for the duration of the shot. In this way, *Motel the Operator* tentatively conjures up in its dying seconds what we might describe as a covertly remodeled version of the traditional bourgeois family that allows for, as it were, "two fathers." Such an arrangement is far from "perfect," far from void of fraught elements, still reliant upon that distinctive conditionality that we've seen again and again in the endings of Yiddish films. And yet, needless to say, it is a far more congenial arrangement than the one at the end of *Where Is My Child?*—and moreover, to invoke a famous Hollywood precedent, than the one at the end of the two adaptations of the 1923 Olive Higgins Prouty novel *Stella Dallas* (the silent version made in 1925, the sound remake in 1937), in both of which, though the kindly, genteel stepmother ensures that the curtains are kept open in order to provide the sacrificing birth mother with a glimpse of her daughter's marriage through the window, a glimpse that prompts a complex, heartened, film-capping smile, the birth mother is still pointedly excluded from the proceedings, kept outside in the pouring rain (in contrast to Motel, who attends the ceremony, blesses his child, and stands nearly next to him), and is not implied to have a future place with the new family, which maintains the traditional bourgeois formal structure of one mother and one father. Such is the power of *Motel the Operator*'s unique mobilization of "silence which is communication"—a silence that, unlike the unidirectional, properly Levinasian silence of the mother in *Stella Dallas* (reinforced in the 1925 adaptation by the daughter staring out the window just before the wedding, and, though appearing to be on the verge of spotting her mother outside amid the crowd of onlookers, seeing only her own reflection in the pane), is met by the ministrations of the righteous child, and thus takes up a place within a reciprocal, dialogical, properly Buberian structure of relations.

At the same time, one can't entirely discount the consequences of the fact that in *Motel the Operator* it is a father rather than a mother who is at the heart of the narrative of parent-child separation, exemplifying a fascinating, gender-swapping variation on maternal melodramas like *Where Is My Child?* and the two versions of *Stella Dallas*. What thus appears operative is a tacit assumption regarding motherhood and its unique claim to, or embeddedness in, "the natural," that resonates with the famous aperçu in James Joyce's *Ulysses*, "Paternity may be a legal fiction." In other words, it is as if motherhood, purportedly "nonfictitious," fundamentally "real" and "natural," lacks a special capacity for elasticity, whereas paternity, purportedly a "fiction," is, somehow (this "somehow" being crucial, as the complex communicative silence in *Motel the Operator* attests) amenable to multiplicity, to a "more than one" condition that, remarkably, in the very face of the dominance of the traditional bourgeois family, allows for a subtle, congenial mutation in the form of such an organization.

7

Groundlessness I (The Nation against the Jew)

The Wandering Jew (1933)

Despite its obscurity in its own day and still today, *The Wandering Jew* (*Der Vandernder Yid*) enjoys a pair of notable distinctions. First, it is the earliest feature film made in America to critique the Nazi regime. That is to say, shot on Long Island in the summer of 1933, mere months after Hitler's rise to power, the film got a massive head start on Hollywood, which, as Thomas Doherty recounts in *Hollywood and Hitler, 1933–1939*, did not substantively sound the alarm about Nazism until many years later. Tracing how the studios possessed "no commercial incentive and plenty of official disincentive"[1] for producing negative representations of Hitler, Doherty judiciously writes: "In the nearly seven years between Hitler's seizure of power and the outbreak of the war in Europe, the meaning of Nazism came slowly to Hollywood, like a picture just out of focus—fuzzy and dimly lit at first, sharp and fully outlined only at the end."[2] *The Wandering Jew*'s second important distinction lies within the smaller domain of Yiddish cinema: that is, it is the only Yiddish film made prior to World War II that involves a *direct* grappling with Nazism (in contrast, say, to a film like *Tevye*, whose evocation of Nazism is refracted through an earlier, trying historical period for Jews, the period around the turn of the century in the Russian Empire). The film takes the form, as Hoberman aptly puts it in an account that was written at a time when *The Wandering Jew* was still considered lost, and thus that derives from reviews and other archival material, as an "exposé *cum* visionary pep-talk."[3] In narrative terms, this translates into a strongly media-centric story about excommunication, a very Yiddish-cinematic story despite its exceptional setting in Nazi Germany, in which a successful, assimilated German Jewish painter and professor at the Berlin Academy of Art, Arthur Levi (played by the debonair Yiddish theater actor and later codirector of *Green Fields*, Jacob Ben-Ami), finds himself increasingly, precariously cut off and cast out from society under the new antisemitic race laws. In this way, the work—directed by George Roland, a major player in Yiddish cinema with a diverse range of credits, and written by Jacob Mestel, a Yiddish theater actor who went on to become an important historian of the Yiddish stage[4]—offers a fascinating enactment of Flusser's key, autobiographically infused, existential concept of "groundlessness" (*Bodenlosigkeit*).

Groundlessness

Flusser most likely took the term "ground" (*Boden*) from his key influence, the founder of phenomenology Edmund Husserl. In Husserl, "ground" refers to the transcendental spatial form that, together with the transcendental temporal form of the "horizon" (*Horizont*), constitutes "the lifeworld" (*Lebenswelt*), the pregiven world that provides the basis for consciousness.[5] Modifying Husserl, however, Flusser strips "ground" of its transcendental import and employs the term in reference to cultural models that habitually *appear* pre-given, and that enable people to invest their fundamentally chaotic, random, and absurd lives with meaning (*Sinngebung*). His usage of the term, that is to say, falls in line with his general view of human communication—informed by information theory—as a "negentropic" activity that opposes "the meaningless context in which we are completely alone and incommunicado, that is, the world in which we are condemned to solitary confinement and death: the world of 'nature.'"[6] As he writes at the outset of his experimental autobiography *Groundless* (*Bodenlos*), a book written in the early 1970s, in both a German and a Portuguese version (neither of which was published in his lifetime), that provides his most sustained meditation on the titular concept: "'The absurd' is a term that means, in the majority of cases, 'groundless,' in the same sense as 'meaningless,' just like the planetary system is groundless when we ask, 'Why do the planets orbit around the Sun in that abyssal void?'"[7]

As Flusser goes on to explain, the concept is for him more specifically associated with his world-shattering experience of the Nazi invasion of Prague, the city where he was born and grew up, and whose ethos he extollingly evokes in the early chapters of *Groundless*. While many other places in interwar Europe were witnessing ominous, rising tides of nationalism, Flusser explains, Prague stood out for the way in which it nurtured and sustained a strong internationalist character. Accordingly, he relates, he spoke "two first languages," Czech and German, which enabled him to be a "natural participant of both Western and Eastern Europe,"[8] while, in fact, he gainfully drew from *three* cultures. He writes: "Between the two Great Wars Prague was the centre of a new Czech culture (inspired by Masaryk), of European Jewish cultural life, and of a trend in German culture that allowed the monarchic tradition of the Habsburgs to flourish. These three cultures were mutually fertilized through struggles and collaborations, which provoked a tremendous richness of ideas."[9] For a curious child like himself of well-off, intellectual Jewish parents, the city was thus, in a word, "inebriating."[10] On top of his teenage encounter with Buber's dialogic philosophy (noted in our introduction), he was exposed to "the Prague Circle, Kafka, Rilke, Čapek's experimental theatre, phenomenology, Einstein at the University, and psychoanalysis with all its various schools."[11] Indeed, it was in Prague, in November of 1935, that the Moravian-Jewish-by-origin Husserl gave the lectures that would become *The Crisis of European Sciences and Transcendental Phenomenology*,[12] the late-career book where he offers his first in-depth exploration of "the lifeworld," the concept with which "ground" is so closely aligned.

In Flusser's telling, the first reaction to the Nazi invasion was disbelief, a denial of the possibility that one's entire "ground" could vanish: "Prague was one's reality, and how could this reality disappear? . . . Prague was eternal: if it disappeared, everything would disappear."[13] In his evolving relationship to the new situation, Flusser thus devoted himself feverishly to intellectual pursuits, in a desperate, self-protective retreat from the world: "One spun many fantasies to avoid a wide-eyed vision of reality that was more fantastic than any fantasy."[14] Eventually, as the new reality set in—a reality in which "from a promising member of the elite, one became a worthless marginal element,"[15] in which Jews like himself "had been reduced to the biological level (according to Nazi 'philosophy')"[16]—Flusser made a profoundly difficult decision to flee the city. In this way, he came to reject the new, hostile "ground" that replaced his old one, and yet, as he explains, the decision to leave everything behind, which included his entire family, far from resolved his absurd condition: "Subsequently, one would never lose the irrational, but existentially valid conviction that 'by right' one should have died in the ovens; that from then on, one lived a borrowed life; that one uprooted oneself from one's own ground (from the ovens) by escaping, and that 'reasonably' (?) the bottomless abyss was one's only possible future."[17]

Flusser's "unforgettable experience"[18] in Nazi-occupied Prague convinced him of the inherent destructibility of all cultural models. In the aftermath of the experience, he thus came to contend with groundlessness by accepting the condition and espousing a kind of philosophical nomadism intended ideally to allow himself to engage in the process of meaning-making with a heightened degree of freedom, intentionality, and self-awareness. As we will see, Arthur's experiences in *The Wandering Jew* reflect those of Flusser in a host of ways, even though the fictional German Jew, envisioned by Yiddish-speaking Jews in America, does not ultimately recoup groundlessness per se but rather redefines it through a redolently Jewish affirmation of the realm of time.

Censorship, Art, and Jewishness

In one of the several expressions of its wide-ranging concern with media, *The Wandering Jew* devotes significant attention to the operations of the *news media* under Nazism. In a lengthy early scene in Arthur's Berlin apartment—a highly aestheticized space, teeming with paintings, statuary, vases, and the like, where the majority of the low-budget film is set—the elegantly suited painter answers a series of questions posed by a veteran, worldly-wise Jewish journalist, who has come over to interview him for a newspaper. (It is in the midst of this interview that the existing print of the film—a film fragment, missing the first reel[19]—begins.) Asked about his newest opus, a work entitled *The Eternal Wanderer*, Arthur explains that the painting deals with the theme of "the Jew as the eternal wanderer among the nations," and that it is his intention to present the piece as a gift to the Art Academy on the occasion of the institution's fiftieth anniversary. At the mere mention of the word "Jew," however, the journalist baulks, smacking his lips, burrowing his tongue in the side of his mouth, and slowly repeating the word as if to flag it in the oral equivalent of red ink. And again he recoils when Arthur casually mentions a detail of his family history—that his parents were *Ostjuden* who immigrated to Germany before he was born. "Better not mention that . . . You know that we do not tolerate newcomers," the journalist cautions, alluding indirectly to the Nazis' particular animus against Jews from Eastern Europe,[20] while crossing out the problematic word from his notepad. As such a real-time expurgation reveals, what the journalist is producing is hardly an honest portrait of the artist but rather a scrubbed and sanitized profile, in conformity with the new, radically constrained journalistic standards of the day.

At the same time, the journalist serves for the aesthete painter, who has yet to accept or even begin to acknowledge the increasing hostility toward Jews circulating in his country, as a kind of mediator with the outside world. As the journalist remarks, accurately and therefore naturally off the record, in response to Arthur's insistence, "I have never considered myself a stranger here": "It seems, Mr. Young Professor, that you live in the dreamland of your art, and do not see the realities on the street. You seem to be overlooking the New German Racial Question." In this moment, the camera pans across the room to a ruminating Arthur and frames him in close-up, over which appears, in double exposure, a documentary image of a Nazi street rally, while a blaring antisemitic harangue comes on over the soundtrack in a vague attempt at ex post facto synchronization (the moment, as we'll see, is one of many in the stylistically varied film to take advantage of the specialty of the director/editor Roland and repurpose archival material, both visual and aural). The layered invocation of the rally creates the impression of the journalist's words all of a sudden mentally materializing for Arthur, or else inducing a nebulous flashback to events witnessed yet insufficiently incorporated into consciousness. Nevertheless, as the imagery of the threatening demonstration fades out, Arthur battens down in his dismissive attitude. "Politics! Nothing to do with art!" he exclaims, recalling Flusser's account of his difficulties accepting reality, or rather, the dissolution of his reality, in the wake of the Occupation, and of his consequent plunge into intellectual abstraction. Buffered by his success in the art world and comfortable assimilation in German society, Arthur fails to register Nazism's politicization of every sphere of life and what that means for himself as a Jew.

Arthur's ignorance and/or denial of the new political reality presents a strange, seemingly paradoxical situation in relation to his painting. Is it simply a coincidence that the utterly and unapologetically apolitical artist has chosen to make a work celebrating his roots at precisely the moment in which those roots have become an object of fierce attack by the state? (The fact that the work is intended to commemorate a specifically state institution adds a further twist.) As we know, many assimilated Jews both within and beyond Germany "came to" their Jewishness through what began to take hold in 1933, through the very antisemitism that would reduce them to their Jewish identity, bearing out a familiar dialectic of oppression, wherein finding oneself attacked on account of one's identity brings about a heightened awareness of that identity, along with a concomitant desire to assert that identity boldly under an opposing, positive valence. Yet, given Arthur's flagrant neglect of "the New German Racial Question," his gravitation toward heroic "racial" depiction, toward a triumphal refashioning of the traditionally antisemitic trope of the Wandering Jew, seems to require a different explanation. To invoke an idea formulated by the movie later on, perhaps a kind of mystical, metaphysical "Jewish Spirit" is unconsciously at work in Arthur, flowing in and through him, managing to be transmitted despite all the dire communicative troubles that German Jews are beginning to face in their everyday lives.

In any case, as if aware of the seeming paradox, the film spends considerable time elaborating Arthur's tenuous yet budding relation to Jewish tradition. This trend begins when the journalist asks the painter to give an estimation of his own work, and the film, or at any rate the surviving film fragment, shows *The Eternal Wanderer* for the first time. Monumentally life-sized, embodying a classical, figurative style befitting a professor and member of the Art Academy (that is, on a formal level, not indicating anything "degenerate," Nazism's disparaging epithet, borrowed from Max Nordau, for avant-garde and modernist art), the painting depicts an archetypal, biblical patriarch figure: long beard, flowing toga, staff in hand. However, as he reveals, Arthur has in fact based the character on his immigrant father, or more accurately, on a dim, dreamlike memory of the man, who died during the painter's childhood. Given this story behind the work, the painter defers the journalist's question to his valet—a slight, sagacious figure in a bow-tie played by the film's writer Jacob Mestel—who knew the father for a significant length of time.

> ARTHUR: So, friend, what do you think? Does his face resemble my father's?
>
> VALET: Yes, his pride, his dignity, his hopefulness. But the stern glance in his eye is not a Jewish characteristic.
>
> ARTHUR: He was a zealous fighter—and isn't Jehovah also a God of strength?

Thus arguing that the painting achieves a successful mimesis of the father's individual, but not "Jewish," traits, the valet in effect critiques the portrait for falling victim to a traditional Christian view of the Old Testament God, and by extension of Judaism as a whole, as being excessively, adversely "stern," bound up with a deleterious overcommitment to (retributive) Law. Indeed, in a corrective vein, the valet goes on to urge Arthur to recall his father's teaching, "His [God's] love of Humanity impelled Abraham to embrace the one God, Jehovah." Or in other words, the valet imparts to Arthur the idea that universalist compassion infuses the Old Testament, too, is right there at the beginning of the relationship between God and what would become His people. Such a sentiment echoes what Hans Kohn—the influential historian of nationalism and key correspondent and biographer of Buber (whom we again invoke later in this chapter)—writes about the universalist strain in Judaism:

> The prophets from Amos to Jeremiah discovered earlier than Greek philosophers the idea of man and humanity, and dug deeper into its meaning than any Greek philosophers before the Stoic period. The dignity of man as

such, regardless of his class, his ancestry, his abilities, was discovered. Something characteristic of all men revealed itself and was summed up in the concept of humanity. All activity and suffering gained meaning, one meaning; the framework of world history, a process binding together generations and peoples in the potential infinity of space and time, was won for human knowledge.... Amos went still further. God was to him not only a God of Israel, manifesting Himself in Jewish history, but the God of all peoples and all history.[21]

However, rather than let this kind of high-minded Jewish notion of "humanity" find straightaway, unequivocal acceptance among the characters, the film has Arthur and the valet debate the matter, showing them laying out their respective positions, in a kind of illustrated version of *pilpul* (Talmudic argumentation of a scrupulously fine-grained sort), with the aid of found-footage montages. Accordingly, in response to the valet, Arthur skeptically questions the validity of the "humanity" concept, and its attendant notion of "*rakhmones* [mercy]," by reflecting on the apocalyptic violence of the First World War: a battle in which he, like many German Jews, fought, and which haunts him to this day (a psychic situation that becomes more apparent later on during a traumatic flashback to the carnage), and which the film conjures in a newsreel-style compilation of documentary footage. Ultimately, though, neither side wins the day. As the valet, in conjunction with a montage of repurposed footage from biblical silent films, counters the painter's reflection on World War I and upholds that the Bible "commands peace and not war," the journalist intervenes and adds his own perspective, a cynical declaration of realpolitik ("We talk and talk of peace till we're involved in War") that prompts his exit and brings the interview to an end.

Antisemitism, Totalitarianism, and the Abandonment of Responsibility

As the interview with the journalist unfolds, the film cross-cuts several times to another room of the apartment, where we are introduced to two important people in Arthur's life. These are the painter's fiancée

Gertrude and friend Paul. Both are gentile, and not incidentally both possess signifiers (i.e., Gertrude's blonde hair, done up in a *volk*ish crown of braids; Paul's full name: "Paul von Eiselen") that positively scream non-Jewish (or alternatively, Aryan) and thus draw attention to the exaggerated importance attributed to racial differences in the new climate. It is through these two characters that the film exposes the fate of personal relations in a state ruled by antisemitism and totalitarianism, and accordingly the deep atrophying of that dimension of Arthur's fragile "ground" constituted by his relationship to others. In the first of the cross-cut scenes, Paul is already engaged in a staggering betrayal of his Jewish friend, trying to woo Gertrude, and doing so by oddly unromantic means, making a case for himself hinging largely on external—social, national—factors. "Imagine yourself as 'Frau Professor . . . Levi,'" Paul challenges Gertrude, hesitating with smarmy revulsion before going through with saying Arthur's last name, insinuating that the prospect of an intermarriage would be so unseemly as to be preposterous, unthinkable. For her part, Gertrude blithely resists Paul's advances and defends her relationship with Arthur, and yet the way that she carries out the defense of her fiancé hardly translates into a robust anti-antisemitism. "Though Arthur is a Jew, I admire him for his artistry, his nobility," she declares, claiming to love Arthur despite his Jewishness and on account of qualities that, in the current context, many would likely consider quintessentially Aryan. That is to say, for Gertrude, it appears that Arthur's individual qualities offset and balance out his Jewishness: a not terribly progressive stance that makes her later breaking up with him seem both plausible and foreseeable.

As a status-conscious rival to his accomplished painter friend, Paul exhibits behavior strikingly in line with Jean-Paul Sartre's characterological portrait of the antisemite in *Anti-Semite and Jew*, a book begun in 1944, in the wake of the Liberation, and first published in 1945. Sartre writes: "The anti-Semite flees responsibility as he flees his own consciousness, and choosing for his personality the permanence of rock, he chooses for his morality a scale of petrified values. Whatever he does, he knows that he will remain at the top of the ladder; whatever the Jew does, he will never get any higher than the first rung."[22] Once Arthur joins his friend and fiancée in the other room after the interview, Paul engages in precisely such a flight from responsibility, which we can also fruitfully think about in terms of

Sartre's concept of "bad faith," which describes a refusal to confront, and thereby to accept and to act upon, the terrifying fact of one's freedom (in this way, Sartre's model antisemite doubles as a model existential failure). For instance, while in a barrage of antisemitic conspiracy theory accusing Arthur of reaping the benefits of having "connections all over the world," Paul at the same time refuses to even utter the word "Jews," deploying instead the vague, second-person plural pronoun *ir*, which gives a sense of "you people." Moreover, after Arthur tries to call him out for "believing such rot," Paul offers the bogus reassurance, "*I* don't accuse you," and goes on to request a meeting later that night at "the German Club," attempting to slip out of the increasingly uncomfortable interaction and deferring a more assertive job of Jew-hatred to an official institution that he knows will refuse entry to the artist.

In *The Origins of Totalitarianism*, her 1951 study that contains another famous account of antisemitism, Arendt resonates with Sartre insofar as her prototypical totalitarian subject exists within "a system that, together with spontaneity, eliminates responsibility."[23] At the same time, however, Arendt departs from Sartre's idea of the antisemite who wishes to "remain at the top of the ladder" by pointing out that the abandonment of responsibility under totalitarianism is best understood not as a form of selfishness but rather as a means of achieving relief precisely from the exigent demands of self-interest. Addressing the immiserated "psychology of the European mass man" that in the wake of World War I provided one of the preconditions for totalitarianism, she writes: "Selflessness in the sense that oneself does not matter, the feeling of being expendable, was no longer the expression of individual idealism but a mass phenomenon. The old adage that the poor and oppressed have nothing to lose but their chains no longer applied to the mass men, for they lost much more than the chains of misery when they lost interest in their own well-being: the source of all the worries and cares which make human life troublesome and anguished was gone."[24] Despite Gertrude ostensibly belonging to the upper class, the mindset that she reveals later on, when she breaks up with Arthur in the wake of his dismissal from his job, chimes strongly with such a psycho-political portrait. Relinquishing her previous thin defense of their relationship, Gertrude attempts to explain to her devastated fiancé: "Understand me, Levi. We cannot stand up against an entire nation [*gants folk*]. I love you, but how can I stand against my people, my nation?" In this way, Gertrude is willing to sacrifice her own personal fulfillment, her clearly unextinguished love for Arthur, in order to relieve herself of the trouble and anguish that comes from being involved with a Jew. Or to translate from Arendt's terms into Buber's: precisely by abandoning her "I," Gertrude abandons her responsibility to the "You."

Nazi Communication: Rallies and Radio

As we saw, a street rally makes a brief, ontologically ambiguous, appearance during the Jewish journalist's interview with Arthur. The film returns to this staple of the Nazi phenomenon later on, when Arthur departs the Art Academy, where a committee is in the midst of deliberations regarding the submission of his painting (just previously, the action is economically clarified for us via a pair of extreme close-ups of an article written about the proceedings in the *Berliner Tageblatt*: dominating shots of the state-controlled newspaper that emphasize Arthur's utter lack of voice and agency in relation to the fate of his work). In long shot, Arthur forlornly descends the shadow-strewn steps to the building, and, midway down, turns to look at something offscreen. Here the film cuts, in an intended eyeline match, to a documentary shot of a vast procession of brownshirts marching and saluting in lockstep, on a street thronged with onlookers. The cut succinctly expresses a sense of the many versus the one, a juxtaposition between majority and minority, enhanced by the difference in texture between the staged image and the archival image, and by the running of the latter image in perceptible slow motion. Meanwhile, over the soundtrack, a layer of militaristic-patriotic marching music blends with an intimidating collective chant, at once guttural and robotic: "*Jude . . . Jude . . . Jude . . . Jude.*" The chant embodies an exemplary instance of Nazi communication, exhibiting a striking marriage of radical extensity and radical restrictiveness, of all-pervasive cannibalization of the airwaves and rigorously policed narrowness of content. Regarding such a dynamic, the focus of the chant on the word "Jew," too, is significant. Whereas earlier, in Arthur's conversations with the journalist and Paul, the word is expressly forbidden to mention, here it is expressly encouraged to mention.

Throughout the film, the ominous chanting of the Nazi rally becomes increasingly prevalent, even flooding through Arthur's apartment windows and finding him at home. Invested with such far-reaching, privacy-penetrating power, the sound of the rally appears to take on the semblance of a kind of radio broadcast, doing so intriguingly in the absence of any literal mention of radio in the film. Relevantly in this respect, the Nazis frequently mobilized radio technology to amplify and carry on the atmosphere and excitement of the rallies. As chief propagandist Joseph Goebbels remarked, giving a speech to representatives of the press in March of 1933: "Our radio propaganda is not produced in a vacuum, in radio stations, but in the atmosphere-laden halls of mass gatherings. In this way every listener has become a direct participant in these events."[25] In fact, such a notion of radio's capacity to create a special sense of immediacy and involvement in its audience comprised one of the main reasons why the Nazis were so legendarily fond of the medium. In his 1933 primer, *Propaganda and National Power: The Organization of Public Opinion for National Politics*, the Nazi's resident specialist in electronic mass media and head of national and regional radio programing (until 1942), Eugen Hadamovsky, wrote: "The real effect of a word or sound carried by radio is much deeper than that, say, of a newspaper or other piece of writing that must be interpreted before it is understood. Radio broadcasting works directly, without that bridge of thought, and has, therefore, greater effectiveness than the printed page."[26] Notably, implying how the history of media theory might be rewritten in particularly unruly, expansive ways, such remarks wrested free of context could easily appear to have been written by McLuhan, for whom radio serves as a powerful vehicle of collectivistic "tribalism." In the context of his oft-repeated claim that the fact that "Hitler came into political existence at all is directly owing to radio and public-address systems,"[27] McLuhan writes: "Radio affects most people intimately, person-to-person, offering a world of unspoken communication between writer-speaker and the listener. That is the immediate aspect of radio. A private experience. The subliminal depths of radio are charged with the resonating echoes of tribal horns and antique drums. This is inherent in the very nature of the medium, with its power to turn the psyche and society into a single echo chamber."[28]

In previous chapters, our discussion of metasemantic modes of communication has focused largely on dialogic potentiality. Recall Flusser's gesture of listening to music as an active receptivity to the resonating pathos of a sonic message, or Buber's silence which is communication as a concerted turning toward another person.

Quite obviously, as Goebbels and Hadamovsky's concern with the propagandistic effectiveness of radio attests, the metasemantic can also be used to advance a program of radical blockage and inhibition of the dialogic. Indeed, in a mass media context where the mass is constituted by what Arendt (who in her reflections on totalitarian propaganda makes extensive references to Hadamovsky) describes as "isolated individuals in an atomized society,"[29] that is, in a context where atomization makes people especially prone to currents of compensatory unification (i.e., to patriotic messaging that encourages a dissolving of the self into the collective), radio's metasemantic prowess can work with deep monologic efficiency. Along similar lines, though independently of the semantic/metasemantic divide, Flusser even goes so far as to suggest that "amphitheatrical" mass media, like radio and television, wherein an emitter "stands in 'empty space'" while broadcasting to a vast number of mutually noncommunicating receivers "who happen to stand in the field of transmission"[30] (i.e., Arthur's predicament exactly as he is unilaterally confronted by the rally chanting, both on the steps of the Academy and in his apartment), offer a perfect structural organization for facilitating the demagogic demands of totalitarianism.[31] Not incidentally, Flusser also points out, "The whole structure [of amphitheatrical media] has, ideally, cosmic dimensions: there is no limit to it."[32] In this way, amphitheatrical media lend themselves uncannily to the particularly imperialistic totalitarian style of the Nazis, to Hitler's ambition, embodied in the notion of *Lebensraum*, to expand the reach of the Third Reich indefinitely and take over the whole world.

Unplugged: Nazi Exclusionary Measures and Book Burning

Places of Remembrance, Renata Stih and Frieder Schnock's permanent Holocaust memorial in Berlin's Bavarian Quarter, offers an instructive, challenging reflection on Jewish life—and the relentlessly increasing assaults upon it—during the Nazi period. Originally installed in 1993, the piece consists of eighty double-sided signs—each of which focuses on a different anti-Jewish measure, alluded to on one side by a colorful, metonymic illustration, and on the other side by a short text summarizing the decree and giving the date of its institution—scattered around the district on lampposts. In 2013, Stih took a walking tour through the installation, which is woven into the neighborhood's everyday fabric with an unnerving subtlety, and explained to an interviewer: "Everything was meant to exclude Jews from daily life, from social structures, and to threaten them. . . . Up ahead is a nasty regulation. The regulation says Jews must give up all electrical devices, like radios or record players. On the reverse side we just showed a plug. You're unplugged. You're cut off from anything social."[33] (The sign in question translates as follows: "Jews must hand over all electrical and optical appliances, bicycles, typewriters, and records. June 19, 1942."[34]) Such measures, of course, affected the entire German Jewish population: a sweepingness evident in the proscription against the use of such ordinary things as bikes, typewriters, and records. And yet, as Saul Friedländer points out, at the start of the Nazis' excommunicative assault on Jews, it was only a relatively small subset of the Jewish population that was targeted. Writes Friedländer in *Nazi Germany and the Jews*: "As peripheral as it may seem in hindsight, the cultural domain was the first from which Jews (and 'leftists') were massively expelled. . . . Even before launching their first systematic anti-Jewish measures of exclusion, the new rulers of Germany had turned against the most visible representatives of the 'Jewish spirit' that henceforth was to be eradicated."[35] In other words, though the Nazis didn't act to disconnect or "unplug" the Jewish community in toto right away, they nevertheless did something intended to have as large an impact as possible, setting their sights on those Jews whose communicative capacity and reach was the greatest, on those Jews who were "most visible" by virtue of having a platform in the cultural arena.

It is thus hardly accidental that *The Wandering Jew* focuses on the plight of a renowned Jewish painter, a high-visibility cultural figure (indeed whose very métier hinges on the visible), who suffers a spiraling, multifaceted excommunication. Arthur's disturbing process of exclusion begins with the rejection and return of *The Eternal Wanderer*, his painting submission to the academy. Turning up at the apartment, an anonymous delivery man drops off the work—which, notably, hasn't been packaged up, as if no concern was taken for its safety—along with a curt note (which, as we shortly find out, explains that the painting has been turned down "on account of New National Convictions"), and procures the signature of the valet. Characteristically, in order to convey the message of rejection, the Nazi-aligned institution employs a means of communication (viz., the disinterested delivery service) that both allows its committee members not to have to face the once-valued member whom they are spurning (a potentially awkward and uncomfortable situation) and prevents Arthur from being able to make an immediate response to their ruling. (By contrast, recall that when Tevye is given his banishment order, the fact that he is given it by actual representatives of the Tsar means that he is at least able to put up a modicum of—sardonic, back-talking—resistance.) Making matters worse, Arthur turns out to be severely limited in his ability to sound an even private response to the situation. "German convictions!" he scoffingly repeats, first in response to the rally chants of *Jude* streaming in from the streets, and next in relation to the framed picture of the *Reichsadler*, the German heraldic eagle, that hangs above his mantelpiece and reveals his one-time pride in his country. However, the valet puts a stop to the outburst, shushing Arthur and reminding him of the threat of state surveillance, of the possibility that "the walls have ears." Meanwhile, the excommunicatory flood proceeds apace. Returning to the apartment, the Jewish journalist apologetically informs Arthur that "the Academy has not only refused your painting, but also you personally. They have also discharged you." And shortly thereafter, Paul also returns, operating under the pretext of rescuing Gertrude from imminent danger and appealing to her with his typical craven circumlocutions: "I warn you, Gertrude, whoever is not with us will be crushed. . . . The country has launched an economic boycott against certain elements. . . . Threatening crowds are massing. . . . Bonfires have been prepared—to burn all Jewish works." In this way, the excommunicative assault against Arthur escalates with wild, exponential force.

While Paul's fearmongering speech references two historical events—the national boycott of Jewish businesses, launched on April 1, 1933, and the book burnings, led by student groups in numerous German cities, on the night of May 10, 1933[36]—and telescopes them into the same day for dramatic effect, the film goes on to represent and model a key scene around the latter: a move that, as Doherty points out, would become a staple of Nazi-themed American films, including similarly early fringe efforts like *Are We Civilized?* (1934) and *I Was a Captive of Nazi Germany* (1936), and later big-budget productions like Frank Borzage's *The Mortal Storm* (1940), all of which incorporate documentary footage of, and/or reenact, the irresistibly spectacular, bibliocidal episode.³⁷ Still lingering in his stubborn denial regarding the Reich, having accused Paul of jealously making up stories, Arthur walks Gertrude, who for the moment remains by his side, back to her apartment. As the two bid each other farewell on the steps outside, however, Gertrude suddenly descries something in the not-far-off distance, at which point the film cuts to a series of archival images of the book burnings, of the massive crowds of youth gathered around the pyres, engaged in what looks like a darkly orgiastic, nighttime pagan ritual. "It has begun. They are burning Jewish books! I must see with my own eyes!" Arthur gasps, moving toward the flames despite Gertrude's mounting, softly heaving protestations. Accordingly, as the film's incorporation of documentary footage once more transfigures the past-tense historicity of the images into a present-tense narrative immediacy, the tactic here contains a canny added twist: namely, the "real-life" images work, at last, to make real, to drive home as real, the direness of the political situation that up to this point Arthur has so stubbornly refused to acknowledge. Indeed, as dramatically recreated flames cast flickering shadows on his and Gertrude's faces, Arthur cries out with the force of a tragic, searingly blinding revelation, before throwing a hand over his too-seeing eyes: "German youths, feeding their own spirit to the flames—what darkness will result!"

The archival footage of the book burnings also plays an evocative part later in the film, where it is, as it were, *re*-remediated, appearing in a traumatic flashback that Arthur experiences at his lowest moment in the film. Sliding back into a treacherous despair from which he had been momentarily rescued, and out of which he will again emerge (as we'll discuss in the next section), Arthur attempts, failingly, to reckon with the cumulative weight of the Jews' historical suffering, his own fraught experience of fighting in World War I, and the new, terrifying antisemitic dispensation in his country. As he delivers a monologue of dismay ("Blood, shame, destruction, annihilation!"), captured in a shot in which the camera dollies in closer and closer to his face, images of the nightmarish thoughts afflicting his psyche appear in cascading double, triple, and quadruple exposure. It is at the end of this compilation of horrors, which includes a rerunning of more repurposed footage from biblical silent films and of the archival footage of the street rallies, and a staged reconstruction of Arthur fatally bayoneting another soldier during World War I, that the film returns to the footage of the book burnings. Consequently, because such images appear superimposed over Arthur, an impression is created of the flames engulfing *the Jewish artist himself*, as he once more, now in extreme close-up, throws his hands over his eyes, unable to bear the (inner) vision (see figure 7.1). In other words, for a loaded second, the double exposure strikingly evokes the famous, minatory Heinrich Heine aphorism that would be so colossally borne out in Nazi Germany in the years following the release of the film: "Where books are burned, in the end, people will also be burned."[38] (As one will recall, the cinematic adaptation of *Tevye* also carries out a dalliance with a classic Heine saying about books, in the scene where Tevye, in the lead-up to his exile, packs up his Jewish library and intimates its status as a kind of "portable homeland.")

Before leaving off the treatment of the book burnings in *The Wandering Jew*, however (and indeed we will return to the matter once again in discussing the film's final moments), it is worth dwelling on Arthur's perhaps surprising comment that brings the initial represen-

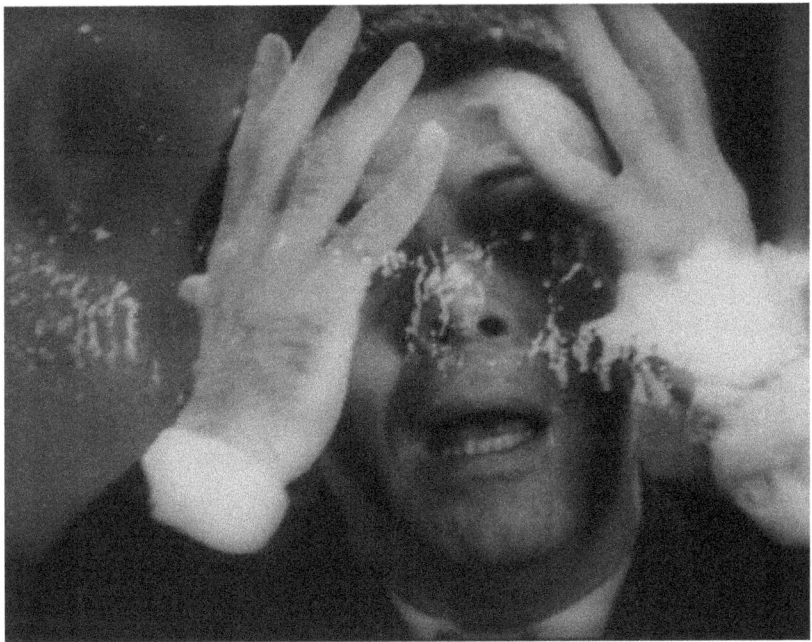

Figure 7.1. Arthur has a disturbing flashback to the book burnings, shown in a double exposure that creates the impression that he himself is being engulfed by the flames. George Roland, *The Wandering Jew* (1933).

tation of the event to an end. To be precise, why does Arthur imagine the German youths "feeding *their own* spirit to the flames," when the frenzied students are clearly engaged in what they believe is an incinerating attack on the so-called "*Jewish* spirit"? In his blistering contemporary essay on the book burnings, "The Auto-da-Fé of the Mind," published in the autumn of 1933 in the French journal *Cahiers Juifs*, Joseph Roth (whose thoughts on shape-shifting Jewish names and identities we encountered in chapter 5) offers a multifaceted possible answer, concluding the piece with a rousing pronouncement that strongly resonates with Arthur's words: "Many of us served in the war, many died. We have written for Germany, we have died for Germany. We have spilled our blood for Germany in two ways: the blood that runs in our veins, and the blood with which we write. We have sung Germany, the real Germany! And that is why today we are being burned by Germany!"[39] According to Roth, on one level, the *self-betraying, auto-destructive* nature of the book burnings stems from the fact that many Jews fought on the German side in World War I—just like Arthur, and indeed just like both Roth himself and the film's writer Jacob Mestel, both Galician Jews who served in the Austro-Hungarian army during the war. Roth's second line of reasoning is considerably less obvious, hinging on the key place of Jewish writers in the pantheon of German literature, or more particularly the pantheon of modern German literature that by the early 1930s had come to be known and celebrated internationally. As Roth writes, "In Germany, more than any other country, there is a 'folk literature' based on region, landscape, tribe, often of high literary value, but necessarily inaccessible to a wider European public. As far as 'abroad' was concerned, there was only that 'Germany' *whose literary mouthpieces were predominantly Jewish writers*. It is through them that the French, the English, the American reader gain their sense of German reality."[40] According to Roth, such a situation arose out of the fact that the distinctly translatable, internationally intelligible element in modern German literature, which he identifies as "the theme of the city," "the urban scene and the spiritual landscape of the city dweller," "the whole diversity of urban civilisation," was a distinctly Jewish innovation—flowing directly out of the Jewish experience rather than being some kind of mark of innate racial character: "This theme was almost imposed on the gifted Jewish writers by the urban milieu from which most of them came, to which their parents had been forced to move, and also by their more highly evolved sensibility and their Jewish aptitude for cosmopolitanism."[41] Of course, as Roth goes on to say, it is precisely the Jewish association with urban life that fuels the spite of German antisemites, and yet, for him, the "Germany" produced by the citified Jewish writers embodies something that fully justifies the name of "Germany," by virtue of providing an essential aspect of the overall picture of "German reality." Accordingly—and it is this that lies behind Arthur's similar outburst—to try, within this context, to differentiate the "Jewish spirit" from the "German spirit" in some neat, purity-retaining way is ludicrous, and it is dismaying that anyone would even attempt to do so.

The Jewish Time Bias

In the face of Arthur's distress, so violently stoked by the book burnings, a potent counterforce arrives that increasingly helps him contend with his unsettled, "groundless" condition. This takes the form of a supernatural incursion, one that exemplifies the recurrent Yiddish-cinematic motif, which we've already encountered before in several permutations, of the still image that bursts to life. Back at his apartment in the wake of witnessing the fires, Arthur desperately protests against the valet's fear that the arsonists will soon come for *The Eternal Wanderer*, and he vows that he will preempt those "with their sharpened claws" and destroy the painting with "[his] own hands." However, as Arthur goes to enact this destruction, raising his palette knife to the portrait in a melodramatic flourish, he is suddenly interrupted by the numinous, acousmatic voice of his father ("Do not do it my child . . . do not do it!"), which instantly, commandingly, causes the relentlessly invasive marching music and *Jude* chanting that have been sounding throughout the scene to cease, and irresistibly calls to mind the disrupted-at-the-last-minute sacrifice in the Abraham and Isaac story in the Bible (except, of course, among things, with the familial roles reversed). In this way, the film, which draws heavily on the cultivation of "reality-effects" through the incorporation of archival, documentary footage, does not demonstrate a shred of hesitation in plunging into deliriously fantastical and mystical territory, exhibiting a certain comfortability with the mixing of modes and registers that in fact typifies large swathes of Yiddish cinema, and compels one to draw an analogy between the strongly hybrid quality of Yiddish film and the strongly hybrid quality of the Yiddish language, or what Max Weinrich, the pioneering historian of the language, refers to as Yiddish's distinctively diasporic, "fusion"[42] quality, meaning the ability to absorb and combine elements from an extensive array of different linguistic pools (Germanic, Slavic, Semitic, etc.).

As Arthur backs away from the painting in astonishment, the life-sized, conveniently 1:1 portrait comes more fully to life, materializing beyond aural form and, in ghostly double exposure, "wandering" off its material support, which consequently turns blank (see figure 7.2). Thenceforth, the interaction between the father (played by the live actor M. B. Samuylow) and the son largely takes the form of an interactive lesson on Jewish history led by the former, who continues to point out, in a tone of erudite calm, that "the Spirit must not—cannot—be destroyed, because the Spirit belongs to the people, to

Figure 7.2. Arthur's portrait, *The Eternal Wanderer*, modeled on his dead father, comes to life and wanders off the canvas. George Roland, *The Wandering Jew* (1933).

all humanity," and that it has been the special "mission" of the Jews to "teach" such a universalist message "since the days when Moses gave the Ten Commandments." Here the father's words begin to be illustrated for us with a dense montage of repurposed footage, as he proceeds to move breathlessly through a chronicle of the last twenty-five hundred years, and cover a litany of infamous, persecutory flashpoints: the Babylonian Siege and Captivity, the Exile after the destruction of the Second Temple, the Crusades, the Spanish Inquisition, the pogroms under the Tsar. However, what the father wishes for Arthur to take away is an optimistic moral. Amid all the woe, he points out, the Jews steadfastly clung to their sense of conscience and endured. And so his disquisition ends on a note of marked hope for the future, making reference to the Russian Revolution, the Second Spanish Republic, and the return of Jews to Palestine (this last glimpsed in a few documentary flashes from the *Yishuv*): "But in time Russia established a New Social Order. The once mighty Spanish inquisitors spread scattered like mice. Now Spain invites our brothers back to help rebuild their country. From out of the ruins of the Old, a New Jewish Homeland is emerging." In other words, as Arthur is meant to extract from the speech, this most recent episode of Jewish suffering and pummeling of the human spirit, perpetrated by Nazism, won't continue on unabated, but will, too, find a resolution "in time," within the rich, resourceful, unfinished history being narrated.

In this way, the father's speech hinges on a valorizing figuration of time as a force of liberation, or on what we might call the distinctive Jewish "time bias" (to adapt a key term from one of the founding figures of media theory, and major influence on McLuhan, Harold Innis). What has been imputed to account for this special attachment to time over space, or preferred orientation within a temporal rather than spatial register, are a number of factors, as intellectual historians of Judaism and Jewish culture have discussed. These factors include: the role of messianism in Judaism, which implies a purposeful directionality to time, and thus promotes a deep sense of historical consciousness (taken up more at length in chapter 8); the sacred place of memory within Judaism (recall chapter 1), which too puts a stress on the temporal; the Second Commandment's "aniconic" proscription against graven images of God, a law that would appear to result in a correlative denigration of space, the visible being an ineluctably spatial category; and the condition of diaspora that Jews have long lived within, involving no anchoring in a single geographical locale. Of course, there is much room for friction, nuance, and contestation in this intellectual complex. Elliot R. Wolfson, for example, explores the several ways that the Jewish mystical tradition operates in tension with the Second Commandment[43] (a phenomenon that dovetails with our discussion of the Kabbalah and *The Dybbuk* in chapter 9), while several critics, particularly art historians keen to push back against the pervasive idea that a rich tradition of Jewish visual art doesn't exist, have questioned the parameters and binding force of the Jewish aniconic imperative.[44] In any case, what we are concerned with is less the actual supportability or justification for a Jewish "time bias" than *The Wandering Jew*'s particular mobilization of the well-trafficked notion—a mobilization that we can better grasp by turning once more to Hans Kohn. Working within the same comparison of "Israel and Hellas" that we saw earlier in his remarks on the Jewish notion of "humanity," Kohn offers a contrast between the spatially oriented Greek and the temporally oriented Jew:

> The Jew lived more in the realm of time than in space. The world as time does not know of separation into a plurality of dimensions. It is one-dimensional: it points to the past, surges towards the future, and overcomes the tension of various directions in the forceful unity of its stream. The world as time is a polar world, suspended in tension between two poles. It is burdened with the tradition of the past, and the forward-driving urge propels it into the uncertain future. It does not know the balance of forces which have developed contiguously and harmoniously. It is itself force, one-sided, tending towards extremes and avoiding compromises, rushing towards the infinite and shattering all form.[45]

Such a passage resonates strongly with the characterization of Arthur's ghostly father, who is burdened with the past (indeed he practically personifies Jewish history), urges a propulsive venturing into the uncertain future, and upholds a profound faith in the redemptive power of such a unified, dynamic temporal "stream." Further, as we'll shortly see, one could hardly ask for a more apt description of the final moment of the film as a depiction of "the world as time . . . rushing towards the infinite and shattering all form."

Arthur relapses into despair following his father's initial mystical appearance, and then this is compounded, in the next scene, by his breakup with Gertrude. However, it is as if the collapse of the engagement, this loss of the last tie binding him to his rapidly crumbling reality, enables Arthur to shake off his remaining doubts and more fully align himself with the paternal apparition. Thus, as a crowd swells to gigantic proportions outside his apartment (portrayed in another archival, documentary insert), and a battery of projectiles shatteringly fly through the window and make a gash in the portrait of the *Reichsadler*, Arthur thunders, repeatedly, to his valet: "We shall go!" Yet a critical question, as Arthur goes on to pose it, hovers over this pronouncement. Now willfully invoking his father, he pleads with open palms and a subtly smoldering sense of indignity: "But where can we go, father, when all gates are closed, when every country raises barriers against us?" The question triggers the father to reappear and deliver another historical monologue, illustrated again for us with found footage, that makes reference to monumental figures who emerged in times of emergency, like Moses and Herzl. Nevertheless, in regard to Arthur's question, the father can only meet it with yet another question. As he remarks, notably resisting to frame Palestine as the only and/or necessary solution to Arthur's refugee crisis, while at the same time obviously viewing the Zionist project through a rosily utopian lens: "Shall it be Palestine, Argentina, Canada, Crimea, or Birobidzhan?"

Unable to designate a definite solution for his son within the realm of geopolitical reality, the father thus turns to a more mystical plane, in a move that calls up the book burnings once more. Here, however, in this climactic final movement of his monologue, the event is depicted not through a return to the documentary footage deployed several times earlier, but through a striking, heavily stylized, single stop-motion animation shot, possibly repurposed, that puts the books themselves at center stage and exhibits yet one more style within the film's magpie arsenal of formal techniques. Against an abstract, black background, we see a series of books by Jewish authors—names loudly emblazoned on the covers—being dropped by an anonymous hand, and falling, with surreal, over-geometric motion, into a raging fire at the bottom of the frame. The cast of authors includes Mendelssohn, Zweig, Toller, Feuchtwanger, Einstein, and, with an entirely unstressed yet, if one is familiar with his famous remark on book burning, oozing irony, Heine (see figure 7.3).

All of this downward motion, however, is finally countered with a surge of upward motion as the ghostly father and his son, in double exposure, now both in biblical togas, appear rising up out of the flames unscathed (see figure 7.4). Meanwhile, amid this ethereal ascent, the father declares, "They may destroy the Written Word . . . but they can never extinguish the Eternal Spirit!": a remark that affirms a form of media transmission that operates within a kind of extraterritorial zone, beyond the strictures of ordinary, material channels, and that the next, and final, shot of the film reinforces. Within the same black, redolently transcendent (non)space, father and son ecstatically exclaim, one after the other, "In all eternity!" before taking leave of

Figure 7.3. In a stop-motion animation sequence that recasts the book burnings, a book by the early nineteenth-century German Jewish author Heinrich Heine is dropped into the flames. George Roland, *The Wandering Jew* (1933).

Figure 7.4. Out of the flames of the burning books, Arthur and the spirit of his father rise up unscathed. George Roland, *The Wandering Jew* (1933).

the spatio-visible realm entirely and "wandering" out of the frame. Hence we never return to the "realistic" register of the film, which, along with Arthur's apartment and Berlin and the whole terrestrial world, seems completely to melt away. It is in this way that the film, finally, to come back to the passage from Kohn, offers up an image of the "world as time . . . rushing towards the infinite and shattering all form," of an unbounded temporal realm where all the excommunicative obstacles and obstructions that the troubled German Jewish artist faces, including the national borders that keep refugees out, do not exist. Indeed, echoing Kohn's words almost literally, the eccentric concluding title of the film, superimposed on the image, reads not "The End" but rather "Ad Infinitum."

As Yiddish films more broadly illustrate, it is most often the changes that time eventually brings, after many years, rather than actions within a momentary context, that provide resolution—family members reuniting, identities being recovered, oppressors waning in power. Arthur's vindication of his groundlessness through time thus finds a wider resonance with several of the films that we discuss, even as *The Wandering Jew*, relative to these other works, unfolds within the shortest narrative time span, that is, a single day or two, aptly conveying the urgent, rapidly worsening nature of the contemporary crisis being represented. At the same time, in its rescuing faith in time, and in its bracing historiographical perspective—the latter of which strongly resonates with Flusser's dialectical discovery, in conjunction with his embrace of groundlessness and adoption of a nomadic mentality, that "history is made not by the expellers but by the expellees. The Jews are not a part of Nazi history. To the contrary, the Nazis are a part of Jewish history"[46]—the film, as we'll see, departs sharply in tone from that of the film that we look at next—the far more pragmatically mired *Long Is the Road*, another film about groundlessness, yet made at the end rather than the beginning of the Nazi reign, in the immediate aftermath of World War II.

8

Groundlessness II (Among the DPs)

Long Is the Road (1948)

ONE OF ONLY A PRECIOUS handful of Yiddish films made in Europe in the raw wake of the Holocaust, *Long Is the Road* (*Lang Iz der Veg*) focuses on the plight of Jewish "DPs" (displaced persons). (*We Live Again*, a 1946 documentary made in France, and *Our Children*, a 1948 hybrid documentary with staged reenactments made in Poland, also deal inescapably with displacement, yet with a specific focus on displaced children, on the orphans of the Holocaust.) Shot near Munich in the American-occupied zone of Germany, in part on location at the Landsberg DP camp, and in part at the Emelka Studios, in 1947, the film was produced by the US Army Information Control Division, on the recommendation of YAFO (Yidishe Film Organisatsie), the Jewish film body initiated the year before by the American Joint Distribution Committee, with a cast drawn from, among other sources, the Munich Yiddish Art Theatre, and, for more minor roles and extras, the actual residents of the Landsberg camp.[1] Regarding the direction, the matter is somewhat complicated. The credits list two directors: Marek Goldstein, a Jewish concentration camp survivor, and Herbert B. Fredersdorf, a German who was active in filmmaking during the Nazi period, and who was engaged to handle the film's technical aspects. However, reportedly, much of the direction was eventually taken over by the film's lead actor, co-scriptwriter, and (semiautobiographical) idea provider, Israel Beker, a thirty-year-old Yiddish theater actor from Bialystok who alone among his family survived the war (before it was too late, Beker found himself in the Soviet Union, spent the war there, and afterward led an unstable, itinerant existence, first back in Poland, then in Germany, before completing the film and immigrating to Palestine with a forged passport[2]). The film, whose realistic linguistic fabric is in fact multiple and consists not only of Yiddish but also of Polish and German, forms an obvious continuity with the last chapter, extending our exploration of groundlessness in the shadow of Nazism. However, it does so with an important difference, insisting on the need to reground in a far more concrete way than, as we saw in *The Wandering Jew*, the ostracized German Jewish painter's flight into a zone of transcendent temporality. That is to say, as intimated by the titular metaphor of "the road," *Long Is the Road* depicts the DP's project of regrounding as one that is compelled to reckon with the world in all its actual, (as yet) unavoidable geopolitical spatial organization.

Displacement, Objectification, Cohabitation

"The Decline of the Nation-State and the End of the Rights of Man," a chapter of Arendt's *The Origins of Totalitarianism* that deals with the problem of statelessness, is today perhaps the book's most famous section, reflecting the dogged persistence and radical expansion of the problem since the time the book was written. For Arendt, the stateless person or person who has lost the protection of a nation is one who has been reduced to "nothing but a man,"[3] to a mere "human being in general":[4] a situation rife with perils that, as she goes on to explain, became even more precarious after World War II as the discourse shifted to a focus on so-called "displaced persons." As Arendt writes: "The term 'stateless' at least acknowledged the fact that these persons had lost the protection of their government and required international agreements for safeguarding their legal status. The postwar term 'displaced persons' was invented during the war for the express purpose of liquidating statelessness once and for all by ignoring its existence."[5] What this denial meant in reality, as Arendt explains, is that displaced persons were expected to be repatriated to their countries of origin regardless of circumstances; that is to say, they were expected to be deported to places that might not want them back and/or refused to acknowledge them as citizens, or that perhaps wished to have them back for the purposes of punishing them.[6] As Mark Wyman, a historian of DPs, notes, a version of this conundrum settled itself pointedly on Jews: "Thousands of Jews returned home, including some 130,000 who had spent the war years in the Soviet Union [a group that included Beker]. But they discovered that the defeat of the Third Reich was not the defeat of anti-Jewish feeling."[7] Currents of antisemitism, in other words, potently, dismally persisted even after the war and the liberation—and full exposure—of the camps. However, on top of this, and the fact that returning often meant returning quite literally to nothing—homes destroyed or repossessed, family members and communities entirely annihilated—Wyman also points to another, less tangible but no less important, factor that hindered Jewish DPs from returning and remaining at home and that made them wish to build their futures elsewhere. He writes: "Europe had become the graveyard of their people, its major monuments not the Eiffel Tower and Saint Peter's but the Nazi death camps where humans were turned into objects and plundered for their labor, gold fillings, hair."[8]

In *Post-History*, Flusser modifies formulations such as Wyman's by effectively dispensing with the underlying binarism and suggesting a certain *continuity* between the legacy of Europe's impressive scientific and cultural achievements and certain forces of radical dehumanization. Rhetorically employing "Auschwitz" as a synecdoche for the Holocaust, he writes in the book's opening essay, "The Ground We Tread," whose title reveals a return to the conceptual terrain of his autobiography: "Auschwitz is not a violation of Western models of behavior, it is, on the contrary, *the result of the application* of such models."[9] Drawing on another of his key concepts, "apparatus," with which he designates a type of mechanism that runs concealed, automated programs, or that operates according to a "black box" structure, Flusser argues more specifically that Auschwitz pried open the black box of the West, unmasking objectification—objectification capable of leading to "the ultimate *reification* of people into amorphous objects, into ashes"[10]—as "one of its inherent virtualities."[11] Or in other words, anticipating the argument of Zygmunt Bauman's better-known, much-debated book,

Modernity and the Holocaust, published six years later in 1989, Flusser conceptualizes Auschwitz not as a pathological aberration from but rather as a structurally encoded, *"characteristic realization"*[12] of the culture in which it arose. Indeed, for him, "Auschwitz" stands as persistently entrenched in the Western-derived, post-industrial society of the present and anticipated future, whose technocratic regimes he aims to critique in the subsequent, wide-ranging essays of *Post-History*. (Later, the Flusser/Bauman argument about the Holocaust will become important to our analysis of *Long Is the Road*'s engagement with bureaucracy, but here we should signal that the shape of the claim in both thinkers bears traces of a limited, Eurocentric framework. As Paul Gilroy has compellingly and sensitively argued, the histories of slavery and colonial domination furnish ample prior examples of outrageous dehumanization carried out in the name of Western "reason," "progress," and so forth, and these can be set alongside the Holocaust to mutually instructive effect.[13])

As part of his idiosyncratic, fluid, academically fugitive style, Flusser rarely cites or even names the thinkers whose ideas serve as springboards for his own. However, thanks to a personal letter sent to his friend, Milton Vargas, that contains a philosophical "key" to the essays in *Post-History*, we know for certain that the primary, submerged interlocutor of "The Ground We Tread" is Arendt.[14] Indeed, Arendt's key concept of "cohabitation"—which she proposes as a model for society that would resist sliding back into and reproducing the paradigm of the nation-state that, as she so insightfully diagnoses, produces problems like statelessness, and genocide, in the first place—seems redolently to inform the essay all over the place. As Judith Butler explains, unpacking an important appearance of the "cohabitation" concept in Arendt's book on the Eichmann trial: "For Arendt, one reason why genocide is radically impermissible is that, in fact, we have no choice with whom to cohabit the earth. . . . This means that unwilled proximity and unchosen cohabitation are preconditions of our political existence, which . . . implies the obligation to live on the earth and in a polity that establishes modes of equality for a necessarily heterogenous population."[15] Echoes of such a pluralist obligation resound in Flusser's remark, "Our culture allowed its mystifying mask to fall at Auschwitz and revealed its real face. The face of a monster that objectifies man. Our culture has shown that it must be rejected in toto if we admit that the purpose of every culture is to allow for the convivial existence of men that recognize each other mutually as subjects."[16] Along similar lines, while remaining attuned to the challenges of ever completely rejecting one's culture, to the fact that cultural models are necessary, meaning-making, madness-staving-off "traps to catch the world,"[17] Flusser concludes the essay with an appeal to let the unmasking of Western culture's inherent virtuality of radical objectification persist in consciousness, in the hopes of challenging the tendency and moving toward the realization of more auspicious projects:

> We have lost faith in our culture, in the ground we tread. That is, we have lost faith in ourselves. It is this hollow vibration that follows our steps toward the future. What remains is for us to analyze the event "Auschwitz" in all its details in order to discover that fundamental project that realized itself there for the first time, so that we may nurture the hope to project ourselves out of that project. Out of the history of the West. This is the "post-historical" climate in which we are condemned to live in from hereon.[18]

As we'll see, *Long Is the Road*'s treatment of the DP strikingly chimes with Flusser and Arendt, insofar as it commits itself precisely to such a critical analysis of objectification, and the more "convivial," subjectifying, and intersubjectively enabling alternatives with which it might be replaced.

Subjectifying Tactics

Take, for instance, the film's basic narrative approach and orientation. This is announced in a revealing intertitle that appears in between the typographically evocative, slantwise-printed credits (the words displaced, as it were, from the condition of standard linearity) and the opening scene: "Driven from their home for political or ethnic reasons, more than 1 million people today still live scattered across Europe. They are known as D.P.s. This is a story out of the life of these people, told as it really took place—told by them." (In English, the intertitle is possibly a substitute for an original intertitle in German, the language of the voice-over narration in the National Center for Jewish Film's restored print of the film.[19]) The text right away declares a commitment to capturing the reality of events, to events as they "really took place," revealing a core principle that resonates with that of Italian neorealism, the influential postwar cinematic movement with which *Long Is the Road* is contemporaneous (notably, as we'll say more about later, while displaying many neorealist proclivities, *Long Is the Road* also, in a fusion-friendly, typically Yiddish-cinematic way, departs from a realist modality on several occasions, for instance resorting to a kind of minimalist expressionism to represent the notoriously "unrepresentable" experience of the camps). Also of crucial importance, however, is the phrase "told by them"—a phrase that assures us that the DPs do not merely serve as the source and/or the subject of the narrative of the film but also function as the enunciating agents of the film. This is particularly unique in the context of other films dealing with the Holocaust made in the immediate aftermath of the catastrophe. As Joshua Hirsch points out in *After Image: Film, Trauma, and the Holocaust*, the earliest film representations of the survivors largely took the form of newsreel- and compilation-style documentaries:[20] that is to say, films that were not made by and told through the perspective of the survivors themselves (i.e., people like Beker and Goldstein) but that rather exhibit what scholars of documentary film call an "expository" mode, wherein, most often, the footage taken from real life is commented on by a voice-over narrator, confidently didactic and almost universally male, who stands at an "objective" distance from the images and is not, properly speaking, "of" the sights on display. It is true that *Long Is the Road* amply employs the expository mode, containing several newsreel-style, documentary sequences, replete with a third-person (male) narrator. Crucially, however, such expository sequences result in only a superficial resemblance to the type of documentary films analyzed by Hirsch. For, aside from the fact that he fleetingly comes and goes and plays a role in only a fraction of the film, the voice-over narrator of *Long Is the Road* is a deeply eccentric figure, constantly offering biting asides on the cold, information-laden commentary that he conveys (several examples of this will appear later in our analysis). Going hand in hand with the intertitle's underscoring of the film's status as an enunciation of the DPs themselves (however potentially ruffled by aporetic difficulties), such differentiation thus comprises yet one more tactic by which the film obsessively strives to mark out its subjects recognizably *as* subjects.

Dissolution of Ground

Notably, *Long Is the Road* begins not by launching into the DP problem as it is outlined in the prefatory intertitle, but rather by going back in time and tracing the origins of the problem. Indeed, the film does not arrive at the postwar moment until about midway through its brief yet packed seventy-seven-minute run time. Accordingly, we begin in the late summer of 1939, in Warsaw, just prior to the Nazi invasion of Poland, with a sequence that interweaves documentary and staged footage (with far more "professional" polish and restraint, one might add, than *The Wandering Jew*), and introduces us to the Polish Jewish Yellin family, right on the cusp of the dissolution of their "ground." Seamlessly stitched in amid a montage of images of the lively, bustling city, David Yellin (the intense, giant-eyed Beker), the only child of the family, appears first, in a proletarian-style flat cap and overalls, jovially engaged in repairing a motor at the garage where he works. However, since we don't yet know that he will become our protagonist, his quick appearance makes it seem as if he were merely one of scores of happy citizens embedded in the almost utopian urban fabric (as we'll shortly see, the film introduces him on an intimate level only once his ground has been destabilized, as if in subjectivizing response to the threat of dehumanization that he consequently faces). Over the images, the voice-over narrator provides us with more context: "It began in Warsaw. The city still looked like a city then. The 'Noviezin,' 'New World Street,' was crowded with shoppers, and through the street noise the bells of the Church of the Holy Cross could be heard. It was a late summer's day, a day like any other. The papers did report political tensions, but the children played with colored balloons, and the people believed in peace." Significantly, inaugurating a characteristically Yiddish-cinematic focus on communication, the narrator evokes the city as a space of striking interconnectivity, as an emphatically smooth-running network: despite the presumably considerable "noise" of the busy commercial prospect, the church bells manage to resist being drowned out and are collectively "heard," possessing extraordinary transmissive reach and resistance to interference. Suddenly, however, such an idyllic vision is dashed. Walking arm in arm, a quartet of teenaged girls are compelled to look up at something in the sky offscreen. What they see, as a craftily executed eyeline match reveals, are scores of *Luftwaffe* bombers descending on the city in menacing formation. The harmonious city symphony thus collapses into a cacophony of destruction, with cascades of falling bombs, buildings blowing up, and crowds scattering in panic. Moreover, represented in close-up with sound accompaniment, an air-raid siren goes off, blaringly spinning its cylinders and effectively replacing the verbally conjured church bells with a similarly centralizing noise, yet one that connects only to warn of disruption.

The more personal introduction to David occurs in an underground bomb shelter, where, along with a crowd of other denizens of the city, he and his parents have taken shelter from the air raids. Carried out over a series of shots, the camera takes us on a roving tour of this space, flickeringly lit and palpably suffused with terror, until finally arriving at the Yellins—David clutching a tool from the garage (now effectively a relic of another era), his bearded and bespectacled father, Jacob (Jakob Fischer), putting a consoling hand on his mother, Hannah (Berta Litwina, a recurrent presence in prewar Polish Yiddish films, including Joseph Green's 1937 *The Purim Player* [*Der Purimshpiler*]). Such a flagrantly deferred introduction to our protagonist also introduces us to a key technique in the composition of the film's visual style: the tracking camera. Perfectly keyed to the thematic of displacement and the winding mission to recover a home, the technique creates an impression of the camera constantly being forced to *locate* its intended object, never permitted to have a focal point presently at hand from the start of a shot. (Irresistibly, one is reminded of the emotionally and philosophically freighted tracking shots in Alain Resnais's 1956 experimental Holocaust "documentary" *Night and Fog*.) When we next return to the Yellins, following an inexorable escalation in the atmosphere of fear, conjured through a series of cutaway shots to people, both Christian and Jewish, in the midst of fervently praying, David suddenly pulls away from the huddle with his parents and approaches a small window at the top of a wall in the background, triggering his mother to call out his name in anxious protest (a maternal appeal that comprises the first diegetic line of the film). Nevertheless, David continues to move toward the danger, toward the hostilities reducing his city to ruins, appearing as something of an anomaly within his family and the larger crowd, and demonstrating an attraction to "the abyss" that later manifests as a kind of irrational compulsion and proves to be one of his defining characteristics.

With the occupation of Poland in the wake of the three-week-long blitzkrieg, the Yellins' situation, like that of all the Jews in the country, becomes even more destabilized. At first, the film shows this decline obliquely, in a montage sequence that, calling back to *The Wandering Jew*, accentuates the Nazis' particular, and particularly dominative, uses of media and modes of communication. In a barrage of rapidly cut images, a series of Nazis, pictured from behind or in featureless silhouette, paste up posters bearing the new anti-Jewish decrees on walls in public places. The textual onslaught suggests a transference of the bombings onto a mediatized, legal plane, while the fact that we never see the faces of the Nazis—an evocative, highly deliberate representational strategy that continues throughout the film—makes a critical point regarding their style of communication. Remaining anonymous, just like the invisible academy members who rule on Arthur's painting in *The Wandering Jew*, the paste-boarding soldiers perfectly capture the virtual authorlessness of Nazi messaging, and the entanglement of this phenomenon with the propagation of power. As Arendt remarks: "The only rule of which everybody in a totalitarian state may be sure is that the more visible government agencies are, the less power they carry, and the less is known of the existence of an institution, the more powerful it will ultimately turn out to be."[21] Relatedly, to come back to Flusser's terms, such cloaking and dispersal of authorship inevitably results in the forestalling of any possibility of "revolution," of the launching of any kind of responsive resistance within the discursive structure of communication, on the part of the recipient of the message. Only later, as we'll see, do we more fully realize that the film's concerted withholding of the faces of the Nazis also serves another, reparative purpose: that is, to direct us more keenly to the faces of those whom they are victimizing.

Suggestively, the first time we see the Yellins back at home, in their modest, upper-floor apartment, the space is revealed as every bit as unsettled as the bomb shelter, similarly providing only the thinnest of buffers from the dangers of the outside world. The scene picks up with the fall of Shabbat. In a tense silence, Hannah prepares the table, while Jacob pulls himself away from the window and paces around the room, nervously awaiting the return of their son, who has gone out to try to gather information. Eventually, as Jacob rashly decides to go out and look for David, a knock is heard at the door, causing a paralyzing chill to run through the couple, and demonstrating how, in the current state of emergency, the normally most innocuous occurrences of daily life become invested with the most threatening possibilities. Fortunately, it turns out to be their son, and yet, swiftly undoing any sense of calm, David hurries inside, redoes the double lock on the door, and, in a single loaded word, delivers the distressing news that he has discovered: "Ghetto." The word (which of course implies that the family will shortly be forced to abandon their home entirely) has an almost winding effect on Jacob, who, in order to try to counteract this, reminds his wife and child that it is Friday night, and that they should continue with the Shabbat meal. As the family stand around the table and Jacob recites a blessing, however, the father chokingly struggles to get out the words (as his wife and son, in a pair of close-ups, notice with concern) and eventually tapers off to a woeful whispering, raising the specter of muteness and "speech pathology" that we've discussed throughout this book, and that indeed (as we'll see) continues to play a large role in *Long Is the Road*.

With the attempt to mitigate and push back against the crisis of displacement through religion thus proving treacherously fragile, the film intriguingly rearticulates the point on a formal plane. At the abortive conclusion of Jacob's prayer, the camera tilts down from his face (which he himself lowers to try to hide his distress) and zeroes in on the table, where we see, framed in between two flickering candles, the ornately embroidered challah bread covering, which boasts a Star of David at the center. From this, the film dissolves into another, yet very different, image of a Star of David. Here, the symbol is in the midst of being drawn, by an anonymous hand belonging to a cropped-out Nazi officer, on a vast map of Warsaw, within the thickly outlined region demarcated for the ghetto (see figures 8.1 and 8.2). With remarkable visual concision, the film thus conveys the usurpation of the Yellins' intimate private sphere, along with the profanation of their religious symbolism, by the Nazis' imperialistic, bureaucratic forces. Or in Flusser's terms, the dissolve puts on display the quite literal dissolving of their ground, their foundation for meaning, and its overpowering replacement by another, nefarious ground. (In fact, in a manner most fitting to the narrative's focus on dislocation and

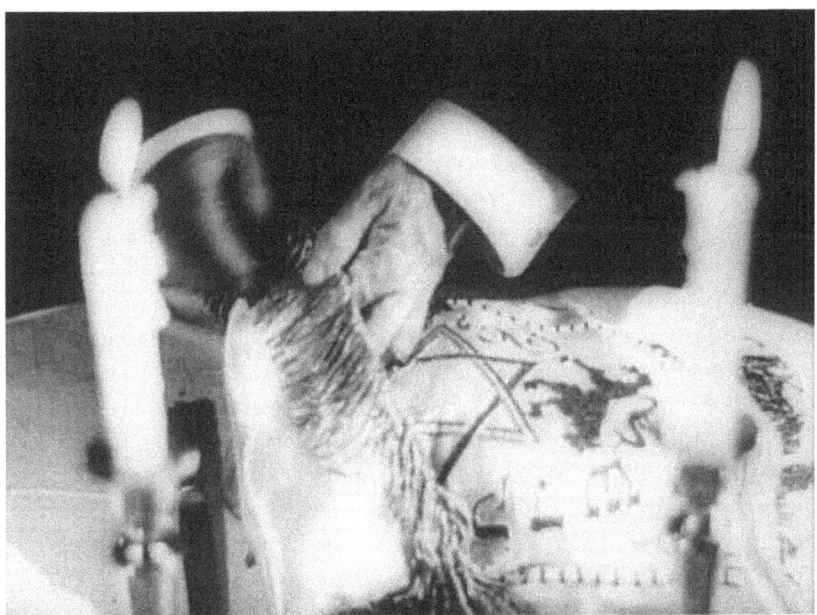

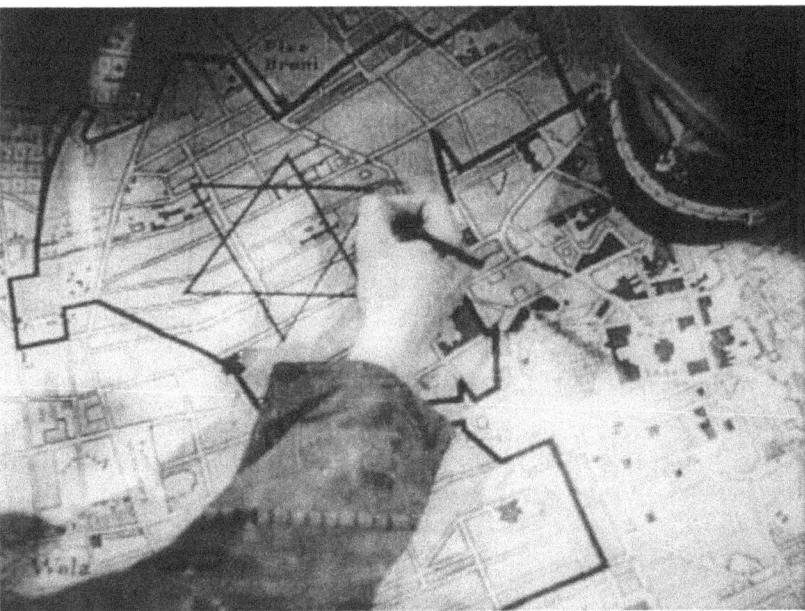

Figures 8.1 and 8.2. In a loaded transition between scenes, the Yellins' challah bread cover with a Star of David dissolves into the hand of a Nazi officer drawing a Star of David on a map of the Warsaw Ghetto. Marek Goldstein and Herbert B. Fredersdorf, *Long Is the Road* (1948).

being in transition, the film frequently makes such charged use of "transitional" devices and shifts between scenes.)

Shortly, the Yellins are shown departing for the Warsaw Ghetto, now all wearing armbands with the Star of David. After taking his last step out of the apartment and locking the door behind him (with keys that his father will in a moment surrender to their Polish neighbour), David puffs on a cigarette with cool disgruntlement and tears the mezuzah down from the doorframe, putting it in his pocket, before joining his parents in front of the building and helping them secure (a modicum of) the family's possessions onto a small, overstuffed wagon (multiple shades of the ending of *Tevye*). Regarding the Yellins' time inside the ghetto itself, however, the film suggestively withholds representing this in the same concrete way. Although a brief recreation shows the family, amid an endless procession of Jews, filing into the ghetto through an arched entryway, thereafter the film switches into an "expository" mode, wherein the voice-over narrator provides an abstract, merely statistical report on ghetto life, or more accurately, ghetto death. "By 1941, 500,000 people were crammed into the ghetto. They decreased rapidly," he reports, as the screen oscillates between the map of the ghetto and an image of a vast pile of dead bodies, over which appears in superimposition a series of numbers corresponding with the fatally decreasing ghetto population. Such a distancing narrative move, this telling of life in the ghetto strictly through statistical figures and impersonal imagery, subtly whiffs of the Nazis' own practices of objectification (for instance, as we see in the case of the ghetto, the unilateral, technocratic replanning of Warsaw and redistribution of the city's inhabitants). Accordingly, the moment calls for one of the narrator's characteristic forays into rueful self-criticality. "But numbers do not tell what people feel who are driven to their deaths," he checks himself, marking out the limits of his cold reportage, and gesturing at, in place of not being able to fulfill, the film's desire to present a vigorous countermotion to objectification in its several, wide-ranging guises.

Leaping into the Abyss

One is hard-pressed to find moments in *Long Is the Road* where the Yellins are not in a state of transition. Accordingly, the next time we see them they are on a train—David in one crowded, windowless boxcar, his parents in another—being transported to the camps. Before showing any of the family members, however, the scene in question begins with a Nazi soldier, who climbs down from his patrolling perch on the roof of the train and continues his surveillance by peering into one of the boxcars, through a slit in the wall, at the human cargo inside. Hence the film shows, in close-up, his anonymous, disembodied eyes framed by the two wooden planks, followed by, in a panning point of view shot, what his scouring gaze is taking in. In the midst of this latter shot, this optical journey through the fearfully hushed, darkened space, the camera arrives at David and stops at him as he, somehow singularly detecting the inspection, suddenly turns his head and, with his enormous eyes, piercingly gazes directly back at the soldier (see figures 8.3 and 8.4). In this way, David manages a "revolution" within the structure of the soldier's intended one-way communication and resists the objectification imposed upon him by the dominative, "panoptic" gaze. Of course, the "revolution" is a quiet one, whose effects on the solider are either minimal or nonexistent, for the Nazi disengages from the unwonted encounter almost instantly and simply moves on, presumably toward the next inspection. However, the moment has a critical impact on David, who, as if emboldened, dares something far more audacious. Shuffling frantically through the crowd, in spite of accusations that he has gone "mad" and will "make it worse" for everyone (or in other words, armed with the conviction that madness is preferable to the status quo and that things could not get any worse for any of them), David pronounces a wild desire "to live," rips some planks from the wall, and makes a desperate leap for freedom—inevitably, into a spray of machine-gun fire coming from more patrolling soldiers on the roof of the train.

In a 1979 autobiographical text, written in a paratactic style that conveys both an urgency and a sense of the fragmentary nature of memory, Beker discusses the parallel between this moment in the film and his own experience at the beginning of the war. "I acted the jump from the train while remembering my own,"[22] he writes, explaining the original incident as follows:

> I am in Lublin, Poland, with a band of actors. The Germans conquer the city, the way home, to Bialystok is barred. In Lublin terror of the victorious Nazi armies prevails. I have

Figures 8.3 and 8.4. On a train transporting Jewish prisoners, a Nazi officer surveils the inside of one of the boxcars through a slit in the wall. As this panoptic gaze comes across David, the latter manages to stare back and resist the objectification imposed upon him: a quiet communicative revolution. Marek Goldstein and Herbert B. Fredersdorf, *Long Is the Road* (1948).

to get to the border and cross it to join my family. I am on a train heading east. Suddenly a rumor is spread among the passengers—the Germans are aboard and are imprisoning Jews. Panic spreads—fear. The stories are known. Jews are taken out and shot. I looked out the window, the train was moving at high speed. I only knew one thing: I had to escape from this train—which was a rat trap for me. They were not going to get me—I said to myself. I jumped out of the window, felt a terrific bang and rolled down the hill—the train was gone, I was badly hurt, but alive—saved.[23]

Just before this, characteristically out of chronology, Beker explains what happened once he did finally make it home to Bialystok, at the beginning of 1945.

Far away you could still hear the cannons booming, while fighting went on, and [in] what used to be a living and vibrant town—a robe of silence spread. I walked through the ruins and started running towards the place where our house once stood. I knew I was in the right place. It was here. Remnants of walls . . . the arched gate . . . above me our balcony hanging in the air with the railing I used to hang [on to] for support because of my weak and ailing legs. I looked up, and for a split second imagined—here just in a moment my mother would appear—would stand and gaze around her at the town clock far beyond, the busy streets, the row of stores, one of which belonged to my father . . . I would reach up and take hold of her dress . . . I knew then that it was just a wild dream—that my imagination was playing tricks with me—they were gone. I stood among the debris and my whole life passed in front of me. My past, my home, everything. Then I started searching among the ruins, I turned bricks and iron bars—I found something which I never believed I would find—an enameled salt cellar which used to hang in our kitchen—on it was engraved in Gothic letters—"SALZ"—here is the evidence. If this salt cellar is in my hand, it proves that they existed once, because it seemed to me that they never existed—no father, no mother, no brothers or sisters—no

> home—no neighborhood—all disappeared—and if so—then possibly I don't exist at all.[24]

What one expects at this point in the retelling is to hear how Beker clung ferociously to the miraculously intact object, as if it were a sacred talisman, given its status as the last remaining tie and testament to his former home and existence. However, continuing to recount how he began to sense someone watching him, "most probably gentiles living in the neighborhood—who wanted to know what this man, looking like a Jew, was looking for here," a group whose "faces prophesied evil," Beker tells that he "threw the salt cellar at them—and fled."[25] On some level, Beker's throwing of the object appears to participate in a kind of repetition or reenactment of his earlier throwing of *himself* off the train, and indeed the author's own, psychoanalytically tinged reading of the event does not exclude such a possibility:

> I always run away. All my memories are full of escapes. Instinctive, almost animal impulses, their reason unknown to me. There is nothing easier for me than to get up and leave a place, to move to the unknown. Something tremendous throws me and I succumb easily. Possibly with an inside joy. Here is the command. This is my fate, it is final and I act accordingly. I know that if I am still alive and doing whatever I am doing, I am here and nowhere else, it is only because I was always loyal to this command.[26]

Beker's paradoxically self-constitutive impulse to throw himself into the unknown—a compulsion that forms a strong parallel with Flusser's existential condition of groundlessness—is precisely embodied in the character he plays in *Long Is the Road*. Indeed, as difficult as it may be for viewers today to grasp, equipped as they are with hindsight about the atrocities of the Holocaust, remaining on the train would at least mean for David remaining upon a certain ground. That is to say, as the film emphasizes through the others in the boxcar who violently disapprove of his urge to flee, many en route to the camps still believed, genuinely or in repressive denial, that the status quo would not necessarily lead to death, to say nothing of mass extermination, and that acclimation to such a state of affairs would somehow be the safest and most prudent option. Rather than remain on this ground, which of course also includes his parents just a few boxcars away, David is thus driven toward an utterly unprecedented situation, toward an abyss lacking any familiar elements whatsoever, over which the possibility of virtually instantaneous death, in spite of his will to live, looms enormously.

Bureaucratic Apparatus in and beyond the Camps

In the wake of David's leap, his parents eventually arrive at Auschwitz, which the film represents, as we mentioned earlier, in a kind of minimalist expressionist style. Indeed, the first scene in the camp consists of just a few spare elements suspended against an all-black background: most prevalently, the faces of those being lined up and sent (as a Nazi officer mechanically utters) "*links* [left]" to death or "*recht* [right]" to enslavement, captured in dignifying, low-angle medium shots and close-ups; the white-gloved hand of the Nazi officer, who is otherwise completely cropped out of the image; and a stretch of barbed wire fencing. Dispensing with any claims to realism, such a stylistic strategy functions as an acknowledgment of the difficulties inherent in attempting to "represent the unrepresentable," to borrow the parlance of trauma theory. Yet this is hardly all the strategy works to do. In so heavily relying on faces, it also strives to engage in a dialectic and radically humanize the camp entrants right as they are being radically dehumanized, treated as objects to be lethally discarded or extracted for labor power. Meanwhile, the accompanying tactic of keeping the perpetrators as anonymous abstractions (i.e., the officer as merely a robotic voice and a gloved hand) allows such reclaimed humanity to emerge all the more vigorously. In other words, the facelessness of the Nazis becomes a foil-like screen for keenly apprehending the fearful but never entirely discomposed (and surely idealized) faces of the Jews. Further, by means of such humanizing, facial foregrounding, the filmmakers stake out yet another contrast with the largely distanciated, "expository" documentaries discussed earlier, in which the survivors of the camps, while periodically glimpsed at close range, often appear shockingly "alien" in their drastic emaciation and traumatized hardening or hollowing out (these sorts of images, in fact, appear later during a synoptic, newsreel-style recounting of the liberation of the camps).

Inevitably, the film's distinctive treatment of the camp, too, calls to mind Levinas's idea of the Face of the Other, which we discussed earlier in relation to the figure of the outcast in *Motel the Operator*. In fact, it does so with especial force given that Levinas conceptualizes the Face of the Other in terms of an ambivalently *homicidal* relation to "the absolutely weak—to what is absolutely exposed, what is bare and destitute," wherein what is brought up in the I in the encounter with the Face of the Other is an urge to kill together with a resistance to that very act (embodied in the biblical commandment that prohibits murder). Obviously, the Auschwitz scene traffics quite literally in murder, and yet because ambivalence is absent in the murderous I (indeed, not only does the biblical commandment not even remotely come into play, but the I itself is absent, rendered completely anonymous), it becomes strictly up to us, the spectators, to take up the urgent, life-and-death call for responsibility, which here (unlike in *Motel the Operator*, which features a resplendent answering figure in the character of the humanitarian lawyer son) goes appallingly unheeded within the sphere of the diegesis. Such a situation is put on display with particularly forceful exemplarity in the case of David's father. After his wife is sent to the right and then hauled away (by another soldier, pictured only as an arm thrust out of the darkness), Jacob reaches the front of the line and is directed, fatally, to the left. At this point, he appears in the tightest, most extreme close-up of the entire, pervasively close-shot scene, looking around anxiously, presumably for his wife. Yet when the film cuts away, in match cut fashion, it pictures not Hannah, who is by now out of eyeshot, but the smoke-belching chimney of a crematorium. The substitution couldn't be more brutal. And so, in a return to the extreme close-up of him (now encroachingly double exposed with the smoke), sensing something ominous, Jacob turns once more to religion, yet with his faith in an even more totteringly challenged position than it was on the Shabbat evening when David arrived with the news of the ghetto. Quietly, in the final moment of the scene, he begins to say the *Shema*—a daily prayer traditionally spoken as a Jew's last words—whose unifying address to the Jewish community takes on especial poignancy in the moment of genocidal atomization: "Hear, O Israel, the Lord is our God, the Lord is One . . ." Accordingly, in parallel to the scene's unique, involved treatment of the Face of the Other, it is left up to us, across an ontological divide, to carry out such critical hearing, whose prospects are even further diminished and tested by the scene fading out before Jacob can finish the prayer.

As for Hannah, condemned to imprisonment in the camp, she becomes another of Yiddish cinema's classic figures of alarming isolation, furthering the film's continuity with the canon of prewar Yiddish films. The film renders this steep descent a few scenes later, reintroducing her in a typically deferred manner and taking us on a roaming cinematographic journey before finally "finding" her. Thus the scene begins with another female inmate, one whom we've never met before, who, in a series of tracking and panning shots that gradually tilt up from her feet to her face, walks into a barracks, makes her way through the crowded room, and takes a seat at a coarse wooden table, empty except for a tiny candle, and begins passing around potatoes, no doubt acquired illicitly, to a group of women who are eager to receive this little bit of nourishment. Only at the end of all this activity does the camera tilt up from the table and discover Hannah, who holds her sullen, begrimed face in her hands, and listlessly needs to be prompted in order to take a potato for herself (indeed, she less takes one than has it thrust into her hand). The unknown woman's gesture toward her fellow prisoners demonstrates a crucial attempt to maintain community amid the desolate conditions, bolstered by another's optimistic words about the need to remain steadfast: "We must all wait for the day of liberation and then we'll gather up our broken families, and begin our lives anew." However, Hannah appears unreachable by any of it, absently, laconically recounting how she was sent to the right and Jacob to the left, how David was perhaps shot during his escape attempt, and how familial restoration and beginning again will be impossible. Plagued by survivor guilt, she counters: "Anew, no. They killed him . . . Why have they spared me?" For Hannah, as shown so often in Yiddish cinema, the severing of critical familial bonds results in the utter shattering of her world.

Hannah manages to survive Auschwitz. However, when we pick up with her in the post-liberation period, her isolation not only fails to improve but becomes drastically exacerbated. As the film intriguingly emphasizes, this owes to the fact that her only chance of recovering her lost relations comes via more entanglement in an objectifying, bureaucratic apparatus. Following her release from the camps, unaware if David is alive or dead, Hannah goes in search of her son and returns to Warsaw. There, at the family's old, now re-tenanted, apartment, she discovers that David, too, returned "home"—that he is alive—and goes on to find out further, at the offices of the Jewish Committee, that he planned to go to Germany, where he thought she might have ended up (in a dilemma all too typical of the DP condition, Hannah cannot acquire a fixed address for David, only the general locale of a country). Accordingly, Hannah takes leave of the offices—a space densely packed with other survivors searching for their lost relations, its walls plastered with missing-persons notices—intently bound for Germany. At this point, as the camera tilts down and focuses on her moving feet (a sign of her continuing displacement), the film launches into a highly evocative montage sequence, one that, as Hoberman justly remarks, "could have been lifted from *Motl der Operator*,"[27] and that also bears much in common with the hypercommunicative "searching" sequence in *Where Is My Child?* However, as we wish to stress, the sequence is notable for reasons that go beyond such intertextual resonances.

At the outset, the film cross-cuts between Hannah and David, who is engaged in a parallel, desperate, furious search for his mother. Thus we oscillate back and forth between close-ups of the two characters, both in constant, probing, ambulatory motion, while such shots are superimposed with a delirious flurry of shots of the offices of various tracing services (some located on-site at DP camps), and the vast archives housed at these institutions (see figure 8.5). As we know, such tracing services significantly relied on the Nazis' own, obsessively kept records of their activities. Indeed, as Jennifer Rodgers writes of the International Tracing Service (ITS), which arose in the postwar period out of the previously existing Central Tracing Bureau and served as a crucial instrument in the DP support effort, "the agency [was] once ominously referred to as 'Hitler's Secret Archive.' "[28] What is so fascinating about the montage sequence in the film, however, is that it portrays the borderline between the original instantiation of the Nazi bureaucracy, which functioned in the service of atomizing people, and its repurposed, postwar instantiation, which functioned in the service of reconnecting people, as radically unstable, as if the "good" remediation ran the risk of relapsing into the "bad" precursor on which it was built. Suggestions of this slipperiness appear midway

Figure 8.5. As Hannah searches for her son after the war, she drowns in an overwhelming bureaucracy, appearing double exposed over images of the vast archives at the various "tracing services." Marek Goldstein and Herbert B. Fredersdorf, *Long Is the Road* (1948).

through the montage, which ceases to include David and shifts to an exclusive focus on Hannah, whose psychological condition drastically deteriorates as a result of all her fruitless inquiries. Indeed, as she encounters a seemingly endless series of tracing services administrators, who, amid their vast edifices of paperwork, confront her with the same punishing, denying word, *nein*, Hannah is launched into a full-on traumatic flashback. Repeating *nein* herself in a nonsynchronous, stammered cry, she is flooded by fragments of sounds (the fatal order of *links . . . links . . . links*) and images (the barbed wire fencing, the white-gloved hand, the smoke, Jacob at the front of the line) from the camps. In this way, the montage effects a striking collapse between the two "respective" forms of administration, merging the Nazi officer, who lethally processes Hannah's husband into the camp, and the tracing services workers, who coldly inform her of their inability to give her any information about her son, into one.

Accordingly, it is possible to read the progressively phantasmatic montage as a kind of uncanny analogue to Flusser's sobering claim about Auschwitz as an unmasking of the Western apparatus. That is to say, both see the camps as distinctly continuous with broader motions and potentialities, or in Flusser's terminology, "virtualities," in the surrounding, preexisting, and/or post-existing culture. As mentioned, Zygmunt Bauman too shares this approach to the Holocaust, giving an account that puts particular emphasis on bureaucracy, or more specifically on what he calls the "the dehumanization of the objects of bureaucratic operation," and that thus offers a way of clarifying even further the theoretical energies of the montage's suggestive conflation. According to Bauman, the acts of outrageous dehumanization that occurred in the camps "represent only an extreme manifestation of a tendency which may be discovered in all bureaucracies, however benign and innocuous the task in which they are currently engaged."[29] Bauman's explanation for why this is comes in a remarkable passage that chimes deeply with media theory, for in it he stakes out a claim for understanding the structural properties of media themselves and indulges in an almost Flusserian conscription of the language of information theory (i.e., "programming") in order to advance such an understanding (recall how Flusser understands the "apparatus" as a technology of opaque automation):

> Contrary to widespread opinion, bureaucracy is not merely a tool, which can be used with equal facility at one time for cruel and morally contemptible, at another for deeply humane purposes. Even if it does move in any direction in which it is pushed, bureaucracy is more like a loaded dice. It has a logic and a momentum of its own. It renders some solutions more, and other solutions less, probable. Given an initial push (being confronted with a purpose), it will—like the brooms of the sorcerer's apprentice—easily move beyond all thresholds at which many of those who gave it the push would have stopped, were they still in control of the process they triggered. Bureaucracy is programmed to measure the optimum in such terms as would not distinguish between one human object and another, or between human and inhuman objects. What matters is the efficiency and lowering of costs of their processing.[30]

The refusal to keep clean lines between radically differing uses of bureaucracy in the montage bears this view out. And, indeed, the scene that follows drives home the point. Showing the consequences of Hannah's breakdown, the screen fades into a shot of a small chalkboard that reads: "*Name: Unbekannt* [Name: Unknown]." The camera then tilts down and reveals Hannah in bed in a German hospital, shaking and continuing to moan *nein*, as a doctor rushes over and tries to calm her, imploring her, in what clearly has been an oft-made attempt, to reveal her name and say if she has any relatives. Utterly shattered, Hannah has become, like so many of Yiddish cinema's drastically disconnected characters, effectively mute, unable to respond to the doctor's questions, only repeating traumatic words from the camp and her failed search for her child (*nein, links, recht* . . .). Accordingly, as a nurse informs the doctor after he pulls away from the bed, all that can be done in order to try to discover the unknown woman's identity is to follow the number tattooed on her arm and check it with the tracing services. In other words, the means by which Hannah was so brutally objectified by the Nazis remains in operation; woefully, still she is being handled in terms of a number.

Shelter in the Other

In "The Road Back for the DP's: Healing the Psychological Scars of Nazism," an essay published in *Commentary* in December of 1948, the American psychoanalyst Paul Friedman writes: "It seems altogether incredible today that when the first plans for the rehabilitation of Europe's surviving Jews were outlined, the psychiatric aspect of the problem was overlooked entirely. Everyone engaged in directing the relief work thought solely in terms of material assistance to the DP's. It took months of first-hand practical experience before anyone would acknowledge a similar, equally pressing need for psychological assistance."[31] Such an interest in psychic matters is something that *Long Is the Road*'s treatment of the DP condition amply shares. (Indeed, one could point to a number of connections between the essay and the film, including the shared metaphor of "the road" in their titles; the fact that the American Joint Distribution Committee—the organization that created the Jewish film initiative, YAFO, that recommended the production of *Long Is the Road*—also funded

Friedman's extensive fieldwork with Jewish DPs in Europe, Cyprus, and Palestine; and the fact that both Beker and Friedman come from Poland—the latter born in Lublin 1899, and immigrating to the US in 1935.[32]) Regarding "the psychological scars of Nazism," the film perhaps most obviously represents these through the character of David's mother, who suffers from traumatic flashbacks to the camps and ends up hospitalized in a state of total mental collapse. Yet it also delves into such territory in its representation of David's complex, obstacle-laden, romantic relationship with an adrift, German Jewish DP named Dora Berkovitz (Bettina Moissi). (Moissi, a German actor with movie star beauty who appeared in a cluster of films during and immediately after the war, was the daughter of the famous stage and screen actor Aleksander Moissi, who, pertinently in the context of his daughter's role in *Long Is the Road*, was both often mistaken for a Jew[33]—his Albanian last name translates to "Moses"—and intrepidly outspoken against the Austrian and German antisemitism of his time.[34]) David and Dora come together by chance on the night that David attempts to return home to his family's apartment in Warsaw. Having survived the leap from the train, and then spending the rest of the war fighting with the Partisans (whom he manages to locate in the woods through the aid of a devout Christian farmer who refuses to turn him in to a Nazi search party[35]), David jovially approaches the city on a train quite literally draped in Polish nationalist sentiments. "*OJCYZNA WAS WITA* [Homeland greets you]," announces a banner festooned on the side of one of the cars. However, forced to make the last part of his journey on foot due to the fact that, as a fellow passenger informs him, "all the bridges are down"—a revealing indication of the city's blasted infrastructure, of the shattered state of Warsaw's material means of connectivity—David quickly faces a hostile, if politely shrouded, (un)welcome. At the apartment, he finds a rowdy, celebratory party being thrown by his former neighbour, Mr. Chodecki, who explains, as if describing a kind of self-evident, unchallengeable state of affairs: "You know the house was given to us." In other words, Chodecki entertains not the slightest thought of returning the place to David, whose reappearance gives him such a shock of surprise that it is almost as if he were encountering a person come back from the dead. Instead, Chodecki grudgingly offers to put David up for the night, making the excuse that he has already had to give up two rooms to another neighbor because of the housing shortage in the bombed-out city, and inviting him in for a drink with the insistence that "we too fought for freedom"—a self-absolving comment that rankles David and triggers his abrupt exit. Wanderingly setting out into the streets of the flattened city in the middle of the night, David encounters Dora amid a crowd of people left behind by an overfilled vehicle bound for far-off Targowa. Dora initiates the conversation—in German (like most German Jews, she knows no Yiddish)—and asks David if she can go with him, sensing perhaps the danger of the situation and his decency. As they continue to roam the streets, she explains the basic details of her situation: that both her parents died, and that, in a cruel irony, she had originally been deported from Germany for being Jewish and now is being forced to leave Poland for being German. In turn, David shares his own sense of disorientation, his troubling loss of the ability to navigate the city that had once been so familiar to him: "Where are we? I don't recognize this street anymore. Everything is destroyed." And before long, the exchange yields a moment of startling intimacy—or more specifically, profoundly stifled intimacy—between the two strangers.

In the void-like darkness, the wearied pair sit down to get some rest. Accepting David's invitation to lean her head on his shoulder, Dora continues to open up about her difficult experiences during the war ("We already had to go once, Mother and I. Then we came into the camp. Maybe it will happen again"), and eventually drifts off to sleep, which brings the two even more closely together. Captured in a tight shot in which all that is largely visible is the faces of the characters (see figure 8.6), the moment possesses a radiant, iconic force, and indeed aptly graces the packaging of the DVD put out by the National Center for Jewish Film. What it suggests is that, in the distressing absence of home, the two characters embody (quite literally, if we attend to their pose) a form of shelter for one another: a notion that irresistibly resonates with Yiddish cinema's stress on interpersonal relations, while providing yet another version of the prevalent "portable home" motif, which we saw earlier when David takes down and pockets the mezuzah in the lead-up to his departure for the ghetto. Importantly, however, and this is something that goes unconveyed by the decontextualized still image on the DVD box, the resonantly interconnective moment is perilously fragile and short-lived. That is to say, as David remains awake and casts a continuingly restless *gaze* around the surrounding ruins—portrayed in a floodlit,

Figure 8.6. In the immediate aftermath of the war, Dora falls asleep on David's shoulder on the ruined streets of Warsaw: an image of the two homeless DPs finding shelter in one another. Marek Goldstein and Herbert B. Fredersdorf, *Long Is the Road* (1948).

panning point-of-view shot—Dora is suddenly plunged into a violent nightmare, which causes her to thrash around, repeatedly cry out *nein*, and pull away from him. Like Hannah, whose cry she echoes, Dora is afflicted by traumatic memories of the camps, though hers are kept more "ineffably" internal, not shown by the film in an audiovisual projection of her psyche. Also notably different is the fact that Dora's flashback occurs in the midst of a moment of togetherness rather than isolation, though strikingly with not dissimilar results, hinting that for the survivor a reentry into the world of intersubjective relations remains fraught with difficulties, even when (and perhaps even especially when) warmly and profusely facilitated. As Friedman writes of the camps, "Human beings simply do not exist in such a situation without making profound internal readjustments. One cannot live for years in a world in which one man kills another for a cigarette, in which cannibalism is a reality, and then revert instantly on liberation to the man one was before. In view of all this, it is truly amazing that the DP's whom we found in Europe were capable of any social expression at all."[36] Such a lingeringly impaired sense of relationality seems to be exhibited by Dora, as if she were unconsciously averse, recoilingly defensive, about her burgeoning attachment to David. Or in other words, on a psychic level, it is no accident that her trauma comes raging back at a point of intense intimacy. Accordingly, the scene's apparent, hopeful trajectory toward connection fails to be picked up; the iconic pose of mutually supporting bodies fails to be reassumed. After he shakes her back into consciousness, David presses Dora to tell him about the dream, but she falls disconcertingly silent, claiming it was "nothing" and averting her eyes, at which point the scene abruptly ends.

Nevertheless, the relationship stands as a work in progress to which the film devotes great attention. The next day, at the offices of the Jewish Committee, where David finds out that his father died at Auschwitz, and that his mother was among the prisoners transferred to Dachau, and therefore may or may not be alive, the female clerk taking down his information glances at Dora beside him and asks him for the name of his wife. The mistaken assumption elicits a bashful smile from Dora, while bringing up the fact that, absurdly, the two don't even know each other's names despite spending the entire night in each other's company. And yet, of course, the comment perceptively taps into what is evolving between the two. Indeed, it even seems to act as a nudge in their relationship, a reminder that each is the only "family" that the other has at this point. For on the way out of the offices, the two agree to venture together to Germany, where David hopes to find his mother and is at least, as he points out, "somewhere" toward which they can direct themselves. Hence the pair take a train bound for Germany, amid a tense crush of displaced people of various ethnicities and national backgrounds, including both Jews from different places and non-Jewish Germans who used to live in a formerly German part of Poland before being expelled: a situation that leads David to make an impassioned speech about the need for coexistence and for hatreds to be laid to rest.[37] And once in Germany, along with a teeming truckload of other Jewish DPs, they continue together to the camp at Landsberg, which, as mentioned, "plays itself" and is portrayed in a distinctly ambiguous light that reveals yet another disturbing continuity between conditions in the concentration camps and in the world of the DPs. "Again there were guards at the door, again barbed wire, barracks," warily remarks the narrator, "but at least it was shelter. This time they were called 'D.P. Camps.'" Touching on the same disquieting likeness, Friedman writes: "Most survivors who have had to remain in the [DP] camps under continuous regimentation have grown more anxious and aggressive. Despite all that continues to be done for them, they see themselves as betrayed and abandoned for a second time."[38] Indeed, the film puts such regimentation explicitly on display when we see Dora and David among a group of new arrivals being assigned to their new quarters by a guard who goes about the process totally indiscriminately, purely out of the administrative need to rationalize the space of the rooms, where multiple families and individuals have been thrown together in a zone that permits no privacy and collapses the places of eating and sleeping. "This area is for six people," remarks the guard, checking a number on the door, opening the door without knocking, and letting Dora inside to find a place among the residents already living there. Following this relatively bleak introduction to the camp, it is thus not surprising that the pair's time in the place (David returns some time later after setting out on a vain search for his mother) proves challenging. As David explains sympathetically to a machine-operator in an almost entirely emptied-out shop, bemoaning the failure of the camp to bestow any kind of meaning on the work carried out there: "The waiting drives them [the workers] to the city to make money. It's better than sitting around in the camp, waiting, working. I've been thinking of leaving soon, too, and beginning a new life."

At a certain point under these limbo-like circumstances, David tries to become less stuck and broaches with Dora the possibility of getting married, doing so in an exterior scene that again exhibits the trials of their intimacy. Suggestively, the scene unfolds against the camp's extensive barbwire fencing, a backdrop that creates an obviously trying setting for a proposal, and that the camera continually emphasizes, both in the lengthy opening tracking shot (which follows the couple as they walk along the fencing and views them through the barrier) and in the subsequent shots (in which the camera joins them on their side of the fence and which largely consist of tight shot/reverse-shots). In fact, from the outset of the scene, the rapport between Dora and David appears relatively cheerful, relaxed, and even touchy-feely, as becomes apparent when the two sit down on what passes for furniture on the campgrounds: the trunk of a chopped-down tree (a subtle, realistically anchored emblem of uprootedness). It is only when David mentions the prospect of marriage, in a notably shy, circuitous way that avoids a direct posing of the question ("I thought if we married . . . that would be good") that trouble arises. For Dora neither responds to the (crypto-)proposal affirmatively or negatively but rather again becomes alarmingly reticent and downcast, again beats a retreat at just the point at which their intimacy begins significantly to escalate.

> DAVID: What is it? You don't want to? Ah, I understand! You think there is no space in the camp. We don't have our own room.
>
> DORA: [continuing silence]
>
> DAVID: What is it then? Did I hurt you? [begins to get up in disappointment]
>
> DORA: Stay! You are right, we are strangers. That's why I can tell you everything. Then you can think what you want. You know, we came into the camp . . .
>
> DAVID: You have told me often enough.
>
> DORA: No, not that. That was still in Warsaw, at the *Umschlagplatz* [holding area where Jews were assembled for deportation].
>
> DAVID: You have to forget, Dora. You must forget what has passed.
>
> DORA: Here I can't.
>
> DAVID: But we won't stay here, and there you will forget.

David's imperative to forget will likely sound jarring to contemporary viewers, who are used to encountering an imperative precisely to the contrary, which has come to assume an important place within the more general Jewish veneration of remembrance. Indeed, the film itself would seem, already, to be taking up this urgent demand to enshrine the Holocaust in memory. At the same time, David's plea to Dora to forget also seems to clash with the film's project, analogous to that of Friedman, precisely to *attend* to the psychic traumas of the survivors. In grappling with these contradictions and ambiguities, however, one can point to two things: first, to the fact that the line might simply be in character for David, who experienced the Warsaw ghetto and deportation on the train though not the concentration camps, and who thus might overoptimistically underestimate the psychic difficulties that Dora is experiencing; second, to the fact that his position is borne out of a kind of situational exigency that, of course, is hardly mutually exclusive with a possible reopening of the question of a reckoning with the past at a later, less pressing and precarious time. At any rate, for now, Dora's entertaining of the potential viability of the demand comes down, as she suggests, to getting out of the DP camp. That is to say, threaded through her fragmentary remarks is an acknowledgment of the disturbing resemblance between the two species of camps discussed earlier, which precisely makes forgetting into an impossibility. It is thus a canny, fitting move by the film that although Dora ultimately agrees to the marriage, in a resonant omission that dovetails with David's encumbered, indirect uttering of the proposal, we never actually *witness* her agreeing and saying, "Yes." Following the dialogue quoted earlier, the scene fades out and the film simply cuts to the wedding ceremony (carried out with a chuppah, Hebrew vows, glass breaking, traditional round-dancing, and other moving recommencements of Jewish practices), generating an ellipsis that attests to the persistence of troubled communication between the couple under the frustrating conditions of the camp.

Similarly, the couple's intimacy continues to face blockage in the aftermath of the ceremony, the nuptials appearing, revealingly, as merely one more event in an uncertain, ongoing train of events, rather than as a closure-inviting object for a concluding scene, which is how weddings so often function in Yiddish cinema. Retreating to their cramped, shared room amid shouts of *"mazel tov"* from the other residents, the smiling newlyweds sit down on a bed and attempt to express their affection and celebrate on a more private plane. Yet repeatedly they are interrupted by ambient intrusions: from offscreen, a sweetly meddlesome woman hollers her apologies for not being able to attend the ceremony; a man, briefly glimpsed in a cutaway shot, crouched in front of a radio, switches the set on in order to listen to, as he announces, an important meeting of the Jewish Congress. This latter, radiophonic interruption (which becomes audible) proves especially, persistently distracting, recalling the "virtual" radio that streams in through Arthur's apartment window in *The Wandering Jew* and producing a figuration of the technology as an explicitly political medium that ineluctably invades private space. Indeed, the man who switches on the radio chimes in with a second announcement to the room—that the meeting will be broadcast for the whole camp—just as the couple (having pensively reassumed the pose of their first night together in Warsaw, and in this way managing to create the absorptive conditions for ignoring their surroundings) drop their guard and mutually go in to kiss one another. In other words, with woeful irony, it turns out that at the very moment in which the couple's internal obstacles subside, external obstacles swoop in and take over. As Dora laments to David, softly yet with unmistakably unleashed desire, "At least tonight I would have liked to be alone with you."

A Call to All to Find the One

The appearance of the radio in the post-wedding scene inaugurates what in fact turns out to be an entire radio sequence, and indeed a broader chain of sequences, extending nearly all the way to the end of the film, in which multiple forms of mass media come prominently into play and are subjected to a typically Yiddish-cinematic form of "dialogic" critique. Hoping to find better prospects for privacy outside, Dora and David pick up and leave their room. However, as they walk through the campgrounds in the darkness, hand in hand, breathing more easily, their search is halted by more unsolicited contact with the (evidently ubiquitous) radio. Turning a corner, they encounter a large assembly of camp residents in a yard-like space listening quietly, intently to the broadcast of the meeting of the Jewish Congress, and they stop in front of the crowd. At this point, not only is the interaction between David and Dora (further) interrupted, but the film radically pulls away from the couple, dissolving from a close-up of the radio to the actual site of the broadcast. Suddenly, invested with privileged audiovisual access to what is being transmitted over the airwaves, we find ourselves at the auditorium where, up on a podium, an elder statesman-like figure is giving an impassioned speech about the urgent need to resolve the DP crisis to an audience of diplomats and officials (as Joshua S. Walden points out, this footage is repurposed from a 1947 documentary about the *She'erit Hapletah*—the "surviving remnant"—by the codirector Marek Goldstein[39]). As the film proceeds to illustrate the speech with a montage of images of life at Landsberg (and in so doing adds to our privileged seeing), the speaker declares, in a conclusion that locates a solution firmly in the Zionist project: "We appeal to the United States of America and to England, open the gates of *Eretz Yisrael* to our wandering masses. Liquidate these camps. Until this shameful remnant of Hitler disappears from the face of the earth, there can and will not be a stable Pax Europa." Such rousing words draw enthusiastic applause from the audience, at which point everyone in the room stands and joins in a collective rendition of *Hatikvah*, the proto-Israeli national anthem. It is amid the performance of this song that the film cuts back to the crowd listening in the yard, and then back to the couple standing close by, wherein David attempts to pull Dora away from the scene in a continued hunt for privacy. However, prompted by Dora's remark, "We will never be alone," the two swiftly surrender to the almost farcical futility of the search, and, finally, passionately kiss for the first time that we see in the film, as the music swells and the camera dollies in and reframes them in close-up. In this way, the film offers up an electric moment in which the radio, now transmitting *Hatikvah* to the whole camp, remarkably appears to transform from a source of dire disruption to the couple's intimacy to a potent facilitator of that very intimacy: a shift that perhaps embodies less an intoxicated, erotically charged affirmation of Zionism per se than an index of how the couple's intimacy problems, inextricably embedded as they are in a political dilemma of homelessness (recall Dora's "Not here"), peel back in the face of a persuasive promise to end that dilemma by whatever means.

In any case, however we think of the euphoric moment of mass-mediated connection (which includes not just Dora and David, but all those at the Congress and those listening to the meeting at a distance), the film goes out of its way to deflate it almost instantly. In the next scene, which takes place the next day at a hall somewhere in the camp, a characteristic, opening, extended tracking shot takes us along a long table at which a number of male DPs wile away their time playing chess, smoking, and reading the newspaper. Ultimately, the camera comes to rest at the far end of the table, where one man reads aloud to two other men a transcription of the speech from the previous day. In its remediated migration from the live radio broadcast to print to the perfunctory private reading, the originally full-throated, high-flown speech suffers a startling diminishment in communicative power. Further, in familiar Yiddish that contrasts with the German of the speech, the two listeners provide a withering commentary on the content of the speech, pointing to an insuperable gap between the official political realm, governed by what feel like impossibly abstract ideals, and their everyday reality. In response to the speech's conclusion that until the DP camps are dissolved "there can and will not be a stable Pax Europa," one of the listeners remarks with scoffing, hardnosed skepticism, "Only in Europe? There won't be any peace in the whole world," to which the other listener adds: "Yes, yes, now the Congress is over, and where is the result of all these beautiful speeches?"

Yet the newspaper that remediates the speech does produce a kind of result—one that emerges, fortuitously, out of one of traditional mass media's more marginal, more intimate communicative capacities. As the man who reads the transcription of the speech (which appears on the front page) continues to hold the paper aloft, the man sitting across from him happens to notice an item on the back page that causes him to perk up. "Wait, wait. A certain Hannah Yellin is looking for her relatives," he imparts to the others excitedly (here, too, thanks to a low-angle close shot, we get a partial glimpse of the masthead that permits an identification of the paper as the *Jidisze Caytung*: a popular Yiddish paper produced out of Landsberg, disseminated throughout DP camps in Germany, and, owing to an unsurprising scarcity of Hebrew type, printed in transliterated Latin characters according to the Polish pronunciation system[40]). Like the article about the mother searching for her lost son printed in the Yiddish newspaper in *A Little Letter to Mother*, the item embodies, of course, a missing person's ad, a modality of mass media that functions, in John Durham Peters's deft phrase, as a "call to all to find the one,"[41] as a wildly public address that aims to foster a distinctly private connection. In *A Little Letter to Mother*, as we saw, the missing persons notice in the Yiddish press proves futile, failing to "find the one" and playing no role in bringing about the reunion between the mother and son. *In Long Is the Road*, the situation is different: the "call to all to find the one" does turn out to reach "the one." Brought the paper while he is in the midst of giving a staid lecture on engine mechanics in a classroom in another part of the camp, David seizes the copy, takes in the ad, and, in a close-up that now offers a full glimpse of the paper's masthead, utters in hushed shock that infinitely, self-reflexively loaded Yiddish word that we've discussed on a number of occasions throughout this book: *mame*.

Nevertheless, within a wider context, the difference between the treatment of the mass-mediated "call to all to find the one" in the two films dissolves in the pervasive Yiddish-cinematic conviction that all mediations mean nothing if the people concerned are themselves not receptive, not capable of being (re)connected. In other words, in the spite of all the (marginal) facilitations of mass media, (re)connection still requires a kind of mysterious "turning" on a basic interpersonal level. Accordingly, as David impatiently arrives at the hospital along with Dora, he finds his mother, but only, as it were, in body. Sitting on a wooden chair in a convalescent patio space, haggard and indifferently tidied up, she looks over at him vacantly, mutely, and, in total nonrecognition, reassumes her gaze emptily outward, seeming even more psychically vacant and withdrawn than she was in Auschwitz. Multiple interlocking mediations have brought us to this point: the number tattooed on Hannah's arm, the tracing services, the newspaper article (presumably placed by someone at the tracing services who was able to identify her through the tattooed number sent by the hospital). And yet, as mentioned, for the brute material reunion to become truly meaningful an inner, fundamentally interpersonal event is required; and this, perhaps not surprisingly for the initiates of Yiddish cinema, the film delivers. After David's pleading questions to his mother if she can "see" him go unanswered, a doctor assures him that she will recover "in time." However, right at this moment, as if the long years that have passed since the separation between her and her son have proven to be time enough, Hannah suddenly awakens from her traumatized trance, gasps David's name, and again turns toward him, now in an electrifying bloom of recognition. Hence, at last, it can be said that a reunion between the two takes place, or at least begins. Amid a chorus of ethereal chanting (notably, the film does not mark the reconnection with a reprise of *Hatikvah*), the two embrace in an emotionally seismic enfoldment, while David's faltering repetition of *mame* gives way to an urgent confession and spate of promises: "I want to get out of here. Mama, I won't leave you. We'll always be together. We'll leave and go far away, to our own land and a new home." As the outpouring suggests, David has in fact been grappling with a relational problematic analogous to (if not identical with) Dora's, held back from any kind of "moving on" by the unresolved situation regarding his missing mother. Accordingly, only now that he has been properly reunited with his mother does he seem capable of imagining a future in more concrete terms, and of taking steps, however constrained by forces beyond his control, toward realizing them. Via the recovery of family relations, that is, David is finally able to start piecing back together his ground.

Regrounding

Such a process is what is captured by the film's open-ended, optimistically tinged epilogue. In a nondescript agricultural landscape, David capably steers a horse-drawn plow across a furrowed open field, while behind him a group of other workers move in the opposite direction, hunched over, sowing. Meanwhile, over the establishing shot, providing an update on the situation of the Jewish DPs, the narrator speaks for the last time: "Another year went by. Still they plow, in a land that considers them a burden." That is to say, we are still in Germany, but, as the dialogue shortly clarifies, no longer in Landsberg but rather in a kibbutz somewhere in the German countryside. Setting down the plow and taking a break from his labor, David walks over to his mother and Dora, who are reposing serenely on a blanket in the shade of a tree close by. In fact, he greets three people, the third being a sleeping baby boy, his and Dora's newborn child, whom his mother, looking significantly recuperated (though still not saying terribly much), cradles affectionately in her arms. David confirms with his mother that it's "quieter, calmer" in the kibbutz than in the "*lager*," and that she'll soon get well. He then turns to Dora, who lies flat on the ground, her hands folded beneath her head, and asks if she's also sleeping, to which she replies that she just awoke from a dream, which she proceeds to recount, dreamily, in a close-up in which she sits up and David hovers over her, the warm breeze rustling both of their hair and the leaves casting shadows on her face: "I saw a field, and you, and a house with a garden, just like here, but it was our own." The abstract, hopeful, future-oriented dream stands in obvious contrast to Dora's earlier traumatic nightmares, suggesting that she has made inroads into working through—or in David's parlance, forgetting—her difficult past. Yet the development is tentative, overlaid with uncertainty: "It will come true, yes?" Dora is compelled to confirm. David responds, "It must," and, as if taking steps toward making the dream a reality, gets up and returns to the plow—to his new agricultural line of work, which, unlike the work that he was doing in the seeming dead-end context of the camp, feels meaningful to him, and which, in being bound up with the earth, affords him a quite literal measure of grounding. Thus trudging through the field, David stares resolutely ahead, shown in a low-angle close-up that evokes the ennobling, sky-framed shots of farm laborers in Dovzhenko's *Earth*, and continues to press on into the distance, captured in a long shot—the last shot of the film—that begins trained on his moving feet, and tilts up to reveal the whole expanse of the field, where several more workers sow and plow in the background. Yet just before the final fade-out there is one last narratorial intervention, delivered not in speech but in (German) text, superimposed on the screen in three straight lines that contrast with the slanted lines of the opening credits and suggest a certain evolution toward stability: "*DOCH LANG IST DER WEG* [But long is the road]." In this way, the film foregoes a standard "The End" title, just as *The Wandering Jew* leaves us with a title that reads "Ad Infinitum." This shared eccentricity, while seeking to offer the audience a dose of fortifying hope (however differently shaded), embodies a marker of the films' unique relation to their historical moments—a relation, that is, characterized by an aspiration to intervene within and influence a political situation that is still very much unfolding, that is still very much shot through with inconclusiveness, that has by no means yet ended.

 In relation to the reality of displaced people that it sets out to capture, *Long Is the Road* represents groundlessness as a highly problematic condition. If the DPs are to be able to begin to resume their lives that have been so severely devastated, the film suggests, then their lack of ground will need to be powerfully mitigated. The film, that is, testifies to the necessity of ground. In doing so, it deviates markedly from Flusser, whose writing on groundlessness amounts to a nuanced, counterintuitive affirmation of the condition. For him, groundlessness, while unignorably agonizing, contains the possibility of opening the self up to an existential freedom, that is, to the capacity to form new, freely chosen relations independent of conditioning structures like the nation. Adapting Arendt's famous formulation of refugees as "the vanguard of their peoples,"[42] he writes: "Each person who is without heimat has at least the potential of representing the awakened consciousness of all those who are settled in a heimat. He can be a vanguard of the future. And it seems to me that we migrants must take this function on ourselves as our profession and calling."[43] Instead of advocating for the migrant to reground through assimilation into cultural systems whose rules she or he consequently becomes unconscious of, Flusser thus proposes a new relational model of heimat (a concept with obvious ties to "ground") that shifts the concept away from its usual basis in land and nation: "For me, heimat consists of the people to whom I choose to be responsible."[44] David begins to rebuild his ground in just this way by cultivating his relations to Dora and his mother. At the same time, as such relations emerge, they require a supporting context in order to thrive. (As Arendt's writing on statelessness reminds us, even as it too delivers a radical critique of the nation-state, to be stranded outside of the system of nation-states that organizes the modern world is to lead an impossible life.) Unsurprisingly, as the film shows, the DP can't ultimately meet Flusser's utopian proposal, which he himself admits is utopian, a philosophical response to the absurdity provoked by his own experience(s) of groundlessness. In reality, what the characters are striving for at the point in their journey in which the film leaves them, namely, at the point where personal relations have been restored, is captured in Dora's dream: the desire for a home of their own, presumably in a welcoming country that will become their new homeland. Or we might say, the material, geopolitical home is not important in itself, but only insofar as it sustains the home embodied by the people to whom one is responsible.

9

Mediating the Mystical

The Dybbuk (1937)

CURRENTS OF MYSTICISM flow regularly through Yiddish cinema, from the songs and melodies possessed of a preternatural ability to cross vast distances and ontological boundaries, to the incredible coincidences and providential plot designs of *shund*, to the compendium of dreams and visions where a photograph or a painting of a long-lost loved one bursts numinously into life. *The Dybbuk* (*Der Dibek*), however, presents us with a Yiddish film that is predominantly *about* mysticism. Taking place in a nineteenth-century Hasidic world pervaded everywhere by the influences of the Kabbalah—the Jewish mystical tradition that so heavily informs Hasidism—and superstition-laden Jewish folklore, the film focuses on the supernatural phenomenon of demonic possession, or invasion by a dybbuk. (As Gershom Scholem, the doyen of Jewish mysticism, points out, the term "dybbuk," while referring to an entity that resembles the bad or evil *ibbur* of the Kabbalah, "incidentally . . . never occurs in Kabbalist literature, but owes its existence to Yiddish folk usage from the seventeenth century on, where it appears as a contraction for 'an attachment from the outside forces,' i.e. the evil spirits."[1]) Made in Poland and directed by the prolific, thirty-three-year-old Michał Waszyński (a "reigning wunderkind"[2] of the 1930s Polish film industry), the film is based on the classic play by S. Ansky, which in turn drew on the ambitious ethnographic expedition that the playwright carried out through the Eastern European Jewish heartlands in the years just prior to World War I, and that yielded a wealth of knowledge and materials about the rapidly disappearing traditional ways of life in these regions.[3] For us, the most striking thing about the film is the way that it brings the viewer into a substantially different type of environment from those that we have encountered before, while it powerfully continues Yiddish cinema's obsession with troubled communication, doing so by engaging with problems of mystical—and more specifically *Jewish* mystical—mediation "between two worlds," to borrow the play's alternate title. Indeed, in his adaptation, Waszyński radically foregrounds such problems, dwelling upon them far more frequently and far more elaborately than does the theatrical source material. Most notably, displaying particularly close ties with Flusser's writing on the supernatural (whose broad relevance to the complexities of communication in the universe of *The Dybbuk* this chapter will be exploring), the adaptation introduces a key motif of "the wind"—a motif, that is, with a rich legacy in traditions of spiritual thought.

Mediating the Mystical

In his 1990 essay "'How Goodly Are Your Tents, Jacob,'" acting like a kind of Talmudist, Flusser takes up a line from the Old Testament and offers an adventurously expansive commentary upon it. The line comes from the story—one of the more folkloric in the Bible—of the pagan soothsayer, Balaam. Directed to go out and curse the Israelites by the powerful Moabite king, Balak, Balaam sets out to do so, and yet he is repeatedly thwarted by God in ways that, intriguingly, all hinge on fantastic interventions of voice. First, as Balaam makes his journey, God thrice puts an invisible messenger in the path of his donkey, which causes the animal to appear recalcitrant, and her owner thrice to lash out and strike her. Hence, after the third whipping, God endows the animal with the ability to speak, which enables her—the donkey—to strike back, as it were, and verbally chastise her owner for what appears to be his senseless cruelty. Regarding the actual cursing of the Israelites, the first two times Balaam attempts to do this, God puts words in his mouth, causing the seer to utter blessings in place of imprecations. And the third time, in a variation on this pattern, God sets His spirit upon the seer, who in turn utters yet another blessing. It is from this last and most extensive encomium, spoken as Balaam gazes out at the Israelite tribes encamped in the wilderness, that Flusser plucks his line to dissect: "How goodly are your tents, O Jacob! / your dwellings, O Israel!"[4] (In fact, clearly working from memory, Flusser misattributes the line to the talking donkey, generating a mix-up that, while nonconsequential for his analysis, contains a potent irony in the face of all the strange vocalic wonders and substitutions in the story.) For Flusser, the line raises the question of why exactly Jacob's tents are so worthy of praise, and this leads him, in a series of speculative leaps, to a consideration of the wind, the predominant environmental factor with which the tent dweller, especially in the desert, must contend:

> Canvas in contrast to solid wall; billowing in the wind in contrast to breaking the wind. . . . Although we can hear the wind (it may roar deafeningly) and may feel it (it can knock us over), what we can see is never the wind but only its disastrous consequences. What I have just said also applies to spirits and ghosts, to gods and to God the Creator. All these words are derived from our experience of the wind. This is attested to in the Hebrew, Greek, and Latin words for wind (and for the movement of air generally)—*ruach*, *pneuma*, and *spiritus*—and in their traditions they also denote the holy spirit.[5]

Given the wide-ranging association of the wind with the supernatural, Flusser figures the tent as a "medium of the fantastic,"[6] as a technology for translating—encoding—spiritual messages into humanly readable form. However, as he goes on to stress, the delivery of the supernatural message is not contingent on the tent alone. As the wind does not unilaterally impose itself on the tent dweller but rather operates as a dialogic solicitation, the tent dweller must be open to the message, must be just as pliably receptive as the structure in which she or he dwells: "The voice calls out to him [the tent dweller]. But he doesn't necessarily have to obey. 'Hear, O Israel,' does not necessarily mean 'follow.' (Israel is Jacob's honorific.) But if he follows nonetheless, then the call of the wind becomes his calling. He then accepts the responsibility for answering that call. Jacob's tents were 'goodly' because he answered the call of the wind, because he accepted the responsibility."⁷

The Dybbuk, too, propounds such a moral, showing again and again how not everyone is equally attuned to spiritual messages, how "the call of the wind" can be blocked by things like materialism and narcissism. Yet another troubling factor, hinted at in Flusser's reference to the wind's "disastrous consequences," lies in the possibility that what is blowing in from the beyond is something malign, something to be feared and that therefore may necessitate gestures of apotropaic protection and resistance. Indeed, this possibility is one of the things that, as Scholem points out, both the Kabbalah and Jewish folklore (these two critical influences on the world of *The Dybbuk*) distinctively allow for and vividly express. Setting up an opposition between the Kabbalists and the traditional Jewish philosophers, Scholem writes:

> To most Kabbalists, as true-seal-bearers of the world of myth, the existence of evil is . . . one of the most pressing problems, and one which keeps them continuously preoccupied with attempts to solve it. They have a strong sense of the reality of evil and the dark horror that is about everything living. They do not, like the philosophers, seek to evade its existence with the aid of convenient formula; rather do they try to penetrate into its depth. And by doing so, they unwittingly establish a connection between their own strivings and the vital interests of popular belief—you may call it superstition—and all of those concrete manifestations of Jewish life in which these fears found their expression.⁸

That is to say, by the same token that both the Kabbalah and Jewish "popular belief" take evil seriously, they both take seriously the project of combatting and fending off such forces of metaphysical malevolence. At the same time, and on a more primordial level, both also confront "pressing problems" in relation to the mediation of the supernatural insofar as they both evoke "the world of myth." As Scholem argues, in one of his central claims about the nature of the Kabbalah, which is equally applicable to the nature of Jewish folk belief, the Kabbalah embodies not only a revival of mythical thinking but a revival that is emphatically *fraught*, shot through with layers of ambiguity if not downright ambivalence, given that those carrying out the revival simultaneously *cling* to another belief system—that is, traditional Judaism—that stands opposed to the object of revival and even bears proud responsibility for having wiped out (or sent into retreat) "the world of myth." As he explains: "In its first and crucial impulse, the Kabbalah was a mythical reaction in realms which monotheistic thinking had with the utmost difficulty wrested from myth. Or in other words: the lives and actions of the Kabbalists were a revolt against a world which consciously they never wearied of affirming."[9] In this scenario, to follow the subtle work of Scholem's modifier "consciously," traditional Judaism plays the role of a kind of Ego, or even Super-Ego, to the Kabbalah's Id, constantly trying to keep the subversive, revolutionary, neoprimitivist energies of the latter in check. In this way, Ansky's alternate title finds another possible meaning, suggesting the "two worlds" of myth and monotheism that the adherents of the Kabbalah and Jewish folk belief find themselves uneasily suspended in between—a suspension that, as we'll see, hangs heavily over the film and creates all sorts of problems for the free flow of mystic current.

Those Who Are to Hear and Those Who Are Not to Hear

In *The Living Orphan*, as one will recall, the function of the opening scene is to provide the viewer with an exclusive, backstage glimpse into a normally opaque media process. Set at the headquarters of WEVD, the prominent Yiddish radio station, the scene allows the viewer to be intimately visually present for a live musical performance that those within the diegesis of the film to whom performance is being broadcast, the listeners at home, take in at a distance and only on an aural level. We get, in other words, a kind of fleeting advantage over the characters in the film, who, it turns out (and this goes even for the performers themselves), repeatedly struggle with the structures of communication within which they are embedded. *The Dybbuk* begins in a similar fashion, with an evocative prelude that follows the credits and that shows a mystical event taking place for our eyes only. In an empty synagogue, the camera lowers from a chandelier of burned-down candles to the *bimah* (podium), on which sits a large Talmudic volume. Suddenly, an unaccountably indoor wind appears (or so, a la Flusser, we are led to deduce from the consequences of the strange pneumatic incident) and blows the book open, flipping the pages with apparent deliberation to a place in the middle. The film then reveals what is on the flipped-to page with a fade to an intertitle that (in Yiddish rather than the Aramaic of the Talmud) conveys the basic premise of the film and looks ahead to the core event of possession: "When a man dies before his time, his soul returns to the earth, so that it may complete the deeds that it has left undone, and experience the joys and griefs it had not lived through . . ." In this way, the book functions as a "medium of the fantastic" in a canny double sense, for not only does it deliver information regarding the existence of the soul after death, but its pages—which, like the canvas of a tent, billow in, rather than break, "the wind"—indicate the presence of an otherworldly entity right there in the room.

Another way to put the meaning of the scene is to say that it sets up a communicative hierarchy regarding the mystical, a structure in which, for the moment, we occupy a privileged position, and those not present in the vacant synagogue are implied to be at a disadvantage, excluded from what we apprehend. Such a situation establishes a template for much that will follow in the film, including the following scene—the first extended scene in the film—that introduces the key character of the zaddik (Avrom Morevsky): a charismatic Hasidic sage who serves, to borrow from Scholem's discussion of such saint-like figures, as an "envoy of the spiritual world"[10] and a "mediator between heaven and earth."[11] The scene features the zaddik surrounded by his devoted disciples in an atmosphere of deep, mystical immersion, and yet, notably, the first thing that we are shown is a group of other people precisely excluded from such goings-on. The scene begins, that is, with an image of a window, taken from an interior, at which a man and two boys, representatives of the uninitiated hoi polloi, struggle to peer within (see figure 9.1). Interestingly, however, such communication blockage continues to play a role even as we encounter those in the zaddik's inner circle who would appear to be ideally placed to receive their master's mystic mediations.

Pulling away from the window, in a lengthy panning and tracking shot, the camera slowly reveals a *Last Supper*-like tableau. At a long table, which spans almost the entire horizontal length of the frame, and at which all the characters are conveniently positioned on one side, facing frontward, the zaddik sits at the center, flanked by

Figure 9.1. The hoi polloi trying to get a glimpse of the mystical practices of the zaddik and his followers. Michał Waszyński, *The Dybbuk* (1937).

both seated and standing tiers of his followers, who sway trance-like and, accompanied by a small band of musicians, chant a languorous, wordless melody. Distinguished by his throne-like chair and all-white garb, only the zaddik remains in silent meditation, vigorously pressing down on a pile of closed books with the fingertips of one hand, as if dispensing with the texts' ordinary readerly functionality and employing them as an obscure, osmotic channel through which to draw invisible energy (see figure 9.2).

Accordingly, as in the opening scene with the wind-swept pages of the Talmudic volume, books again emerge as a "medium of the fantastic," while the fact that the zaddik engages with a stack of *closed* books nicely conveys what Scholem describes as Hasidism's distinctive elevation of "emotional enthusiasm" over "rabbinical learning."[12] Eventually, the singing comes to an end and the zaddik begins to hold forth ("Once a year, at a certain hour, these four supreme sanctities

Figure 9.2. A medium between heaven and earth, the zaddik sits amid his followers and appears to draw invisible energy from a pile of closed books. Michał Waszyński, *The Dybbuk* (1937).

of the world were united . . ."), staring at an invisible object aloft and gesticulating extravagantly, while his audience listens silently in a state of rapt attention. The resonantly Kabbalistic speech goes on for some time, and yet, notably, instead of staying trained on the speaker, the camera, engaging in one of the film's characteristic adaptive moves and drawing attention to a dilemma of troubled communication, suddenly at one point "wanders" away from the zaddik, panning across the table to the right in order to reveal all the disciples seated and standing there, young and old alike, cupping their ears and/or leaning toward the speaker in a struggle to "hear" what he is saying, even though his vocal delivery appears to be at a perfectly, even amply, audible volume (see figure 9.3). In other words, the film fascinatingly shows the zaddik's disciples wrestling with the reception of their master's mystic message, which ultimately concerns the dangers faced by souls who "strive to reach the heights,

Figure 9.3. During a speech about the Kabbalistic heights, the zaddik's followers strangely strain to hear him. Michał Waszyński, *The Dybbuk* (1937).

their Source, the Throne of Glory," just as much as those excluded from the proceedings on the other side of the window. *Everyone*, no matter where a person is situated, it seems, must contend with a kind of barrier that prevents the mystic message from fully coming through. As in Buber's Hasidic tale with which we began this book, wherein we are told that "those who are to hear, will hear even at a distance[, and] those who are not to hear, will not hear no matter how near they come," the moment gives in to a kind of leveling of distance, to the idea that the hearing of the vital message requires a kind of *inner* attunement—an idea, that is, that unsettles the apparent hierarchical distinction between those possessed of the privilege of being physically "near" the zaddik and those not. Of course, within this communicative configuration, the zaddik remains uppermost, the central "broadcaster" and sole "emitter" of mystic signals from the "station" of his throne, and yet, as we'll see, he too eventually runs into profound communicative difficulties, coming to doubt his powers as a special emissary of the transcendent.

All of this activity, it should be noted, transpires within a time frame not represented in Ansky's play. The basic story of *The Dybbuk*, around which the event of demonic possession revolves, is that of two best friends, recently graduated yeshiva students, who make a pact to marry their future children to one another, if one should have a boy and the other a girl, and of the disastrous fallout that occurs when, long after the death of one of the friends, the living one violates the pact. Ansky dramatizes only the time of the violation of the pact, keeping the time of the making of the pact within the realm of backstory: a narratological move that compresses the plot into a relatively short period that, according to the classical unity of time, is best suited to theatrical representation. By contrast, the film makes present what Ansky consigns to the past, bringing us immediately into the time (and space) of the making of the pact and showing us the two friends as they were when they were younger: both newly married and with a child on the way, and employing the pact as a means of overcoming the various distances now between them (among other things, they live in separate towns). Such an adaptive alteration results in several interesting and important effects, including, as Eve Sicular points out in her work on the queer dimensions of Yiddish cinema, emphasizing and fleshing out the deep bond between the two friends, which in the handling of Waszyński, who was reputedly gay, betrays a feverish blurring of any purported line between the homosocial and the homosexual.[13] For us, however, as we've already begun to lay out, what is most striking about the move, which amounts to a roughly twenty-minute-long "prologue" to the events depicted in the play, is its contribution to Waszyński's equally feverish emphasis on the problems involved in the mediation of the mystical.

Within this stretch of film, the two friends, Sender (Mojżesz Lipman) and Nisn (Gerszon Lemberger), reunited temporarily in their old student haunt of Miropolye to celebrate the holiday of *Sukkot*, wish to share with the zaddik the news of their newly compacted, sacred vow. However, such an ostensibly approval-seeking communication to this figure who stands as a kind of father figure to them proves wildly difficult, failing to come across no less than five times. The first three times occur in the extended opening scene, in which the friends sit immediately next to the zaddik on the side over which the camera pans and reveals the "hearing" struggles of the disciples. Once the zaddik finishes his Kabbalistic speech, the two privately confer with one another about making their move. "Now's the time. Tell the Rebbe," insists Sender, to which Nisn replies: "Just me? I'm afraid." In other words, they waffle in anxiety. Next, while somewhat able to manage their fear and get some words out, they are bedeviled by external sources. First, they are cut off mid-speech by the Messenger (Ajzyk Samberg)—a strange, supernatural, embedded choral figure (whom we'll have more to say about shortly)—who suddenly turns up on the scene bearing gifts for the zaddik. Second, as the pair pick up where they were interrupted and Nisn remarks, "We decided . . . ," the zaddik abruptly intervenes and, putting a hand on theirs, utters a firm admonishment: "Decided? Man does not make decisions, my children." The fourth attempt comes in the following scene, which takes place on an idyllic, leafy promontory, where the zaddik and his train stop to rest during a constitutional around town (in reality, Kazimierz, where several scenes of the film were shot on location). Again the two go to make their move, as Sender repeats, "Now's the time," and Nisn begins to address the reposing zaddik, "I wanted to tell you, Rebbe . . ." However, again the zaddik interrupts him, refusing to hear the remainder of the disclosure and instead bidding Nisn to sing "Song of Songs," the biblical song that exhibits a rare focus on romantic love, and that Nisn, evidently, has a particular knack for performing in a distinctive melody. Accordingly, Nisn obliges the zaddik, who is held rapt by the heavenly performance (as is Sender, deliriously so), and yet the moving musical transmission does not lead to a communication of the vow. At the end of the performance, now somewhat tired out from the day, the zaddik straightaway announces that it's time to go and gets up and leaves. Finally, in the next scene, which takes place at the synagogue during the prayer service for *Hoshana Rabbah*, the last day of *Sukkot*, amid a momentary pause of the soaring, acousmatic flight of the cantor (in reality, a craftily deployed recording of the famed Gershon Sirota), Nisn takes his turn at the phrase, "Now's the time," and Sender responds, "Let's tell him about our vow." Yet the whispers prompt a harsh shushing from a battery of offscreen congregants, and the attempt, once more, ends up failing. Taken together, the five incidents knit up into a pattern that serves to cultivate, or rather reveal, an aura of disquieting mystery around the oath that the friends themselves fail to acknowledge, or else intuit dimly (otherwise why the initial fear?) and try to repress. In this way, coincident with all their failures to deliver their message to the zaddik, the pair also exhibit a series of reception failures, above and beyond their straining to "hear" the zaddik's Kabbalistic oration. Indeed, not only do they fail to heed the zaddik's fateful warning that man does not make decisions, but they also repeatedly overlook warnings imparted by the Messenger. At the end of the synagogue scene on *Hoshana Rabbah*, for instance, the Messenger again suddenly turns up, and, knowing all about their plan without having to be told, remarks, in his characteristic, steely, vatic voice: "You cannot pledge something as yet unborn." However, the warning is totally lost on Nisn and Sender, who merely look back and forth at one another in baffled silence.

Like the spiritual "envoy" of the zaddik with whom he joins Yiddish cinema's extensive cast of messenger figures, the Messenger occupies a unique position in the film's hierarchy of mystical communication. Or rather we might say that the Messenger sits not so much alongside or even above the zaddik (who, as mentioned, comes to face significant obstacles in his capacity as a spiritual "envoy") within the hierarchy of mystical communication, but rather supremely outside of the hierarchy altogether. As Ansky wrote in a letter to his friend Khaim Zhitlovsky, "My play, needless to say, is a realistic drama about mystics. Its only nonrealistic element is the Messenger, not Leah's dialogue or vision."[14] And, as he continues, explaining that he incorporated the character only in a late version of the play, at the suggestion of Konstantin Stanislavsky, the eminence of the Russian theater: "The Messenger comes from a higher world, a world in which 'Its fire melts the highest mountain tops, / dissolving them into the deepest valleys.'"[15] Accordingly, the Messenger appears effectively omniscient, tapped wholesale into the mysterious workings of destiny, as befits his status as a kind of choral figure, while he possesses the ability (rendered by the film through a primitive special effects combination of superimposition and dissolves) to spontaneously materialize out of, and evanesce back into, what appears to be nowhere. Bearing such exceptionality in mind can help us grasp one of the most indelible features of the Messenger as performed by Ajzyk Samberg, who, Hoberman points out, was "a specialist in proletarian and gangster roles," and whose "rough-hewn" style he contrasts with the "intellectual style"[16] of Avrom Morevsky, who plays the zaddik (a role with which he was much familiar, having played it, in 1920, in a theatrical production of

The Dybbuk with the Vilna Troupe). What we're referring to here is Samberg's odd, highly stylized *mechanicalness*, to employ the word in a purely descriptive rather than evaluative register. Such a quality of unflappable rigidity and austerity appears at the level of body language, in Samberg's measured slowness (he doesn't need to move quickly, or indeed at all, since, as mentioned, he can appear anywhere at will), and monumental stillness once he emerges on the scene. But it also, and perhaps most conspicuously, comes out at the level of voice, in his severe, undeviating monotone, which sharply contrasts with Ansky's play's most prevalent stage direction, "In a trembling voice," a cue of precisely fluctuating vocality faithfully manifest all over the film and meant to communicate the characters' fearful reactions to awesome mystic forces above and beyond the words that they're saying. In short, the Messenger's status as an entity from "a higher world," as an ontologically exceptional, constitutively mystical character, grants him a radical exemption from the hectic vocalic flux (which we might liken to Flusser's billowing of the tent canvas in "the wind") exhibited by virtually every other member of the dramatis personae.

Memory and Forgetting

At the end of *Sukkot*, in front of their horse-drawn wagons, Nisn and Sender bid farewell in high spirits, mutually reinforcing their oath despite still not having been able to share it with the zaddik. Shortly thereafter, Nisn meets his death. On his way home, crossing a body of water on a small skiff during a storm, he is propelled overboard, bellowing in the liminal, abyss-like moment just before he spills into the water: "Sender! *Gedenk! Yizkor!*" Such a demand to his friend with whom he has made a pact to "remember"—a demand whose force is redoubled by the fact that it is uttered in both Yiddish (*gedenk*) and Hebrew (*yizkor*)—eventually forms, of course, in its failure to be heeded, the drama's central-animating instance of troubled communication. Yet such a dilemma is hinted at straightaway. From the tempestuous, preternaturally lightning-flashed, fatal scene on the waters, the film cross-cuts to Sender's house, where the owner (who not long before arrived to discover that his wife died while giving birth to a girl), frantically races out on to the porch and affirms, "I could have sworn someone called out my name," while his sister, Frade (Dina Halpern),[17] who follows him out, reacts with perplexity, evidently having heard nothing. In this way, some part of Nisn's message comes through over the channels of mystic telecommunication. Importantly, however, Sender fails to hear *all* of the message, demonstrating an incomplete receptivity and missing the crucial, redoubled bit about memory.

This proves prescient, for in the years that follow, the once pious yeshiva student becomes a wealthy businessman whose materialistic obsessions result in him forgetting not only his promise to his friend but effectively all his personal relations and the spiritual world in toto. The film cannily portrays such an amnesiac devolution in an extended transitional sequence (think the iterative breakfast montage of marital decline in *Citizen Kane*) that condenses the passage of the next eighteen years and centers on Sender's (non)relationship with his daughter Leah, who repeatedly attempts—and fails—to sway her father from a fixation on counting his money. In front of his desk, covered in growing piles of coins and bills and real estate contracts, she turns up three times at three different ages—as a bawling infant, a bored adolescent, and a poised young woman (this last appearance finally introducing us to Lili Liliana, who would later star in *Kol Nidre* over in the realm of American Yiddish film production)—and issues a fervent appeal that Sender petulantly dismisses, worried that he'll make a mistake in his calculations. Such incorrigible neglect of his daughter presages the neglect of the vow that occurs next, and that, of course, Leah is inextricably bound up with. Never, so far as we can see, bothering to find out if his tragically deceased best friend's wife gives birth to a son (which she does, as the film conveys in a brief insert of her in bed on the morning after her husband's drowning), nor mourning Nisn (whose cry on the verge of death can also be read as a plea that Sender remember *him*), Sender arranges a marriage between Leah and a different man from a rich family, treating the matter as if it were merely another one of his business transactions.

Nisn's appeal on the verge of oblivion, so drastically disregarded by his friend, powerfully resonates with Judaism's fervent valorization of memory: a phenomenon that we've encountered several times throughout this book, and whose philosophical foundations it is now an apt time to delve into further. As Yosef Hayim Yerushalmi writes in his influential 1982 study *Zakhor: Jewish History and Jewish Memory*: "Its [the Hebrew Bible's] injunctions to remember are unconditional, and even when not commanded, remembrance is always pivotal. Altogether the verb *zakhar* appears in its various declensions in the Bible no less than one hundred and sixty-nine times, usually with either Israel or God as the subject, for memory is incumbent upon them both. The verb is complemented by its obverse—forgetting. As Israel is enjoined to remember, so it is adjured not to forget."[18] Or in more incisive terms: "Forgetting, the obverse of memory, is always negative, the cardinal sin from which all others will flow."[19] As Yerushalmi argues, the philosophical underpinning for this value system lies in Judaism's distinctive, revolutionary conception of time as "linear" and "historical," as opposed to, as found in religions rooted in myth, "cyclical." Thus, he writes:

> It was ancient Israel that first assigned a decisive significance to history. . . . The primeval dream-time world of the archetypes, represented in the Bible only by the Paradise story in Genesis, was abandoned irrevocably. With the departure of Adam and Eve from Eden, history begins, historical time becomes real, and the way back is closed forever. . . . Thrust reluctantly into history, man in Hebrew thought comes to affirm his historical existence despite the suffering it entails, and gradually, ploddingly, he discovers that God reveals himself in the course of it. Rituals and festivals in ancient Israel are themselves no longer primary repetitions of mythic archetypes meant to annihilate historical time. Where they evoke the past, it is not the primeval, but the historical past, in which the great and critical moments of Israel's history were fulfilled.[20]

Indeed, within this framework, remembrance becomes ineluctably critical since it provides the only means by which one can gain access to and honor the sacred, revelatory events of time past: "Not history, as is commonly supposed, but only mythic time repeats itself. If history is real, then the Red Sea can be crossed only once, and Israel cannot stand twice at Sinai. . . . If there can be no return to Sinai, then what took place at Sinai must be borne along the conduits of memory to those who were not there that day."[21]

To bear in mind this context is to allow for a full appreciation of the dire extent of Sender's failure to heed Nisn's call of "*Gedenk!*

Yizkor!" As the drama emphasizes, such a violation triggers a truly massive slide into oblivion since it leads to the successive deaths of both of the friends' children—each of whom, not incidentally, is an "only" child—and thus to a cessation of both of their family lines. In other words, because of Sender's "cardinal sin" of forgetting, both friends face a foreclosure of the ability to be mourned—as is the custom, by a surviving family member—and thus to be borne forth in time "along the conduits of memory." This dilemma comes up explicitly in the lead-up to the eccentric, inter-ontological trial scene, where the spirit of Nisn appears for a reckoning with the injustice that Sender has committed against him by breaking their promise. As the zaddik gravely impresses upon Sender: "Because of you, Nisn ben Rivke has no one to bear his name, no memory, no heir, no one to say a prayer for his soul." Though more obliquely, the problem too arises in the devastating graveyard scene on the day of Leah's wedding in which, with extreme rawness, without any of the underscoring that attends such melancholy, separation-haunted cradle songs that we have encountered elsewhere in Yiddish cinema, Leah kneels down at the tombstone of her dead lover and sings a lullaby to the children that they will never have together: "Bayu, bayu, my babies, without clothes, without a bed, unborn children, never mine, lost forever, lost in time."

No doubt, from the perspective of the ardently mnemo-philic Hebrew Bible, the drama ends in calamity. However, such a sense of catastrophe doesn't tell the whole story. That is to say, the deep Kabbalistic and Jewish-folkloric inflections of *The Dybbuk* (inflections that, one will recall from Scholem, involve a conflicted resuscitation of the value system of the world of myth) significantly complicate the situation, introducing sentiments relating to forgetting and annihilation quite other than disquiet and dismay. As Flusser writes in "Mythical, Historical, and Posthistorical Existence," a 1981 essay whose categories are eminently compatible with the opposition between myth and Judaism that structures both Scholem's understanding of the Kabbalah and Yerushalmi's understanding of Jewish memory (the three thinkers, indeed, form a generative cluster within contemporary Jewish thought), time in the world of myth

> sets everything in its proper place in space from which it has distanced itself. It sets things right. It circulates in

space and does not allow trees to grow into the heavens. Because human existence is the movement from birth to death, it [human existence] generates disorder in time and space; it "goes against the world." It is justifiably punished. Time sets it back into its proper place in space. But human existence can also forgo its deserved punishment, if it takes the initiative and offers "sacrifice" in advance.[22]

Similarly, in *The Dybbuk*, the death of the lovers provides a sense of expiation for Sender's treacherous forgetting of the oath that derails the union from its predestined, "proper" path. Their joint demise, that is, appears to bring events full circle and "set things right." As David G. Roskies writes of the play: "Then as now, audiences who knew no Yiddish and had never set eyes on a Hasid could come away inspired by the story of Khonon [Nisn's son] and Leah. Alone and in the face of all odds, these young rebels had restored the moral and metaphysical order by sacrificing their own earthly pleasures."[23] Or to put it in Yerushalmi's terms, the sacrificial death of the couple might be said to assume the lineaments of one of those mythic rituals or reenactments in which, with overtones of exaltation rather than alarm, "historical time is periodically shattered and one can experience again, if only briefly, the true time of the origins and archetypes."[24]

By the Middle Ages, as Yerushalmi points out, Jews did in fact develop observances—recitations, fasts, festivals, and so on—that, in transposing Biblical events within structures of serial recurrence, synthesized linear and cyclical modalities of time. Of such rites, Yerushalmi remarks, offering a certain nuancing "correction"[25] of the opposition between linear and cyclical time while defending the heuristic force of the opposition in its essentials: "To be sure, all this is still far removed from any notion of an 'eternal return,' or of mythic time. The historical events of the biblical period remain unique and irreversible. Psychologically, however, those events are *experienced* cyclically, repetitively, and to that extent at least, atemporally."[26] This evidently unproblematic fusion operative at the level of phenomenology, though, doesn't so much apply in the case of *The Dybbuk*, which presents a far more uneasy copresence of the two temporal modes, in line with the richly fraught ambivalence that Scholem identifies in the Kabbalists' split between an attraction to the reactivated world of myth and a continuing devotion to the old (and yet newer) world of monotheism. In other words, while Sender's forgetful, humanly meddlesome betrayal of the vow is problematic from either the perspective of myth or Judaism, the obliteration of historical time that attends the fatal ending emerges as an event both catastrophically unwelcome and ecstatically welcome.

Silence and Music

Raising what he describes as "one of the fundamental problems of mystical thought throughout the ages," Scholem asks: "How is it possible to give lingual expression to mystical knowledge, which by its very nature is related to a sphere where speech and expression are excluded? How is it possible to paraphrase adequately in mere words the most intimate act of all, the contact of the individual with the Divine?"[27] Or to put it otherwise, how does one grapple with what William James, in his landmark 1902 study *The Varieties of Religious Experience*, calls the "ineffability" of the mystical experience?[28] (Offering a useful account of mystical states of consciousness, James proposes four defining, fairly broad qualities: "ineffability," "noetic quality," "transiency," and "passivity.") In *The Dybbuk*, in keeping with what Scholem describes as the Kabbalists' distinctive "metaphysically positive attitude towards language as God's own instrument,"[29] there is little evidence of that disparagement or belittlement of language that often gets generated as a by-product of wrestling with ineffability in mystical literature. At the same, however, the film engages copiously with the limits of language through the lovers' recurrent recourse to metasemantic modes of communication in moments of intense, mystically inflected contact between one another. Indeed, in taking to silence and music (metasemantic modes that one will recall from discussions in previous chapters) with striking, ecstatic success, the lovers forge a notable counterpoint to all the other characters in the film who, like Sender, for various reasons, face significant communicative blockage in their encounters with the mystical.

Nisn's son, Khonon (Leon Liebgold, who would also go on to appear in *Kol Nidre*, where he plays the impressive young rabbi whom Lili Liliana's character eventually marries), makes his first grown-up appearance in the film right after the money-counting transitional sequence that brings us into the main time frame of the narrative.

On a sunlit, winding country road, Khonon journeys on foot toward Brinitz—Sender's town, where he plans to study at the yeshiva—while totally immersed in a book, giving the impression of not needing to navigate his way and instead being mysteriously drawn toward the town. Shortly, the dreamy *yeshiva bokher* crosses paths with Sender as the latter nearly barrels into him in a hurtling carriage. As a result, at the urging of the Messenger, who suddenly materializes and warns that "the Sabbath may overtake him [Khonon] on the road," Sender gives Khonon a lift in his chauffeured vehicle. Yet during the ride the interaction between the two is stymied by an awkward silence, somewhat reminiscent of the baffled silence between Sender and Nisn in reaction to the Messenger's warning on *Hoshana Rabbah* so many years earlier. This is largely perpetuated by Sender, who not only refrains from asking Khonon any questions about who he is or where he comes from, as would be expected from an elder in a meeting such as this one, but recoils from a brief exchange of glances with an abrupt swiveling of his head toward the road. Such silence is important, since it provides a striking contrast with the next scene, where silence operates in an astonishingly communicative capacity. Now in the dining room of Sender's house, where the foreign student has been invited for Shabbat, Khonon and Leah stand across from one another at the ritually prepared table, while Sender says a blessing before the meal. Once Sender finishes and his servant is about to bring out the food, however, the two young people remain standing in a state of silent, mutual enthrallment, their gazes interlocked, as conveyed in a series of alternating, eyeline-matched close-ups that give the impression of the rest of the world, of whatever lies beyond the scope of such absorptive looking, utterly falling away. Such intuitive connectivity beyond language recalls Buber's "silence which is communication," according to which the turning of two people toward one another is not only a prerequisite for dialogue but embodies a form of dialogue in itself. Here, however, amid a mythologically infused world where every human action contends with secret forces beyond the scope of the will, such turning exceeds a strictly Buberian understanding. In other words, the two lovers turn to one another not only out of a sense of responsibility that transforms the Other into a You, but also out of a mythically primordial bond that precedes them and over which they have no control. (Notably, in his early 1960s guidebook to world cinema that contains a glowing entry on *The Dybbuk*,

Parker Tyler singles out this moment for special consideration and includes a still from it with the caption: "Two lovers, a rich girl and a poor student, silently and secretly communicate during a religious ceremony at her home."[30])

Like silence, music also works to foster the lovers' swiftly flourishing connection with one another, and, accordingly, it seems no coincidence that James cites music and love as exemplary analogues to the mystical experience in his discussion of "ineffability." He writes:

> In this peculiarity mystical states are more like states of feeling than like states of intellect. No one can make clear to another who has never had a certain feeling, in what the quality or worth of it consists. One must have musical ears to know the value of a symphony; one must have been in love one's self to understand a lover's state of mind. Lacking the heart or the ear, we cannot interpret the musician or the lover justly, and are even likely to consider him weak-minded or absurd.[31]

Blending considerations of the heart and the ear, Khonon and Leah take turns singing to one another in a kind of protracted mutual wooing process that unfolds as Khonon settles into the town: a cramped space of twisty cobblestone streets that the film represents through a heavily stylized, Gothic studio set. First, while sewing a large piece of floral drapery with two of her female companions, Leah sings a pining love song, and while she does so, Khonon happens to be strolling by the house and is irresistibly drawn to the window, which he approaches in order to hear the music more closely, recalling the prying crowd at the window of the zaddik's chambers at the beginning of the film (the difference being that here the mystic sounds extravagantly, nonhermetically stream out, and the "interloper" appears to have little trouble apprehending them). Not long afterward, the circuit of transmission is reversed. Over at the synagogue, in a cloistered study hall off to the side of the main prayer space, accompanied by a diegetic choir of honey-throated yeshiva boys who rock back and forth in front of their Talmudic tomes, Khonon gives a reprise performance of his father's renowned version of "Song of Songs," and while he does so, Leah happens to be in the adjoining space, on a visit whose officially stated purpose is to make a close-up examination of the embroidered ark hangings. As in the previous musical scene involving the couple, the singer is positioned behind a partition that results in the song assuming numinously acousmatic form (a form, it is well worth noting, with which one can draw a productive parallel with that of "the wind," whose mystical purchase too derives in large measure from invisibility). As well, the disembodied music has a formidably hypnotic effect on the listener. For Leah is compelled to turn her attention away from the ark hangings—these objects significantly relating to traditional Judaism, proudly unfurled and put on display for her by the synagogue caretaker, Meyer—and cast her eyes toward the hidden source of the sound. Indeed, this rechanneling of focus necessitates Frade, Leah's watchful chaperone, to tap, delicately yet concernedly, on Leah's shoulder in an attempt to break Khonon's musical spell. Yet the effort is in vain. For even when the song concludes, Khonon and Leah remain riveted to one another. As the former steps out of the study room and the two are finally brought face to face, they switch back to their other favored metasemantic communicative mode, gazing at one another with lasered fascination in fastidiously unbroken silence.

However, to linger some more over Khonon's repeat performance of "Song of Songs" in his father's signature melody, the more one thinks about it the more its aura of mysticality appears to grow. For one thing, how exactly did Khonon come to learn the melody, given that he never knew his father, his birth being practically coincident with his father's death? To provide an instructive comparison, in *A Little Letter to Mother*, for all the throbbingly mystical aura that music possesses in that film, the *nign* that the son sings during the HIAS benefit concert and that serves as the critical agent of recognition and reunion is one that we directly see, in the first part of the film, the father directly teaching to his son while the latter is a young boy. To come back to *The Dybbuk*, one might explain away the problem by speculating about a possible route of transmission hinging on Khonon's mother. That is, we might posit Khonon's mother as a missing link, as an unspecified mediator who, being familiar with her late husband's melody, eventually taught it to their son. However, the film provides next to no motivation for making such a deduction, stringently sidelining her in a move very much in keeping with the narrative's focus on fathers. Indeed, following the quick insert of her in bed with her newborn baby, she is never so much as mentioned again, such that, even though she survives childbirth and presumably goes on to raise Khonon, she comes to constitute an absence every bit as great as Leah's dead mother. Consequently, we are left to posit another means of transmission, one in which the song appears to have traveled from (the spirit of) the dead father to the living son in a decidedly supernatural fashion, recalling Y. L. Perets's 1901 short story, "A Gilgul fun a Nign [The Transmigration of a Melody]," in which a tune is passed down, through several otherwise unrelated people and over the course of many years, in a wildly fateful, mystically infused chain of events.[32] (The Kabbalistic term *gilgul*, as Scholem points out, means "literally, 'turning over' or 'rolling over'—i.e. of souls."[33])

And yet still we are not yet done with "Song of Songs." For it again turns up in the scene that directly follows Leah and Khonon's musical encounter in the synagogue. From Khonon retreating to the study hall, where the chorus of yeshiva boys resume their ethereal chanting, the film cuts to Leah back at home, seated on a lavish, high-backed chair, softly swaying with lowered eyelids, still clearly in a potent trance state. For a beat, she is alone, but eventually, in the out-of-focus background, unnoticed by her, Sender enters the room. In this moment, she begins singing Nisn's version of "Song of Songs," soulfully, in a prolongation of her rapturous experience in the synagogue, adding yet another incarnation to the melody's journey of "transmigration." In this way, Sender too becomes caught in the web of "chance" overhearings, and, recalling his dead friend's melody, finally recognizes that Khonon is Nisn's son. Or to put it more accurately, the ancient melody finally forces him to acknowledge what he has always known unconsciously yet violently repressed (to take one example, in the Shabbat dinner scene, he dozes off at the table after the meal and begins dreaming about Nisn, whose name he uneasily mumbles, as if sensing deep down the connection between his old friend and the "stranger" in his house). All too characteristically, however, Sender's reception of the song proves fitful, coming up against a practically instant, reactionary resetting up of his momentarily defeated defenses. Having just returned from finalizing the deal to marry Leah to the boy from the rich family, he doubles down on his transgression of the vow with Nisn, monomaniacally boasting to Leah, "They agreed to ten years room and board! Ten years! Ten years!" And when, faced with this news for the first time, Leah storms out of the room in a series of painful, tearful moans, he does not chase after her, or consider annulling the freshly made match, but rather collapses back down on his chair and, in a rapidly tightening close-up that punctuates the scene, declares with a shuddering hand and lowering of his head, "Nisn, dear friend, it's too late now. Too late . . ." That is, Sender falls back into a resigned, faux-fatalism that merely justifies his own prerogatives (besides, unlike the Messenger, he is hardly in a position to *know* the workings of fate that would dictate if an action is too late). Hence, while the melody of "Song of Songs" makes a spectacular, "transmigratory" journey all the way to Sender—a journey that, notably, comprises another of the film's mediatically rich, adaptive additions to the material—and delivers the all-important message at last (like music so often does in Yiddish cinema), Sender refuses to receive the song in a meaningful, enduring way. In stark contrast to Leah and Khonon's profuse, profound, metasemantic exchanges of music and silence, he troubles the train of continuing transmission and brings the *gilgul fun a nign* to a disturbing halt.

The Wind

Unwilling merely to accept the plan for Leah's marriage and hoping to win her for himself, Khonon launches a desperate resistance mission that hinges on a treacherous, antinomian-tinged excursus into deep mystical territory. As all his peers vacate the synagogue in order to go to Sender's house for a party celebrating the engagement, Khonon remains behind, alone in the main prayer space. There, he enacts a series of black-magical rituals, including a species of *gematria* (mystically loaded alphanumeric calculation) involving his and Leah's names, and an appeal to "Satan [*tayvl*]" in which he offers up, among other things, his "soul [*neshome*]" and "learning [*toyre*]." However, in doing so, he goes too far, recalling the zaddik's warning about those souls that "strive to reach the heights, their Source, the Throne of Glory" and are suddenly "overwhelm[ed]" by "evil" and "stumbl[e]" and "fal[l]." Indeed, as the room fills up with rising, amorphous clouds of smoke, the daring young Kabbalist stretches out his arms to an invisible, transcendental something and collapses fatally to the floor with a hideous shriek.

Out of Khonon's death, "the wind" makes a vital resurgence from its early appearances in the film (i.e., the mysteriously blown-open book in the synagogue, the tempest on the waters in which Nisn perishes). Suddenly, the sound of gusting emerges as the film cross-cuts from the fatal scene in the synagogue to a lit-up window outside of Sender's house, where, amid the blustery darkness, the Messenger turns up and taps on the pane with his staff, intending to deliver news of the death. As he is met by Sender's servant, however, the latter reacts fearfully to the request to speak to his master and proceeds to reclose the shutters, redo the latch, and fully draw the curtains that were only half-drawn before. In other words, acting as a kind of psychic extension of Sender and his tendency to repress anything to do with the oath, the servant, to borrow Flusser's language, fails to heed the call of "the wind," which presently fills the outdoors and has become ineluctably associated with Khonon's just unleashed spirit. Indeed, as it continues, the sequence becomes a kind of protracted attempt on the Messenger's part to communicate such a call, which the intended recipient does everything in his power to block out.

Inside the house, the party—thrown by Sender despite the recent revelations about Khonon's identity and his daughter's extreme despair over the match, or rather precisely because of those things and intended as a way of distracting himself from and ignoring them—rolls on in boisterous fashion. The male revelers (it is an all-male affair) ecstatically sing and dance, belting out a vivacious, wordless melody and whirling around in bodily interlocking, concentric circles (*freylekhs*, the traditional Hasidic round dance). Notably, with another man, Sender forms the innermost circle, in a positioning that, given his psychic state, allows him to occupy a kind of enclosure within the enclosure of the house that provides him with a second layer of wall-like defense against the mysterious, proverbial "outside." However, neither the dance nor the house proves to be windproof, as it were. First, the dance is broken up, the chains of bodies coming apart, as Khonon's yeshiva-mate Henekh, by now having found out about the death, bursts into the room, urgently grabs Sender, and, in a naked moment of troubled communication, futilely attempts to deliver the news in a series of terrified, spastically stuttered verbal fragments: "Jews! Khonon!" (Interestingly, while the anxious, wary Henekh serves as the main "check" on Khonon's occult ventures, he at the same time betrays a wild fascination with them, this ambivalence combining in the film's most deliriously homoerotic moment, when Henekh follows Khonon to the *mikve*, the Jewish ritual bath, and, through a befogged window, spies on his sweaty, shirtless friend in the midst of performing obscure sacraments.[34]) Next, as Henekh continues trying to get his words out and Sender emphatically misreads the disjointed attempt at an articulation ("Khonon! Where is he? Invite him here to dance with us," the host remarks with wobbly, boozy incomprehension), the shutters of the window, where the Messenger had previously appeared, spontaneously unlatch and fling open toward the outside, allowing the wind to blow furiously, commandingly in, and consequently plunge the candle-lit room in semidarkness. Similarly, in the same uncannily autonomous fashion, a door to the room swings open and allows the entrance of the Messenger, whose appearance causes the men to recoil for a second time in fear and form a tight horizontal huddle of bodies, over which the camera lingeringly tracks back and forth, and which, like the concentric rings of the round dance, attempts to instantiate a kind of makeshift defensive structure. Nevertheless, it is at this point that the Messenger is finally able to deliver his curt, disturbing message: "Khonon is dead."

In the split second before the scene fades out, however, in an ingenious formal move, the film contrasts the "wall" of affrighted men with a striking, surprising heeding of the call of "the wind." Straight after the Messenger's line, while the camera is still trained, in a low-angle medium shot, on his daunting, unblinking presence, we hear Leah, who up to this point has played no role in the all-male scene, yearningly cry out Khonon's name from an undisclosed location offscreen. That Leah should be the one who answers the Messenger makes eminent sense given that she is the one most intimately connected to Khonon and most brutally affected by his death. Yet to include her in the scene as an acousmatic entity is a brilliant added touch, since the move has her responding to the message on the same plane as "the wind," indeed almost as if she were *of* the same invisible stuff as the otherworldly phenomenon. In other words, it is a moment that beautifully capitalizes on the implicit association between the acousmatic and "the wind" mentioned earlier and thus works to hint at the still hotly operative communication lines between the couple in the face of Khonon's death.

As Leah's unwanted wedding approaches, such moments of contact accordingly become more and more explicit. In the much-celebrated dance sequence, choreographed by Judith Berg, that puts the class structure of the shtetl on display, from the hobbled, desperately clutching poor to the smug, sumptuously dressed, stately waltzing rich, Leah takes part in a danse macabre with a sleek-moving personification of Death (played by Berg), whose disguised, skeleton face provides a screen for Khonon's face (softly, seductively smiling) to appear in ghostly double exposure. Further, later on the same day—the day of the wedding, which is also the day on which Leah, prior to the dance, visits her lover's tombstone—Khonon appears in another guise. In an atmosphere redolent of a Victorian spirit photograph, Leah sits at a circular parlor table while her excited, ebullient bridesmaids fuss over her and try to prepare her for what they perceive as a happy event. Startled and aghast, they come upon a number of dirty creases—vestiges of her passionate, knelt-down visit to Khonon's grave—on her all-white, silken wedding gown. However, Leah is totally unresponsive to their concerns, plunged in a silent, motionless, hypnotic state that conveys that her concerns are rather with the other world, where her true love lies. Indeed, the moment she is left alone in the room, the camera suddenly, spectrally, swoops toward Leah, and a hushed, acousmatic susurration, a redolently liminal breath-entity halfway in between a human voice and a gust of wind, and thus between the linguistic and the nonlinguistic, addresses her: "Le-ye . . ."

Not surprisingly given all this, the actual wedding ceremony, too, is powerfully windswept. At the start of the scene, which takes place in the streets after sundown with scores of shtetl residents looking on, the blustery sound of a looming tempest provides not only aural ambience but nearly drowns out the band of klezmer musicians that lead the march of the terrified groom toward the chuppah. Such noise quiets down during the melodious recital of the *badkhn*, the traditional wedding entertainer, and the prayers of the swaying, officiating rabbi. However, during the latter, "the wind" makes a striking visual appearance. As the film cuts from a wide shot that takes in a significant portion of the crowd to a medium shot that focuses on just the two being betrothed, the groom oozes fear, looking nervously, fidgetily over at his bride, as if there were another presence enfolding her. And indeed there appears to be, for Leah's veil—which consists of an almost immaterial material, a fabric so gossamer thin as to be almost completely transparent in those places, toward the center, where there is no bunching—catches the wind and billows all across the frame (see figure 9.4). In this way, the garment, like Jacob's tents, serves as an exemplary "medium of the fantastic," allowing what would

Figure 9.4. A mystical wind causes Leah's wedding veil to billow, while the groom looks on in fear. Michał Waszyński, *The Dybbuk* (1937).

appear to be Khonon's spirit—or its allied energy—to manifest visually, and exhibiting the mysteriously equipoised bride's untrammeled openness to it.

"The wind," however, makes its most emphatic appearance once Khonon's spirit interrupts the ceremony (right as the shivering groom attempts to put the ring on the bride's finger) and invades Leah.[35] "You buried me, but I have come back to my destined bride [*basherte*] and will not leave her," declares the spirit (via his host speaking in a lowered, "masculine" register) to the horror-struck crowd, after which the menacingly impending storm finally breaks out and reveals that "the wind" is not something that has been contained (i.e., shut up inside Leah's body) as a result of the possession but rather embodies a source of mystic energy far greater than Khonon's spirit alone. Accordingly, the crowd disperses in chaos, and while this is happening the film offers up a small, quick, tantalizing detail. Tasked by sources unknown, a group of boys, scurrying across the frame, contends with the unwieldy task of shuffling the collapsed chuppah away to safety.

Given that a chuppah is a type of tent, and, moreover, one that evokes a sense of exemplary receptivity (indeed, it is often said that the chuppah is modeled on the design of Abraham and Sarah's tent, which, according to Midrashic tradition, was open on all four sides in an expression of radical hospitality and openness toward strangers), the detail irresistibly brings us back to Flusser's speculations on Jacob's "goodly" tents. Here, however, it is as if "the wind" is simply too much for the mediating capacity of the tent to handle, the apparent divine message of angry disapproval causing the structure (unlike Jacob's tents—as well, one might add, as Leah's veil) to break down under the sheer force of the message.

Struggles of the Zaddik

In an inspired, laudatory description of Morevsky's performance, Hoberman refers to the zaddik as "an instrument tuned to a frequency that no one else can hear."[36] Such a metaphor seems almost certainly to derive from the moment, lingered over earlier in our own analysis, when the zaddik gives his speech about the Kabbalistic heights and his disciples—like the uninitiated outside at the window attempting to eavesdrop—struggle to take in his words. It is a moment in which the zaddik emerges as a surpassingly self-assured "mediator between heaven and earth." *Even though* his audience struggles to hear him, *even though* not much of what he is saying appears to be coming through to them—and indeed perhaps it would be more accurate to say that these potential receivers grapple with hearing a frequency to which he alone has access and which he is accordingly trying to channel *on* to them—this struggle appears not to register with him, not at all to cloud his sense of himself as an effective spiritual liaison. Over time, however, the situation becomes radically changed. When Sender brings Leah to Miropolye in the hopes that the zaddik can resolve the crisis of possession, the old master, now nearly two decades older and showing it, is himself plunged in an acute state of crisis, deeply shaken in terms of his capacities of mystic communication. Now, it is as if he has become acutely aware of his audience's struggles with hearing, to say nothing of his own attune-ability to the divine "frequency," and has allowed these doubts to color his entire self-perception. Now, we find him vacillating wildly between moments of extreme, often muteness-addled despair and moments of bombastic, overcompensatory hypercommunication. In this way, the film's treatment of troubled communication fascinatingly broadens out to encompass an emissary character who appears initially, in a certain sense like the Messenger, exempt from the condition.

The film reintroduces the zaddik in a sequence that cross-cuts back and forth between his chambers and the adjoining, supplicant-packed waiting room into which Sender, Leah, and Frade arrive from an anxious, close-huddled wagon journey from Brinnitz. The first time that we are brought into the former space, the camera pans away from a group of the zaddik's disciples sitting at a table and chanting the same melody from the tableau at the beginning of the film, and over to another part of the room (whose dimensions suddenly appear to expand exponentially, far beyond our initial impression of them), where, in the distance, captured in deep focus, below the arched, high ceiling, there is a double door. Shortly, as the door opens and the zaddik walks in, attended by his candelabra-bearing assistant Mikhoel, along with a support system of several more men, it appears as if it might take an eternity for him to cross the expanse, so slowly and falteringly does he proceed, at one point even, unwisely, brushing Mikhoel's steadying arm aside. This arduous journey across the room powerfully conveys the zaddik's startling deterioration since the last time that we saw him and prepares the way for what follows. Once he finally arrives at the table and takes a seat, Mikhoel begins to tell him about Sender's case, which he somehow already knows about, and to which he responds, rising precariously from his chair in astonished exasperation:

ZADDIK: How could he [Sender] bring her [Leah] to me, when the "I" in me is not here?

MIKHOEL: Rebbe, all the world comes to you.

ZADDIK: All the world . . . It's a blind world. Blind sheep following a blind shepherd. If they were not blind, they would not come to me, but to "Him" who can say "I," the only "I" in the world.

Finished with a longing gaze toward the heavens and an overwhelmed throwing of a hand over the eyes (the other hand clasping Mikhoel for balance), the zaddik's remarks suggestively resonate with another conversation happening out in the waiting room that we see in between his entrance and the exchange with his assistant. As Sender listens in a state of captivation to a man tell "wondrous tales" of the sort that appear in Buber's *Tales of the Hasidim*, and clamors to hear another, the Messenger spontaneously appears and takes over the role of the storyteller. Relating a parable that is sourced from the play and that perhaps provides one of the bases for the film's obsession with windows (these physical manifestations of a borderline "between two worlds"), the Messenger remarks: "A window and a mirror are both made of glass. But the glass of the mirror is covered with silver. And owing to the silver, man no longer sees others, and he sees only himself." Suggestively, whereas the parable focuses on a problematic, greed-driven excess of ego that blocks one's ability to see other people, the zaddik's lament, "the 'I' in me is not here," focuses on a problematic dearth of ego, a sense of no longer possessing *enough* of a self in order to help others. Indeed, the zaddik seems to be saying that if only people weren't so blind, then they would be able to appreciate that his spiritual mediatorship is hardly needed, for they are themselves capable of going on their own, directly, to "Him," to God, whose self is, on the contrary, replete and exclusively so ("the only 'I' in the world").

Nevertheless, despite all of his self-deprecations and self-doubts, the zaddik agrees to see Sender, and conducts the meeting like a kind of psychoanalyst, brushing aside the immediate circumstances of the possession and seeking after the underlying cause of the crisis in the deep past. In this way, he elicits a confession from his old disciple and calls for a rabbinical trial in which Sender will have to "answer" to Nisn for the breaking of their sacred vow: a wrongdoing whose gravity, as we mentioned earlier, the zaddik stresses in terms that elaborate the key theme of memory and forgetting. From this point, as the film characteristically expends considerable energy showing, the zaddik and his followers take steps of an intricate and involved nature in order to arrange the unusual process of legal "mediation" between the living and the dead. Tasking Mikhoel with summoning Nisn to the trial, the zaddik provides his assistant with a series of esoteric hailing instructions, explaining how the latter must take his master's special gilt-handled staff, go to the cemetery, and utter a distinctive address to the "blameless departed" (all of which the film then shows being enacted, Mikhoel walking with his eyes shut through the cemetery, stopping at the first headstone that he encounters, tapping on it with the staff, and repeating the tactful subpoena). Next, in the synagogue where the trial is set to take place, the zaddik's men string up a lengthy white sheet that is meant to serve as a precise and protective "partition" that Nisn will be commanded not to step cross, that is to say, that will be mobilized, despite the superficial material resemblance between the two, considerably unlike the exorbitantly, fluidly welcoming fabric of Jacob's tents. Further, in the moments just before the trial, the zaddik guides his men in draping their tallises over their faces: a maneuver seemingly aimed to provide, on top of the partition, a second line of defense. And, finally, once Nisn's spirit arrives, entering the room through a spontaneously opening door and with a loud blast of "the wind" over the soundtrack (and thus echoing the entrance of the Messenger in the engagement party scene), the same men, arrayed in a tight-knit row over which the camera tracks, offer a coordinated reaction that stands as one of the most elaborate flourishes of Waszyński's communicative imaginary. In an escalating, trepidatious sequence of relayed transmission that evokes the game "Telephone," the man closest to the door whispers into the ear of the man beside him, "He's here," which the latter man subsequently whispers into the ear of the man beside him, and so on down the line.

As for the trial itself, in contrast to the much ado that precedes it, this transpires in a strikingly hurried fashion, which, too, is revealing. Indeed, whereas in the play the trial consists of long stretches of argumentation, testimonial, and cross-examination, the zaddik dispenses with all such due process and skips straightaway to the verdict—which is that Sender ought to be absolved, given the Torah's position (earlier adduced by the Messenger) that "an agreement pertaining to a thing not yet created is not binding." Accordingly, it is only *after* the zaddik renders such a decision that he addresses the ghostly plaintiff, asking Nisn's spirit whether he has heard and accepts the ruling. In response, though it requires a second address, a massive "wind" blows into the shadow-covered partition, causing the sheet to billow and the onlooking men, who now hold their tallises over their heads and reveal their faces, to tremble in fear. Of course, as any reasonable effort at decoding would imagine,

Nisn's answer to the zaddik is a vigorous "No." However, the zaddik takes the "articulation" for a "Yes" (or else ignores it altogether) and declares the trial over. Further, as the Messenger turns up and correctively intervenes, pointing out that Nisn did not utter an "Amen," the zaddik responds by imperiously doubling down. Swatting away two of his men in order to clear a path for himself, he approaches the Messenger on the steps leading up to the ark, and pronounces: "Even if it had been otherwise decided in the worlds above, I would reverse the decision." And, finally, he implores Sender to "send the swiftest horses for the bridegroom's party"—that it to say, to make hasty preparations for the resumption of Leah's wedding. In this way, the zaddik not only imagines himself, but acts as if he were, in fact, invested with an authority that exceeds that of the heavens. Notably, such grandiosity is facilitated by the film's strategic, streamlining elimination of the troika of traditional religious authorities, Reb Shimshon and two rabbinical judges, who co-officiate the trial in the play: a move, that is, that makes the zaddik into the lone officiator of the proceedings, in spite of the reality, reflected in the play, that a zaddik possesses only limited jurisdiction in a rabbinical court.[37] (Related to this change, whereas in the film it is "the wind" that conveys the mysterious communications of Nisn's spirit, in the play these are translated, as it were, for the court by Reb Shimshon. At the same time, in an exchange that produces an extraordinary chiasmus, the two rabbinical judges evoke the memorable, ambiguous voice/wind entity that addresses Leah at the parlor table before her wedding. "I hear a voice, but I don't hear any words," the first one remarks upon hearing the spirit "speak" for the first time, to which the second adds, "I hear words, but I don't hear a voice."[38])

The zaddik's shift from tottering deference in the face of "the only 'I' in the world" to thunderous insistence that he is able to reverse decisions "in the worlds above" initiates a cyclic pattern that repeats several times in short order. By the morning after the trial, all of the much-vaunted (ostensible) self-assurance that he displays during the court proceedings has evaporated. Finding the zaddik in his chambers, where he has spent the night in his chair, Mikhoel gingerly wakes him up and passes him a note from one of his supplicants. Screwing the paper up to one of his failing eyes, the zaddik laments: "What do they want from me? I'm old. And I'm weak. My soul yearns for solitude . . . I cannot go on." However, in response to such a denial of the normally strongly communitarian role of zaddikim (these uniquely nonhermetic, nonreclusive mystics), the assistant gives his master a loving, heartfelt pep talk that reminds him of his illustrious lineage, of his grandfather Reb Velvele the Great, who was "a pupil of the Baal Shem," namely, the very founder of the Hasidic movement, and this effort from the trusty Mikhoel works its own kind of wonder on the wonder rabbi. Indeed, so re-persuaded of his powers does the zaddik become that, turning his attention back to Sender's unfinished case, he calls for the dybbuk to be brought to the synagogue, where he plans to exorcise it, just like his ancestors used to do, "simply with a command." Yet the jackknifing cycle of self-doubt and self-inflation, weary resignation and fevered exertion, continues to grind away. After the dybbuk proves defiant and unbudging in the face of the naked exhortation, which forces his adversary to take the last resort and call for a *cherem* (a formal religious excommunication), the zaddik breaks down into a deflated, pitiable, tearful whimpering. And in the *cherem* scene that immediately follows, the zaddik suddenly appears, from his crumpled state of muteness, without any intermediate steps, right back in the thick of titanic efforts of hypercommunication.

The *cherem* scene, the film's last big set piece, strongly ties into Yiddish cinema's recurrent fascination with excommunication and places the phenomenon in a context that we have yet to encounter. In a book on Spinoza—arguably the most famous target of a *cherem* ever issued—Steven Nadler usefully explains the way that a *cherem* was normally carried out in reality: "The ceremony of pronouncing a strict *cherem* was usually held in a synagogue, where a rabbi or *chazzan* read the ban either in front of the Torah in the open ark or from the pulpit. The *shofar* (ram's horn) would be blown, while members of the congregation held candles (sometimes black) that were extinguished after the *cherem* was proclaimed."[39] Reproducing several of these elements, the *cherem* scene in the film takes place in the main room of the synagogue, where the zaddik stands on the pulpit in front of an open book and forcefully addresses the ban to the intent-looking, singularly black-garbed host of the dybbuk, who stands directly across from him on the steps leading up to the ark, while the zaddik's men, gripping long black candles, encircle the two opponents. Strikingly, as he makes his way through the utterance (whose severity is far more extreme than the exorcism, for it calls for an evacuation not only from Leah, but from the entire "body" of

"Israel"), the zaddik furiously whirls his hands, one around the other, as if a magician at the pivotal "abracadabra" moment of enacting an occult feat (not incidentally, pointing out "the close connection between mysticism and magic throughout the history of the Hasidic movement,"[40] Scholem describes the Baal Shem as a "master of practical Kabbalism, a magician"[41]). Such a memorable, ostentatious gesture suggestively evokes the key motif of "the wind," generating a quite literal "wind" with which to counter the dybbuk, this entity associated with so many of the blustery, mystic incursions that we have "seen" throughout the film. And indeed the effort pays off, for at the blowing of the shofars that answers the zaddik's expectant, uncertainty-tinged *Tekiah*, and concludes the excommunicative speech act, the dybbuk becomes dislodged (indicated by a spasm in Leah's shoulders) and then capitulates fully, asking with melancholy exhaustion that kaddish be recited for him. (Fittingly, the zaddik delegates the saying of the prayer of mourning to Sender, who manages to finish it, unlike at the hurriedly arranged, nervous burial for Khonon, in which he falters midway through, necessitating his servant finish it for him.)

Satisfied that the *cherem* has achieved its aim and that the dybbuk has been ousted, the zaddik goes over to the steps of the ark—where Leah sits in an unconscious, slumbering state—and rescinds the excommunication. Indeed, in keeping with the fact that all throughout their warring he has maintained deep sympathy for Khonon, he begs God to take mercy on "this tortured and wandering soul" and "grant [him] eternal rest in thy palaces." However, the more the zaddik tries to bring order and closure to the situation, the more his struggles appear to linger. Following the removal of the ban, he clears his men out of the synagogue and enjoins, with flailing arms, in a conspicuous echoing of the desperate, churningly hypercommunicative conclusion of the (mis)trial: "Sender! Sacred congregation, welcome the groom's party. Remove your white robes. Put away your prayer shawls. Faster, faster, hurry." And, in fact, as will shortly become clear in our discussion of the film's final moments, such a plan for the resumption of Leah's wedding turns out to be thoroughly dashed by forces outside his control. In other words, the film leaves us with an impression of the zaddik, despite his extraordinary feat of exorcising the dybbuk, still grappling, in a valiant, all-too-human way, with his mediatory insecurities and limitations.

In order more fully to grasp, and appreciate, such struggles, it is useful to turn for a brief moment to Grigori Roshal's 1928 Soviet Yiddish silent film, *His Excellency* (*Zayn Ekstelents*), which also includes a *cherem* scene and yet treats the ritual, not surprisingly, far differently. The film is loosely based on the life of Hirsch Lekert, a shoemaker and member of the Bund, who, in 1902, in retaliation for the arrest and punitive flogging of a group of May Day demonstrators, tried to assassinate the governor of Vilna.[42] In a fascinating sequence of quintessential dialectical montage, the excommunication scene appears intercut with another scene in which Jewish workers who have taken to the streets on May Day are being (a la the Odessa Steps scene in Sergei Eisenstein's *Battleship Potemkin*) brutally, violently suppressed by the powers that be. At the synagogue, a rabbi—played by the Moscow Art Theatre's Leonid Leonidov, who, in a canny move of double casting, also plays the governor—stands at the podium and rails against the protestors to an acquiescently spellbound congregation, hierarchically split, as the film repeatedly emphasizes, along gender lines, with the women squirreled away in a balcony. As this character—who appears every bit as sinister as the Orthodox priests in the stridently antireligious Soviet cinema—utters the *cherem* and the order is completed by the blowing of the shofar (just as we saw in *The Dybbuk*), the film cuts back to the demonstration, where a Cossack on horseback takes aim at and fires on a protestor trying to hide on a huge, multilevel, ruinous arcade. In this way, and as the film continues to switch back and forth between the scenes, the editing generates a highly suggestive analogy between the infliction of social death and the infliction of real death, equating the man blowing the shofar, at the behest of the rabbi, with the sniper shooting the protestor, at the behest of the government authorities. As different as the contexts are, such a parallel puts one in mind of the tropological mingling between social death and real death that takes place in several of the scenes of familial excommunication that we have encountered so far. Recall, for instance, in *Kol Nidre* and *Tevye*, the way that the father speaks about sitting shiva (or withholding the custom, or performing it in some curtailed form) in relation to the daughter whom he is cutting off from the family. Yet, in relation to *The Dybbuk*, the most salient aspect of the sequence is the striking contrast that it enables us to form with the representation of the zaddik. Though portrayed as part of an ethos of superstitious cowardice, Leonidov's rabbi does not quaver at all in his wielding of authority (which is effectively subsumed into the authority of the worldly and violence-monopolizing institution of the state), while he refuses all sympathy for those whom he is excommunicating, whom he considers a mob of irredeemable apostates. In other words, when set beside Leonidov's one-dimensional, "typological" rabbi, the energetic performance of which is in its own way remarkable, the complex multidimensionality of Morevsky's zaddik—this highly unique figure deriving authority from an opaque mystical realm, charged with responsibility toward the gravely wronged "rebel" whom he is compelled to excommunicate, contending unresolvedly with self-doubt, and ostensibly very near to the end of his life—comes that much more radiantly into focus.

Dialogue and *Unio Mystica*

Throughout this chapter, we have explored how *The Dybbuk* displays a series of critical tensions shared by the Kabbalah and Jewish folklore. To conclude, we would like to delve into one more such tension, one that is reflected in the very scholarship on the Kabbalah, and that emerges out of the question of *unio mystica*, or mystical union with the divine, which appears as a time-honored idea in many mystical traditions. According to Scholem, the Kabbalistic notion that appears most proximate to *unio mystica* is *devekut*, a notion that is "frequently mentioned as the highest ideal of the mystical life as the Kabbalists see it," and that goes beyond the common Hebrew sense of "attachment or devoutness" to refer to "close and most intimate communion with God." As Scholem expends an enormous amount of energy clarifying, however, *devekut* critically departs from its conceptual kinfolk in other mysticisms by virtue of the fact that it stops short of connoting *all-out* union with the divine. He explains: "It [*devekut*] is not union, because union with God is denied to man even in that mystical upsurge of the soul, according to Kabbalistic theology. But it comes as near to union as a mystical interpretation of Judaism would allow."[43] Accordingly, discussing the concept within the context of Hasidism, in which it is enshrined as a kind of lodestar, he remarks: "The performance of the commands is in itself an act of *devekut*, as is shown by an etymological pun. According to the Baal Shem, *mitzvah* means a bond. The talmudic adage, 'each good deed brings about another one,' is taken to mean that every communion with God leads to ever closer communion. *Devekut* is thus not a state but is in itself a path comprising an infinity of ever more intimate communions."[44] As one might thus imagine the situation, the practice of *devekut* echoes Zeno's famous paradox of motion: one moves ever closer to a union with God but never quite arrives at such a point. Scholem, it is true, goes on to question his own assessment and ask whether there are "in original Hasidic teaching, more radical formulations of *devekut* than those we have been considering," and consequently points out that there is "a definite turn toward a more mystical formulation of it [*devekut*] in the teaching of the Maggid of Mezritch and some of his pupils."[45] However, more closely examining the teaching of this famous pupil of the Baal Shem who goes "far on the way of what must be described as mystical intoxication,"[46] Scholem finds only further justification for his core position. Taking up the Great Maggid's virtuosic commentary on the Torah verse, "Make thee two trumpets of silver, of a whole piece shall thou make them,"[47] and offering an equally virtuosic metacommentary on it, he concludes: "This, then, is the deepest meaning of *devekut* of which Hasidism knows, and the radical terms should not blind us to the eminently Jewish and personalistic conception of man which they still cover. After having gone through *devekut* and union, man is still man—nay, he has, in truth, only then started to be man, and it is only logical that only then will he be called upon to fulfill his destiny in the society of men."[48]

Moshe Idel, whom Harold Bloom has described as "Scholem's leading revisionist,"[49] stakes out a powerful alternative position on the question of *unio mystica* in the Kabbalah. Departing more broadly from Scholem's methodology and emphasizing the experiential, phenomenological dimensions of the Kabbalah over its speculative, theoretical offerings, Idel writes: "Far from being absent, unitive descriptions recur in Kabbalistic literature no less frequently than in non-Jewish mystical writings, and the images used by the Kabbalists do not fall short of the most extreme forms of other types of mysticism."[50] Accordingly, returning to the Great Maggid's commentary on the two trumpets, Idel points out that Scholem's metacommentary "is no more than one of the many possibilities inherent in the Hasidic text," and with impressive hermeneutic dexterity shows how the same commentary can in fact be interpreted to affirm a "radical" mystical perspective, wherein the individual does not emerge and return from the experience of *devekut*, but is utterly annihilated, "absorbed in the depth of the Godhead,"[51] without any residuum whatsoever. Indeed, turning to his amply marshaled textual evidence, Idel supports such a position by discussing a number of the Great Maggid's disciples, including R. Levi Isaac of Berdichev, from whom he cites a passage in which Moses serves as an ideal figure for the zaddikim on account of a unique ability to overcome the "problem of human nature, which can hardly sustain a state of continuous immersion in a contemplative/annihilative experience."[52] Wrestling with the "transiency" of the mystical experience, to borrow William James's term, the author thus contrasts the zaddik, who "cleaves to the nought and nevertheless returns afterward to his essence,"[53] with Moses, who "was annihilated all the time since he was constantly contemplating the grandeur of the Creator, blessed be he, and did not return to his essence at all, as it is well known, since Moses our master, blessed be his memory, was constantly cleaving to the nought, and from this aspect he was annihilated."[54] Such an extreme description that thoroughly troubles a "personalistic conception of man," Idel shows, takes up a place within a range of similar evocations of self-annihilation (i.e., the mystic as droplet of water in the divine ocean, the mystic as object of divine swallowing or devouring) that pervade the corpus of Kabbalistic—and particularly Hasidic—writings.

Let us now return to *The Dybbuk*, whose final moments don't so much settle the question of the Kabbalah and *unio mystica* as evocatively rehearse it, presenting us with the two positions side-to-side, or rather back-to-back, in a state of suspended conflict. After the zaddik and his men clear out of the room in the synagogue where the *cherem* and its commutation have taken place, the film stays with Leah, who remains unconscious on the stairs to the ark. However, as the slow, looping, eerie music from the danse macabre scene returns, she is stirred awake by a long-drawn-out, vaguely erotic sigh (yet another species of "the wind") originating from a mysterious source offscreen. Accordingly, Leah rises, and, while conversing with the unseen entity, follows it up to the podium (as captured by a spectrally, sinuously backward-tracking camera), where she yearningly stretches her arms out to it. The exchange between the two—the voice, of course, belongs to Khonon—runs as follows:

LEAH: Who sighs here so deeply?

KHONON: I [do].

LEAH: Who are you?

KHONON: I have forgotten who I am. Only in your thoughts I can remember myself.

LEAH: Oh, my heart was drawn to you as to a bright star. On silent nights I wept for you. Why have you forsaken me again? Why?

KHONON: I departed from your body to return to your soul.

LEAH: Take my soul, my bridegroom, my husband.

Especially in relation to what has come before, the interchange is remarkable, even startling, among other things, for its communicative *ordinariness*, constituting neither of the special metasemantic modes, silence and (long-distance) song, that the lovers have been forced to resort to in order to elude external policing forces. Moreover, the conversation contrasts sharply with the situation brought about by the possession, which, so far as we can see, never involves the lovers speaking to or with one another. That is, we only ever see one of them speaking at a time: either Khonon speaking through Leah (signaled by Leah's lowered, "masculine" voice) or Leah speaking as herself (signaled by her frightened, "normal," "female" voice, which returns when the dybbuk periodically loosens his grip and goes dormant). By contrast, in the late moment when they are finally alone together, Khonon's spirit speaks to Leah from outside her body, and this restoration of distance facilitates a basic form of dialogue. Indeed, as Buber recurrently points out, relation fundamentally presupposes the maintenance of some measure of distance between the "I" and the "You"[55] (in this sense, we can think of separation as an even more primordial dialogic foundation than "turning"). It is accordingly no wonder that Khonon's remark, "I have forgotten who I am. Only in your thoughts can I remember myself,"[56] feels almost as if it could have been written by Buber—or by the neo-Buberian Flusser, for whom, recall, the central Jewish idea is that my "immortality" consists "in the memory of others." In a similar way, one can read into the moving moment of burgeoning, separation-preserving reconnection hints of Scholem's notion of Kabbalistic *devekut*, which never involves the two entities finally collapsing into one another: *devekut*, that is, as "communion" rather than "union," and no "*mere* communion" but rather "communion" that makes something profound out of "the eminently Jewish and personalistic conception of man."

Of course, however, all of this only tells one part of the story. Throughout the exchange, the black cape that was previously wrapped all the way around Leah during the *cherem* is parted, slung over her shoulders and revealing her white bridal gown beneath. As if a chrysalis being shed, this garment finally falls off entirely when Leah reaches out to Khonon and surrenders her soul to him. Leah, that is, appears to be moving on to a different reality, on to another ontic plane. Indeed, when the film returns to her after momentarily turning our attention to Mikhoel entering the room and crying out at the sight of her, she appears lying on the bench at the back of the podium with perfect, rigorous straightness, as if in obedience to some minute sacrificial specification, dead. Here, intimations of Idel's "radical" notion of Kabbalistic *devekut* come into play, for it appears as if the death of the lovers has resulted in a merger of their souls, and concomitantly a collapse of the distance required by dialogue, by "the memories of others," and indeed by all communication (barring, of course, to recall our introduction, what Peters describes as the contradictory dream of "perfect communication"). From a moment of poignantly raw dialogue shot through with mnemonic energy, that is, the end of the film pivots to what appears to be a moment of *unio mystica* in the full sense of the term, percolating with the energy of ecstatic self-annihilation. And yet the shift happens without displacing what has just come before. Rather, the two moments seem almost as if superimposed, suspended in an in-between state, thus offering yet one more iteration of the tension that flows so powerfully throughout the Kabbalistic, Jewish-folkloric film. Meanwhile, the concluding title card, which announces *koniec*, or "the end" in Polish, fittingly reinforces such ambivalence by featuring an illustrated, mythico-monotheistic image of a Star of David—layered on top of a menorah—flanked at the base by a pair of vigilant sphinxes.

In this way, the mediation of the mystical remains a fraught matter to the end, while its continuation, in the wake of the lovers' (earthly) demise, and in the face of the inexorable dying out of their respective family lines, is left up to others—namely, to the film itself, and to us, its spectators. As Flusser writes, bringing his audacious biblical exegesis to bear on the history of media, and envisioning the film screen, among other mediatic canvases, as a communicative analogue to Jacob's "goodly tents": "The tent wall, billowing in the wind, gathers experiences, processes them, and then passes them on."[57]

Coda

EXPLORING THE MANY, multifaceted connections between Yiddish cinema and Flusser's media philosophy, this book has attempted to read the collective body of Yiddish movies as a dramatically embodied "Jewish media theory from below." Naturally, there are other ways that one might enact the needful task of bringing Yiddish cinema, as it were, out of "the ghetto" that it unfortunately mostly still occupies, and into aesthetic and philosophical spheres where it might find a broader reception. For instance, one might build bridges with other cinemas, particularly those that, too, fall under the banner of the "minor" (Deleuze and Guattari),[1] the "narrowcast" and/or the "accented" (Naficy),[2] the "ethnic," and the "transnational,"[3] and that have increasingly proliferated since the time of the end of Yiddish cinema's "golden age." Or stretching out the timeline of Yiddish cinema into the "postvernacular" phase of the language, one might forge links with more recent Yiddish film and media, including works about Hasidic and other Haredi communities (where, of course Yiddish still retains a vernacular purchase) like the global sensation, Netflix-streaming series *Shtisel* (2013–).[4] For us, however, the connection with Flusser and media theory has been especially compelling, perhaps because of the truly wide-ranging resonance, in our own, radically media-saturated moment, with Flusser's central hypothesis, endlessly born out in Yiddish cinema, that "the structure of communication is the infrastructure of human reality," or as he elsewhere puts it, that "we know and experience the world, and . . . we act in it, within the structures that are imposed on us by the codes that inform us."[5]

As we have stressed, this notion as it is expressed in both Flusser and Yiddish cinema in no way implies a strict technological determinism but rather allows room for, and indeed insists upon the importance of, the sort of "turning" that can be read into Buber's retold tale, "Those Who Are to Hear, Hear." In fact, to come back to the other communication-obsessed Jewish storyteller with whom we began, intimations of such a critical dual framework can also be seen to animate Kafka's "Introductory Talk on the Yiddish Language," which he delivered as a preamble to an evening of recitations by the Yiddish actor Yitzhak Löwy, held at the Jewish Town Hall, in Prague, in 1912. Writes Kafka, in the closing movement of the talk:

> You begin to come quite close to Yiddish if you bear in mind that apart from what you know there are active in yourselves forces and associations that enable you to understand Yiddish intuitively. It is only here that the interpreter can help, reassuring you, so that you no longer feel shut out from something and also that you may realize that you must cease to complain that you do not understand Yiddish. This is the most important point, for with every complaint understanding diminishes. But if you relax, you suddenly find yourself in the midst of Yiddish. Once Yiddish has taken hold of you and moved you—and Yiddish is everything, the words, the Chasidic melody, and the essential character of this East European Jewish actor himself—you will have forgotten your former reserve.[6]

According to Kafka, Yiddish—whose codes he not incidentally defines in a wide-ranging, trans-linguistic way ("Yiddish is everything") that resonates powerfully with the capacious aims of media theory—possesses a vast reservoir of intersubjective powers. At the same time, he suggests, in order to enter into a rapport with this extensive, reserve-melting communication system, one must open oneself to it, must tap into mysterious, metasemantically operative, "intuitive" forces within oneself.

Notably, at the last minute, regarding the enlivening experience that he ideally imagines for and hopes to cultivate in his audience, Kafka anxiously adds: "How could it last, fed only on the memory of a single evening's recitations!" Luckily for us, however, engraving performances like Löwy's on celluloid, Yiddish cinema allows us to feed on them copiously, to take more than a *bisl*—a little bit—of nourishment from them, and so perpetuate the memory of Yiddish—whose fragility Kafka seemed to sense even more than a century ago—that much longer.

Acknowledgments

We would like to extend our sincerest thanks to the National Center for Jewish Film, in Waltham, Massachusetts, for the colossal project of rescuing Yiddish movies en masse and making them available to viewers like ourselves with a fanatical appetite for them; to the Vilém Flusser Archiv, at the Universität der Künste, Berlin, for providing an accessible home for Flusser's papers and other Flusseriana, and warmly hosting Monika during an invaluable stint as a researcher in 2013–2014; to Murray Pomerance, editor of the Horizons of Cinema series, for bigheartedly sustaining his belief in this project through many incarnations and offering much sage advice; to our two anonymous reviewers for their generous engagement with the manuscript, shrewd criticisms, and useful recommendations for improvement; to James Peltz at State University of New York Press, for graciously advocating for the book and navigating us through the publication process; and to George Toles, at the University of Manitoba, and Polona Tratnik, at Nova Univerza (Nova Gorica, Slovenia), for deeply cherished mentorship, inspiration, and friendship over the years.

Notes

Introduction

1. Martin Buber, *Tales of the Hasidim, Book Two: The Later Masters*, trans. Olga Marx (New York: Schocken Books, 1991), 115.

2. Franz Kafka, "An Imperial Message," trans. Willa and Edwin Muir, in *The Complete Stories* (New York: Schocken Books, 1971), 4.

3. Adding to its ties with Buber's Hasidic tale, "An Imperial Message" possesses subtle but crucial Jewish resonances inasmuch as it, to quote Robert Alter, "resembles the classical midrashic parable, or *mashal*, in exploiting (though only implicitly) a correspondence between terrestrial monarch and celestial King." Robert Alter, *Necessary Angels: Tradition and Modernity in Kafka, Benjamin, and Scholem* (Cambridge: Harvard University Press, 1991), 101.

4. Kafka, "An Imperial Message," 5.

5. Vilém Flusser, *The Surprising Phenomenon of Human Communication* (n.p.: Metaflux, 2016), 154. The polyglot Flusser originally composed the lectures in both French and English—two of the four languages, in addition to German and Portuguese, that he regularly wrote in and translated between. The Metaflux edition of the lectures is based on Flusser's "original" English text.

6. See Rodrigo Maltez Novaes, editor's note in *The Surprising Phenomenon of Human Communication*, 10–11.

7. Flusser describes the moving encounter in "Conversation between Vilém Flusser and Patrik Tschudin," in *The Freedom of the Migrant: Objections to Nationalism*, trans. Kenneth Kronenberg, ed. Anke K. Finger (Urbana: University of Illinois Press, 2003), 93–94.

8. See Martin Buber, *I and Thou*, trans. Walter Kaufmann (New York: Simon & Schuster), 1996.

9. Vilém Flusser, "On the Problem of Being Jewish. (Focus on 'Chosen People' and 'Honesty')," unpublished essay, Vilém Flusser Archiv (2768), Berlin, 5. For similar formulations, see Flusser's critical texts on Zionism, "Two Different Kinds of Jew. (To Be Discussed at the Meeting of the Study Circle

on Contemporary Jewry and Zionism at Hillel House, London, on October 29, 1980)," unpublished document, Vilém Flusser Archiv (2812), Berlin, and "The Jewish War. (A Testimony of Commitment)," unpublished essay, Vilém Flusser Archiv (2793), Berlin. These two texts—the latter addressing the 1973 Yom Kippur War—were written in English, like "On the Problem of Being Jewish." A selection of Flusser's Jewish writings is contained in the German-language collection, *Jude Sein: Essays, Briefe, Fiktionen*, ed. Stefan Bollmann and Edith Flusser (Mannheim: Bollmann Verlag, 1995).

10. Hannah Arendt, "Concern with Politics in Recent European Thought," quoted in John Durham Peters, *Speaking into the Air: A History of the Idea of Communication* (Chicago: University of Chicago Press, 1999), 280. Arendt's essay is collected in *Essays in Understanding, 1930–1954: Formation, Exile, and Totalitarianism*, ed. Jerome Kohn (New York: Schocken Books, 1994).

11. Peters, *Speaking into the Air*, 1.

12. Peters, *Speaking into the Air*, 263.

13. J. Hoberman, *Bridge of Light: Yiddish Film Between Two Worlds* (New York: Museum of Modern Art and Schocken Books, 1991), 10.

14. Nahma Sandrow, *Vagabond Stars: A World History of Yiddish Theater* (New York: Limelight Editions, 1986), 98–99.

15. Peter Brooks, *The Melodramatic Imagination: Balzac, Henry James, and the Mode of Excess* (New Haven: Yale University Press, 1995).

16. Brooks, *The Melodramatic Imagination*, 55.

17. Brooks, *The Melodramatic Imagination*, 55.

18. See Jeffrey Shandler, *Adventures in Yiddishland: Postvernacular Language and Culture* (Berkeley: University of California Press, 2006).

19. All of the films that we write on come from the DVD offerings of the National Center for Jewish Film, save *The Dybbuk*, for which we use the DVD released in 2017, with French and English subtitles, by Lobster Films. (Toward the end of our work on this project, Kino released a Blu-ray box set, *The Jewish Soul: Ten Classics of Yiddish Cinema*, based on restorations by Lobster Films.) Generally, in reproducing dialogue, we follow the English subtitles—which might be hard-encoded on the print, newly made, or a mix of the two—while quoting the original Yiddish when it is critical to a point or provides an essential added resonance. In keeping with this strategy, we refer to the films by their English titles, including the Yiddish in parenthesis in the first mention and in the beginning of chapters. Our transliterations of Yiddish adhere to the YIVO system, aside from names and in cases where the word has become incorporated into English.

Chapter 1

1. See Eric A. Goldman, *Visions, Images, and Dreams: Yiddish Film, Past and Present*, revised and expanded (Teaneck: Holmes & Meier, 2011), 78–80.

2. For the full lyrics of the song, see Solomon Smulevitz, "A brivele der mamen," Milken Archive of Jewish Music, https://www.milkenarchive.org/music/volumes/view/great-songs-of-the-american-yiddish-stage/work/a-brivele-der-mamen/, accessed January 12, 2019. For more on the song, and the genre of "letter-songs" that it helped spawn, see Mark Slobin, *Tenement Songs: The Popular Music of the Jewish Immigrants* (Urbana: University of Illinois Press, 1982), 124–26, 152–53.

3. Vilém Flusser, *Gestures*, trans. Nancy Ann Roth (Minneapolis: University of Minneapolis Press, 2014), 111–12. The collection of linked essays, which Flusser prepared shortly before his death, first appeared in German in 1991.

4. Flusser, *Gestures*, 113.

5. Flusser, *Gestures*, 113.

6. Flusser, *Gestures*, 114.

7. Flusser, *Gestures*, 114.

8. Flusser, *Gestures*, 112.

9. Flusser, *Gestures*, 116.

10. Flusser, *Gestures*, 116.

11. Flusser, *Gestures*, 117.

12. See Michel Chion, *The Voice in Cinema*, trans. Claudia Gorbman (New York: Columbia University Press, 1999), 23–27.

13. Flusser, *Gestures*, 114.

14. Daniel Boyarin, *Unheroic Conduct: The Rise of Heterosexuality and the Invention of the Jewish Man* (Berkeley: University of California Press, 1997), 158.

15. Boyarin, *Unheroic Conduct*, xxii.

16. Boyarin, *Unheroic Conduct*, 66.

17. Boyarin, *Unheroic Conduct*, fn. 89.

18. See, in addition to Boyarin's *Unheroic Conduct*, Natalie Zemon Davis, *Women on the Margins: Three Seventeenth-Century Lives* (Cambridge: Harvard University Press, 1995).

19. For an insightful, Boyarin-inspired analysis of *Green Fields* as an attempt to work out a dialectical synthesis of the *yeshiva bokher* type and the opposing *musklyid* (muscle Jew) type, see Vincent Brook, "Forging the 'New Jew': Ulmer's Yiddish Films," in *The Films of Edgar G. Ulmer*, ed. Bernd Herzogenrath (Lanham: Scarecrow Press, 2009).

20. Vilém Flusser, "Family Unit," unpublished essay, Vilém Flusser Archiv (2742), Berlin, 1.

21. See Hannah Arendt, "What Is Authority," in *Between Past and Future: Eight Exercises in Political Thought* (New York: Penguin Books, 1993), 122.

22. Flusser, "Family Unit," 2.

23. See Goldman, *Visions, Images, Dreams*, 92.

24. Hoberman, *Bridge of Light*, 290.

25. Hamid Naficy, *An Accented Cinema: Exilic and Diasporic Filmmaking* (Princeton: Princeton University Press, 2001), 101.

26. Naficy, *An Accented Cinema*, 105.

27. Naficy, *An Accented Cinema*, 106.

28. Hoberman, *Bridge of Light*, 9. For more on the longstanding associations between Yiddish and maternality—and the feminine more broadly—see Naomi Seidman, *A Marriage Made in Heaven: The Sexual Politics of Hebrew and Yiddish* (Berkeley: University of California Press, 1997).

29. Flusser, *The Surprising Phenomenon of Human Communication*, 33.

30. Vilém Flusser, "On Religion, Memory and Synthetic Image. Interview with Vilém Flusser in Budapest, April 7, 1990," interview by László Beke and Miklós Peternák, in *"We Shall Survive in the Memory of Others": Vilém Flusser*, ed. Miklós Peternák (Köln: Verlag der Buchhandlung Walter König, 2010).

31. Goldman, *Vision, Images, and Dreams*, 188.

Chapter 2

1. *Mayn Zundele* is the title of the Sholem Secunde play from which the screenplay of the film is adapted.

2. "The best remembered and most powerful of all the Yiddish radio stations. . . . Created in 1927 by the Socialist Party to honor its recently deceased leader, Eugene Victor Debbs, the station was taken over in 1932 by the leading Yiddish newspaper, *The Forward*." "The Yiddish Radio Dial," Yiddish Radio Project, accessed December 16, 2018, https://www.yiddishradioproject.org/exhibits/history/. See also J. Hoberman and Jeffrey Shandler, *Entertaining America: Jews, Movies, and Broadcasting* (Princeton: Princeton University Press, 2003), 108; and "WEVD: Yiddish Radio in New York," Mapping Yiddish New York, October 9, 2017. http://jewishstudiescolumbia.com/myny/arts/wevd-yiddish-radio-in-new-york/.

3. Flusser, *The Surprising Phenomenon of Human Communication*, 73.

4. Vilém Flusser, "Mutation in Human Relations," unpublished manuscript, 1977/78, Vilém Flusser Archiv (1712), Berlin, 21.

5. Flusser, "Mutation in Human Relations," 22.

6. Flusser, *The Surprising Phenomenon of Human Communication*, 70.

7. Flusser, "Mutation in Human Relations," 13.

8. Flusser, "Mutation in Human Relations," 13.

9. Flusser, *The Surprising Phenomenon of Human Communication*, 70.

10. Flusser, "Mutation in Human Relations," 21.

11. Theodor W. Adorno, *Current of Music*, ed. Robert Hullot-Kentor (Cambridge: Polity, 2009), 99. *Current of Music* was never published in Ador-

no's lifetime, appearing, in reconstructed form, for the first time in 2006 as part of Adorno's collected posthumous writings.

12. Adorno, *Current of Music*, 91.
13. Adorno, *Current of Music*, 54.
14. Adorno, *Current of Music*, 55.
15. Adorno, *Current of Music*, 107.
16. Adorno, *Current of Music*, 113.
17. Flusser, "Mutation in Human Relations," 21.
18. Flusser, "Mutation in Human Relations," 17.
19. Flusser, "Mutation in Human Relations," 17.
20. Silvia Federici, "On the Meaning of Gossip," in *Witches, Witch-Hunting, and Women* (Oakland: PM Press, 2018), 35–43.
21. Flusser, *The Surprising Phenomenon of Human Communication*, 69.
22. Flusser, "The Gesture of Telephoning," in *Gestures*, 140.
23. Flusser, *Mutation in Human Relations*, 17.
24. Brooks, *The Melodramatic Imagination*, 45.
25. Flusser, "Mutation in Human Relations," 17.
26. Brooks, *The Melodramatic Imagination*, 56.
27. Arendt, *Between Past and Future*, 93.
28. See Hoberman and Shandler, *Entertaining America*, 111.
29. Neal Gabler, *An Empire of Their Own: How the Jews Invented Hollywood* (New York: Random House, 1989).

Chapter 3

1. Hoberman, *Bridge of Light*, 154.
2. See Goldman, *Visions, Images, and Dreams*, 51–58, and Hoberman, *Bridge of Light*, 154–57.
3. Flusser, "Family Unit," 4.
4. Flusser, "Family Unit," 3.
5. Flusser, "Family Unit," 3–4.
6. Flusser, "Family Unit," 4.
7. Raymond Williams, *Television: Technology and Cultural Form* (New York: Routledge, 2003), 135.
8. Flusser, "Family Unit," 4.
9. Flusser, "Family Unit," 4.
10. Marshall McLuhan, *Understanding Media: The Extensions of Man* (Cambridge: MIT Press, 1994), 303. McLuhan's book was originally published in 1964.
11. McLuhan, *Understanding Media*, 300.

12. L. Honors, "Radio–Phonograph: That's the Bone of Contention in Jewish Families These Days," in J. Hoberman and Shandler, *Entertaining America*, 109.

13. L. Honors, "Radio–Phonograph," 109.

14. L. Honors, "Radio–Phonograph," 109.

15. Of course, American Jews also did use radio—in a complex dialectic, as it were—to serve traditional ends presumably appealing to the older generation: for instance, as Shandler tells in a longer discussion of the interplay between Judaism and radio in America, through a show like *The Eternal Light*, a highly popular instance of Jewish "ecumenical broadcasting" that began near the end of World War II on NBC radio and eventually became a television show. Jeffrey Shandler, "Turning on *The Eternal Light*," in *Jews, God, and Videotape: Religion and Media in America* (New York: New York University Press, 2009), 57.

16. Walter Benjamin, "Reflections on Radio," in *The Work of Art in the Age of Technological Reproducibility and Other Writings on Media*, ed. Michael W. Jennings, Brigid Doherty, and Thomas Levin, trans. Rodney Livingstone (Cambridge: Harvard University Press, 2008), 391. Unpublished in Benjamin's lifetime, the text was written no later than November 1931 (392).

17. Walter Benjamin, "The Work of Art in the Age of Its Technological Reproducibility: Second Version," in *The Work of Art in the Age of Its Technological Reproducibility and Other Writings on Media*, ed. Michael W. Jennings, Brigid Doherty, and Thomas Levin, trans. Edmund Jephcott and Harry Zohn (Cambridge: Harvard University Press, 2008), 33. Unpublished in this form in Benjamin's lifetime, the essay was written between late December 1935 and the beginning of February 1936 (42).

18. Benjamin, "The Work of Art," 33–34.

19. Brooks, *The Melodramatic Imagination*, 56.

20. Alexander R. Galloway, Eugene Thacker, and McKenzie Wark, "Introduction: Execrable Media," in *Excommunication: Three Inquiries in Media and Mediation* (Chicago: University of Chicago Press, 2014), 15.

21. J. L. Austin, *How to Do Things with Words* (Cambridge: Harvard University Press, 1962), 155.

22. Austin, *How to Do Things with Words*, 156–57.

23. Austin, *How to Do Things with Words*, 155.

24. Pierre Bourdieu, *Language and Symbolic Power*, ed. John B. Thompson, trans. Gino Raymond and Matthew Adamson (Cambridge: Polity Press, 1991).

25. Shoshana Felman, *The Scandal of the Speaking Body: Don Juan with J. L. Austin, or Seduction in Two Languages*, trans. Catherine Porter (Stanford: Stanford University Press, 2003). Felman's book was originally published in French in 1980.

26. Judith Butler, *Excitable Speech: A Politics of the Performative* (New York: Routledge, 1997), 155–56. The new edition of *The Scandal of the Speaking Body* also includes an afterword by Butler.

27. Brooks, *The Melodramatic Imagination*, 56.

28. Brooks, *The Melodramatic Imagination*, 56.

29. Brooks, *The Melodramatic Imagination*, 72.

30. Dan Miron, *A Traveler Disguised: The Rise of Modern Yiddish Fiction in the Nineteenth Century* (Syracuse: Syracuse University Press, 1996), 35–36. Miron's book was originally published in 1973.

31. Quoted in Miron, *A Traveler Disguised*, 43.

32. Quoted in Miron, *A Traveler Disguised*, 64.

33. See Sander L. Gilman, *Jewish Self-Hatred: Anti-Semitism and the Hidden Language of the Jews* (Baltimore: Johns Hopkins University Press, 1986).

34. For more on the role of the cantor in Yiddish American film and Jewish American culture, see Jeffrey Shandler, "Cantors on Trial," in *Jews, God, and Videotape*.

35. We discuss another such montage more at length in our discussion of *The Wandering Jew* in chapter 7. For more on techniques of repurposing in Yiddish cinema, see chapter 14, "The *Faryidisht* Film," in Hoberman's *Bridge of Light*.

Chapter 4

1. In the stories, Chava's suitor is named Chvedka. Producing a more distinct rhyme with "Tevye," the changed name in the film produces an intensified sense of antagonism between lover and father.

2. Yuri Slezkine, *The Jewish Century* (Princeton: Princeton University Press, 2004), 163.

3. Sholem Aleichem, *Tevye the Dairyman and Motl the Cantor's Son*, trans. Aliza Shevrin (New York: Penguin Books, 2009), 72.

4. Dan Miron, introduction to Sholem Aleichem, *Tevye the Dairyman and Motl the Cantor's Son* (New York: Penguin Books, 2009), xvii–xix.

5. See Chava Weissler, "Tkhines," in *The YIVO Encyclopedia of Jews in Eastern Europe*, http://www.yivoencyclopedia.org/article.aspx/Tkhines, accessed January 12, 2018.

6. Alain Brossat and Sylvie Klingberg, *Revolutionary Yiddishland: A History of Jewish Radicalism*, trans. David Fernbach (London: Verso, 2016). *Revolutionary Yiddishland* was originally published in French in 1983.

7. Quoted in Slezkine, *The Jewish Century*, 164.

8. Aleichem, *Tevye the Dairyman*, 79.

9. See Slezkine, *The Jewish Century*, 325–27.

10. See Butler, *Excitable Speech*, 71–82.

11. Benjamin Harshav, *The Meaning of Yiddish* (Stanford: Stanford University Press, 1999), 114.

12. The issue of the proscription against Jewish burial in the countryside is also alluded to in *Green Fields*. The father of the young girl who falls in love with the scholar reflects on his own father's death and the family's rural existence: "When I went to the city to bury him . . . I didn't want to leave for the village. This must be God's will . . . that we should live far from the Jews, and be buried among them."

13. Butler, *Excitable Speech*, 141.

14. Butler, *Excitable Speech*, 148.

15. Butler, *Excitable Speech*, 163.

16. Butler, *Excitable Speech*, 163.

17. Hoberman, *Bridge of Light*, 11. For more on the concept of "Yiddishland," see Shandler, *Adventures in Yiddishland*, 31–58.

18. George Steiner, "Our Homeland, the Text," *Salmagundi*, no. 66 (Winter–Spring 1985): 5. Heine's phrase literally means "the written-down fatherland." For more on Judaism and the idea of textual homeland, see Daniel Boyarin, *A Traveling Homeland: The Babylonian Talmud as Diaspora* (Philadelphia: University of Pennsylvania Press, 2015).

19. The film doesn't make clear what Tevye considers the difference to be between Palestine and the Holy Land.

20. Jacqueline Rose, *The Last Resistance* (London: Verso, 2017), 17.

21. Miron, Introduction, xxiv.

22. Peters, *Speaking into the Air*, 8.

Chapter 5

1. See Mary Anne Doane, *The Desire to Desire: The Woman's Film of the 1940s* (Bloomington: Indiana University Press, 1987), 36.

2. Editor's note, in Flusser, *The Freedom of the Migrant*, 1. In this book, an English translation of Flusser's *Von der Freiheit des Migranten: Einsprüche gegen den Nationalismus* that also includes his essays "Nomaden" and "Vom Fremden," the word "heimat" is left untranslated and unitalicized throughout.

3. Flusser, *The Freedom of the Migrant*, 6–7.

4. Flusser, *The Freedom of the Migrant*, 7.

5. Jacqueline Rose, *Mothers: An Essay on Love and Cruelty* (New York: Farrar, Straus and Giroux, 2018), 1.

6. Rose, *Mothers*, 12.

7. Rose, *Mothers*, 12.

8. Rose, *Mothers*, 12.

9. Rose, *Mothers*, 18.

10. See Donald Crafton, *The Talkies: American Cinema's Transition to Sound, 1926–1931* (Berkeley: University of California Press, 1997).

11. Erving Goffman, *Asylums: Essays on the Social Situation of Mental Patients and Other Inmates* (New York: Anchor Books, 1961), 12–13.

12. See Austin, *How to Do Things with Words*, 14–16.

13. Rose, *Mothers*, 8.

14. Rose, *Mothers*, 8.

15. In many of the National Center for Jewish Film (NCJF) restorations of the films, including *Where Is My Child?*, this nonremovable, often quite spare, original subtitle track is supplemented by further, newly translated titles, printed with comparative typographic uniformity.

16. Harshav, *The Meaning of Yiddish*, 90.

17. Vilém Flusser, *Does Writing Have a Future?*, trans. Nancy Ann Roth (Minneapolis: University of Minnesota Press, 2011), 104. Flusser's book was first published in German in 1987.

18. Important scenes with still images also appear in *Bar Mitzvah*, *Mamele*, *Two Sisters*, and *American Matchmaker* (*Amerikaner Shadkhn*, 1940).

19. Plucking love letters out of Elick's mail bag, the couple take turns reading the missives aloud, in the process appropriating the amorous sentiments and redirecting—or better: rerouting—them at one another. The number recalls *Tevye* and *Green Fields* in providing another instance of the invigorating interaction between desire and reading/texts/literacy.

20. Since Raymond Bellour's seminal 1984 essay "The Pensive Spectator," trans. Lynne Kirby, republished in *Wide Angle* 9, no. 1 (1987): 6–10, the critical literature on the dynamic between stillness and motion in cinema has grown immensely. See, for especially notable contributions, Garrett Stewart's *Between Film and Screen: Modernism's Photo Synthesis* (Chicago: University of Chicago Press, 1999) and Laura Mulvey's *Death 24x a Second: Stillness and the Moving Image* (London: Reaktion Books, 2006).

21. Azoulay's work focuses largely on documentary photography, with special emphasis on images of injury from the Israeli Occupation. See Ariella Azoulay, *The Civil Contract of Photography* (New York: Zone Books, 2008), 14.

22. Goffman, *Asylums*, xiii.

23. Goffman, *Asylums*, 12.

24. Goffman, *Asylums*, 14.

25. Goffman, *Asylums*, 14.

26. Goffman, *Asylums*, 16.

27. Goffman, *Asylums*, 20.

28. See Georges Didi-Huberman, *Invention of Hysteria: Charcot and the Photographic Iconography of the Salpêtrière*, trans. Alisa Hartz (Cambridge: MIT Press, 2003).

29. Doane, *The Desire to Desire*, 43.

30. Michel Foucault, *The Birth of the Clinic: An Archaeology of Medical Perception*, trans. A. M. Sheridan Smith (New York: Random House, 1973), 107. *The Birth of the Clinic* was originally published in French in 1963.

31. Michel Foucault, *Madness and Civilization: A History of Insanity in the Age of Reason*, trans. Richard Howard (New York: Random House, 1965), 70. *Madness and Civilization* was originally published in French in 1961.

32. Foucault, *Madness and Civilization*, 250.

33. One could also draw a fruitful parallel between the Foucauldian "medical gaze" and Marshall McLuhan's notion of the "culture of the eye," which the latter argues is embodied with particular force by Western culture in the wake of the development of the printing press. See Marshall McLuhan, *The Gutenberg Galaxy* (Toronto: University of Toronto Press, 1962), 54–58, 159–61. In chapter 8, we discuss modes of objectification, visual and beyond, in Western culture more broadly.

34. Goffman, *Asylums*, 130.

35. Goffman, *Asylums*, 19.

36. Goffman, *Asylums*, 19.

37. Goffman, *Asylums*, 35–36.

38. Foucault, *The Birth of the Clinic*, xviii.

39. Goffman, *Asylums*, 82.

40. Goffman, *Asylums*, 81.

41. Goffman, *Asylums*, 82.

42. Goffman, *Asylums*, 12.

43. Cesar Baio, "Functionary," in *Flusseriana: An Intellectual Toolbox*, ed. Siegfried Zielinski et al. (Minneapolis: Univocal, 2015), 184.

44. Baio, "Functionary," 184–85.

45. Baio, "Functionary," 185.

46. Doane, *The Desire to Desire*, 43.

47. Doane, *The Desire to Desire*, 54.

48. See Mark Wyman, *DPs: Europe's Displaced Persons, 1945–51* (Ithaca: Cornell University Press, 1998), 92–95.

49. Emma Wilson, *Cinema's Missing Children* (New York: Wallflower Press, 2003), 61. Wilson also comments on the treatment of this difficulty in the context of the Holocaust, briefly mentioning the Kindertransport documentary *Into the Arms of Strangers* (2000) (61).

50. Wilson, *Cinema's Missing Children*, 61.

Chapter 6

1. R. Murray Schafer, *The Soundscape: Our Sonic Environment and the Tuning of the World* (Rochester: Destiny Books, 1994), 256.

2. Martin Buber, "Dialogue," in *Between Man and Man*, trans. Ronald Gregor-Smith (London: Routledge, 2007), 3.
3. Buber, "Dialogue," 9.
4. Buber, "Dialogue," 19.
5. Flusser, *Does Writing Have a Future?*, 98.
6. See Karl Marx, "Economic and Philosophic Manuscripts of 1844," in *The Marx-Engels Reader*, second edition, ed. Robert C. Tucker (New York: W. W. Norton, 1978), 70–81.
7. Abraham Cohen, *Everyman's Talmud: The Major Teachings of the Rabbinic Sages* (New York: Schocken Books, 1995), 196.
8. Quoted in Cohen, *Everyman's Talmud*, 196.
9. Emmanuel Levinas, *Entre Nous: On Thinking-of-the-Other*, trans. Michael B. Smith and Barbara Harshav (New York: Columbia University Press, 1998), 119–20.
10. Irving Howe, *World of Our Fathers: The Journey of the East European Jews to America and the Life They Found and Made* (New York: Simon & Schuster, 1976), 297.
11. Howe, *World of Our Fathers*, 298.
12. Quoted in Howe, *World of Our Fathers*, 299.
13. Quoted in Howe, *World of Our Fathers*, 300.
14. Levinas, "Philosophy, Justice, and Love," in *Entre-Nous*, 104.
15. See Levinas, "Philosophy, Justice, and Love." Levinas also elaborates upon this paradox of the Face in the essay "Ethics and Spirit," collected in *Difficult Freedom: Essays on Judaism*, trans. Seán Hand (Baltimore: Johns Hopkins University Press, 1997). Notably, a French copy of *Difficile Liberté* is contained in Flusser's library, housed at the Vilém Flusser Archiv.
16. Levinas, "Philosophy, Justice, and Love," 104–05.
17. Joseph Roth, *The Wandering Jews: The Classic Portrait of a Vanished People*, trans. Michael Hofmann (New York: W. W. Norton, 2001), 59.
18. Roth, *The Wandering Jews*, 99–100.
19. Uriel Weinreich, *Modern English-Yiddish Yiddish-English Dictionary* (New York: Schocken Books, 1977), 386.
20. Solon Beinfeld and Harry Bochner, eds., *Comprehensive Yiddish-English Dictionary* (Bloomington: Indiana University Press, 2013), 682.

Chapter 7

1. Thomas Doherty, *Hollywood and Hitler, 1933–1939* (New York: Columbia University Press, 2013), 45.
2. Doherty, *Hollywood and Hitler*, 12.
3. Hoberman, *Bridge of Light*, 195.

4. See "Jacob Mestel," Yiddishkayt, https://yiddishkayt.org/view/mestel/, accessed January 10, 2021.

5. See Michael Lewis and Tanja Staehler, *Phenomenology: An Introduction* (New York: Continuum, 2010), 33–46.

6. Vilém Flusser, "What Is Communication?," in *Writings*, ed. Andreas Ströhl, trans. Erik Eisel (Minneapolis: University of Minnesota Press, 2002), 4.

7. Vilém Flusser, *Groundless*, trans. Rodrigo Maltez Novaes (n.p.: Metaflux, 2017), 19. Maltez Novaes's translation is based on the Portuguese version of the book.

8. Flusser, *Groundless*, 25.

9. Flusser, *Groundless*, 24.

10. Flusser, *Groundless*, 31.

11. Flusser, *Groundless*, 24.

12. The constructively polyglot, polycultural atmosphere of Prague described by Flusser is amply on display in Husserl's remarks appended to the initial publication of parts 1 and 2 of the *Crisis*: "The work has grown from the development of ideas that made up the basic content of a series of lectures I gave in November, 1935, in Prague (half in the hospitable rooms of the German university, half in those of the Czech university), following a kind invitation by the 'Cercle philosophique de Prague pour les recherches sur l'entendement humain.'" Edmund Husserl, *The Crisis of European Sciences and Transcendental Phenomenology*, trans. David Carr (Evanston: Northwestern University Press, 1970), 3.

13. Flusser, *Groundless*, 31.

14. Flusser, *Groundless*, 35–36.

15. Flusser, *Groundless*, 34.

16. Flusser, *Groundless*, 37.

17. Flusser, *Groundless*, 38.

18. Flusser, *Groundless*, 37.

19. See the title card at the beginning of the 1999 restoration by the National Center for Jewish Film.

20. Singling out immigrant *Ostjuden* early on, the Nazis, in March of 1933, introduced policies aimed at "prohibition of further immigration, cancellation of name changes made after 1918, and expulsion of a certain number of those who had not yet been naturalized." Saul Friedländer, *Nazi Germany and the Jews, Volume I: The Years of Persecution, 1933–1939* (New York: Harper Perennial, 1998), 27.

21. Hans Kohn, *The Idea of Nationalism: A Study in Its Origins and Background* (New York: Macmillan, 1961), 40–41.

22. Jean-Paul Sartre, *Anti-Semite and Jew*, trans. George J. Becker (New York: Schocken Books, 1976), 27.

23. Hannah Arendt, *The Origins of Totalitarianism* (New York: Harcourt, 2003), 437.

24. Arendt, *The Origins of Totalitarianism*, 315.
25. Quoted in David Welch, *The Third Reich: Politics and Propaganda* (London: Routledge, 1995), 30.
26. Eugen Hadamovsky, *Propaganda and National Power: The Organization of Public Opinion for National Politics*, trans. Randall Bywerk, https://research.calvin.edu/german-propaganda-archive/hadamovsky.htm, accessed August 10, 2020.
27. McLuhan, *Understanding Media*, 300.
28. McLuhan, *Understanding Media*, 299.
29. Arendt, *The Origins of Totalitarianism*, 357.
30. Flusser, *Mutation in Human Relations*, 21.
31. See Flusser, *The Surprising Phenomenon of Human Communication*, 73.
32. Flusser, *Mutation in Human Relations*, 21.
33. Ian Johnson, "'Jews Aren't Allowed to Use Phones': Berlin's Most Unsettling Memorial," *New York Review of Books*, https://www.nybooks.com/daily/2013/06/15/jews-arent-allowed-use-telephones-berlin-memorial/, accessed February 25, 2019.
34. Renata Stih and Frieder Schnock, "'Signs from Berlin' Presentation at the Jewish Museum in New York 2003/2004," http://www.stih-schnock.de/jmny.htm, accessed November 7, 2021.
35. Friedländer, *Nazi Germany and the Jews, Volume I*, 12.
36. See Friedländer, *Nazi Germany and the Jews*, 57.
37. See Doherty, *Hollywood and Hitler*, 93–95.
38. For a wider consideration of book burning in Jewish history, see Stephen J. Whitfield, "Where They Burn Books . . . ," *Modern Judaism* 22, no. 3 (October 2002): 213–33.
39. Joseph Roth, "The Auto-da-Fé of the Mind," in *What I Saw: Reports from Berlin 1920–1933*, trans. Michael Hofmann (New York: W. W. Norton, 2004), 217.
40. Roth, "The Auto-da-Fé of the Mind," 216.
41. Roth, "The Auto-da-Fé of the Mind," 215.
42. Max Weinreich, *History of the Yiddish Language, Volume 1*, trans. Shlomo Noble, ed. Paul Glasser (New Haven: Yale University Press, 2008), 29. For Benjamin Harshav, who offers a persuasive, complementary modification of Weinreich, Yiddish is better characterized as a fusion language *and* an "open language"—that is, a language that "openly" allows elements from disparate linguistic pools to coexist while not necessarily causing them to melt into each other. See Harshav, *The Meaning of Yiddish*, 49.
43. Elliot R. Wolfson, *Through a Speculum That Shines: Vision and Imagination in Medieval Jewish Mysticism* (Princeton: Princeton University Press, 1994).
44. See Elisheva Revel-Neher, "'With Wisdom and Knowledge of Workmanship': Jewish Art without a Question Mark," and Margaret Olin,

"Graven Images on Video? The Second Commandment and Jewish Identity," in *Complex Identities: Jewish Consciousness and Modern Art*, ed. Matthew Baigell and Milly Heyd (New Brunswick: Rutgers University Press, 2001). For a broader intellectual history of Jewish aniconism in a critical vein, also see Kalman P. Bland, *The Artless Jew: Medieval and Modern Affirmations and Denials of the Visual* (Princeton: Princeton University Press, 2000).

    45. Kohn, *The Idea of Nationalism*, 33. In a footnote to this passage, Kohn adds, radically expanding the reach of his claim: "Contemporary Jewish philosophers emphasize the basic importance of time. Bergson has made time the vehicle of his world conception" (584). The intellectual historian Stephen Kern has, too, associated Bergson's fixation on time with the philosopher's Jewishness, while making parallel claims about Freud and Proust. See Stephen Kern, *The Culture of Time and Space: 1880–1918* (Cambridge: Harvard University Press, 1983), 50–51.

    46. Flusser, "Exile and Creativity," in *The Freedom of the Migrant*, 85.

Chapter 8

    1. For the film's production details, we rely on Goldman, *Visions, Images and Dreams*, 125–29; Hoberman, *Bridge of Light*, 331–36; Ira Konigsberg, "Our Children and the Limits of Cinema: Early Jewish Responses to the Holocaust," *Film Quarterly* 52, no. 1 (Autumn 1998): 7–19; and Joshua S. Walden, "'Driven from Their Home': Jewish Displacement and Musical Memory in the 1948 Movie *Long Is the Road*," in *Dislocated Memories: Jews, Music, and Postwar German Culture*, ed. Tina Frühauf and Lily E. Hirsch (New York: Oxford University Press, 2014).

    2. See Israel Beker, "Stage of Life," trans. Carmella Cohen, *Zchor*, May 2007, http://www.zchor.org/beker/beker.htm#english.

    3. Arendt, *The Origins of Totalitarianism*, 300.

    4. Arendt, *The Origins of Totalitarianism*, 302.

    5. Arendt, *The Origins of Totalitarianism*, 279.

    6. Arendt, *The Origins of Totalitarianism*, 279.

    7. Wyman, *DPs*, 142.

    8. Wyman, *DPs*, 132.

    9. Vilém Flusser, *Post-History*, trans. Rodrigo Maltez Novaes, ed. Siegfried Zielinski (Minneapolis: Univocal, 2013), 7. As Maltez Novaes points out, "The Ground We Tread" was especially important to Flusser, who, aside from placing it first in the book, left behind twelve different versions of the essay, in four languages. Translator's introduction in Flusser, *Post-History*. Maltez Novaes's translation is based on the Portuguese version of *Post-History*, originally published in 1983.

10. Flusser, *Post-History*, 5–6.
11. Flusser, *Post-History*, 4.
12. Flusser, *Post-History*, 4, emphasis original.
13. See Gilroy, *The Black Atlantic*, 213–17.
14. Maltez Novaes, Translator's introduction, xii.
15. Judith Butler, *Parting Ways: Jewishness and the Critique of Zionism* (New York: Columbia University Press, 2014), 24.
16. Flusser, *Post-History*, 7.
17. Flusser, *Post-History*, 7.
18. Flusser, *Post-History*, 10.
19. In Ruth Walk's documentary about Beker, *The Balcony* (2000), there is a scene in which *Long Is the Road* is projected on the outside of Beker's Tel Aviv apartment building, and the voice-over narration is clearly in English. Accordingly, multiple "original" versions of the film, with differing linguistic constitutions, appear to exist.
20. See Joshua Hirsch, *After Image: Film, Trauma, and the Holocaust* (Philadelphia: Temple University Press, 2004), 32–41.
21. Arendt, *The Origins of Totalitarianism*, 403.
22. Beker, "Stage of Life."
23. Beker, "Stage of Life."
24. Beker, "Stage of Life."
25. Beker, "Stage of Life."
26. Beker, "Stage of Life."
27. Hoberman, *Bridge of Light*, 333.
28. Jennifer Rodgers, "Bernd Joachim Zimmer: International Tracing Service Arolsen," *Sehepunkte*, 2012, http://www.sehepunkte.de/2012/10/21188.html. For more on the history of tracing services and their key role in war and its aftermath, see "History of the Central Tracing Agency of the ICRC," International Committee of the Red Cross, July 15, 2002. https://www.icrc.org/en/doc/resources/documents/misc/57jqrj.htm.
29. Zygmunt Bauman, *Modernity and the Holocaust* (Ithaca: Cornell University Press, 2000), 102.
30. Bauman, *Modernity and the Holocaust*, 104.
31. Paul Friedman, "The Road Back for the DP's: Healing the Psychological Scars of Nazism," *Commentary* 6, no. 6 (December 1948), https://www.commentary.org/articles/paul-friedman/the-road-back-for-the-dpshealing-the-psychological-scars-of-nazism/.
32. "Dr. Friedman, 73, Is Dead; Psychiatrist and Suicide Expert," *New York Times*, October 13, 1972, https://www.nytimes.com/1972/10/13/archives/dr-paul-friedman-73-is-dead-psychiatrist-and-suicide-expert.html.
33. See chapter 4, "Searching for Redemption: The Salzburg Festival Meets Yiddish Theater," in Lisa Silverman, *Becoming Austrians: Jews and Culture between the World Wars* (Oxford: Oxford University Press, 2012).

34. "Alexander Moissi, "Non-Jewish Actor Indicts Christian World for Its Persecution of the Jew," *The Jacobean*, December 4, 1931, https://ufdc.ufl.edu/UF00001408/00010/images/4.

35. As Beker recounts in his memoir, the selfless farmer was based on a real-life person, Antony Militzky, who helped him cross the Bug River, over the border and into safety. Beker, "Stage of Life."

36. Friedman, "The Road Back for the DP's."

37. Beker was well aware of the riskiness of including such a speech, exposing the film to the charge of too simply and easily granting absolution to those responsible for the horrors of the war. Nevertheless, he insisted on it, recounting: "We waited until the film was almost done to do this scene. It felt right to include such a scene, and every member of the crew agreed. It was not easy, but it was the right thing to do" (quoted in Konigsberg, "Our Children and the Limits of Cinema," 10–11). Commenting on the scene, Walden writes: "Whatever brief partnership and understanding may be inferred from this scene and the collaboration between Jewish and non-Jewish filmmakers [the latter including not only the codirector Herbert Fredersdorf but also the co-scriptwriter Karl Georg Külb and the composer Lothar Brühne], however—whether their motive for working together was pressure from the U.S. military, the practical need for skilled crew members, or even a moral desire for fruitful interaction with recent enemies—the film's message was ultimately no more reconciliation than it was of retribution. It was instead a farewell to Europe, one that would prove permanent for Beker himself" (Walden, "Driven from Their Home," 126). Walden's point about the unknowability of motivations is astute, and yet we view the film as constituting *both* a farewell to Europe (along the lines discussed earlier in relation to Flusser and Wyman) and a work whose overarching concern with relationality could potentially encompass an interpersonal, conciliatory rapport between "enemies." In any case, despite the humanitarian/universalist thrust of the scene, Hoberman points out that the film was still seen by some contemporary reviewers as marred by Jewish parochialism: "*Variety* called it 'honest propaganda' and 'a sure bet for the art house circuit,' while the *New York Herald Tribune* pointed out that only 20 percent of Europe's DPs were Jews and scored the film for its special pleading" (Hoberman, *Bridge of Light*, 335–36).

38. Friedman, "The Road Back for the DP's."

39. Walden, "'Driven from Their Home,'" 124.

40. See Ruth Gay, *Safe among the Germans: Liberated Jews after World War II* (New Haven: Yale University Press, 2002), 71–72.

41. John Durham Peters, "Mass Media," in *Critical Terms for Media Studies*, ed. W. J. T. Mitchell and Mark B. N. Hansen (Chicago: University of Chicago Press, 2010), 269.

42. Hannah Arendt, "We Refugees," in *The Jewish Writings*, ed. Jerome Kohn and Ron H. Feldman (New York: Schocken Books, 2007), 274.

43. Flusser, "The Challenge of the Migrant," in *The Freedom of the Migrant*, 15. This 1985 paper also appears in the German version of *Groundless* (*Bodenlos*), under the title "Wohnung beziehen in der Heimatlosigket" (Taking residence in homelessness).

44. Flusser, "The Challenge of the Migrant," 11.

Chapter 9

1. Gershom Scholem, *On the Mystical Shape of the Godhead: Basic Concepts in the Kabbalah*, trans. Joachim Neugroschel, ed. and rev. Jonathan Chipman (New York: Schocken Books, 1991), 223.

2. Hoberman, *Bridge of Light*, 282.

3. For more on the expedition, see David G. Roskies, Introduction to S. Ansky, *The Dybbuk and Other Writings*, trans. Golda Werman, ed. David G. Roskies (New Haven: Yale University Press, 2002), xix–xx; xxii–xxvi. Sections from a questionnaire used on the expedition dealing with dybbuks and other beliefs in the supernatural are usefully reproduced in *The Dybbuk and the Yiddish Imagination: A Haunted Reader*, trans. and ed. Joachim Neugroschel (Syracuse: Syracuse University Press, 2000).

4. *The Five Books of Moses*, Numbers 24:4, trans. Robert Alter (New York: Norton, 2004), 811.

5. Vilém Flusser, "How Goodly Are Your Tents, Jacob," in *Freedom of the Migrant*, 61–62.

6. Flusser, "How Goodly Are Your Tents, Jacob," 64.

7. Flusser, "How Goodly Are Your Tents, Jacob," 64.

8. Gershom Scholem, *Major Trends in Jewish Mysticism* (New York: Schocken Books, 1995), 36.

9. Gershom Scholem, *On the Kabbalah and Its Symbolism*, trans. Ralph Manheim (New York: Schocken Books, 1996), 98.

10. Scholem, *On the Mystical Shape of the Godhead*, 128.

11. Scholem, *On the Mystical Shape of the Godhead*, 134.

12. Scholem, *Major Trends*, 335.

13. See Eve Sicular, "*A Yingl mit a yingl hot epes a tame*: The Celluloid Closet of Yiddish Film," in *When Joseph Met Molly: A Reader on Yiddish Film*, ed. Sylvia Paskin (Nottingham: Fives Leaves, 1999). For more on Ansky's play and issues of queerness, also see Naomi Seidman, "The Ghost of Queer Loves Past: Ansky's 'Dybbuk' and the Sexual Transformation of Ashkenaz," in *Queer Theory and the Jewish Question*, ed. Daniel Boyarin, Daniel Itzkovitz, and Ann Pellegrini (New York: Columbia University Press, 2003).

14. S. Ansky, "From a Letter to Khaim Zhitlovsky," in *The Dybbuk and the Yiddish Imagination*, 1.

15. Ansky, "From a Letter to Khaim Zhitlovsky," 1.

16. Hoberman, *Bridge of Light*, 282.

17. Frade's role in the film is slightly changed from that in the play, where she is Sender's daughter's nurse. Still, in both cases, she embodies a kind of devoted, surrogate maternal figure for the motherless child.

18. Yosef Hayim Yerushalmi, *Zakhor: Jewish History and Jewish Memory* (Seattle: University of Washington Press, 1996), 5.

19. Yerushalmi, *Zakhor*, 108.

20. Yerushalmi, *Zakhor*, 8–9.

21. Yerushalmi, *Zakhor*, 10.

22. Vilém Flusser, "Mythical, Historical, and Posthistorical Existence," in *Writings*, 117–18.

23. Roskies, Introduction, xxix.

24. Yerushalmi, *Zakhor*, 6–7.

25. Yerushalmi, *Zakhor*, 120.

26. Yerushalmi, *Zakhor*, 42.

27. Scholem, *Major Trends*, 14–15.

28. See William James, *The Varieties of Religious Experience: A Study in Human Nature* (New York: Modern Library, 2002), 414–16.

29. Scholem, *Major Trends*, 15.

30. Parker Tyler, *Classics of the Foreign Film: A Pictorial Treasury* (Secaucus: Citadel Press, 1962), 120. In the estimation of Tyler, one of the great stylists of American postwar film criticism and an important champion of the cinematic avant-garde, the film version of *The Dybbuk* stands as "one of the most solemn attestations to the mystic powers of the spirit the imagination has ever purveyed to the film reel" (120).

31. James, *The Varieties of Religious Experience*, 414.

32. For a discussion of the story, see the introductory pages of Slobin's *Tenement Songs*.

33. Scholem, *On the Mystical Shape of the Godhead*, 201.

34. See Sicular, "The Celluloid Closet of Yiddish Film," 242.

35. Relative to the larger, centuries-old body of Yiddish stories and accounts of demonic possession, the representation of the phenomenon in *The Dybbuk* is radically unique insofar as it figures the invading spirit as a *lover*, that is, as a far from outright malevolent entity to which the host is in many ways actively "attached." At the same time, however, the drama is standard insofar as it features a male spirit and a female medium. As Neugroschel comments on dybbuk gender dynamics, while the invading spirit is nearly always a male, the possessed is a female in roughly twice the number of cases as it is a male. Joachim Neugroschel, introductory note to *The Possession* by

Jacob Ben Abraham of Mezritch, in *The Dybbuk and the Yiddish Imagination*, 59.

36. Hoberman, *Bridge of Light*, 283.

37. As Roskies points out in a footnote, "Ansky is careful to distinguish between the zaddik's charismatic powers and the rabbinic authority vested in the rabbi, Reb Shimshon. The latter has sole jurisdiction over matters pertaining to Halacha (Jewish law), but at critical moments abdicates authority to the zaddik." Ansky, *The Dybbuk and Other Writings*, 214.

38. Ansky, *The Dybbuk and Other Writings*, 41.

39. Steven Nadler, *Spinoza's Heresy: Immortality and the Jewish Mind* (Oxford: Oxford University Press, 2001), 12. Interestingly, citing an early biographer and personal acquaintance of Spinoza, Nadler goes on to point out that while the 1656 ban against the young philosopher (for reasons that still remain nebulous) by the Amsterdam Sephardic community was singularly harsh, its actual execution, as sometimes happened, was quite stripped down and did not involve the aforementioned ritual elements.

40. Scholem, *Major Trends*, 348.

41. Scholem, *Major Trends*, 349.

42. See Don Levin, "Lekert, Hirsch," *The Yivo Encyclopedia of Jews in Eastern Europe*, https://yivoencyclopedia.org/article.aspx/Lekert_Hirsh, accessed November 20, 2020.

43. Gershom Scholem, *The Messianic Idea in Judaism and Other Essays on Jewish Spirituality* (New York: Schocken, 1995), 204–05.

44. Scholem, *The Messianic Idea in* Judaism, 211.

45. Scholem, *The Messianic Idea in Judaism*, 225.

46. Scholem, *The Messianic Idea in Judaism*, 226.

47. Quoted in Scholem, *The Messianic Idea in Judaism*, 226.

48. Scholem, *The Messianic Idea in Judaism*, 227.

49. Harold Bloom, Foreword to Moishe Idel, *Enchanted Chains: Techniques and Rituals in Jewish Mysticism* (Los Angeles: Cherub Press, 2005).

50. Moshe Idel, *Kabbalah: New Perspectives* (New Haven: Yale University Press, 1988), 60.

51. Idel, *Kabbalah*, 66.

52. Idel, *Kabbalah*, 72.

53. Quoted in Idel, *Kabbalah*, 72.

54. Idel, *Kabbalah*, 72.

55. See, for instance, Buber, *I and Thou*, 131–43, and, for useful commentary, Elliot R. Wolfson's "The Problem of Unity in the Thought of Martin Buber," *Journal of the History of Philosophy* 27, no. 3 (July 1989): 423–44.

56. In Golda Werman's translation of the play, the lines are only slightly different: "I have forgotten [who I am]. It is only through your thoughts that I can remember who I am." Ansky, *The Dybbuk*, 48.

57. Flusser, "How Goodly Are Your Tents, Jacob," 63.

Coda

1. See Gilles Deleuze and Felix Guattari, *Kafka: Toward a Minor Literature*, trans. Dana Polan (Minneapolis: University of Minnesota Press, 1986).

2. See Hamid Naficy, "Between Rocks and Hard Places: The Interstitial Mode of Production in Exilic Cinema," in *Home, Exile, Homeland: Film, Media, and the Politics of Place*, ed. Hamid Naficy (New York: Routledge, 1999); and Naficy, *An Accented Cinema*.

3. See, for example, Nataša Ďurovičová and Kathleen Newman, eds., *World Cinemas, Transnational Perspectives* (New York: Routledge, 2010).

4. For an insightful discussion of the multilingual verbal texture of the series, see Shayna Weiss, "*Shtisel*'s Ghosts: The Politics of Yiddish in Israeli Popular Culture," *In Geveb: A Journal of Yiddish Studies* (blog), March 6, 2016, https://ingeveb.org/blog/shtisel-s-ghosts-the-politics-of-yiddish-in-israeli-popular-culture.

5. Vilém Flusser, "On the Theory of Communication," in *Writings*, ed. Andreas Ströhl, trans. Erik Eisel (Minneapolis: University of Minnesota Press, 2002), 16.

6. Franz Kafka, "An Introductory Talk on the Yiddish Language," trans. Ernst Kaiser and Eithne Wilkins, in *Reading Kafka: Prague, Politics, and the Fin de Siècle*, ed. Mark Anderson (New York: Schocken Books, 1989), 266.

Bibliography

Adorno, Theodor W. *Current of Music*. Edited by Robert Hullot-Kentor. Cambridge: Polity, 2009.

Aleichem, Sholem. *Tevye the Dairyman and Motl the Cantor's Son*. Translated by Aliza Shevrin. New York: Penguin Books, 2009.

"Alexander Moissi, Non-Jewish Actor Indicts Christian World for Its Persecution of the Jew." *The Jacobean*, December 4, 1931. https://ufdc.ufl.edu/UF00001408/00010/images/4.

Alter, Robert. *Necessary Angels: Tradition and Modernity in Kafka, Benjamin, and Scholem*. Cambridge: Harvard University Press, 1991.

Ansky, S. *The Dybbuk, or Between Two Worlds: A Dramatic Legend in Four Acts*. In *The Dybbuk and Other Writings*, translated by Golda Werman, edited by David G. Roskies. New Haven: Yale University Press, 2002.

———. "From a Letter to Khaim Zhitlovsky." In *The Dybbuk and the Yiddish Imagination: A Haunted Reader*, translated and edited by Joachim Neugroschel, 1–2. Syracuse: Syracuse University Press, 2000.

———. "From the Ethnographic Expedition: Questionnaire." In *The Dybbuk and the Yiddish Imagination: A Haunted Reader*, translated and edited by Joachim Neugroschel, 53–58. Syracuse: Syracuse University Press, 2000.

Arendt, Hannah. *Between Past and Future: Eight Exercises in Political Thought*. 1968. Reprint, New York: Penguin Books, 1993.

———. "Concern with Politics in Recent European Philosophical Thought." In *Essays in Understanding, 1930–1954: Formation, Exile, and Totalitarianism*, edited by Jerome Kohn, 428–47. New York: Schocken Books, 1994.

———. *Eichmann in Jerusalem: A Report on the Banality of Evil*. 1963. Reprint, New York: Penguin Books, 1994.

———. *The Origins of Totalitarianism*. New York: Harcourt, 2003.

———. "We Refugees." In *The Jewish Writings*, edited by Jerome Kohn and Ron H. Feldman, 264–74. New York: Schocken Books, 2007.

Austin, J. L. *How to Do Things with Words*. Cambridge: Harvard University Press, 1962.
Azoulay, Ariella. *The Civil Contract of Photography*. New York: Zone Books, 2008.
Báez, Fernando. *A Universal History of the Destruction of Books: From Ancient Sumer to Modern Iraq*. Translated by Alfred MacAdam. New York: Atlas, 2008.
Baio, Cesar. "Functionary." In *Flusseriana: An Intellectual Toolbox*, edited by Siegfried Zielinski et al., 184–87. Minneapolis: Univocal, 2015.
Bauman, Zygmunt. *Modernity and the Holocaust*. Ithaca: Cornell University Press, 2000.
Beinfeld, Solon, and Harry Bochner, eds. *Comprehensive Yiddish-English Dictionary*. Bloomington: Indiana University Press, 2013.
Beker, Israel. "Stage of Life." Translated by Carmella Cohen. *Zchor*, May 2007. http://www.zchor.org/beker/beker.htm#english.
Bellour, Raymond. "The Pensive Spectator." Translated by Lynne Kirby. *Wide Angle* 9, no. 1 (1987): 6–10.
Benjamin, Walter. "Reflections on Radio." In *The Work of Art in the Age of Technological Reproducibility and Other Writings on Media*, edited by Michael W. Jennings, Brigid Doherty, and Thomas Levin, translated by Rodney Livingstone, 391–92. Cambridge: Harvard University Press, 2008.
———. "The Work of Art in the Age of Its Technological Reproducibility: Second Version." In *The Work of Art in the Age of Its Technological Reproducibility and Other Writings on Media*, edited by Michael W. Jennings, Brigid Doherty, and Thomas Levin, translated by Edmund Jephcott and Harry Zohn, 19–55. Cambridge: Harvard University Press, 2008.
Bland, Kalman P. *The Artless Jew: Medieval and Modern Affirmations and Denials of the Visual*. Princeton: Princeton University Press, 2000.
Blondheim, Menahem. "The Jewish Communication Tradition and Its Encounters with (the) New Media." In *Digital Judaism: Jewish Negotiations with Digital Media and Culture*, edited by Heidi A. Campbell, 16–39. New York: Routledge, 2015.
Bloom, Harold. Foreword to Moishe Idel's *Enchanted Chains: Techniques and Rituals in Jewish Mysticism*. Los Angeles: Cherub Press, 2005.
———. *Kabbalah and Criticism*. New York: Seabury Press, 1975.
Bourdieu, Pierre. *Language and Symbolic Power*. Edited by John B. Thompson, translated by Gino Raymond and Matthew Adamson. Cambridge: Polity Press, 1991.
Boyarin, Daniel. *A Traveling Homeland: The Babylonian Talmud as Diaspora*. Philadelphia: University of Pennsylvania Press, 2015.

———. *Unheroic Conduct: The Rise of Heterosexuality and the Invention of the Jewish Man*. Berkeley: University of California Press, 1997.

Boyarin, Jonathan, and Daniel Boyarin. *Powers of Diaspora: Two Essays on the Relevance of Jewish Culture*. Minneapolis: University of Minnesota Press, 2002.

Brook, Vincent. "Forging the 'New Jew': Ulmer's Yiddish Films." In *The Films of Edgar G. Ulmer*, edited by Bernd Herzogenrath, 71–85. Lanham: Scarecrow Press, 2009.

Brooks, Peter. *The Melodramatic Imagination: Balzac, Henry James, Melodrama, and the Mode of Excess*. 1976. Reprint, New Haven: Yale University Press, 1995.

Brossat, Alain, and Sylvie Klingberg. *Revolutionary Yiddishland: A History of Jewish Radicalism*. Translated by David Fernbach. London: Verso Books, 2016.

Buber, Martin. "Dialogue." In *Between Man and Man*, translated by Ronald Gregor-Smith, 1–45. 1947. Reprint, London: Routledge, 2007.

———. *I and Thou*. Translated by Walter Kaufmann. New York: Simon & Schuster, 1996.

———. *Tales of the Hasidim, Book Two: The Later Masters*. Translated by Olga Marx. New York: Schocken Books, 1991.

———. *The Way of Man: According to the Teaching of Hasidism*. London: Routledge, 1994.

Butler, Judith. Afterword to Shoshana Felman's *The Scandal of the Speaking Body: Don Juan with J. L. Austin, or Seduction in Two Languages*. Stanford: Stanford University Press, 2003.

———. *Excitable Speech: A Politics of the Performative*. New York: Routledge, 1997.

———. *Parting Ways: Jewishness and the Critique of Zionism*. New York: Columbia University Press, 2014.

Chion, Michel. *The Voice in Cinema*. Translated by Claudia Gorbman. New York: Columbia University Press, 1999.

Cohen, Abraham. *Everyman's Talmud: The Major Teachings of the Rabbinic Sages*. 1949. Reprint, New York: Schocken Books, 1995.

Crafton, Donald. *The Talkies: American Cinema's Transition to Sound, 1926–1931*. Berkeley: University of California Press, 1997.

Davis, Natalie Zemon. *Women on the Margins: Three Seventeenth-Century Lives*. Cambridge: Harvard University Press, 1995.

Dean, Martin. *Robbing the Jews: The Confiscation of Jewish Property in the Holocaust, 1933–1945*. Cambridge: Cambridge University Press, 2010.

Deleuze, Gilles, and Felix Guattari. *Kafka: Toward a Minor Literature*. Translated by Dana Polan. Minneapolis: University of Minnesota Press, 1986.

Didi-Huberman, Georges. *Invention of Hysteria: Charcot and the Photographic Iconography of the Saltpêtrière*. Translated by Alisa Hartz. Cambridge: MIT Press, 2003.

Doane, Mary Anne. *The Desire to Desire: The Woman's Film of the 1940s*. Bloomington: Indiana University Press, 1987.

Doherty, Thomas. *Hollywood and Hitler, 1933–1939*. New York: Columbia University Press, 2013.

"Dr. Friedman, 73, Is Dead; Psychiatrist and Suicide Expert." *New York Times*, October 13, 1972. https://www.nytimes.com/1972/10/13/archives/dr-paul-friedman-73-is-dead- psychiatrist-and-suicide-expert.html.

Ďurovičová, Nataša, and Kathleen Newman, eds. *World Cinemas, Transnational Perspectives*. New York: Routledge, 2010.

Federici, Silvia. "On the Meaning of Gossip." In *Witches, Witch-Hunting, and Women*. Oakland: PM Press, 2018.

Felman, Shoshana. *The Scandal of the Speaking Body: Don Juan with J. L. Austin, or Seduction in Two Languages*. Translated by Catherine Porter. Stanford: Stanford University Press, 2003.

The Five Books of Moses. Translated by Robert Alter. New York: W. W. Norton, 2004.

Flusser, Vilém. *Does Writing Have a Future?* Translated by Nancy Ann Roth. Minneapolis: University of Minnesota Press, 2011.

———. "Family Unit." Unpublished essay. Vilém Flusser Archiv (2742), Berlin.

———. *The Freedom of the Migrant: Objections to Nationalism*. Translated by Kenneth Kronenberg, edited by Anke K. Finger. Urbana: University of Illinois Press, 2003.

———. *Gestures*. Translated by Nancy Ann Roth. Minneapolis: University of Minnesota Press, 2014.

———. *Groundless*. Edited and translated by Rodrigo Maltez Novaes. N.p.: Metaflux, 2017.

———. "The Jewish War. (A Testimony of Commitment)." Unpublished essay. Vilém Flusser Archiv (2793), Berlin.

———. *Jude Sein: Essays, Briefe, Fiktionen*. Edited by Stefan Bollman and Edith Flusser. Mannheim: Bollmann Verlag, 1995.

———. *Language and Reality*. Translated by Rodrigo Maltez Novaes. Minneapolis: Univocal, 2018.

———. "Mutation in Human Relations." Unpublished manuscript, 1977–1978. Vilém Flusser Archiv (1712), Berlin.

———. "Mythical, Historical, and Posthistorical Existence." In *Writings*, translated by Erik Eisel, edited by Andreas Ströhl, 117–25. Minneapolis: University of Minnesota Press, 2002.

———. "On Religion, Memory and Synthetic Image: Interview with Vilém Flusser in Budapest, April 7, 1990." Interview by László Beke and

Miklós Peternák. In *"We Shall Survive in the Memory of Others"*: *Vilém Flusser*, edited by Miklós Peternák, 32–35. Köln: Verlag der Buchhandlung Walter König, 2010.

———. "On the Problem of Being Jewish. (Focus on 'Chosen People' and 'Honesty')." Unpublished essay. Vilém Flusser Archiv (2768), Berlin.

———. "On the Theory of Communication." In *Writings*, edited by Andreas Ströhl, translated by Erik Eisel, 8–20. Minneapolis: University of Minnesota Press, 2002.

———. *Philosophy of Language*. Translated by Rodrigo Maltez Novaes. Minneapolis: Univocal, 2016.

———. *Post-History*. Translated by Rodrigo Maltez Novaes, edited by Siegfried Zielinski. Minneapolis: Univocal, 2013.

———. *The Surprising Phenomenon of Human Communication*. N.p.: Metaflux, 2016.

———. "Two Different Kinds of Jew. (To Be Discussed at the Meeting of the Study Circle on Contemporary Jewry and Zionism at Hillel House, London, on October 29, 1980)." Unpublished document. Vilém Flusser Archiv (2812), Berlin.

———. "What Is Communication?" In *Writings*, edited by Andreas Ströhl, translated by Erik Eisel, 3–7. Minneapolis: University of Minnesota Press, 2002.

Foucault, Michel. *The Birth of the Clinic: An Archaeology of Medical Perception*. Translated by A. M. Sheridan Smith. New York: Random House, 1973.

———. *Madness and Civilization: A History of Insanity in the Age of Reason*. Translated by Richard Howard. New York: Random House, 1965.

Friedländer, Saul. *Nazi Germany and the Jews, Volume I: The Years of Persecution, 1933–1939*. New York: Harper Perennial, 1998.

Friedman, Paul. "The Road Back for the DP's: Healing the Psychological Scars of Nazism." *Commentary* 6, no. 6 (December 1948), https://www.commentary.org/articles/paul-friedman/the-road-back-for-the-dpshealing-the-psychological-scars-of-nazism/.

Gabler, Neal. *An Empire of Their Own: How the Jews Invented Hollywood*. New York: Random House, 1989.

Galloway, Alexander R., Eugene Thacker, and McKenzie Wark. "Introduction: Execrable Media." In *Excommunication: Three Inquiries in Media and Mediation*. Chicago: University of Chicago Press, 2014.

Gay, Ruth. *Safe among the Germans: Liberated Jews after World War II*. New Haven: Yale University Press, 2002.

Gilman, Sander L. *Jewish Self-Hatred: Anti-Semitism and the Hidden Language of the Jews*. Baltimore: Johns Hopkins University Press, 1986.

Gilroy, Paul. *The Black Atlantic: Modernity and Double Consciousness*. Cambridge: Harvard University Press, 1993.

Goffman, Erving. *Asylums: Essays on the Social Situation of Mental Patients and Other Inmates*. New York: Anchor Books, 1961.

Goldberg, Judith N. *Laughter through Tears: The Yiddish Cinema*. Rutherford: Fairleigh Dickinson University Press, 1983.

Goldman, Eric A. *Visions, Images, and Dreams: Yiddish Film, Past and Present*. Revised and expanded. Teaneck: Holmes & Meier, 2011.

Hadamovsky, Eugen. *Propaganda und nationale Macht: Die Organisation der öffentlichen Meinung für die nationale Politik*. Oldenburg: Gernhard Stalling, 1933.

———. *Propaganda and National Power: The Organization of Public Opinion for National Politics*. Translated by Randall Bywerk. https://research.calvin.edu/german-propaganda-archive/hadamovsky.htm. Accessed August 10, 2020.

Harshav, Benjamin. *The Meaning of Yiddish*. Stanford: Stanford University Press, 1999.

Hirsch, Joshua. *After Image: Film, Trauma, and the Holocaust*. Philadelphia: Temple University Press, 2004.

"History of the Central Tracing Agency of the ICRC." International Committee of the Red Cross. July 15, 2002. https://www.icrc.org/en/doc/resources/documents/misc/57jqrj.htm.

Hoberman, J. *Bridge of Light: Yiddish Film Between Two Worlds*. New York: Museum of Modern Art and Schocken Books, 1991.

Hoberman, J., and Jeffrey Shandler. *Entertaining America: Jews, Movies, and Broadcasting*. Princeton: Princeton University Press, 2003.

Hoffmann, Michael. Translator's preface to *The Wandering Jews*. In Joseph Roth, *The Wandering Jews: The Classic Portrait of a Vanished People*. New York: W. W. Norton, 2001.

Honors, L. "Radio–Phonograph: That's the Bone of Contention in Jewish Families These Days." In J. Hoberman and Jeffrey Shandler, *Entertaining America: Jews, Movies, and Broadcasting*, 109. Princeton: Princeton University Press, 2003.

Howe, Irving. *World of Our Fathers: The Journey of the East European Jews to America and the Life They Found and Made*. With the assistance of Kenneth Libo. New York: Simon & Schuster, 1976.

Husserl, Edmund. *The Crisis of European Sciences and Transcendental Phenomenology*. Translated by David Carr. Evanston: Northwestern University Press, 1970.

Idel, Moishe. *Kabbalah: New Perspectives*. New Haven: Yale University Press, 1988.

Insdorf, Annette. *Indelible Shadows: Film and the Holocaust*. Third edition. Cambridge: Cambridge University Press, 2003.

"Jacob Mestel." Yiddishkayt. https://yiddishkayt.org/view/mestel/. Accessed January 10, 2021.

James, William. *The Varieties of Religious Experience: A Study in Human Nature*. New York: Modern Library, 2002.
Johnson, Ian. "'Jews Aren't Allowed to Use Phones': Berlin's Most Unsettling Memorial." *New York Review of Books*. https://www.nybooks.com/daily/2013/06/15/jews-arent-allowed-use-telephones-berlin-memorial/. Accessed February 25, 2019.
Judt, Tony. *Postwar: A History of Europe since 1945*. London: Penguin Books, 2006.
Kafka, Franz. "An Imperial Message." Translated by Willa and Edwin Muir. In *The Complete Stories*, 4–5. New York: Schocken Books, 1971.
———. "An Introductory Talk on the Yiddish Language." Translated by Ernst Kaiser and Eithne Wilkins. In *Reading Kafka: Prague, Politics, and the Fin de Siècle*, edited by Mark Anderson, 263–66. New York: Schocken Books, 1989.
Kern, Stephen. *The Culture of Time and Space: 1880–1918*. Cambridge: Harvard University Press, 1983.
Kohn, Hans. *The Idea of Nationalism: A Study in Its Origins and Background*. New York: Macmillan, 1961.
Kohn, Jerome. "Preface. A Jewish Life: 1906–1975." In Hannah Arendt, *The Jewish Writings*, edited by Jerome Kohn and Ron H. Feldman. New York: Schocken Books, 2007.
Konigsberg, Ira. "The Only 'I' in the World: Religion, Psychoanalysis, and 'The Dybbuk.'" *Cinema Journal* 36, no. 4 (Summer 1997): 22–42.
———. "Our Children and the Limits of Cinema: Early Jewish Responses to the Holocaust," *Film Quarterly* 52, no. 1 (Autumn 1998): 7–19.
Learning Voices of the Holocaust. "Anti-Jewish Decrees." British Library. https://www.bl.uk/learning/histcitizen/voices/info/decrees/decrees.html. Accessed February 22, 2019.
Levin, Don. "Lekert, Hirsch." *The Yivo Encyclopedia of Jews in Eastern Europe*. https://yivoencyclopedia.org/article.aspx/Lekert_Hirsh. Accessed November 20, 2020.
Levinas, Emmanuel. *Difficult Freedom: Essays on Judaism*. Translated by Seán Hand. Baltimore: John Hopkins University Press, 1997.
———. *Entre Nous: On Thinking-of-the-Other*. Translated by Michael B. Smith and Barbara Harshav. New York: Columbia University Press, 1998.
Lewis, Michael, and Tanja Staehler. *Phenomenology: An Introduction*. New York: Continuum, 2010.
Maltez Novaes, Rodrigo. Editor's note. In Vilém Flusser, *The Surprising Phenomenon of Human Communication*, 9–19. N.p.: Metaflux, 2016.
———. Translator's introduction to Vilém Flusser, *Post-History*, edited by Siegfried Zielinski. Minneapolis: Univocal, 2013.

Marx, Karl. "Economic and Philosophic Manuscripts of 1844." In *The Marx-Engels Reader*, second edition, edited by Robert C. Tucker, 66–125. New York: W. W. Norton, 1978.
Matisoff, James A. *Blessings, Curses, Hopes, and Fears: Psycho-Ostensive Expressions in Yiddish*. Philadelphia: Institute for the Study of Human Issues, 1979.
McLuhan, Marshall. *The Gutenberg Galaxy*. Toronto: University of Toronto Press, 1962.
———. *Understanding Media: The Extensions of Man*. Cambridge: MIT Press, 1994.
McLuhan, Marshall, and Eric McLuhan. *Laws of Media: The New Science*. 1988. Reprint, Toronto: University of Toronto Press, 2007.
Miron, Dan. Introduction to Sholem Aleichem's *Tevye the Dairyman and Motl the Cantor's Son*. Translated by Aliza Shevrin. New York: Penguin Books, 2009.
———. *A Traveler Disguised: The Rise of Modern Yiddish Fiction in the Nineteenth Century*. Syracuse: Syracuse University Press, 1996.
Mulvey, Laura. *Death 24x a Second: Stillness and the Moving Image*. London: Reaktion Books, 2006.
Nadler, Steven. *Spinoza's Heresy: Immortality and the Jewish Mind*. Oxford: Oxford University Press, 2001.
Naficy, Hamid. *An Accented Cinema: Exilic and Diasporic Filmmaking*. Princeton: Princeton University Press, 2001.
———. "Between Rocks and Hard Places: The Interstitial Mode of Production in Exilic Cinema." In *Home, Exile, Homeland: Film, Media and the Politics of Space*, edited by Hamid Naficy, 125–47. New York: Routledge, 1999.
———. "Palestinian Exilic Cinema and Film Letters." In *Dreams of a Nation: On Palestinian Cinema*, edited by Hamid Dabashi, 90–104. London: Verso, 2006.
Neugroschel, Joachim, ed. *The Dybbuk and the Yiddish Imagination: A Haunted Reader*. Translated by Joachim Neugroschel. Syracuse: Syracuse University Press, 2000.
Olin, Margaret. "Graven Images on Video? The Second Commandment and Jewish Identity." In *Complex Identities: Jewish Consciousness and Modern Art*, edited by Matthew Baigell and Milly Heyd, 34–50. New Brunswick: Rutgers University Press, 2001.
Paskin, Sylvia, ed. *When Joseph Met Molly: A Reader on Yiddish Film*. Nottingham: Five Leaves, 1999.
Peters, John Durham. "Mass Media." In *Critical Terms for Media Studies*, edited by W. J. T. Mitchell and Mark B. N. Hansen, 266–79. Chicago: University of Chicago Press, 2010.

———. *Speaking into the Air: A History of the Idea of Communication*. Chicago: University of Chicago Press, 2000.

Revel-Neher, Elisheva. "'With Wisdom and Knowledge of Workmanship': Jewish Art without a Question Mark." In *Complex Identities: Jewish Consciousness and Modern Art*, edited by Matthew Baigell and Milly Heyd, 12–33. New Brunswick: Rutgers University Press, 2001.

Rodgers, Jennifer. "Bernd Joachim Zimmer: International Tracing Service Arolsen." *Sehepunkte*, 2012. http://www.sehepunkte.de/2012/10/21188.html.

Rose, Jacqueline. *Mothers: An Essay on Love and Cruelty*. New York: Farrar, Straus and Giroux, 2018.

———. *The Last Resistance*. London: Verso, 2017.

Roskies, David G. Introduction to S. Ansky's *The Dybbuk and Other Writings*, translated by Golda Werman, edited by David G. Roskies. New Haven: Yale University Press, 2002.

Roth, Joseph. "The Auto-da-Fé of the Mind." In *What I Saw: Reports from Berlin 1920–1933*, translated by Michael Hofmann, 207–17. New York: W. W. Norton, 2004.

———. *The Wandering Jews: The Classic Portrait of a Vanished People*. Translated by Michael Hofmann. New York: W. W. Norton, 2001.

Sandrow, Nahma. *Vagabond Stars: A World History of Yiddish Cinema*. 1977. Reprint, New York: Limelight Editions, 1986.

Sartre, Jean-Paul. *Anti-Semite and Jew*. Translated by George J. Becker. 1965. Reprint, New York: Schocken Books, 1976.

Schafer, R. Murray. *The Soundscape: Our Sonic Environment and the Tuning of the World*. Rochester: Destiny Books, 1994.

Scholem, Gershom. *Major Trends in Jewish Mysticism*. 1961. Reprint, New York: Schocken Books, 1995.

———. *The Messianic Idea in Judaism and Other Essays on Jewish Spirituality*, 1971. Reprint, New York: Schocken Books, 1995.

———. *On the Kabbalah and Its Symbolism*. Translated by Ralph Manheim. New York: Schocken Books, 1996.

———. *On the Mystical Shape of the Godhead: Basic Concepts in the Kabbalah*. Translated by Joachim Neugroschel, edited and revised by Jonathan Chipman. New York: Schocken Books, 1991.

Sconce, Jeffrey. *Haunted Media: Electronic Presence from Telegraphy to Television*. Durham: Duke University Press, 2000.

Seidman, Naomi. "The Ghost of Queer Loves Past: Ansky's 'Dybbuk' and the Sexual Transformation of Ashkenaz." In *Queer Theory and the Jewish Question*, edited by Daniel Boyarin, Daniel Itzkovitz, and Ann Pellegrini, 228–45. New York: Columbia University Press, 2003.

———. *A Marriage Made in Heaven: The Sexual Politics of Hebrew and Yiddish*. Berkeley: University of California Press, 1997.

Shandler, Jeffrey. *Adventures in Yiddishland: Postvernacular Language and Culture*. Berkeley: University of California Press, 2006.

———. *Jews, God, and Videotape: Religion and Media in America*. New York: New York University Press, 2009.

Sicular, Eve. "*A Yingl mit a yingl hot epes a tame*: The Celluloid Closet of Yiddish Film." In *When Joseph Met Molly: A Reader on Yiddish Film*, edited by Sylvia Paskin, 231–44. Nottingham: Five Leaves, 1999.

Silverman, Lisa. *Becoming Austrians: Jews and Culture between the World Wars*. Oxford: Oxford University Press, 2012.

Slezkine, Yuri. *The Jewish Century*. Princeton: Princeton University Press, 2004.

Slobin, Mark. *Tenement Songs: The Popular Music of the Jewish Immigrants*. Urbana: University of Illinois Press, 1982.

Smulevitz, Solomon. "A brivele der mamen." Milken Archive of Jewish Music. https://www.milkenarchive.org/music/volumes/view/great-songs-of-the-american-yiddish-stage/work/a-brivele-der-mamen/. Accessed January 12, 2019.

Steiner, George. "Our Homeland, the Text," *Salmagundi*, no. 66 (Winter–Spring 1985), 4–25.

Stewart, Garrett. *Between Film and Screen: Modernism's Photo Synthesis*. Chicago: University of Chicago Press, 1999.

Stih, Renata, and Frieder Schnock. "'Signs from Berlin' Presentation at the Jewish Museum in New York 2003/2004." http://www.stih-schnock.de/jmny.htm. Accessed November 7, 2021.

Tyler, Parker. *Classics of the Foreign Film: A Pictorial Treasury*. Secaucus: Citadel Press, 1972.

Walden, Joshua S. "'Driven from Their Home': Jewish Displacement and Musical Memory in the 1948 Movie *Long Is the Road*." In *Dislocated Memories: Jews, Music, and Postwar German Culture*, edited by Tina Frühauf and Lily E. Hirsch, 121–38. New York: Oxford University Press, 2014.

Walk, Ruth. *The Balcony*. Documentary, Self-published, 2000.

Weinreich, Max. *History of the Yiddish Language, Volume 1*. Translated by Shlomo Noble, edited by Paul Glasser. 1980. Reprint, New Haven: Yale University Press, 2008.

Weinreich, Uriel. *Modern English-Yiddish Yiddish-English Dictionary*. New York: Schocken Books, 1977.

Weiss, Shayna. "*Shtisel*'s Ghosts: The Politics of Yiddish in Israeli Popular Culture." *In Geveb: A Journal of Yiddish Studies* (blog), March 6, 2016. https://ingeveb.org/blog/shtisel-s-ghosts-the-politics-of-yiddish-in-israeli-popular-culture.

Weissler, Chava. "Tkhines." *The YIVO Encyclopedia of Jews in Eastern Europe*. http://www.yivoencyclopedia.org/article.aspx/Tkhines. Accessed January 12, 2018.
Welch, David. *The Third Reich: Politics and Propaganda*. 1993. Reprint, London: Routledge, 1995.
"WEVD: Yiddish Radio in New York." Mapping Yiddish New York, October 9, 2017. http://jewishstudiescolumbia.com/myny/arts/wevd-yiddish-radio-in-new-york/.
Whitfield, Stephen J. "Where They Burn Books . . ." *Modern Judaism* 22, no. 3 (October 2002): 213–33.
Williams, Raymond. *Television: Technology and Cultural Form*. New York: Routledge, 2003.
Wilson, Emma. *Cinema's Missing Children*. London: Wallflower Press, 2003.
Wolfson, Elliot R. "The Problem of Unity in the Thought of Martin Buber." *Journal of the History of Philosophy* 27, no. 3 (July 1989): 423–44.
———. *Through a Speculum That Shines: Vision and Imagination in Medieval Jewish Mysticism*. Princeton: Princeton University Press, 1994.
Wyman, Mark. *DPs: Europe's Displaced Persons, 1945–51*. Ithaca: Cornell University Press, 1998.
Yerushalmi, Yosef Hayim. *Zakhor: Jewish History and Jewish Memory*. Seattle: University of Washington Press, 1996.
"The Yiddish Radio Dial." Yiddish Radio Project, 2002. https://www.yiddishradioproject.org/exhibits/history/.

Index

acousmatic/offscreen sound, 12, 16, 88, 139–40, 174, 209, 265, 274–75, 279, 280, 292–93
Adler, Celia, 126, 142
Adler, Julius, 100
Adorno, Theodor, 4, 43–45, 306–7n11
After Image: Film, Trauma, and the Holocaust (Hirsch), 222
Aleichem, Sholem (née Rabinovitch), 93–95, 108
Allegretto of the Seventh (Beethoven), 43
American Joint Distribution Committee, 217, 239–40
Ansky, S., 255–56, 259, 264, 266–67, 319n13, 321n37
Anti-Semite and Jew (Sartre), 199
antisemitism, 5
  and Jewish languages, 87
  Jews' reaction to, 196
  See also under *Long Is the Road*, antisemitism in
  in Nazi Germany, 203–4, 208–9
  in post-war Europe, 219
  See also under Sartre, Jean-Paul, on antisemitism
  See also under *Tevye*, antisemitism in
  See also under *Wandering Jew, The*, antisemitism in
Arendt, Hannah, 201
  influence on Flusser, 3, 50, 220
  on statelessness, 218–19, 253
  on totalitarianism, 200, 203, 218, 225
  on violence, 63, 106–7
Are We Civilized? (film), 205
Arnon, Ceril, 155
Asylums (Goffman), 143, 144
Auschwitz, 233–35, 243, 250
Austin, J. L., 81–83, 117, 133
"Auto-da-Fé of the Mind, The" (Roth), 208
Azoulay, Ariella, 142–43

Baal Shem, the, 287–88, 290, 291
Baio, Cesar, 153
Bar Mitzvah (*Bar Mitsve*) (film), 25–26, 142
Battleship Potemkin (Eisenstein), 289
Bauman, Zygmunt, 4, 219–20, 238–39
Beker, Israel, 218, 222, 229–32, 240, 318n37
Ben-Ami, Jacob, 15, 96, 192
Benjamin, Walter, 78–79
Berdichev, R. Levi Isaac of, 292

335

Berg, Judith, 279–80
Berger, Gustav, 38
Berliner Tageblatt (newspaper), 201
Bernstein, Blanche, 139
Birth of the Clinic, The (Foucault), 146
Bloom, Harold, 291
Blue Angel, The, (film), 62
Bolshevik Revolution, 6, 93, 167–68
Borkin, Ida, 48
Borzage, Frank, 205
Bourdieu, Pierre, 82
Boyarin, Daniel, 305n19
    on Jewish gender roles, 14–15, 37
Bozyk, Max, 13
Bridge of Light: Yiddish Film Between Two Worlds (Hoberman), 8
Brooks, Peter, 6, 59, 62, 84–85
Brossat, Alain, 102
Bruner, Irving, 12
Buber, Martin, 147, 175, 197, 294
    on dialogue, 163–64, 180, 293
    influence on Flusser, 3, 193
    I-Thou relationship, 3, 151–52, 178, 201, 293
    retellings of Hasidic legends, 1–2, 263, 284, 298
    on "silence which is communication," 163, 188, 202, 273
    on "turning," 163–64, 180, 293, 298
Bulman, Gertrude, 16
Bund, the, 132, 289
Butler, Judith, 4, 83, 112, 116–18, 220

Cahiers Juifs (journal), 208
Čapek, Karel, 193
Cashier, Jennie, 48
Central Tracing Bureau, 236
Charcot, Jean-Martin, 146

Children Must Laugh (Mir Kumen On) (film), 132
Chion, Michel, 12
Christianity, 197
    See also under *Long Is the Road*, Christianity in
    See also under *Tevye*, Christianity in
cinema, 46, 73, 78, 80, 142–43, 222, 297
    "accented cinema," 23–24, 297
    See also Hollywood
    Italian neorealism, 222
    See also under melodrama, maternal melodrama, medical melodrama, the "woman's film" about missing children, 157–58
    See also *shund*
    Soviet cinema, 289
Citizen Kane, 268
Cohen, Abraham, 168
Crisis of European Sciences and Transcendental Phenomenology, The (Husserl), 193

Dachau, 243
Deleuze, Gilles, 297
Derrida, Jacques, 117
Der Tog (newspaper), 181
dialogue
    See under Buber, Martin, on dialogue
    See under Flusser, Vilém, on dialogue, on discourse and dialogue
"Dialogue" (Buber), 163
Diderot, Denis, 84
Displaced Persons (DPs)
    See under Arendt, Hannah, on statelessness
    See under *Long Is The Road*, Displaced Persons (DPs) in,

displacement in, post-war psychological trauma in
Doane, Marianne, 146, 154–55
Does Writing Have a Future? (Flusser), 137, 164
Doherty, Thomas, 191, 205
Dovzhenko, Alexander, 252
Dybbuk, The (play), 255–56, 264, 266–67, 284, 285–86, 320–21n35
Dybbuk, The (*Der Dibek*) (film), 7, 320n30
  books in, 259–60, 261
  cinematography, 262
  excommunication in, 287–90
  filming of, 265, 274
  Hasidism in, 255, 261, 278, 287–88, 290
  hypercommunication in, 283, 286–88
  Jewish holidays in, 264–67, 273–74, 276
  Kabbalistic inflections of, 212, 258, 270, 272, 276–77, 288, 290, 292, 294
  impaired reception of the mystical in, 256, 258–59, 260–67, 272, 278–79, 281–82, 282
  liminality in, 259, 267, 280, 284
  and memory, 267–72, 284, 294
  music in, 261, 265, 270, 274–78, 280
  queer dimensions of, 264, 278–79
  religious rituals/trappings in, 274–75, 276, 278–82, 285–88, 294
  silent communication in, 273–75
  source material for, 255–56, 264, 266–67, 284–86
  Talmud in, 259–61, 274
  and tension between myth and monotheism, 258–59, 269, 270–72, 290, 292–94
  wind motif in, 256–58, 259–60, 267, 275, 277–82, 285, 286, 288, 292, 295
  zaddik figure in, 260–67, 270, 277, 282–90, 292

Earth (Dovzhenko), 252
East and West (*Mizrekh un Mayrev*) (film), 133
Eichmann, Adolf, 220
Einstein, Albert, 193, 214
Eisenstein, Sergei, 289
Emelka Studios, 217
Entertaining America: Jews, Movies, and Broadcasting (Hoberman and Shandler), 76
epistolarity/letter-writing, 9–10, 20, 22, 23–25, 30, 41–42, 44–45, 111, 137–39, 176, 311n19
  theories of, 23–24, 137–38
Eternal Wanderer, The (fictional painting), 195–96, 204, 209–11

family
  as all-important, 76, 122, 152
  bourgeois family, 14, 16, 37, 46–48, 50, 58, 70–71, 73, 187–89
  See also under Flusser, Vilém, on the family unit
  the mass media family, 70–73, 76, 87–88, 90
  as organism, 110–11
  traditional Jewish family, 14–16, 37, 49, 70, 76
Federici, Silvia, 50
Felman, Shoshana, 4, 83, 116
Feuchtwanger, Lion, 214
Fiddler on the Roof (film), 94, 109

Fiddler on the Roof (musical), 93–94, 109
Field, Harry, 49
Fischer, Jakob, 224
Flusser, Vilém
  on amphitheatrical discourse, 41–47, 203
  and Buber, 3, 163–64, 193, 294, 297–98
  on dialogue, 3, 38, 41–42, 44, 50, 52, 71, 126, 128
  on discourse and dialogue, 3, 38, 41–42, 50, 225
  on experience of Nazism, 193–94
  on the family unit, 15–16, 32, 46, 50
  on the functionary, 153
  on groundlessness (*Bodenlosigkeit*), 192–94, 232, 252–53
  on the Holocaust, 194, 216, 219–21, 238
  on human communication as negentropic, 192
  on human freedom, 73
  intellectual development of, 2–3, 193–94
  on Jewishness, 3, 126, 303–4n9
  on letters, 137–38
  on mass media, 41–42, 45, 70
  on the mass media family, 70–73
  on memory in Jewish tradition, 32–33, 108, 294
  on migrants and homelands, 127–28
  on music, 11–13, 31–32, 43, 163, 202
  on myth, 270–71
  on the patriarchal father, 16, 71–72
  as polyglot, 303n5
  phenomenological approach of, 3, 164, 192–93
  on responsibility as response-ability, 41, 44–45, 60, 126
  on revolution, 41, 46, 60, 71, 163–64, 225
  on the structure of communication, 2–3, 72, 297–98
  on subjects and apparatuses, 154
  on the supernatural, 256–58, 267, 278, 282, 295
  and Talmudic exegesis, 256
  on telephone communication, 52, 54
  on theatrical discourse, 46–47, 57, 60–61, 71, 163
Ford, Aleksander, 132
Fostel, Simche, 13
Foucault, Michel, 143–44, 146–47, 151–52, 312n33
Frankel, Izidor, 168
Fredersdorf, Herbert B., 217–18, 318n37
Friedman, Paul, 239–40, 242–44, 246
From Here to Eternity (film), 135

Gabler, Neal, 65
Gehrman, Lucy, 14
Gilman, Sander, 87
Gilroy, Paul, 220
Glikl of Hameln, 15
God (Old Testament), 89, 122, 184, 197–98, 211, 256, 284
Goebbels, Joseph, 202–3
Goffman, Erving, 4, 132, 143–45, 148, 150–52
Goldberg, Judith N., 8
Goldin, Sidney M., 133, 142, 161
Goldman, Eric A., 8
Goldstein, Marek, 217, 222, 248
Goodman, Benny, 75–76, 89, 103
Gorky, Maxim, 95–97, 99–103

Gotlober, Avrom-Ber, 87
Green Fields (*Grine Felder*) (film), 15, 96–97, 112, 192, 305n19, 310n12
Green, Joseph, 9–10, 12, 35, 224
Grossman, Helen, 106
Groundless (Flusser), 192, 319n43
"Ground We Tread, The" (Flusser), 219–20, 316n9
Grudberg, Izak, 17
Guattari, Felix, 293

Hadamovsky, Eugen, 202–3
Halpern, Dina, 267–68
Harris, Al, 114
Harshav, Benjamin, 113, 136–37, 144, 315n42
Hart, Bertha, 74, 177
Hasidism
   See also under Buber, retellings of Hasidic legends
   See also under *Dybbuk, The* (film), Hasidism in
   in *Dybbuk, The* (play), 271
   Idel on, 292
   Kafka on, 298
   recent film and media about, 297
   See also under Scholem, Gershom, on Hasidism
Haskala (Jewish Enlightenment), 86–87
Hebrew, 13, 74, 86, 99, 112, 184, 246, 249, 257, 267, 290
   ascendancy of in Israel, 7
Hebrew Bible/Old Testament, 89, 98, 105, 120, 178, 197, 209, 234, 256, 268–70
Hebrew Immigrant Aid Society (HIAS)
   See under *Little Letter to Mother, A* (1938 film), Hebrew Immigrant Aid Society (HIAS) in
Heine, Heinrich, 5, 119–20, 207, 214
Herzl, Theodor, 213
Hirsch, Joshua, 222
His Excellency (*Zayn Ekstelents*) (film), 289
His Wife's Lover (*Zayn Vaybs Lubovnik*) (film), *142*
Hitler, Adolf, 148, 202, 236, 248
   "ambitions" of, 203
   rise of, 7, 191
Hoberman, J., 76, 236
   on *The Dybbuk*, 266, 282
   on Joseph Seiden, 69
   on the thematics of Yiddish cinema, 24–25
   on *The Wandering Jew*, 192
   on Yiddish American melodramas, 6
   on Yiddish cinema's development, 8
   on Yiddish movies as *Yidishland*, 118
Hollywood, 6, 9, 34, 65, 69, 125, 130, 155, 157, 188
   response to Hitler, 191
Hollywood and Hitler: 1933–1939 (Doherty), 191
Holocaust, the, 5, 7, 132, 217
   Bauman on, 219–20, 238–39
   Beker's memories of, 229, 231–32
   films about, 222, 224, 312n19
   See also under Flusser, Vilém, on the Holocaust
   family reunions after, 157
   See also under *Long Is the Road*, Holocaust in
   memorials to, 203
Howe, Irving, 169
"'How Goodly Are Your Tents, Jacob'" (Flusser), 256

Husserl, Edmund, 12
  influence on Flusser, 3, 192–93, 314n12
hypercommunication, 28–29, 54, 135–37, 181, 236, 283, 286–88
  definition of, 5–6

Idel, Moshe, 291–92, 294
Immigration Act, the, 129
"Imperial Message, An" (Kafka) 1, 303n3
information theory, 192, 238
Innis, Harold, 211
International Tracing Service (ITS), 236
"Introductory Talk on the Yiddish Language" (Kafka), 298
I Was a Captive of Nazi Germany (film), 205

James, William, 272, 274, 292
Jannings, Emil, 62
Jewish Century, The (Slezkine), 95
Jewish culture
  and assimilation, 7, 65
  and diaspora, 13, 211–12
  gender roles in, 14–16
  in Germany, 204, 208–9
  Jewish folklore, 136–37, 173, 255, 256, 258–59, 270, 290, 294
  "questioning" modality of, 113
  ritual observances, 271
  and textual homeland, 119–20
  and transportable objects, 119
  and visual art, 212
Jewish Daily Forward (newspaper), 76
Jidisze Caytung (newspaper), 249
Joyce, James, 188
Judaism (traditional), 258–59
  and aniconism, 211–12
  Christian stereotypes of, 197

  conception of time, 211–13, 269
  and ethical responsibility, 5, 41, 102, 126, 152–53, 157, 169
  importance of memory, 5, 32–33, 108–9, 185–86, 211, 245–56, 268–70, 293–94
  and messianism, 211
  and myth/mysticism, 212, 258–59, 269–72, 294
  and universalism, 102, 103, 197–98, 210–11
Judea Pictures, 69

Kabbalah, the, 212, 255, 258–59, 270, 288
  and *devekut*, 290–92, 294
  self-annihilation in, 292
  and *unio mystica* (mystical union), 290–92, 294
Kafka, Franz, 1–2, 193, 298–99
Klingberg, Sylvie, 102
Kohn, Hans, 4, 197–98, 212, 215, 316n45
Kol Nidre (film), 93–94, 155, 162, 184, 268, 272
  assimilation in, 76–77
  bilingualism in, 74
  clashes involving radio in, 69–70, 75–79, 81, 88–89
  crises of authority in, 69–70, 73–74, 79–80
  daughterly rebellion in, 70, 75–77, 81, 83
  excommunication in, 81–83, 109, 116, 126, 289
  feminist rebellion in, 70, 78–80
  and "mass media family" structure, 70–73, 76, 87–88, 90
  music in, 74, 77–80, 85–88, 90–91
  muteness in, 81, 83–87, 89, 162

religious rituals/trappings in, 73–74, 87–88, 289
restoring of patriarchal authority in, 87–90
reunions in, 88, 120
silencing of characters in, 78–80, 90, 162
"the speaking body" in, 83
voices of religious authority in, 89–90
Krause, Gertrude, 177
Kristallnacht, 104
Kroner, Maurice, 176

Landsberg DP camp, 217, 243, 248–49, 251
Laughter through Tears: The Yiddish Cinema (Goldberg), 8
Lederman, David, 77
Leff, Abraham, 125
Lekert, Hirsch, 289
Lemberger, Gerszon, 264
Lemlich, Clara, 169–70
Leonidov, Leonid, 289–90
Levinas, Emmanuel, 4, 169, 175, 178, 180, 188, 234
Lewin, Chana, 14
Liebgold, Leon, 74, 95, 272
Liliana, Lili, 74, 268, 272
Lillian, Anna, 131
Lipman, Mojzesz, 264
"Little Letter to Mother, A" ("A Brivele der Mamen") (ballad), 9–10, 28
Little Letter to Mother, A (A Brivele der Mamen) (1911 film), 24–25
Little Letter to Mother, A (A Brivele der Mamen) (1938 film), 48, 51, 89, 162, 167
  depiction of America, 21–23, 27–28, 37

family dynamics and authority in, 14–20, 32, 38
Hebrew Immigrant Aid Society (HIAS) in, 26–27, 29–30, 275
hypercommunication in, 28–29
Jewish holidays in, 20–21, 33
letter-writing in, 20, 23–25, 111
and mass media, 26–29, 32, 37–38, 65
messenger figures in, 25, 59, 137
missing persons ads in, 27–29, 249–50
music in, 9–14, 16, 18, 21, 23, 26, 30–34, 38, 275
and the Smulevitz ballad, 9–11, 23, 24, 28, 30
yeshiva bokher type in, 14–15
Litwina, Berta, 224
Living Orphan, The (Der Lebediker Yosem) (film), 26, 69, 90, 165, 175
  alternate title of, 37
  amphitheatrical discourse in, 41–43
  bilingualism in, 61–62, 65
  dialogic revolution in, 60–61
  depiction of America, 37, 48, 55–56
  estranged characters in, 55–56, 59, 61, 126, 140, 162
  excommunication in, 54–55, 126
  family dynamics in, 46–59, 62–64, 66–68, 110
  gender roles in, 37–38, 48–50, 52, 67–68
  hypercommunication in, 54
  and mass media (esp. radio), 37–47, 51–54, 56–58, 259
  messenger figures in, 58–59, 61, 64, 137, 140, 156
  music in, 38–39, 42–43, 45–46, 48, 57–61, 65–66, 259

Living Orphan, The (Der Lebediker Yosem) (film) *(continued)*
  muteness in, 63–64, 81
  mystical communication in, 63–64
  reunions in, 62, 64
  and telephone, 41–42, 44–45, 51–54
  theatrical discourse in, 46, 57, 60–61
Long Is the Road (Lang Iz der Veg) (film)
  antisemitism in, 219, 225, 240
  bureaucracy in, 26, 220, 235–39, 243
  Christianity in, 224, 240
  displaced persons (DPs) in, 7, 217–18, 218–19, 221, 222, 223, 236–38, 239–40, 242–47, 247–49, 251–53
  displacement in, 135, 175, 224, 226, 228, 232, 235–37, 239–44, 246–49, 251–53
  expository mode in, 222–23, 228, 233–34
  filming/production of, 217–18
  German spoken in, 218, 221–22, 233, 237, 239, 241, 249, 252
  groundlessness in, 223, 226, 232–33
  Holocaust in, 228, 229, 232–33, 233–39, 241, 246
  hypercommunication in, 236
  and Italian neorealism, 222
  missing persons ads in, 249–50
  muteness in, 226, 239, 250
  narrative approach of, 221–23, 228
  Nazism in, 223–28, 228–29, 233–39
  and objectification, 219–21, 228–30, 233, 235–39
  and post-war psychological trauma, 239, 242–43, 245–46, 250
  religion and ritual in, 224–28, 234–35, 241, 246
  reunions in, 250–51
  "regrounding" in, 218, 251–53
  scenes of destruction in, 224–25, 240–42
  and trauma theory, 233
  verisimilitude in, 218, 222–23, 243, 248
  visual style of, 222, 223, 224, 227–28, 233
  Yiddish in, 218, 249
  Zionism in, 248
Love and Sacrifice (Libe un Laydnshaft) (film), 26
Löwy, Yitzhak, 298
Lubelski, Paula, 98
"Lullaby Song, The," 142
Lynn, Henry, 125

Madness and Civilization (Foucault), 143, 146
Maggid of Mezritch, the, 291–92
Makarenko, David, 106
Marcus, Betty, 98
Marcus, Vicki, 98
McLuhan, Marshall, 45, 76–77, 202, 211, 312n33
Meaning of Yiddish, The (Harshav), 113
Medem Sanitorium, 132
mass media, 5, 22–23, 26–27, 28–29, 37–38, 79, 90, 95, 103, 202–3, 247, 249–50
  See also under family, the mass media family
  See also under Flusser, Vilém, on amphitheatrical discourse, on mass media

See also print
See also radio
See also television
media theory, 3, 211, 238, 297–98
  axioms of, 4
melodrama
  as expressionistic, 6, 84
  maternal melodrama, 25–26, 125, 142, 188
  medical melodrama, 125, 146, 144–45
  and pathological states (esp. muteness), 6, 80, 83–86, 107
  See also *shund*
  the "woman's film" 25–26, 125, 142, 146, 154–55, 188
  and the *voix du sang*, 59, 140, 153
  Yiddish vs American, 6

Mendelssohn, Felix, 214
Mendelssohn, Moses, 87
Mestel, Jacob, 192, 197, 208
metasemantic communication, 5, 12–13, 163, 202–3, 272, 275, 277, 293, 298
Mirele Efros (film), 26
Miron, Dan, 86–87, 98, 122
Modernity and the Holocaust (Bauman), 220
Moissi, Aleksander, 240
Moissi, Bettina, 240
Morevsky, Avrom, 260, 266–67, 282, 290
Mortal Storm, The (film), 205
Moscow Art Theatre, 289
Moses, 211, 213, 292
Motel the Operator (*Motl der Operator*) (film), 69, 236
  assimilation in, 182
  fabricated names/identities in, 181–82, 186

  family crises in, 170–71, 173–75, 182
  hypercommunication in, 181
  "the Face of the Other" in, 178–80, 188, 234
  Marxist messages in, 167–69
  music in, 165–67, 171, 176, 182, 185
  oppressive institutions in, 165, 169, 172, 180
  outcast figure in, 126, 161–62, 170
  phantasmatic dialogue in, 140, 174, 182–83
  rescue of main character, 161–62, 178–85, 187
  as *shund*, 162, 176, 180
  silencing of workers in, 168, 171–72
  "silence which is communication" in, 162–63, 178–85, 186–89
  Talmud in, 168–69, 185–86
  and "turning," 163–64, 180
  workers' protests/rebellion in, 168–72
Mothers: An Essay on Love and Cruelty (Rose), 128
Mothers of Today (*Hayntige Mames*) (film), 26
Mulvey, Laura, 146
Munich Yiddish Art Theatre, 217
"Mythical, Historical, and Posthistorical Existence" (Flusser), 270

Nadler, Steven, 287, 321n39
Naficy, Hamid, 23–24, 297
National Center for Jewish Film, 222, 241, 304n19
Nazi Germany and the Jews (Friedländer), 204

Nazism, 2, 217, 229, 314n20
  in American films, 205–6
  See also under Flusser, Vilém, on experience of Nazism
  See also under *Long Is the Road*, Nazism in
  See also under *Tevye*, and Nazism
  See also under *The Wandering Jew*, Nazism in
  use of media/communication, 201–3, 225
Netflix, 297
Night and Fog (Resnais), 224
Nordau, Max, 197

Oppenheim, Menasha, 74
Origins of Totalitarianism, The (Arendt), 200, 218
Orwell, George, 73
Our Children (Unzere Kinder) (film), 132, 217
"Our Homeland, the Text" (Steiner), 119
Oysher, Moishe, 166–67

Palestine, 120, 211, 213, 218, 240, 310n19
Paskin, Sylvia, 8
Perets, Y. L., 276
performative speech acts, 82
  and the body, 83, 109–10, 116
  excommunication, 55, 81–83, 107–9, 111–18, 133–35, 204–5, 287–90
  insurrectionary speech, 114–18, 205
  "performative abuse," 133–34
  sovereign performatives, 111–12, 116–18
Peters, John Durham, 4–5, 249, 294
Picon, Molly, 133
Pinel, Philippe, 147

Places of Remembrance (Holocaust memorial), 203
Possessed (film), 154
Post-History (Flusser), 219, 220
Princeton Radio Research Project, the, 43
Propaganda and National Power: The Organization of Public Opinion for National Politics (Hadamovsky), 202
print
  books, 66, 74, 94–103, 112, 114–15, 119–20, 122, 164, 205–9, 213–15, 259–62, 273, 277–78, 287
  newspapers, 27–29, 32, 41–42, 45–46, 56–59, 156, 181, 194–95, 201–2, 249–50
Prouty, Olive Higgins, 188
Purim Player, The (Der Purimshpiler) (film), 224

radio, 21–23, 27, 38–49, 52, 54, 59, 62–63, 64–66, 69–72, 74–81, 88–90, 94–95, 103, 201–4, 247–49, 259, 306n2, 308n15
"Radio-Phonograph: That's the Bone of Contention in Jewish Families These Days" (article), 76
Rappel, Malvina, 170
Rechtzeit, Seymour, 177
Resnais, Alain, 224
Revolutionary Yiddishland (Brossat and Klingberg), 102
Rilke, Rainer Maria, 193
Riselle, Miriam, 95
"Road Back for the DP's: Healing the Psychological Scars of Nazism, The" (Friedman), 239
Rodgers, Jennifer, 236
Roland, George, 192, 195

Rose, Jacqueline, 4, 121, 128–29, 135
Rosen, Herman, 53
Rosenberg, Jerry, 57
Roshal, Grigori, 289
Roskies, David G., 271, 319n3
Roth, Joseph, 4, 181–82, 208–9
Rousseau, Jean-Jacques, 84
Rubina, Fania, 49

Samberg, Ajzyk, 265–67
Samuylow, M. B., 210
Sandrow, Nahma, 6
Sartre, Jean-Paul
  on antisemitism, 199–200
Satz, Ludwig, 142
Schafer, R. Murray, 162
Schnock, Frieder, 203
Schoengold, Joseph, 74, 173
Scholem, Gershom, 4
  critics of, 291–92
  on Hasidism, 261, 288, 290–92
  on the ineffable, 272
  on Kabbalists and Kabbalah, 255, 260, 276, 290–91, 294
  on myth/mysticism, 258–59, 270–72
Schwartz, Maurice, 93, 109, 161
Seiden, Joseph, 37–38, 43, 45, 69, 93, 161, 162, 165, 167
Shandler, Jeffrey, 76, 309n34, 308n15
  on "postvernacular" Yiddish, 7
She'erit Hapletah, 248
Shock (film), 154
Shtisel (television series), 297
shund, 7, 59, 62, 65, 88, 125, 131, 146, 157–58, 162, 176, 180, 255
  See also melodrama
Sicular, Eve, 264
Silberkasten, Morris, 131

Singing Blacksmith, The (Yankl der Shmid) (film), 166–67
Sirota, Gershon, 265
Slezkine, Yuri, 95, 102
speech act theory, 82
Spinoza, Baruch, 287
Smulevitz, Solomon, 9–10, 23–24, 28, 30
"Song of Songs," 264, 274–77
Soundscape, The (Schafer), 162
Speaking into the Air: A History of the Idea of Communication (Peters), 4
Stanislavsky, Konstantin, 266
Stein, Alexander, 12
Steiner, George, 119–20
Stella Dallas (film), 188
Stella Dallas (novel), 188
Sternberg, Josef von, 62
Stih, Renata, 203–4
still images
  painting, 194–97, 201, 204, 205, 209–10, 225, 255
  photography, 27, 29, 51, 139–43, 174, 182–83, 255, 280
Strassberg, Morris, 131
Stutchkof, Mischa, 145
"Surprising Phenomenon of Human Communication, The" (lecture series) (Flusser), 2

Tales of the Hasidim (Buber), 1, 284
Talmud, the
  See also under Dybbuk, The (film), Talmud in
  See also under Flusser, Vilém, and Talmudic exegesis
  See also under Motel the Operator, Talmud in
  See also under Wandering Jew, The, *pilpul* in

Talmud, the *(continued)*
  wisdom in, 290–91
  See also under *yeshiva bokher*
Tauber, Chaim, 164
telegrams, 53–55, 58–59, 64, 66
telephone, 41–42, 44–45, 51–54, 143–44, 176
television, 41–42, 45–46, 70–73, 78, 203, 308n15
Television (Williams), 71–72
Tevye (film), 7, 134, 155, 228
  and Aleichem's stories, 93–95, 98, 103, 107–9, 120, 309n1
  as allegory, 94, 191
  antisemitism in, 103–4, 106, 111–14, 118
  assimilation in, 104
  books in, 94–103, 112, 114–15, 119–20, 122, 207
  Christianity in, 100, 103, 106, 121
  citational speaking style in, 97–99, 105, 121–22
  daughterly rebellion in, 93, 99, 103
  demand for child's return in, 105–6
  excommunication in, 107–10, 111–18, 126, 289
  exile in, 119–20, 122–23, 207
  on the family as organism, 110–11
  "insurrectionary speech" in, 114–18, 205
  Jewish ethics in, 102, 121
  Judeophilia in, 95
  literary-mediated desire/courtship in, 95–100, 103, 311n19
  loss of authority in, 94–95, 99, 103, 105–7, 111, 118, 134, 162
  memory in, 108–9
  music in, 105
  muteness in, 111, 118
  and Nazism, 94
  objects of importance in, 119–20
  patriarchal transmission of tradition in, 112
  political radicalism in, 102–3
  recovery of authority in, 93–94, 107, 109–10, 116, 118, 122–23
  religious objects/customs in, 108, 112, 119–21, 289
  reunions in, 120–23
  silencing of characters in, 105–6, 114–16
  "the speaking body" in, 109–10, 116
  and textual homeland, 119–20, 207
  tradition/modernity tension in, 94
  Yiddish in, 118
Tevye the Dairyman (Aleichem), 93–95, 103, 107–9, 120, 309n1
"Those Who Are to Hear, Hear" (Buber), 1, 298
Toller, Ernst, 214
Tolstoy, Leo, 100–1, 103
Torah, the
  commentary on, 291
  gendered roles regarding study of, 15–16, 70
  role in Jewish culture, 14
  in *The Dybbuk*, 285
"Transmigration of a Melody, The" ("A Gilgul fun a Nign") (Perets), 276
troubled communication
  definition of, 4–5
Trystan, Leon, 9
Tsar Alexander II, 129
Tuke, William, 147
Two Sisters (Tsvey Shvester) (film), 26
Tyler, Parker, 273–74, 320n30

Ulysses (Joyce), 188
Ulmer, Edgar G., 15, 96, 166–67
Uncle Moses (film), 161–62
Unheroic Conduct: The Rise of Heterosexuality and the Invention of the Jewish Man (Boyarin), 14
US Army Information Control Division, 217

Vargas, Milton, 220
Varieties of Religious Experience, The (James), 272
Visions, Images, and Dreams: Yiddish Film, Past and Present (Goldman), 8

Walden, Joshua S., 248, 318n37
Waldman, Louis (Liebele), 88, 185
Wandering Jew, The (Der Vandernder Yid) (film)
  antisemitism in, 192, 195–96, 198–201, 204, 206–9
  art and artists in, 192, 194–97, 203–5, 207–12
  assimilation in, 196
  book burnings in, 205–9, 213–15
  censorship in, 195
  exclusionary measures/ excommunication in, 192, 203–5, 215
  fantastical/mystical elements in, 140, 209–10, 213–15
  denial of new political reality in, 195–96, 206
  filmic techniques, 195, 201, 205–6, 209–11, 213–15
  groundlessness in, 192, 194, 199, 209, 216
  Jewish "time bias" in, 194, 211–13, 215–16
  Jewish universalism in, 197–98
  Nazism in, 7, 191–92, 194–97, 201–7, 211, 216, 225
  news media in, 194–95, 201
  pilpul in, 198
  radio in, 201–4, 247
  "regrounding" in, 218
  responsibility in, 199–201
  street rallies in, 195, 201–3, 205–6
  traumatic memories in, 198, 206–7
  Zionism in, 213
Wandering Jews, The (Roth), 181–82
Warsaw Ghetto, the, 226–28, 246
Waszyński, Michał, 255–56, 264, 285
Weinrich, Max, 210
We Live Again (Mir Lebn Do!) (film), 132, 217
Wendorf, Ruben, 137
When Joseph Met Molly: A Reader on Yiddish Film (Paskin), 8
Where is My Child? (Vu Iz Mayn Kind?) (film), 26, 161–62, 173, 177, 181, 184, 187–88
  asylum/mental institution in, 125–26, 134, 143–55
  corruption in, 131–35, 139, 143, 153–54, 156
  disconnection in, 125–26, 129–31, 144–49, 158–60
  excommunication in, 133–34, 144–49, 158–60, 187
  gender politics of, 154–55
  hypercommunication in, 135–37, 236
  "hysterical" speech in, 147–49
  institutions in, 127–28, 131–32, 134–35, 138–40, 143–54, 156, 162, 165
  Jewish ethical responsibility in, 126, 152–53, 157

Where is My Child? (Vu Iz Mayn Kind?) (film) *(continued)*
  as maternal melodrama, 125, 142, 188
  as medical melodrama, 125, 146, 154–55
  messenger figures in, 137–39, 156
  migrants and migration in, 125–30, 133
  mother-child separation in, 125, 131–35, 139–43, 149–53
  motherhood in, 126, 128–29, 131, 135–36, 154–55, 156–60
  music in, 130, 141–43
  outcast figure in, 126–29, 131–32, 152–53, 160–61
  "performative abuse" in, 133–34
  reunions in, 156–60
  as *shund*, 125, 130–31, 145–46, 157–58
  silencing of characters in, 134–35, 145, 148–49, 150–51
  still images in, 139–43
  surrogate objects in, 139–43, 149–50
  as "woman's film," 125, 142, 146, 154–55
  whistleblowers in, 139, 168
Williams, Raymond, 71–72
Wittgenstein, Ludwig, 3
Wolfson, Elliot R., 212, 312n55
World War I, 9, 25, 193, 200, 198, 206, 208, 256
World War II, 6, 26, 218–19
  Beker's memory of, 229–32
  See also under Flusser, Vilém, experience of Nazism
  See also under *Long Is the Road*, Holocaust in, Nazism in
Wyman, Mark, 219

YAFO (Jewish film body), 217, 239

Yerushalmi, Yosef Hayim, 268–71
yeshiva bokher, 96–97, 133, 273, 274, 276, 305n19
  See also under *Little Letter to Mother, A* (1938 film), *yeshiva bokher* type in
Yiddish, 271
  "afterlife" of/postvernacular phase of, 7, 297
  negative attitudes towards, 86–87
  decline of, 6–7
  hybrid quality of, 209–10
  Kafka on, 298–99
  and labor/working class politics, 161
  See also under *Long Is the Road*, Yiddish in
  and the maternal/as *mame-loshn*, 24–26, 61–62, 110–11, 118, 140, 250, 306n28
  as modern "vernacular" language, 297
  native speakers' attitude toward, 136–37
  newspapers in, 27–32, 181, 249, 306n2
  radio broadcasting in, 65, 77
  See also under *Tevye*, Yiddish in
  translation into English, 136–37
Yiddishland, 65, 118, 140
Yiddish Art Theatre, 93
Yiddish literature, 7, 86–87
Yiddish theater, 6, 93
  actors in, 9, 126, 192, 217–18, 266, 298–99
  adaptations of, 7, 255–56
Yishuv, the, 120, 211, 248
Young, Boaz, 114

Zakhor: Jewish History and Jewish Memory (Yerushalmi), 268
Zanger, Jacob, 48, 165
Zayenda, Edmund, 27
Zhitlovsky, Khaim, 266

Zinnemann, Fred, 135
Zionism
  See under *Long Is the Road*,
    Zionism in
  See under *Wandering Jew, The*,
    Zionism in
Zweig, Stefan, 214
Zwerling, Yetta, 77, 173

www.ingramcontent.com/pod-product-compliance
Ingram Content Group UK Ltd.
Pitfield, Milton Keynes, MK11 3LW, UK
UKHW041915140426
5217IPUK00013B/164